# Critical Theory Ethics for Business and Public Administration

A volume in
*Ethics in Practice*
Robert A. Giacalone and Carole L. Jurkiewicz, *Series Editors*

# Critical Theory Ethics for Business and Public Administration

*Edited by*
## David M. Boje
*New Mexico State University*

INFORMATION AGE PUBLISHING, INC.
Charlotte, NC • www.infoagepub.com

**Library of Congress Cataloging-in-Publication Data**

Critical theory ethics for business and public administration / edited by David M. Boje.
    p. cm. – (Ethics in practice)
 Includes bibliographical references.
 ISBN 978-1-59311-785-6 (pbk.) – ISBN 978-1-59311-786-3 (hardcover)
1. Business ethics. 2. Business administration–Moral and ethical aspects. 3. Public administration–Moral and ethical aspects. I. Boje, David M.
 HF5387.C75 2008
 174'.4–dc22

                                2008017758

Printed in the United States of America

# CONTENTS

Series Editors' Preface ............................................................. ix

Foreword: Critical Theory, Ethics, and the Critique of Business ......... xi
    *Douglas Kellner*

## PART I

### INTRODUCTION TO CT ETHICS IN BUSINESS
### AND PUBLIC ADMINISTRATION

1   Contributions of Critical Theory Ethics for Business
    and Public Administration ........................................................ 3
    *David M. Boje*

2   Ethics in the World of Management?: Making the Case
    with Critical Theory ............................................................. 29
    *Adrian N. Carr*

3   Practicing Critical Theory in Public Administration ...................... 55
    *Lisa A. Zanetti*

4   Business Ethics and Its World .................................................. 79
    *Martin Fuglsang*

# PART II

## CT ETHICAL ANSWERABILITY AND ACCOUNTABILITY

**5** Story Ethics ................................................................. 97
*David M. Boje*

**6** No Alibi in Ethics: Bakhtin's Philosophy of the Act and the
Question of Answerability in Business ................................ 119
*Olga Belova*

**7** The Critical Issue of Accountability ................................. 135
*Harro M. Höpfl*

# PART III

## CT ETHICS FOR ORGANIZATIONAL CONTEXTS

**8** Legal Fictions: Critical Theory Criticality and the State
of Economics and Management ........................................ 159
*Robin Matthews*

**9** Monsters of Accounting: An Ante-Ethics Approach .................. 185
*Alexis A. Downs, Rita A. Durant, and William L. Smith*

**10** Strategy and Critical Theory Ethics ................................ 211
*David M. Boje and Usha C. V. Haley*

**11** International Business and Critical Ethics ........................ 229
*George Cairns and Martyna Sliwa*

**12** Techno-Futurist Ethics ............................................. 259
*Stewart Clegg and Nelson Phillips*

# PART IV

## CT ETHICS FOR SOCIAL ISSUES

**13** Morality in Context: Reflections on Voice and Exclusion ........... 283
*Gabrielle Durepos and Albert J. Mills*

**14**   Ethics of Recognition: I / you (thou) / they.................................. 299
*Hugo Letiche*

**15**   Good Order: Ethics and Disposition ............................................... 319
*Heather Höpfl*

**16**   Critical Spirituality, Moral Philosophy, and Business Ethics ......... 333
*Michael Whitty and Jerry Biberman*

**17**   Critical Pedagogy and Ethics: An Epic Four-Quadrant Model...... 347
*Grace Ann Rosile, Mark Horowitz, Stephen DeGiulio, and Janet Marta*

**18**   Environmental Ethics and Business: Toward a Habermasian
Perspective ..................................................................................... 373
*Robert P. Gephart, Jr. and Michael Kulicki*

# SERIES EDITORS' PREFACE

The *Ethics in Practice* series provides a forum for the exploration and discussion of organizational ethics issues that may otherwise be overlooked in the usual venues of academic journals and books. The focus of the series is interdisciplinary, which includes not only a focus on ethical issues in the public, private, and nonprofit sectors, but on the body of knowledge on ethics that can be found in other disciplines as well. The series, therefore, seeks to help readers better understand organizational ethics from a variety of vantage points, including business, public and nonprofit administration, psychology, sociology, anthropology, criminology, and victimology. There is much each discipline can learn from each other, with the common thread being organizational ethics.

As editors, our goal is to provide scholars, instructors, and professionals in ethics and social responsibility with a meaningful collection of books in key areas that will expand thinking on issues of research and pedagogy. We see the series as a consortium where new ideas can be surfaced and explored, future inquiry stimulated, and where old ideas can be seen through different lenses.

David Boje's *Critical Theory Ethics for Business and Public Administration* fits the goals of this series perfectly. As Editors, we have long believed that the critical voice in organizational ethics was largely absent. Much of the research in organizational ethics explicates the problems found in the work environment, but often these are reactive in nature, cast within the rubric of the values and interests of corporations and governments. A critical voice provides for a different conception of how business ethics can be defined and how business practices be executed and understood. Such criticism is invaluable in encouraging a deeper understanding of and greater confidence in the findings of ethics research.

As Kellner notes in his foreword to this volume, "Thus a diverse and wide-ranging set of critical perspectives on ethics and business such as is assembled here can help point out problems to be addressed and transformations to be made in society, the economy, and our individual ways of thinking and acting."

We hope you will agree and find the chapters in this book to be a provocative challenge to organizational ethics "as usual," and that it will stimulate further inquiry in all aspects of research, practice, and pedagogy.

**Robert A. Giacalone**
**Carole L. Jurkiewicz**
Editors, *Ethics in Practice*

FOREWORD

# CRITICAL THEORY, ETHICS, AND THE CRITIQUE OF BUSINESS

**Douglas Kellner**

Since the 1960s, there has been a wave of critical theories throughout the disciplines, accompanying the radical movements of the epoch. Critical theories have put in question the major assumptions of philosophy, social theory, and the Humanities, as well as criticizing specific fields of social science like sociology, political science, or economics. Some critical theories are influenced by the classical models of the Frankfurt School, while others have been influenced by poststructuralist and other critical discourses emerging from Europe.

The proliferation of these modes of thought now looks like an era of the emergence and dissemination of critical theory throughout the world and throughout all academic disciplines, as part of the flow of globalization. Of course, dominant academic disciplines and most academics resist critical theory in all forms, sometimes like the plague, since it can endanger one's career and salary. Business has been perhaps one of the most resistant fields to critical theory perhaps because there is more at stake in the domain of economics and capital than in superstructural concerns like philosophy

*Critical Theory Ethics for Business and Public Administration,* pages xi–xvii
Copyright © 2008 by Information Age Publishing
**xi**

and art history, and perhaps because capitalism itself is resistant to ethics and reflective critique on its ends and effects in the relentless drive for power and profit.

It is thus welcome to discover a volume that is dedicated to *Critical Theory Ethics in Business and Public Administration Practice.* The contributors to this volume deploy a wide range of critical theories, branching from different versions of the Frankfurt School to poststructuralist and a range of other critical theories that are dedicated to developing robust ethical discourse and critique in the areas of business, management, and organization. To help set up this project, I will offer some contextualizing comments on the critical theory of the Frankfurt School, a section on the emergence of other critical theories from poststructuralism through the political movements of the 1960s like feminism and postcolonial theory; and conclude with some comments on the subject matter and contributions of this book.

## THE FRANKFURT SCHOOL AND CRITICAL THEORY

"Critical theory" stood as a code for the quasi-Marxist theory of society of a group of interdisciplinary social theorists collectively known as the Frankfurt School. The term "Frankfurt School" refers to the work of members of the *Institut für Sozialforschung* (Institute for Social Research) that was established in Frankfurt, Germany, in 1923 as the first Marxist-oriented research centre affiliated with a major German university. Max Horkheimer became director of the institute in 1930, and gathered around him many talented theorists, including Erich Fromm, Franz Neumann, Herbert Marcuse and T. W. Adorno. Under Horkheimer, the Institute sought to develop an interdisciplinary social theory that could serve as an instrument of social transformation. The work of this era was a synthesis of philosophy and social theory, combining sociology, psychology, communication studies and political economy, among other disciplines.

In a series of studies carried out in the 1930s, the Institute for Social Research developed theories of monopoly capitalism, the new industrial state, the role of technology and giant corporations in monopoly capitalism, the key roles of mass culture and communication in reproducing contemporary societies, and the decline of democracy and of the individual. Critical theory drew on Hegelian dialectics, Marxian theory, Nietzsche, Freud, Max Weber, and other trends of contemporary thought. It articulated theories that were to occupy the center of social theory for the next several decades. Rarely, if ever, has such a talented group of interdisciplinary intellectuals come together under the auspices of one institute. They managed to keep alive radical social theory during a difficult historical era and provided aspects of a neo-Marxian theory of the changed social reality and new historical situation in the transition from competitive capitalism to monopoly capitalism (see Kellner 1989).

During the Second World War, the Institute split up due to pressures of the war. Adorno and Horkheimer moved to California, while Lowenthal, Marcuse, Neumann and others worked for the US government as their contribution in the fight against fascism. Adorno and Horkheimer worked on their collective book *Dialectic of Enlightenment* (1947 [trans. 1972]), which discussed how reason and enlightenment in the contemporary era turned into their opposites, transforming what promised to be instruments of truth and liberation into tools of domination. In their scenario, science and technology had created horrific tools of destruction and death, culture was commodified into products of a mass-produced culture industry, and democracy terminated into fascism, in which masses chose despotic and demagogic rulers. Moreover, in their extremely pessimistic vision, individuals were oppressing their own bodies and renouncing their own desires as they assimilated and made their own repressive beliefs and allowed themselves to be instruments of labor and war.

After the Second World War, Adorno, Horkheimer and Pollock returned to Frankfurt to re-establish the Institute in Germany, while Lowenthal, Marcuse and others remained in the USA. In Germany, Adorno, Horkheimer and their associates published a series of books and became a dominant intellectual current. At this time, the term "Frankfurt School" became widespread as a characterization of their version of interdisciplinary social research and of the particular critical theory developed by Adorno, Horkheimer, and their associates. They engaged in frequent methodological and substantive debates with other social theories, most notably "the positivism dispute," where they criticized more empirical and quantitative approaches to theory and defended their own more speculative and critical brand of theory.

The Frankfurt School eventually became best known for their critical theories of "the totally administered society," or "one-dimensional society" (see Marcuse 1964), which analyzed the increasing power of capitalism over all aspects of social life and the development of new forms of social control. During the 1950s, however, there were divergences between the work of the Institute relocated in Frankfurt and the developing theories of Fromm, Lowenthal, Marcuse and others who did not return to Germany, which were often at odds with both the current and earlier work of Adorno and Horkheimer. Thus it is misleading to consider the work of various critical theorists during the post-war period as members of a monolithic Frankfurt School. Whereas there were both a shared sense of purpose and collective work on interdisciplinary critical theory from 1930 to the early 1940s, thereafter critical theorists frequently diverge.

## CRITICAL THEORIES PROLIFERATE AND GO GLOBAL

In both the humanities and social sciences, the term critical theory more generally over the past decades has signified the use of critical and theoretical approaches to the subject matter of specific disciplines and more broadly to society, while a more specialized usage has described the work of the Frankfurt School. While critical theories were entering many disciplines throughout the world, a proliferation of new theoretical approaches from France, often associated with structuralism and then poststructuralism and postmodern theory (see Best and Kellner 1991), generated new discourses that were also assimilated to the cover concept of critical theory.

The development of structuralism and poststructuralism in France in the 1950s and 1960s and rapid global transmissions contributed to development of an interdisciplinary mode of theory. Whereas structuralism had ambitions of attaining the status of a super science, which could arbitrate among competing truth claims and provide a foundational discipline, poststructuralism challenged any single disciplines' claim to primary status and promoted more interdisciplinary modes of theory. Poststructuralism turned to history, politics, and an active and creative human subject, away from the more ahistorical, scientific, and objectivist modes of thought in structuralism.

The poststructuralist moment was a particularly fertile one as important theorists like Barthes, Lyotard, and Foucault, wrote new poststructuralist works and younger theorists like Derrida, Baudrillard, Virilio, and others entered into productive periods. The poststructuralist turn was evident in the famous 1966 conference on "Critical Languages and the Sciences of Man" at Johns Hopkins University, which featured an important intervention by Jacques Derrida, "Structure, Sign, and Play in the Discourse of the Human Sciences" (in Derrida 1977: 278ff). Rejecting structuralist theories of language, Derrida stressed the instability and excess of meaning in language, as well as the ways that heterogeneity and difference were generated. Derrida also questioned the binary opposition between nature and culture upon which Levi-Strauss had erected his system (1969), thus undermining a certain glorification of the human sciences in the humanities and opening the discipline for more appreciation of philosophy, literature, and less scientific modes of discourse.

Poststructuralism stressed the openness and heterogeneity of the text, its embedded in history and desire, its political and ideological dimensions, and its excess of meaning. This led critical theories to more multilevel interpretive methods and more radical political readings and critique. Foucault (1980) described how texts and discourses are embedded in power; Edward Said (1979) articulated the "orientalism" of western-centric ideology and construction of non-western cultures in both colonial and postcolonial discourses; and feminists described how patriarchy and relations of domination and subordination are inscribed in texts (Tong 1988).

French poststructuralist critical theory is extremely hard to categorize as it combines social theory, cultural and political commentary, philosophy, literary stylistics, and many social and human sciences in their work, crossing boundaries between academic disciplines and fields. This interdisciplinary focus links French critical theory to Frankfurt School critical theory and to certain types of feminism and other cultural theories that practice "border crossing" (i.e. cross the borders between disciplines and traditional division of topics and academic labor).

Critical theories were also developed within feminism, critical race theory, gay and lesbian theory, and other groupings associated with post-1960s political movements, making critical theory part of political struggle inside and outside the university. Feminists, for instance, demonstrated how gender bias infected disciplines from philosophy to literary study and was embedded in texts ranging from classics of the canon to the mundane artifacts of popular culture. In similar ways, critical race theorists demonstrated how racial bias permeated cultural artifacts, while gay and lesbian theorists demonstrated sexual bias (see Essed and Goldberg 2002 and Corber and Valocchi 2002).

These critical theories also stressed giving voice to groups and individuals marginalized in the dominant forms of Western and then global culture. Critical theory began going global in the post-1960s disseminations of critical discourses. Postcolonial theory in various parts of the world developed particular critical theories as a response to colonial oppression and to the hopes of national liberation. Frantz Fanon in Algeria, Wole Soyinka in Nigeria, Gabriel Marquez in Latin America, Arrundi Roy in India, and others all gave voice to specific experiences and articulated critical theories that expanded its global and multicultural reach (see Padmini 1996).

The past decades has thus witnessed a proliferation of critical theory to the extent that the very concept is a contested terrain. At present, conflicting models of critical theory are utilized by different individuals and groups in various fields of inquiry in different parts of the world. There is also a tendency to combine critical theories in one's work, following a recommendation by Foucault in the 1970s that many have taken up. Others who took up the anti-theory discourse of Rorty (1989) and various critics of Theory have called for rigorous empirical and contextual engagement with topics and subject matter. Critical theory is thus a multidimensional term that continues to take on differing connotations and uses and is embedded in many different disciplines and debates in the contemporary moment.

## ETHICS AND THE CRITIQUE OF BUSINESS

Critical theories recognize that academic disciplines and domains of social life are contested terrains. Thus not only do corporations, enterprises, media, and states compete to define and control the field of business, but competing academic conceptions strive to define and evaluate economic and business institutions and practices and their academic discourses. As noted, business itself in the contemporary capitalist moment is often resistant to ethics, although the field of business ethics has emerged as a flourishing, if not particularly profitable enterprise, one criticized by contributors to this book.

And yet ethics itself has competing conceptions including Kantian universalist ethics, Hegelian social ethics, utilitarian ethics of consequences, dialogical ethics, and a diversity of other ethical positions, as evident in this collection. The studies in this volume indeed contain a variety of ethical perspectives reflecting competing, or complementary, perspectives on business and ethics, or on critical ethics in business, as Campbell Jones puts it.

In an introductory article, editor David Boje notes how Horkheimer and Adorno attempt to go beyond the abstract and universalist perspectives of Kantian ethics for a more socially responsible and political ethics. Drawing on Bakhtin, Boje calls for an "answerability ethics" where individuals are accountable for their actions and to others, not just by avoiding eating McDonald's or buying Nike shoes, but by acting to try to create more ethical practice and institutions.

Adrian Carr uses critical theory to explore a reflexive ethics in the world of management and how dialectics, properly understand, can help make connections and carry out ethical critique. Lisa Zanetti discusses intersections between critical theory and public administration, while David Boje uses critical theory to develop a story ethics against narrative ethics, creating a more open-ended and less dogmatic way of talking about the world ethically and politically.

Other contributors like Harro Hopfl call for an ethics with accountability a key feature, while Heather Hopfl seeks an ethics of goodness. Hugo Letische proposes an ethic of recognition, while Martin Fuglsang explores the rhizomatics of critical ethics. Olga Belova develops an ethics of dialogism, while Hugo Letische proposes a postmodern ethics and Stewart Clegg outlines a technofuturist ethics. Alexis Downs, Rita Downs, and Bill Smith explore the connections between critical theory and accounting ethics, while George Cairns examines international business and critical ethics. Bob Gephart connects environment ethics and business, while Gerald Biberman and Michael Whitty work toward a critical spirituality approach to business ethics. Usha Haley, in turn, discusses why critical theory is ignored in business strategy, and Gabrielle Durepos and Albert Mills query where race and ethnicity factor into business ethics.

The contributors to this value offer a rich diversity of perspectives on ethics and business and their contributions and positions cannot be easily summarized. My own position is that we need a variety of critical perspectives in order to account for all forms of political, economic, and social oppression, subjugation, and exploitation. Likewise, we need a wide range of ethical critique to depict flaws, problems, and negative features of business institutions and practices and to indicate the limitations of its academic defenses. Thus a diverse and wide-ranging set of critical perspectives on ethics and business such as is assembled here can help point out problems to be addressed and transformations to be made in society, the economy, and our individual ways of thinking and acting.

## REFERENCES

Best, S., & Kellner, D. (1991). *Postmodern theory: Critical interrogations.* London and New York: Macmillan and Guilford Press.

Corber, R. J., & Valocchi, S. (Eds.). (2002). *Queer studies: An interdisciplinary reader.* Malden, MA: Blackwell.

Derrida, J. (1977). *Writing and difference.* Chicago: University of Chicago Press.

Essed, P., & Goldberg, D. T. (Eds.). (2002). *Race critical theories.* Malden, MA: Blackwell.

Foucault, M. (1980). *Power/Knowledge.* New York: Pantheon.

Horkheimer, M. (1972). *Critical theory.* New York: Seabury.

Horkheimer, M., & Adorno, T. W. (1972). *Dialectic of enlightenment.* New York: Herder and Herder.

Jameson, F. (1991). *Postmodernism, or the cultural logic of late capitalism.* Durham, NC: Duke University Press.

Kellner, D. (1989). *Critical theory, Marxism, and modernity.* Baltimore and Cambridge, UK: Johns Hopkins University Press and Polity Press.

Levi-Strauss, C. (1969). *The raw and the cooked.* New York: Harper and Row.

Mongia, P. (Ed.). (1996). *Contemporary postcolonial theory: A reader.* London: Arnold.

Rorty, R. (1989). *Contingency, irony, and solidarity.* Cambridge, MA: Harvard University Press.

Said, E. (1979). *Orientalism.* New York: Vintage.

Tong, R. P. (1998). *Feminist thought.* Boulder: Westview.

# PART I

INTRODUCTION TO CT ETHICS IN BUSINESS
AND PUBLIC ADMINISTRATION

CHAPTER 1

# CONTRIBUTIONS OF CRITICAL THEORY ETHICS FOR BUSINESS AND PUBLIC ADMINISTRATION

**David M. Boje**

The structure of this book introduction is to give the reader a brief overview that addresses the question, What is Critical Theory? The overview includes looking at the contributions of the two directors of the Frankfurt School Institute for Social Research, as well as the several historical phases that constitute shifts in the direction of its theory. I then look at several scholars associated with Critical Theory, and conclude with some contemporary work being done in lowercase "critical theory" (the conventional way to designate those contributing to projects begun by the Frankfurt School directors and associates). I turn to the issue of where the feminist scholars are in Critical Theory. I conclude by positing some ways to develop an ethics of responsibility in business and public administration, and situate the contributors to this book into "critical theory."

Figure 1.1 represents the interplay of three interdependent ethical positions. The formal ethics of Kantian categorical imperative and the content-

*Critical Theory Ethics for Business and Public Administration*, pages 3–27
Copyright © 2008 by Information Age Publishing
All rights of reproduction in any form reserved.

**Figure 1.1**  Interdependency of three types of ethics.

sense ethics, which takes in a more utilitarian ethics, compete in organizational discourse with what we propose in this book as a "*critical ethics*" of answerability. Whereas formal ethics asks each person to do the right thing, it does not answer with a description of what is required to change systematically. As Adorno (1963/2000: 174) often repeats, "There is no right behavior within the wrong world." One way of thinking of this is through the concept of answerability from Mikhail Bakhtin (1990, 1993). "An answerable act or deed," according to Bakhtin (1993, p. 42) "is precisely that act which is performed on the basis of an acknowledgment of my *obligative (ought-to-be) uniqueness.*" What is necessary is an answerable organizing with others to bring the maxim about. It is recognizing that one is a unique participant in Being, in once-occurent, irreplaceable times and places, where there is no alibi not to answer what is going on in an organization. Horkheimer (1933/1993) puts it this way: "In the attempt to actually apply the Kantian imperative, it immediately becomes clear that the general interest of the moral will is concerned about would not be helped in the least" (p. 22). Rather, to be answerable is to be witness, to organize with others to bring about changes.

Content-sense ethics can be defined as "an indiscriminant conglomeration of various principles and evaluations" (Bakhtin, 1993, p. 23). Bakhtin

(1993) raises two challenges to content ethics. Content-sense ethics tries to find special grounding for its principles in ways that are sometimes quite relativistic and utilitarian (see also Horkheimer, 1947, p. 22). Content-sense ethics bounces between universal and relativist concerns, grounding ethics in theoretic disciplines, in concepts such as equity, commitment, loyalty, and not blowing whistles on activities outside one's own job. In short, "the ethical ought is tacked on from the outside" by the theory/concept (Bakhtin, 1993, p. 23). When the content-sense theory tries to generalize, it becomes flawed in its attempts at universality (Bakhtin, 1993, p. 25). It then shares the same "radical defect" as formal ethics (Bakhtin, 1993, pp. 23–25).

A *critical ethics of answerability* does not ignore formal or content ethics. It adds the criterion that each unique participant in an organization (be it public or private) has a "concrete, unique and compellent oughtness" to change the system producing the ethical problems (Bakhtin, 1993, p. 46). We are complicit participants as consumers, producers, owners, or critics. We participate in *Being* and are answerable.

> What underlies the unity of an answerable consciousness is not a principle [or set of ethic codes] as a starting point, but the fact of acknowledgement of one's own participation in unitary Being-as-event. (Bakhtin, 1993, p. 40)

I intend to trace how answerability has its parallel in the early writings of the Frankfurt School of Critical Theory (Adorno, Benjamin, Fromm, Horkheimer, and Marcuse). Adorno (1963/2000) talks about it as the distinction between Kant's ethics of conviction and an ethics of responsibility.[1] Horkheimer's challenge is how can any "society of isolated individuals," acting with an ethics of conviction, bring about meaningful change in the social order (Horkheimer, 1933/1993, p. 25)? In short, individuals ought to organize to join the dialectical processes in history, hopefully joining the antithesis of exploitative global capitalism.

The *critical ethics of answerability* is a matter of contention in *business and public administration ethics*. I shall argue, in what follows, that answerability is being actively co-opted. To make this case, I begin by defining terms, and provide a brief genealogy of Critical Theory and its influences.

## DEFINING TERMS AND CONTRIBUTION OF THE BOOK

### What is Critical Theory (CT)?

Critical Theory (CT) designates the philosophy, theory, and practice of the directors and associates of the Frankfurt School Institute for Social Research from 1931 until several decades ago. The Frankfurt School was founded in Frankfurt in 1923. The Frankfurt School learned from the work of Kant, Hegel, Marx, Weber, Lukacs, and Freud (Held, 1980, p. 16).

Key directors include Theodor Adorno and Max Horkheimer. Jurgen Habermas's recent leadership sought to refocus Critical Theory. Key associates include Walter Benjamin, Henry Gossmann, Arkadij Gurland, Eric Fromm (often excluded by historians), Otto Kirchheimer, Leo Lowenthal, Herbert Marcuse, Franz Newmann, and Freidrich Pollock. CT developed a critique of moral philosophy that still provides a way to associate the "ethics of conviction" (how to reflect upon moral good of our own life) and the "ethics of responsibility" (what is our answerability for changing the macro social, political, economic, and cultural systems that are responsible for exploitation, oppression, injustice, and inequity around the world).

## What is critical theory (ct)?

The "ct" (lowercase) is what is commonly referred to as the work of contemporary scholars, particularly in the fields of business management and public administration, who are making contributions by changing, revising, and critiquing the earlier work of CT (Frankfurt School).

I am working with Bakhtin's (1993) *Toward a Philosophy of the Act*, written in his notebooks between 1919 and 1921. We effect our signature in an emotional-volitional tone that we give to sense-content in the once-occurent act of a domain such as telling or hearing a story with the signature of answerability. Our emotional-volitional tone is a signature acknowledgment of one's obligation. It is "answerably acting or acting-performing" of story "consciousness" that participates in the actual moment (p. 38). When I tell a story in emotional-volitional tone or hear it and the tone is experienced in my living consciousness, then, in that moment, I make a unique answerable signature to some ongoing event that has being-as-event with an "ought-to-be attitude" or morally valid answerability (p. 36). This is the power of a story. "This is the way in which a living consciousness and a cultural consciousness becomes embodied in a living consciousness" (p. 33).

## What is Critical Postmodern Theory?

Put simply, critical postmodern theory is defined as the intersection of Critical Theory with postmodern theory. There is a nexus of some Critical Theory and some avenues of postmodern theory that focus on human subjectivity, on the interpretation of socioeconomic conditions. As with Critical Theory, postmodern theory is not one theory, but many theories (some quite co-opted) and some not. My own work is situated in this nexus of Critical Theory and postmodern theory.

## What is Managerialism?

One of the barriers to the emergence of the revolutionary agent, the critical business ethicist, is managerialism. Managerialism is defined as ethics seen through the viewpoint of managers, the owner's agents of capital. Managerialism is a *reification* of the multifaceted panorama of logics and worldviews of diverse stakeholders (employees, unions, community, nature, etc.). *Reification* means to treat a subjective process as objectified, treating social phenomena as an object or thingness. Authority, power, justice, and ethics are frequently reified. The social relations that constitute ethical phenomena become redefined as object-like relations.

## What is Surplus Value?

Surplus value is produced by surplus labor, the labor in excess of what is needed to compensate the laborer plus cost of cools and materials used in the production process. Classical Marxism views surplus value (and surplus labor) as the primary source of exploitation in capitalism. In short, in classical Marxism, *surplus value is the primary form of capitalist exploitation of labor.* Analytic Marxists, on the other hand, regard "organization exploitation" as the primary source of capitalist exploitation. *Organizational exploitation* is defined as "exploitation based upon unequal control of organizational assets" (Mayer, 1994, p. 333). *Status exploitation* is defined as "economic inequality based upon possession of organizational or bureaucratic position" (Mayer, 1994, p. 338).

## DEFINING CONTRIBUTION

## Contribution

*Business ethics* and *public administration ethics* has been co-opted, and can be reinvented with *Critical Theory.* In this book we assert that what passes for ethical theory and practice is a co-opted version of moral philosophy that denies the responsibility of citizens to change and resist the exploitations of late modern capitalism. In our time, *business ethics,* its conferences, journals, and consulting, has taken the low road: corporate codes of conduct, compromised monitoring of said codes, creative accounting to subvert accountability, submission to neoliberal market ethics legitimating exploitative practices, bait and switch to make it appear unethical business practices are not happening, and a lack of critical thinking skills being taught to students.

## What is Ethics and Moral Philosophy?

*Ethics* is defined simply as "doing the right things in the right way" (Clegg, Kornberger, & Pitsis, 2005, p. 253). In CT, there are two types of ethics, and both are necessary. First, there is the "ethics of conviction" to lead a right life in the right way. Second, is the "ethics of responsibility," or what Mikhail Bakhtin (1990) calls the ethics of "answerability," to understand the systems we are a part of, and to take action to change those systems so they stop producing the same, let us say "evil" results. For me, Bakhtin is an example of someone doing "ct." Like CT directors and associates of the Frankfurt School, Bakhtin critiqued Immanuel Kant's work on moral philosophy. Moral philosophy is much more encompassing and less shallow and mundane than what passes for business ethics and public administration ethics in our time. Indeed we are in a crisis. We inherit ethics from Greek moral philosophers who asked what is the meaning of the "good life" and "what is 'good' and what are 'bad' relationships to the *Other* (Jones, Martin, & ten Bos, 2005, pp. 2, 75).

The academic fields of business ethics and public administration ethics are in crisis. Their ethics serves as a shield to hide unethical practice. These fields emerged in the 1970s and have become apologists for doing the least that has to be done, ethically. These ethics disciplines present Kant's categorical imperative (to make each individual's maxim a universal law in human conduct) into an alternative to Kant's practical reason (sorting out what is in our self-interest). The problem with this line of ethical theory and practice is that it ignores the teachings of the "ethic of answerability" with its injunction to become involved and change the status quo, and the recognition that it's impossible to lead a good moral life within a society or global capitalism that frames a bad moral life. For practical business purposes, contemporary business ethics and public administration ethics endorse a *supposed right to lie* and to *right to exploit* because of practical concerns; it is co-opted! It does this by privileging the individualistic explanation, that our society and global capitalism gives us freedom by making us responsible only for being individualistic, and not social. In our administered business and public world, organizations are said to be in charge of changing the systems that exist, while we "individuals" are just supposed to not lie, cheat, or steal (thus making us "good" corporate workers and good citizens). As apologists for the status quo, and noninvolvement of citizens in changing the practices of global capitalism, business ethics and public administration ethics writers do debate the ethics of child labor, bribery, and pollution, while treating most other issues, such as wage rates and right to organize, as if they do not present ethical concern to the business or public sector.

The result is the dumbing-down of ethics by acts of exclusion of answerability. A short list of the excluded topics includes employment contracts, 9-to-5 routines of work, inequalities of race, ethnicity, and class, as well as our concern with areas of Critical Theory (and critical theory) such as business participation in postmodern war; biotechnology' sweatshop labor in computer, apparel, sneaker, toy, and other industries; wage slavery; the supposed right of corporations to lie in advertising; and the virtual control over consumption practices CT calls the culture industry (the control of media by big business and big political parties). The main objective is to keep any thoughts of an ethics of answerability from entering the minds of citizens. Otherwise, these individuals might get self-organized (instead of administratively organized) in their local community, and petition the state to de-charter and dissolve the unethical corporations and recall politicians who are taking the moral low road.

Business ethics, as well as public administration ethics, substitutes "*McEthics*" in what sociologist George Ritzer (1993/2002) calls the "McDonaldization of society" where "Just Lovin' It" substitutes clown-fun and exhalation of performativity for an ethical inquiry into paying poverty wages, anti-unionism, robotic jobs, exploiting children in advertising, and a diet of unhealthy food, killing animals, and the destruction of the rainforest for cattle grazing. Add to this list Wal-Martization, Disneyfication, and Las Vegasization.

Business ethics refuses to question or challenge basic assumptions about 'normal' business practices. And in public administration ethics, the collapse of Enron and Arthur Andersen did not raise questions about the complicity of consultancy fees, role of SEC, Congress/Senate contributions, Whitehouse campaign contributions, or endowments to the Business School. A few individuals are handcuffed and put on trial; the judicial spectacle of theatrics forecloses the need to investigate the wider, systemic areas of contemporary business practices. Anything to keep citizens from beginning to adopt an "ethics of answerability"!

## DIRECTORS OF THE FRANKFURT SCHOOL AND THEIR CRITICAL THEORY

Theodor Wiesengraund Adorno (1903–1969) and Max Horkheimer (1895–1973) were each directors of the Frankfurt School Institute for Social Research. Horkheimer was director after 1931. After their death, Jurgen Habermas assumed the mantle of leadership of the Frankfurt School. Next I put the history into historical phases. My caveat is that as scholars translate more of the early work of CT, that history does change, the history tends to focus on the directors and forgets the work of the associates, and as I shall conclude at the end of this introduction, that the work of feminist CT and ct authors is largely being marginalized.

## HISTORICAL PHASES OF THE DIRECTORS OF FRANKFURT SCHOOL

Critical Theory (hereafter, CT) has three phases of historical development.

### CT Phase One

The early phase of CT was to develop an empirical and historically ground interdisciplinary research program to overcome the inadequacies of Hegelian, Marxist, and Kantian theories. There was hope that the Enlightenment could be salvaged in critical interdisciplinary projects. Then the Nazis came to power. Horkheimer's (1974a, p. vii) *Critique of Instrumental Reason* (a collection of his writing from the mid-1940s to 1967) asserted that business goals once achieved become instrumental means to new goals, and that this progression is without ethical moorings. Reason without spiritual (transcendental reflexivity) substance becomes the curse of science made into technology instrumentally deployed by business and public administration. Horkheimer (1974, p. ix), for a time thought that CT would, after Nazism's defeat, begin a new day of "authentically human history" brought about by "reforms or revolution." Yet new forms of dictatorship emerged.

Critical theorists, such as Adorno and Horkheimer, contend that ethics is an emasculation of moral philosophy, an emasculation that would horrify Kant. Nevertheless, Kant's work has been instrumentally transformed in ways that promote business ethics as emasculated moral philosophy. In short, business ethics since Kant has privileged an ethics of conviction over an ethics of responsibility. And the ethics of conviction is a specific product of the culture industry, business and public administration schools (and their academies).

Adorno and Horkheimer are particularly critical of Immanuel Kant's (1781/1900) *Critique of Pure Reason*. This jeopardizes Habermas's reading of Kant as a "communicative ethics" with "communicative rationality." As Hunter (1993, p. x) puts it, "Horkheimer's 1933 essay 'Materialism and Morality,' [is] arguably the most decisive materialist critique of Kantian ethics ever written." Horkheimer (1933/1993, p. 25) points out, for example, how the Kantian doctrine of the categorical imperative anticipates the end of morality, and helps it along by making a "distinction between interest and duty." Adorno (1963/2000) talks about it as the distinction between Kant's ethics of conviction and an ethics of responsibility. Their thesis is that Kant's writings were influenced and contextualized by the dawn of the industrial revolution. This revolution is the gemstone of the Enlightenment, the purge of the transcendental from science, technology, and for our purpose, administrative reason in business and public administration. As the industrial revolution gave way to the post-industrial revolution of late modern capitalism, Kant's writings on moral philosophy have been transformed to achieve currency in a field known as "business ethics" in the Academy of Management, and public administration ethics, in the Academy of Public Administration.

Kant (1785/1993, p. 30) wrote of categorical imperative, "Act only according to that maxim whereby you can at the same time will that it should become a universal law." Horkheimer's (1933/1993, p. 25) critique is the basis for an ethics of responsibility:

> If people want to act in a way that their maxims are fit to become universal laws, they might bring about an Order in which this intention—so dubious in the cases invented by Kant—can really be carried out according to criteria.

Horkheimer's challenge is how can any "society of isolated individuals" acting with ethics of conviction bring about meaningful change in the social order (1933/1993, p. 25)? Each individualistic ego in the administered marketplace is concerned for their own property, consumption, and profit. Kant's is an impossible, idealist philosophy that becomes appropriated by power, "the structure of the bourgeois order" (Horkheimer, 1933/1993, p. 9). Kant's conceptions of morality are "idealist delusions" (Horkheimer, 1933/1993, p. 24). Concerns for the moral will of individualistic culture does not help in the least and, in fact, is appropriated by exploitative power to further the spread and depth of exploitation. A conviction of individualistic consciousness (ethics of conviction) to do "good" in their own life does not change oppressive organizations or global patterns of global exploitation. It's what Horkheimer derides in Kant as a "refined form of the primitive belief in the omnipotence of thought" by the individual.

At the close of phase one of CT, it was business as usual for the capitalist *and* Marxist-inspired states: exploitation reined. Horkheimer and Adorno's (June 1947) introduction could well be describing 2006:

> When public opinion has reached a state in which thought inevitably becomes a commodity, and language the means of promoting that commodity, then the attempt to trace the course of such depravation has to deny any allegiance

to current linguistic and conceptual conventions, lest their world-historical consequents thwart it entirely.

## CT Phase Two

Horkheimer and Adorno's (1947/1972) *Dialectic of Enlightenment* is regarded as a turning point in CT, and the marker of its second phase, the aesthetic critique of the culture industry. The Nazi fascism of World War II left them disillusioned that any positive program of empirical study or the goal of ultimate emancipation were derivable, or useful from the Enlightenment. Why, because even after the fall of the Third Reich, disaster radiated triumphant (Horkheimer & Adorno, 1947/1972, p. 3). Horkheimer and Adorno turned in this second phase to more Weberian and Nietzchean skepticism themes to contend with the dark reality of their age: "This skepticism," according to Hunter 2000, p. ix), "regarding the emancipatory potential of science as a whole during this period lead them to abandon the former goal of an empirical, scientific interdisciplinary research program and to focus their theoretical attention increasingly on culture and aesthetic criticism." Adorno (1963/2000, p. 170) ends his series of 1963 lectures by declaring, "There is no ethics… in the administered world." Adorno says he owes Nietzsche "the greatest debt" for his skepticism (p. 172). The individualistic society is absent the social to protest against the administered world. The skills of moral reflexivity, so important to redeem in phase one of CT, have atrophied.

## ASSOCIATES OF CRITICAL THEORY

Besides the directors, Horkheimer and Adorno, CT has several prominent associates.

**Walter Benjamin (1892–1940)** achieved posthumous fame. In Germany, one writes two dissertation theses. The first that Benjamin wrote ensured he would not be invited to write a second. It criticized the very scholars who, understanding power, ensured nothing else would follow. Benjamin could not get a regular position at university, so he became a contributor of literary criticism to magazines and newspapers. Along the way Benjamin, who wrote few books but many essays, became more of a poet than a theorist (Arendt, 1955/1968). He chose suicide on September 26, 1940, during the fall of France. He left safe Paris for the front lines, thinking it was safer. Ironically, Paris was never bombed. Few outside of Adorno, Horkheimer, and the playwright Bertolt Brecht knew the name Benjamin. Fifteen years later, his only disciple, Adorno (1955/1966), edited and published two volumes of his writing in Germany, and Benjamin's fame spread. Arendt (1955/1968), writing the introduction to Benjamin, compares his posthumous fame to that of Kafka, a genius, who introduces absolute originality (p. 3). Arendt writes that Adorno and Horkheimer considered what "Benjamin's thinks… undialectic" (p. 10). Yet, these leaders of the Frankfurt School ensured Benjamin's financial support. "Benjamin probably was the most peculiar Marxist ever produced by this movement, which God knows has had its full share of oddities" (Arendt, 1955/1968, p. 11).

Benjamin's curse was to be a surrealist, to "attempt to capture the portrait of history in the most insignificant representations of reality, its scraps, as it were" (*Beiefe* II, 685, as cited in Ardendt, 1955/1968, p. 11). Benjamin set about discovering archetypes in the world of seemingly insignificant appearances. Benjamin's refusal to do metaphysics, and his undialectic approach to Marxism, could have ended his financial support by the Frankfurt School, but for one good fortune. "Adorno and Scholem blamed Brecht's 'disastrous influence' … for Benjamin's clearly undialectic usage of Marxian categories and his determined break with all metaphysics" (Ardendt, 1955/1968, p. 15).

Benjamin's (1936) essay "The Storyteller" sets up my own contribution to this book. Benjamin argues that the only proper way to view the storyteller is from a great distance. "It teaches us that the art of storytelling is coming to an end" because "less and less frequently do we encounter people with the ability to tell a tale properly" (Benjamin, 1936, p. 83). Our ability as storytellers to exchange experience is dying. Why? Because "experience itself has fallen in value" (pp. 83–84). Arendt (1955/1968) has argued that Benjamin is a surrealist. It is then no accident that another surrealist, Gertrude Stein (1935), would make a similar claim a year earlier. Both saw that storytelling has left the newspaper business, unable to tell stories of the external or the moral world. We have grown poorer in communicative experience so that we can barely storytell with word of mouth or in writing: reality, meanwhile, grows ever more surreal.

**Erich Fromm (1990–1980)** His CT mixes Freud's psychoanalysis of unconscious drives (biological determinism) with Marx's socioeconomic context (economic and class determinism) (1941, 1947, 1955, 1956, 1973). Fromm joined the Frankfurt School Institute for Social Research as their psychology expert in 1929. In 1934 he left Germany for New York, continuing his association with the Institute for Social Research. According to Douglas Kellner, Fromm was one of the few associates of the Frankfurt School that seriously developed a Marxist feminist critique of gender differences in relation to class.[2] Fromm held that "psychoanalytic characterology… is indispensable to the development of ethical theory (1947, p. 32). The same words in traditional Aristotelian virtue ethics can take on radically different meaning with psychoanalytic differences of the human character's unconscious. "The subject matter of ethics is *character*, and only in reference to the character structure as a whole can value statements be made about single traits or actions" (Fromm, 1947, p. 33). Fromm critiques Freudian ethical inquiry for being relativistic (pp. 34–35).

**Herbert Marcuse (1898–1979)** His CT takes a more radical revolutionary position. Marcuse's (1964, p. xv) *One-Dimensional Man* had two hypotheses: "(1) that advanced industrial society is capable of containing qualitative change for the foreseeable future; (2) that forces and tendencies exist which may break this containment and explode the society." One-dimensional man is that "*happy consciousness* which facilitates acceptance of the misdeeds of this society" (p. 76). "It reflects the belief that the real is rational, and that the established [technological-economic] system, in spite of everything, delivers the goods" (Marcuse, 1964, p. 79). The "technological rationality" of the private sector has become the "political rationality" of the public sector (Marcuse, 1964, p. xvi). The result is a tendency toward totalitarian society, defined as "economic-technical manipulation of needs by vested interests" (p. 3) using the "indoctrinating power of the 'media'" (p. 8). In public and private spheres all opposition to economic-technical rationality is absorbed (p. 18). Marcuse (1964, p. 32) explains the failure of the working class to change the established society since working class and managerialist class are being absorbed into the "technological veil" that conceals "inequity and enslavement." A two-dimensional or dialectical thought does not emerge. Marcuse references Kant's agreement with Locke, "in justifying revolution *if and when* it has succeeded in organizing the whole and in preventing subversion" (p. 15). One-dimensional thought and behavior as such as subversion. Marcuse held that in late capitalism the social conditions for revolution had changed, since opposition of the dialectic was being "rendered illusory or meaningless" (p. 15). One-dimensional habits of thought were being socialized in the masses by education and media that made opposition to established universes of discourse unthinkable. Opposition lines are blurred and opposition has no easy target. Centrifugal forces of social change or revolution do not go beyond the framework of national or group interest (p. 37). "And, to the degree to which the slaves have been preconditioned to exist as slaves and be content in that role, their liberation necessarily appears to come from without and from above" (Marcuse, 1964, p. 40). Marcuse's (196, pp. 32–33) *Essay on Liberation* questions Kant's transcendental reason for limiting it only to space and time a priori thinking, when Marcuse wanted a more material constitutive form, and "rupture with the vocabulary of domination." In terms of my Figure 1.1, at the beginning of this introduction, Marcuse (p. 37) is setting out a social liberation, as a revolution in sense-content, as a "new sensorium" that could critique the "reason and rationality of the established system" and fulfill Kant's aim of "reconstruction of society," which is consistent with the *critical ethics of answerability* that I have been summarizing in CT scholars.

## CT in Phase Three

Since 1970, Jurgen Habermas has led the third phase of CT, by steering it on the famous "linguistic turn" (Hunter, 2000, p. ix). Habermas rejected the phase 2 CT focus on aestheticized critique and tried to redeem the phase 1 CT project: the Enlightenment ideal of emancipatory potential of social science using neo-Kantian moral philosophy (p. ix), which Habermas calls "communicative ethics" (p. x). Habermas has most recently changed his lens from Frankfurt School (phase 1) to elaborating Luhmann as well as Parson's structural-functionalist system theory. The result, in my view, is a move away from *critical ethics of answerability*, and a return to formal, absolutist, universalistic ethics to which Adorno, Horkheimer, Fromm, and Marcuse would, I think, most certainly see as insufficient to the problems posed by the culture industry.

## "CRITICAL THEORY" IN LOWERCASE

I use lowercase "critical theory" to refer to critical theory authors who came after the Frankfurt School. The "critical theory" (ct) authors include Douglas Kellner, who writes the introduction to this book. I like to include Mikhail Bakhtin as a critical theorist, as well as Frederick Jameson, and my neighbor in Texas, Steve Best. Contemporary writers in this volume are not all self-identified with "critical theory." These are regular presenters at "critical theory" and "critical management studies" conferences, and in journals serving that community, such as Ephemera, Electronic Journal of Radical Organization Theory (EJ-ROT), Critical Perspectives on International Business, Critical Discourse Journal, Organization: The Critical Journal of Organization, Theory and Society, as well as the fledgling journal I founded: Tamara: Journal of Critical Postmodern Organization Science (whose title is meant to be ironic). Several I recruited with the assignment to read Critical Theory, and critical theory, to explore the "unfinished ethics thesis." The "ct" movement has resulted in regular "Critical Management Studies" (CMS) meetings in the United Kingdom, and in a full-fledged division forming in the Academy of Management under that name. In the United Kingdom, there are several universities that have CMS programs of study. In particular, Leister and Essex Universities have such programs. In the United States, there is token faculty in some of the Business and Public Administration Schools doing "ct" work, but they do not run the curriculum for the mass of students coming through their doors. I would say the same is true of "ct" faculty in Australia, New Zealand, Canada, and elsewhere. On the horizon is the possibility that "ct" will be gaining increasing control of the curriculum of a Business or Public Administration school near you.

There is something about the current historical era that is prompting this intrusion of "ct" into the belly of the beast.

Business ethics and public administration ethics are fashioned differently in each historical age. What these two bedfellows do not want is any close encounters of their "administered life" with moral philosophy, especially critical theory. It would become painfully obvious that business ethics and public administration ethics have emasculated moral philosophy. Ethics, in our contemporary era, has removed something effective, the forces of answerability and responsibility from the playing field. To act with moral philosophy of answerability is considered offensive to business and public administration.

## State of the Ethical Arts

In the current Ethics texts, one finds apologies for free market capitalism, which is seen to be quite capable of sorting out the good life. Business Ethicists, in particular, have become apologists for global sweatshop practices. Maitland (1997), for example, defends letting the market alone determine sweatshop wages and standards. He argues that attempts to create living wages may have unforeseen tragic consequences. Raising sweatshop wages, he argues, penalizes those in the informal sector, discourages further multinational corporate investment, and leads to higher unemployment, greater poverty, less exports, and more inequity. Therefore, the business ethicist is advised to pay market-determined rates. He mouths what the World Bank advocates pay minimum wages in industrialized nations, but never in the Third World. He gleefully quotes Nike's Phil Knight, pointing out his ethics. Is it any wonder that Nike has been accumulating business ethics awards? The moral compass is broken! For Maitland, and the business ethicists, what does not conform to free market determination is excess baggage. It's just another step in the progress of the Enlightenment. "For the Enlightenment, whatever does not conform to the rule of computation and utility is suspect" (Horkheimer & Adorno, 1947/1973, p. 6). The Enlightenment is a program to disenchant the world, dissolve myths, and everything transcendental, especially moral philosophy.

## The Culture Industry

Public administration ethics does not provide a critique of the administered life. The enlightened public administrator radiates disaster triumphant. Public administrators govern by opinion polls, focus groups, and the advice of consultants to the culture industry. Business schools and public administration schools are training those who are running the Culture Industry of mass deception. In the culture industry all is identical: Home Depot, Wal-Mart, and McDonald's make the housing décor, the apparel, and the food all identical. Wal-Mart is no longer concerned to conceal its monopoly, proud of the "Wal-Mart effect." Movies, radio, video games, and Internet are just businesses, not art, which needs some kind of ideology that legitimates the artless rubbish produced (Horkheimer & Adorno, 1947/1973, p. 121). Culture industry...

> It is alleged that because millions participate in it, certain reproduction processes are necessary that inevitably require identical needs in innumerable places to be satisfied with identical goods.

Now the culture industry claims that global standards are based on consumer needs, that sweatshop workers in the Third World cannot possibly be paid living wages, and for these reasons globalization is accepted with so little resistance. The culture industry advocates a business ethics and public administration ethics that sacrifices any distinction between ethics of conviction at work and ethics of answerability for the system of globalization. The culture industry controls individual consciousness, advocating the ethics of conviction, without the ethics of answerability. We listen to radio stations, videos, films, and school lectures, and read newspapers and magazines that are all exactly the same. There is no rejoinder to the conservative talk shows babbling hatred across the airways of the U.S. Bible belt. The public favors the culture industry system, and wants to be part of the system, but does not look too closely at who owns the mass media. Films, music, video games, etc., are put into consumer classifications (X, R, PG-13, PG, G), so that none may escape (p. 123).

Critical theory ethics argues that an ethics of responsibility is a necessary compliment to the ethics of conviction. Individuals ought to organize to join the dialectical processes in history, hopefully joining the antithesis of exploitative global capitalism. Ethics of responsibility ensures that the external arrangement to effect changes in the power structure come into being.

The ethics of conviction is all about obedience, sacrifice, and is a path to postmodern mysticism. Do the right thing in your cubicle, and all will be well. Leading a virtual life is admirable, but it does not change anything about the contradictions and miseries in late modern global capitalism. It takes, at the very least, a "constellation of social groups" to effect any meaningful change in the balance of power of dialectic forces of history (Horkheimer, 1933/1993, p. 21). If the dynamic network organizations of the Empire (WTO, G8, NAFTA, World Bank, etc.) are to be balanced with an antithesis, it will take more than postmodern street threater actors wearing masks and waving signs. Rather, it takes organizing the grassroots individuals to bring about a counterforce of change.

> To be sure the individual cannot fulfill the demand to rationally shape the whole. (Horkheimer, 1933/1993, p. 21)

The individual is already incorporated in the directed labor process and being asked to act with the ethics of conviction, while scuttling the ethics of responsibility to change the whole production and consumption system of global capitalism, and its bed-partners, business and public administration.

Joining one side or other of the dialectic of history is a critical theory that rescues business and public administration ethics from being another emasculated moral philosophy. Business ethics stands on shaky ground by invoking Kantian categorical imperative (ethics of conviction) as an alternative to instrumental ethics (free market capitalism). It is shaky because both are ways to give power over responsibility to the greedy. Kant is mired in egoistic activity of consciousness, moral reflection, and idealism that in contemporary culture is filtered through the distorted lens of the culture industry.

Adorno's critique of Marx's *Capital* critiques the deducing of society from the principle of exchange (Hullot-Kentor, 1989, p. xvi). "As Adorno became a Marxist, a complete break from [Kantian] idealism was made" (Hullot-Kentor, 1989, p. xvi). Adorno's critique of "false immediacy" (or false organic nature) has as its outcome the resituation of a "true immediacy." That is because, in the aesthetics of film, as well as organic system theory, the composition of image and voice into some stylistic organicity tends toward "stiltedness" (Hullot-Kentor, 1989, p. xvii). It is the role of business ethics to obscure this stiltedness, so that spectators do not deconstruct the spectacle. Kierkegaard's critique of idealism is destructive. Yet, Adorno situates Kierkegaard in the Enlightenment idealist tradition.

## The Subterfuge of Ethics

I claim business ethics, in particular, is a subterfuge. The ethics of conviction is a doctrine to establish islands of individuals who do not enter the economic struggle on any ocean whatsoever. As Adorno put it, "Freedom from the economy is nothing else than economic freedom and remains restricted to a small circle of people as a luxury" (1973, p. 56, as cited in Hullot-Kentor, 1989, fn 34, p. xvii)

CT acquires its socioeconomic content in resistance to modern capitalism. Business ethics coverts the positive good it portends into negative evil. Business ethics joins the brotherhood of what moral philosophy formerly rejected. "The metamorphoses of criticism into affirmation [of business and public administration] do not leave the theoretical content untouched, for its truth evaporates" (Horkheimer & Adorno, 1947/1973, p. xii).

## Lack of Reflexivity

Business ethics and public administration ethics lack reflexivity on issues of answerability in terms of the administered global world order. The administered world of organizations, including the network organizations of WTO, NAFTA, World Bank, IMF, etc., rule the world more than the United Nations, or nations singly. Business ethics and public administration ethics churn out their apologetic ideology. As Adorno (1963/2000, p. 174) often repeats, "There is no right behavior within the wrong world." BE and PAE are ideologies imposed upon the oppressed, schooled to act with ethics of conviction, cogs in the global machine. We are told by business ethicists that there is no social change outside of market forces that can deal effectively with the circumstances giving rise to injustice, oppression, imperialism, and the globalization empire. BE and PAE have degenerated into ideological masks to cover up dirty business and market forces with ethics plaques.

## "CRITICAL THEORY" AND FEMINIST SCHOLARSHIP

The usual candidates for CT (Frankfurt School) are all males. Yet, there are feminist scholars who have contributed to CT. At the 2006 Academy of Management meetings in Atlanta, several feminist scholars (Joanne Martin, Linda Smircich, Marta Calas, and Anne Cunliffe, among others) put out a challenge to "ct" and "CT" to begin to do more than cite the usual list of white male scholars. To be answerable to this challenge, I would like to suggest how several feminists not usually cited in "ct" can contribute: Susan Bordo, Judith Butler, Hélène Cixous, Donna Haraway, Lucé Irigaray, and Julia Kristeva.

## Susan Bordo

Bordo's work links the spectacle of consumer image-dominated culture industry (TV, ads, etc., in CT) to formation of gendered bodies, to how images of the slender body train women to a constellation of disorders: agoraphobia, anorexia, bulimia, and hysteria (Bordo, 1990, 1993). Knowledge of the body is produced by spectacle from a standpoint of male/female dualism. Bordo is critical of treating body as just text. For example, the body-spectacle on popular media—TV, ads, and magazines—is a form of domination over sensemaking (i.e., what is a beautiful body). Resistance to the received body style depends on being able to decode and deconstruct the images. Recent work looks at male bodies from female (image) perspectives.

## Judith Butler

Butler's work is related to other poststructuralist and critical theorists: Kristeva, Lacan, Irigaray, Derrida, and Foucault (Butler, 1997a, 1997b, 1999). She cites Adorno in her desire to break with the bonds of traditional academic styles of writing and language. Sex, sexuality, and gender categories are narrated with an apparent natural-seeming coherence construction that is accomplished through stylized rhetorical acts of telling. Sex and gender control narrative coherence, which is accomplished within what Foucault calls *regulatory discourse*. Butler challenges biological accounts of body to decode what I call *control narrative constructions* (i.e., how systems are constructed as "natural," "organic," etc.). Control-narratives are products of regulatory discourses of sensemaking (Boje, 2006). Butler's ethics approach is that we should assume responsibility (what Bakhtin [1990, 1993] terms "answerability") for our narrative accounts, their incompleteness (or unmerged parts, unfinalizability wholeness). This is where, as George Herbert Mead puts it, our "I" is dialectical in relation to many "we's." Since we are in the ontology of intertextuality, our I–we has ethical responsibility, an answerability to change the social situation. This critique of narrative-control is at the core of an ethic-answerability practice.

## Hélène Cixous

Cixous founded the first center for women's studies in Europe (Paris) and is one of the mothers of feminist poststructuralist theory, with Irigaray and Kristeva (Cixous, 1975a, 1975b; Cixous & Calle-Gruber, 1997; Cixous & Clement, 1986). For Cixous sexuality is socially constructed by what we narrate in society. Her critical theory is influenced by Derrida and Lacan. From Derrida stems her interest in phallologocentric (masculine-centered hierarchy of language terms) binaries and, from Lacan, the split of unconscious self by duality of language and emotion.

## Donna Haraway

Haraway began by looking at the function of masculine (biased) metaphors and narratives in shaping biology science (i.e., toward reproductive competition by aggressive males seeking receptive females) (Haraway, 1985, 1990a, 1990b, 1991, 1992). She also looks at persistent narratives of racial and gender differences (1989, p. 377). She turned her focus to our love/hate relation to machines. In terms of answerability ethics, Haraway cannot be silent about the masculinity bias in science narratives. In terms of critical postmodern theory, she argues against any kind of essentialism or universalism.

## Lucé Irigaray

Irigaray is one of the founding mothers of feminist poststructuralist theory, with Kristeva and Cixous (Irigaray, 1985a, 1985b, 1993, 2000). She attended Lacan's seminars, and applies Derrida's phallologocentric concept. Irigaray deconstructs male ideology underlying whole-system thinking. She creates a feminine countersystemicity with positive sexual identity for women, and intersubjectivity between man and woman.

## Julia Kristeva

Kristeva is another of the mothers of feminist poststructuralist theory, with Cixous and Irigaray (Kristeva, 1980). She was influenced by Bakhtin's (1990, 1993) philosophy of language and the carnivalesque, and Lacan's psychoanalysis (from a less structuralist perspective). Kristeva's work develops carnivalesque reading of intertextuality (see Boje, 2001). It is in the intertextual in-betweenness that the local responsibility for our ethics is situated, rather than some universalistic claim.

## HOW TO BE ANSWERABLE IN A WRONG WORLD

I resist what the world has made me. I am answerable for what I consume.

- I don't wear Nike.
- I don't shop at Wal-Mart.
- I don't eat at McDonald's.
- I don't vote for Empire.

These are acts of resistance, but these acts alone do not serve the ethics of answerability. Getting arrested for nonviolent protest against war, being told by the university administration that I am not "corporate enough" to be an administrator of anything—that gets closer to Kierkegaard's self-sacrifice, but is still not bringing about answerability by creating viable alternatives.

My writing and speaking can begin to reflect upon how I am involved and totally complicit in the systemicity I protest. I am no saint, and cannot avoid the temptation to join in the culture industry, to go to its movies, read its news, rent its videos, ride its motorcycles and cars. The culture industry is my biggest addiction. What I obtain from the culture industry is so deformed and distorted that I must meditate hours to get clarity about how to live the "good life." Yet, as CT writers have stressed, my ethical convictions are not changing the systems that exist. To do that, I would need to actively change the culture industry. In truth, I am no match for it. My fledging website does not change consumer behavior, does not change corporate behavior, and barely interests students.

## SUMMATION

There is a critical ethical tradition represented by CT and ct that informs CMS (critical management studies). The purpose of this book is to develop those ethical traditions. For example, Horkheimer's books Eclipse of Reason and Critique of Instrumental Reason (1974a, 1974b), and his early and now classic essay Materialism and Morality (1933) ask for a reformation of Kantian ethics. The reform sought is that categorical imperative in an individualism capitalism serves to worsen the difference between business ethics and moral philosophy. That is, it is not enough to try to be good or ethical as individuals when it is the systemic processes that must be dealt with. Therefore, Horkheimer asks that the maxim that would be made universal be done at the level of people organizing with others to change the social system that is producing the unethical behaviors.

Adorno's (1963/2000) writing, in *Problems of Moral Philosophy*, also called for a reformation of ethics to a higher plane of moral philosophy. As I have summarized the history above, in the early phase of CT (Frankfurt School), Horkheimer and Adorno sought this reform of Kantian ethics to make it into what Bakhtin (1990, 1993) would call "answerability" ethics. Indeed, Horkheimer and Adorno were quite skeptical of the term *ethics* because it had been given over to instrumental and practical reasons to legitimate many forms of exploitation.

In their second phase of CT, Horkheimer and Adorno (1972, pp. 120–167) switched to a *Culture Industry* (aesthetic critique) in 1944 (German Edition of the book). The Culture Industry was "enlightenment as mass deception" (Horkheimer & Adorno, 1972, p. 120). They thought that a reform of *business as well as public administration ethics* was not going to get to a moral philosophy plane. Adorno (1972/1991, p. 98) followed up (without Horkheimer), writing a second book, *The Culture Industry*. The culture industry sufficiently socializes and manipulates people to be docile and complicit in exploitation. "The entire practice of the culture industry transfers the profit motive naked onto cultural forms" (Adorno, 1972/1991, p. 99).

Besides the directors of CT (Frankfurt School), associates had their contribution to a *Critical Ethics* (the theme of this book). Erich Fromm's (1947) book, *Man For Himself*, has the subtitle of, *An Inquiry into the Psychology of Ethics*. Fromm's differentiation between *absolute authority formalism* and more *practical ethics* is not quite the same as where Adorno and Horkheimer go in their early phase of CT. It is, however, another critique of Kantian ethics. Fromm brings Freudian and Marxism together into an ethical treatise.

Herbert Marcuse (1964, 1969) develops an ethics that is much more akin to early Marxism, to promoting the revolution. He misses the realization that Adorno and Horkheimer had made, that the *culture industry* rules, effectively subverting and co-opting ethics from achieving the ideals of moral philosophy.

Walter Benjamin (1955/1968) has his own approach to ethics. Benjamin foresaw the demise of storytelling, and its reduction to rather formalistic beginning, middle, and end, control narratives, where storytelling was once a product of oral community practices. Changes in the division and hierarchical control of labor did away with the community fabric where craftspeople practiced their telling and listening skills. *Managerialism* and *The Culture Industry* took over narrative, incorporating it into socialization and other forms of control over the labor process. The result is a narrative ethics that co-opted story ethics. I will develop this point in my chapter in this book, and will not belabor the point here.

In the late phase of CT, Habermas's project constitutes a return to the formalist, even absolutist, and universalism ethics, in ways Adorno, Horkheimer, Fromm, Benjamin, and even Kant himself would object to. The objection would be that it remakes the critical ethics of the Frankfurt School into an overly rationalist ethics and communicative principle ethics. Some CMS scholars are persuaded by Habermasian ethics, others by the Horkheimer, Adorno, Marcuse, and Fromm reforms of Kant, and still others by the vision Benjamin had. I think these strands need to be sorted out in CMS scholarship. It is my hope that this book contributes to such a project.

After the various strands and phases of CT, what came after was little ct. In this introduction I have focused on Mikhail Bakhtin, whose writing preceded the writing of the Frankfurt School. Bakhtin's project, like that of CT, was neo-Kantian. However, Bakhtin sorted Kant differently than the Frankfurt School. Bakhtin (1990, 1993) in writing between 1919 and the 1920s, looks at differences between his preference for answerability ethics, and the stalled Kantian formal ethics (e.g., categorical imperative) as well as content-sense ethics. Bakhtin calls for answerability, in ways similar to Horkheimer, Adorno, and Marcuse, to go beyond Kant's maxim (golden rule) and actually change the systemicity, a term I use in my own work to describe unfinishedness and unfinalizability of systems (Boje, 2006) so that it produces less unethical and more ethic behaviors. Bakhtin, Adorno, and Horkheimer call for intervening in the systemicity. Marcuse goes further and calls for revolution in the Marxist sense. Fromm has concerns with authoritarian ethics for it was part of the Holocaust, and the genocides before and after.

Besides Bakhtin, I have tried to show the contributions of a number of feminist scholars to ct. I recall at a CMS conference a few years back, Joanne Brewis saying CMS was cynical, but not prone to intervening. In short, for me, there is too much on Alvesson and Deetz, and not enough coverage of the roots of ethical positions in CT and ct.

## ABOUT THIS BOOK AND CRITICAL ETHICS THEORY

Robert A. Giacalone and Carole Jurkiewicz (Series Editors) approached me to request I undertake this project. They gave me freedom to choose whom I wanted to invite to write chapters. For their gracious freedom, I am eternally thankful. Each chapter was peer-reviewed and revised. I invited philosopher Douglas Kellner to write the preface to the book. I am thankful to the contributing authors of this book for taking on the topics I outlined, and for changing them into what they wanted most to do. The book is organized into several sections.

The first section sets the stages, beginning with a challenge to the field of social responsibility in business and public administration (Jones, Ten bos, & Parker have a new book out that is smashing). Then, we turn to Carr and to Zanettic who each have done critical theory work in public administration. This is followed by Heather Hopfl, who edited an issue on ethics of goodness, and does the kind of writing that makes deep connections.

The next set of chapters make topic connections: rhizomatics, dialogics of co-experience, story/narrative, and postmodern.

The third set of topics focus on application: technofuturist, international business, economics, university, environment, accounting, spirituality, strategy, and ending with Mills' work on silence of race/ethnicity in business (and public administration) ethics writing.

## ACKNOWLEDGMENT

Thanks to Stuart Clegg for his helpful comments on this chapter.

## NOTES

1. Kantian "ethics of conviction" not measuring up to an "ethics of responsibility" comes form Horkheimer (1947, pp. 6–7). Horkheimer is convincing that ethics is an emasculation (p. 24) of moral philosophy. Business ethics, in particular, is an ethics of conviction (or as Bakhtin, 1993, calls it, a content ethics) created outside of moral philosophy. As more philosophy professors have begun to teach "business ethics," the avoidance of responsibility/answerability by business ethics, as taught by those growing up in the business school, is a more obvious gap.
2. See Kellner's website Erich Fromm, Feminism, and the Frankfurt School, accessed August 28, 2006, at http://www.uta.edu/huma/illuminations/kell8.htm

## REFERENCES

Adorno T. W. (1955/1966). Walter Benjamin, Schriften, Frankfurt a.M., Schrkamp Verlag, 1955, 2 vols, and briefe, Frankfurt A.M., 1966, 2 vols.

Adorno, T. W. (1963/2000). *Problems of moral philosophy.* Stanford, CA: Stanford University Press.

Adorno, T. W. (1972/1991). *The culture industry: Selected essays on mass culture.* London: Routledge.

Arendt, H. (1955/1968). Introduction. In W. Benjamin, *Illuminations* (pp. 1–58). New York: Harcourt, Brace & World.

Bakhtin, M. M. (1990). *Art and answerability* (M. Holquist & V. Liapunov, Eds. & V. Liapunov, Trans.). Austin: University of Texas Press.

Bakhtin, M. M. (1993). *Toward a philsophy of the act* (M. Holquist & V. Liapunov, Eds. & V. Liapunov, Trans.). Austin: University of Texas Press.

Benjamin, W. (1955/1968). *Illuminations* (H. Zohn, Trans.). New York: Harcourt, Brace & World.

Benjamin, W. (1936/1955/1968). The storyteller: Reflections on the works of Nikolai Leskov. In W. Benjamin, Illuminations (pp. 83–110). New York: Harcourt, Brace & World.

Boje, D. M. (2006). *Storytelling organization.* London: Sage.

Bordo, S. (1993). *Unbearable weight: Feminism, Western culture, and the body.* Berkeley: University of California Press.

Bordo, S. (1990). Reading the slender body. In M. Jacobus, E. F. Keller, & Shuttleworth (Eds.), *Body/politics: Women and the discourse of science* (pp. 83–112). London: Routledge.

Butler, J. (1993). *Bodies that matter: On the discursive limits of sex.* New York: Routledge.

Butler, J. (1999). *Gender trouble: Feminism and the subversion of identity.* London: Routledge.

Butler, J. (1997a). Performative acts and gender constitution. In K. Conboy, N. Medina, & S. Stanbury (Eds.), *Writing on the body: female embodiment and feminist theory* (pp. 401–417). New York: Columbia University Press.

Butler, J. (1997b). *The psychic life of power: Theories in subjection.* Stanford, CA: Stanford University Press.

Cixous, H. (1975a). The Laugh of the Medusa

Cixous, H. (1975b). Sorties.

Cixous, H., & Calle-Gruber, M. (1997). *Rootprints: Memory and life writing.* London: Routledge.

Cixous, H., & Clement, C. (1986). *The newly born woman* (B. Wing, Trans.). Minneapolis: University of Minnesota Press.

Fromm, E. (1941). *Escape from freedom.*

Fromm, E. (1947). *Man for himself: An inquiry into the psychology of ethics.* New York: Rinehart and Company.

Fromm, E. (1955). *The sane society.*

Fromm, E. (1956). *The art of loving.*

Fromm, E. (1973). *The anatomy of human destructiveness.*

Haraway, D. (1985). *A cyborg manifesto: Science, technology, and socialist-feminism in the late twentieth century.*

Haraway, D. (1990a). A manifesto for cyborg: Science, technology, and socialist feminism in the 1980s. In L. Nicholson (Ed.), *Feminism/postmodernism* (pp. 190–233). New York: Routledge.

Haraway, D. (1990b). *Simians, cyborgs and women: The reinvention of the nature.* New York: Routledge.

Haraway, D. (1992). *Primate visions: Gender, race and nature of the world of modern science.* London: Verso.

Haraway, D. (1991). I'd rather be a cyborg than a goddess.

Held, D. (1980). *Introduction to critical theory: Horkheimer to Habermas.* Berkeley: University of California Press.

Horkheimer, M. (1933/1993). Materialism and morality. In *Between philosophy and social science: Selected early writings, Max Horkheimer* (pp. 15–49). Cambridge, MA: MIT Press.

Horkheimer, M. (1974a). *Critique of instrumental reason.* New York: Seabury Press.

Horkheimer, M. (1974b). *Eclipse of reason.* New York: Seabury Press.

Horkheimer, M., & Adorno, T. (1972). *Dialectic of enlightenment* (J. Cumming, Trans.). New York: Herder and Herder.

Hullot-Kentor, R. (1989). Foreword: Critique of the organic. In *Adorno's Kierkegaard, Construction of the aesthetic* (pp. x–xxxiii). Minneapolis: University of Minnesota Press.

Hunter, F. (1993). Introduction. In *Between philosophy and social science: Selected early writings, Max Horkheimer* (pp. vii–x). Cambridge, MA: MIT Press.

Irigaray, L. (1985a). *Speculum of the other woman* (G. Gill, Trans.). Ithaca, NY: Cornell University Press.

Irigaray, L. (1985b). *This sex which is not one* (C. Porter, with C. Burke, Trans.). Ithaca, NY: Cornell University Press.

Irigaray, L. (1993). *An ethics of sexual difference* (C. Burke & G. Gill, Trans.). Ithaca, NY: Cornell University Press.

Irigaray, L. (2000). *The wedding between body and language, to be two.* London: Athlone Press.

Kant, I. (1781/1900). *Critique of pure reason.* New York: The Colonial Press.

Kant, I. (1785/1993). *Grounding for the metaphysics of morals: On a supposed right to lie because of philanthropic concerns.* Indianapolis, IN: Hackett.

Kristeva, J. (1980). *Desire in language: A semiotic approach to literature and art.*

Maitland, I. (1997,September). *The great non-debate over international sweatshops.* British Academy of Management Annual Conference Proceedings, pp. 240–265.

Marcuse, H. (1964). *One-dimensional man: Studies in the ideology of advanced industrial society.* Boston: Beacon Press.

Marcuse, H. (1969). *An essay on liberation.* Boston: Beacon Press.

Mayer, T. (1994). *Analytic Marxism.* Thousand Oaks, CA: Sage.

Ritzer, G. (1993/2002). *The McDonaldization of society.* Newbury Park, CA: Pine Forge.

Stein, G. (1935). *Narration: Four lectures.* Chicago: University of Chicago Press.

CHAPTER 2

# ETHICS IN THE WORLD OF MANAGEMENT?

## Making the Case with Critical Theory

**Adrian N. Carr**

In the last decade or so, we have witnessed somewhat of a revival of interest in critical theory. For example, special issues of journals have sought to link critical theory and management and a number of book publishers have commissioned volumes that will carry very recent translations of correspondence and hitherto unpublished papers of the founders of critical theory.[1] The reasons for this revival of interest is open to some speculation. I have expressed the view that this revival is in large part a reaction to the turbulence that has been created by postmodernist theorizing, such as that related, for instance, to the findings of noncritical management praxis surrounding the fall of Enron's world (Carr, 2005). Alternatively, another organization I have investigated used critical theory to some degree of success but without necessarily knowing that it was the concepts of dialectics being applied (Lapp & Carr, 2005b). It is because of the continuing anxiety that arises from the dominant structural-functionalist and other conservative positivistic paradigms' failures to account for the social world and the

*Critical Theory Ethics for Business and Public Administration,* pages 29–54
Copyright © 2008 by Information Age Publishing
**29**

changes within it that critical theory is becoming not a response but *the* response to making a case for ethics in the world of management.

Postmodernist theorizing has raised many issues previously raised by critical theorists, but the proposed "solutions" are quite different. Elsewhere on such solutions regarding management development, I have maintained that, in spite of appearing to be a radical perspective, postmodernism leads to a very conservative political agenda (see Carr, 1996; Zanetti & Carr, 1999). In my view, there is a problematic disconnect of postmodernist theory to the "body politic" that has been described as "derealization": "the avant-gardes are perpetually flushing out artifices of presentation which make it possible to subordinate thought to the gaze and to turn it away from the unpresentable" (Lyotard, 1984, p. 10). On the other hand, critical theory espouses a firm connection with the body politic, a connection that brings the issues of ethics and morality clearly into focus. As we will shortly note, critical theory must at all times be self-critical, but in so doing it must be explanatory, practical, and normative all at the same time—as Bohman (1996) noted: "it must *explain* what is wrong with current social reality, *identify* actors to change it and provide clear norms for criticism and practical *goals* for the future" (p. 190, italics added; see also Carr, 2005, p. 485). The goal of critical theory is, as Horkheimer originally described it: "the emancipation of human beings from the circumstances that enslave them" (1937/1976, p. 219). "For the sake of efficiency, principles are adjusted too quickly, so reflexivity is sacrificed and the consequence is internalization of substandard best worst and worst best principles in a poor exchange for what is perceived to be ideal" (Carr & Lapp, 2005, p. 45).

The brief of critical theory is emancipation, but to move in such a direction requires recognition of its *own* political import and an ability to be self-conscious of the political context in which it relates to practice (Carr, 1986; Carr & Mason, 1997; Mason & Carr, 1999). Ben Agger (1991) aptly observed that "there is something profoundly unreflexive about a theory that forgets its own connection to the body politic" (p. 187). Critical theory requires the recognition of such a connection and in so doing, rejects any separation of "facts" and "values." *It is in its critique of logical positivism and its embrace of a form of "logic" called dialectics that critical theory carries an ethical trajectory.*[2] In this chapter, it is argued that critical theory brings us to a point of recognizing that social science facts cannot be separated from values, but our major decisions involve us in making choices between these bipolar "visions" (Greenfield, 1977/1993b). This is what has previously been alluded to as being a moral disconnect from which ethics becomes contextually valued *or* scientifically bound so as to create situational ethics (Lapp & Carr, 2005a). So, my task, first, is to convince those in the world of management that this is so. Then, we need to engage in a dialectical discourse in regard to the choices on offer. And finally, to discuss how decisions among and over the selection of these alternatives are to be achieved. It will be noted that after almost 10 years of study on and with critical theory, I have found that an ethical trajectory has become a series of recursive ethical moments in the controlling of private and public worlds of moral, amoral, and yes, even immoral management: "If the other can be conquered; if the other can be made to be like self, then self cannot be consumed by other: a much different someone else cannot engulf and de-differentiate me" (Lapp & Carr, 2006).

## DO YOU KNOW CRITICAL THEORY? NO, BUT IF YOU HUM A FEW LINES, I THINK I CAN REMEMBER THE TUNE!

Before proceeding further, I want to bring us back to the issue of the revival of interest in critical theory. With many "revival movements" we find zealots and worshippers. Some of the zealots' tendencies are to choose one critical theorist and then only substantiate those claims of "criticalness." Some of the worshippers have "forgotten," or have never known the original "script," and therefore have a somewhat hazy understanding of the original concepts. And, unfortunately, and somewhat ironically, some of the worshippers get to go to print with views that distort or contain misrepresentations of the original ideas and, in so doing, may aid and abet the detractors of critical theory. It is in such a context, particularly at this early stage of this book volume, that it seems appropriate to provide a clear understanding of what critical theory is and is not. So, as a means to identify and clarify some common misconceptions that have appeared in the discourse, I continue with a discussion of the critical purchase of critical theory.

## CRITICAL THEORY: MANAGING CONTAMINATION THROUGH CRITICAL PURCHASE[3]

I currently live in the pretty city of Sydney, Australia. Sydney is arguably best known for the Opera House and the "coat hanger"—the latter term being the local way of referring to the bridge across Sydney harbor. Sydney harbor is a working harbor and until 2006 allowed commercial fishing. But, commercial fishing has now been suspended. The reason for the suspension of fishing in the harbor is that the fish were found to contain higher than acceptable levels of dioxin and other chemical pollutants. The pollution is thought to have leached from soil of nearby contaminated industrial sites, although in part, dumping may also be from the direct discharge of industrial waste before enacted regulation was in place. The government's "critical purchase" was to buy out all of the licences of those commercial fishing operations directly affected by the suspension. It was a sublime example of the colloquial assurance that I'm from the government and *I'm here to help you!*

At this point, my readers might wonder why I have begun a section of the chapter that is supposed to be about critical theory with the story of contamination. I see this story as somewhat of a metaphor in relation to the use of the term "critical theory" and the associative term of "dialectics," both of which have been "mis-cased." In some earlier work, I naively suggested (see Carr, 2000b) that the organization discourse should declare a moratorium on the use of these terms for they had clearly been heavily contaminated. This contamination comes from a variety of sources, but the major source is a lack of understanding of the work of those who founded the terms. It is not uncommon to read a paper on critical theory and not find one reference, either original or secondary source, to those who originated the term and championed this school of thought. It is to the introduction of the correct casing of critical theory that I now turn our attention.

## THE WORLD OF THE FRANKFURT SCHOOL

In the social sciences, the term critical theory became part of the vocabulary largely through the work of Max Horkheimer (1937/1976) and the group of scholars with whom he worked. This group of scholars were located at the Frankfurt University and they were members of a social research collective at the Institut für Sozialforschung—the Institute for Social Research. Collectively, they became known as the "Frankfurt School." Established in February 1923, the key figures associated with the Institute were Theodor Adorno (1903–1969), Erich Fromm (1900–1980), Max Horkheimer (1895–1973), Otto Kirchheimer (1905–1965), Leo Lowenthal (1900–1993), Herbert Marcuse (1898–1979), Franz Neumann (1900–1954), Friedrich Pollock (1894–1970), and somewhat outside of the inner group, Walter Benjamin (1892–1940). This group is most often regarded as the "first generation" of the Frankfurt School. The time period and the major themes they had as the focus of their work somewhat separated them from those that later were also to be associated with the Frankfurt School—theorists such as Klaus Elder, Jürgen Habermas, Oskar Negt, Claus Offe, Alfred Schmidt, and Albert Wellmer, who as a group are sometimes referred to as the "second generation."

While the term critical theory is sometimes used to refer generally to the body of work of the Frankfurt School, the manner in which the term is invoked as a form of self-conscious critique that has a specific interest is the defining and uniting element among these scholars. The actual terms "critical" and "theory" have an etymology that is noted in many dictionaries. The word "critical" is derived from the Greek *krites*, meaning to judge or reflect. "Theory" is derived from the Greek word *theoria*, meaning view or speculation. As a form of self-conscious critique or judgment, critical theory in the Frankfurt School tradition goes further than the etymology of the individual terms "critical" and "theory" might suggest. In the Frankfurt School tradition, critical theory is not merely reflective speculation or to mount a critique, but it is an approach that has *cognitive content* (Geuss, 1981, p. 2). Cognitive content provides *a form of critical purchase* with *an explicit intention* of realizing an emancipatory interest. Thus, the aim is not simply criticism or reflection per se, but a specific form of *liberation*. Comprehending the social world through an optic of dialectics[4] is vital in gaining the aforementioned critical purchase, but at the same time critical theory requires that we are self-conscious and reflective about the manner in which that critical purchase is obtained. To explore this further, an essential starting point in the realization of this aim is to understand how the social sciences are very different to those of the natural sciences.

## FACT AND FRICTION

It was in his critique of "traditional theory," and its adherence to the natural sciences, that Horkheimer (1937/1976) challenged the positivistic assumptions that external reality is the author of truth or "fact." In his critique, Horkheimer sought to replace such assumptions with a dialectical appreciation of "facts."

Horkheimer commenced his critique of traditional theory by arguing that it had as its objective the discovery of generalizations about aspects of the world. This was the case whether these generalizations were derived deductively (i.e., as with Cartesian theory), inductively (i.e., as with John Stuart Mill), or phenomenologically (i.e., as with Husserlian philosophy). Horkheimer argued that the social sciences were different to the natural sciences. In social sciences, generalizations could not be easily made from so-called "experiences", because the understanding of experience itself was being fashioned from ideas that were in the researchers themselves. The researcher is both part of what he or she is researching while at the same time, being caught in a historical context in which ideologies shape the thinking. Thus, theory would be conforming to the ideas in the mind of the researcher rather than from the experience itself. Clearly, the "facts" emerged from the interpretative framework of the researcher/observer.

> The facts which our senses present to us are socially performed in two ways: through the historical character of the object perceived and through the historical character of the perceiving organ. Both are not simply natural; they

are shaped by human activity, and yet the individual perceives himself (sic) as receptive and passive in the act of perception. (Horkheimer, 1937/1976, p. 213)

In the course of making this point, Horkheimer (i.e., by injecting the Marxist, and most specifically, the Lukács notion of reification into his argument) argued that the development of theory "was absolutized, as though it were grounded in the inner nature of knowledge as such or justified in some other ahistorical way, and thus it became a reified, ideological category" (Horkheimer, 1937/1976, p. 212). For Horkheimer, Marxism was based on materialist reification of the forced "centered subject," created by scientific management. On the other hand, Lukacs represented idealist notions of the "'decentered subject' or the illusion of the coherent self or ego [that] is set off against more traditional Frankfurt School defenses of psychic 'autonomy'" (Jameson, 1984, p. x). Later, this was to become the basis for another charge that traditional theory maintained a strict separation between thought *and* action. In contrast, critical theory was about insight leading not only to emancipatory theory but to emancipatory praxis. Along with other first-generation Frankfurt School scholars, Horkheimer insisted that approaches to understandings in the social sciences could not simply imitate those in the natural sciences. Rasmussen (1996, p. 18) framed Horkheimer's resolution to the dilemma well, by saying that:

> Although various theoretical approaches would come close to breaking out of the ideological constraints which restricted them, such as positivism, pragmatism, neo-Kantianism and phenomenology, Horkheimer would argue that they failed. Hence, all would be subject to the logico-mathematical prejudice which separates theoretical activity from actual life. The appropriate response to this dilemma is the development of a critical theory.[5]

What is required, Horkheimer would argue, is "a radical reconsideration not of the scientist alone, but of the knowing individual as such" (1937/1976, p. 221). Through epistemology, this solution to the problem is an approach of such significance it cannot be overestimated. Notwithstanding the fact that the Horkheimer paper can be seen as deeply influenced by the Hegelian-Marxist idea of the individual alienated from society, it signified how critical theory was not simply reflective of orthodox "materialism" Marxism; and nor purely ideological or philosophical Hegel. Indeed, it was Marx's *Capital: Critique of Political Economy* (1906) that largely served as the touchstone paradigm from which resonance and departures were made by the early scholars at the Frankfurt School. However, the epistemological turn gave critical theory a "critique" of a different kind. Critical theory was about being *self*-critical and rejects any pretensions to absolute truth. In contrast to much Marxist and Hegelian doctrine, critical theory defends the primacy of neither matter (materialism) nor consciousness (idealism), arguing that both epistemologies distort reality to the benefit, eventually, of some group. In this approach, what critical theory attempts to do is to place itself outside of philosophical strictures and the confines of existing structures. Yet, by turning idealism, through materialism, on itself, Horkheimer became the mediator of the dialectic of materialism and idealism—and his own ideology became privileged. To decontaminate the criticalness of theory and praxis, it is then that one must first recognize contamination. Decontaminated critical theory, however, is the means to eliminate recontamination, which means to review the full case of dialectics.

## DIALECTICS

The inability of researchers to separate themselves from the subject of their research and to produce "facts"—absolutist metaphysical entities—led Horkheimer to suggest that subject–object relationships need to be conceived as dialectic. Horkheimer (1968/1992) asserted:

> The subject–object relation is not accurately described by the picture of two fixed realities which are conceptually fully transparent and move towards each other. Rather, in what we call objective, subjective factors are at work; and in what we call subjective, objective factors are at work. Consequently, for the historical understanding of a given theory we must grasp the interplay of both aspects, the human and the extrahuman, the individual and the classifiable, the methodological and the substantive, and not separate any of these, as realities, from the others. (p. 29)

Object and subject are mediated by each other, so the idea of valid knowledge being detached (i.e., and therefore neutral) from a knowing subject must be rejected. Horkheimer's colleague Herbert Marcuse (1960/1997) reinforced this advocacy of dialectical thought when he argued:

> Dialectical thought invalidates the a priori opposition of value and fact by understanding all facts as stages of a single process—a process in which subject and object are so joined that truth can be determined only within the subject–object totality. All facts embody the knower as well as the doer; they continuously translate the past into the present. The objects thus "contain" subjectivity in their very structure. (p. 445)

Like others in the Frankfurt School, Adorno put forth the view that there was a constant interplay of the particular and the universal of moment[2] and totality. Lukács (1922/1972) captured this point well when he remarked:

To leave empirical reality behind can only mean that the objects of the empirical world are to be understood as objects of a totality, i.e., as the aspects of a total social situation caught up in the process of historical change. Thus the category of mediation is a lever with which to overcome the mere immediacy of the empirical world, and as such it is not something (subjective) foisted onto the objects from outside, it is no value-judgment or "ought" opposed to their "is." It is rather the manifestation of their authentic objective structure. (p. 162)

Thus, for critical theory, the relationship between totality and its moments are reciprocal. All cultural phenomena are *mediated* through the social totality (Adorno, 1967).

The Frankfurt School's appreciation of dialectics is one that owes much to the work of Hegel, who, alongside other important aspects, viewed the universal and the particular as being interdependent. Hegel's notion of "development" came together in what he viewed as fundamental "laws" of dialectical thought. Namely, these were:

The law of the transformation of quantity into quality, and vice-versa.

The law of the unity (interpenetration, identity) of opposites.

The law of the negation of the negation. (Guest, 1939, p. 45)

As a means of gaining critical purchase, the second of these laws was particularly significant to the Frankfurt School scholars in relation to dialectics. This law is not simply about the essentially contradictory character of reality, but that the "opposites…do not remain in stark, metaphysical opposition, but exist in unity" (Guest, 1939, pp. 47–48). Hegel expressed this relationship as follows:

Positive and negative are supposed to express an absolute difference. The two however are at bottom the same; the name of either might be transformed to the other. … The North Pole of the magnet cannot be without the South Pole and vice versa. … In opposition the difference is not confronted by any other, but by its other. (cited in Wallace, 1975, p. 222)

For Hegel, dialectical thought is akin to "dialogue" in which the conflict of opinion results in the emergence of a "new" viewpoint. The dialectic, as such, was conceived as a "motion" involving three "moments": thesis, antithesis, and synthesis. McTaggart captured this dynamic when he noted:

The relation of the thesis and the antithesis derives its whole meaning from the synthesis, which follows them, and in which the contradiction ceases to exist as such…. An unreconciled predication of two contrary categories, for instance Being and not-Being, of the same thing, would lead in the dialectic

... to scepticism if it was not for the reconciliation in Becoming.... [Thus] the really fundamental aspect of the dialectic is not the tendency of the finite category to negate itself but to complete itself. (1896, pp. 9–10)

Lenin was to describe contradiction as "the salt of dialectics" and argued that "the division of the one and the cognition of its contradictory parts is the *essence* of dialectics" (cited in Guest, 1939, p. 48). The Frankfurt School scholars did not accept the notion of "dialectical laws of nature" and any notion of absolute truth, but they firmly embraced the notion of contradiction, the unity of opposites, and the underlying rejection of the Cartesian linear logic of foundationalism. Dialectical logic is a processual logic that begins with a "thesis"—any definable reality. Reflection progresses and this thesis is seen to encompass its opposite, or "antithesis," as part of its very definition. One "moment" of the dialectic process gives rise to its own negation, which means that it has, at the same time, a rise and a fall. However, it is that we cannot understand the reason for the next rise unless we have experienced the fall or the consequence. As such, for many, dialectics remain incomplete: "The process is comparable to tragedy in which the protagonist is brought down as a result of the dynamics inherent in his/her own character" (Carr & Zanetti, 2000, p. 907). What emerges from the dialectic of affirmation and negation is a transcendent moment that at once negates, affirms, and incorporates all the previous moments. Thus, the thesis should be understood to have possessed the seeds of its antithesis all along. If thought focuses appropriately on the reciprocal relationship between the thesis and antithesis, a synthesis emerges. The synthesis is the understanding of the unity that holds between the two apparent opposites, and which permits their simultaneous existence. The synthesis is not a kind of middle ground or compromise but a "new working constellation of the thesis and antithesis, a new 'working reality' so to speak" (Gebhardt, 1997, p. 398).

Adorno (1970/1997) was to remark "that *each pole realizes itself only in the other, and not in some middle ground*" (p. 44, italics added). So, it is from the synthesis of these views that: (a) one choice automatically creates its opposite; (b) each opposite affects and effect each other and continually, over a period of time; (c) from the synthesis of their interrelationships, consequences arise; (d) the realization *and* the privation of these consequences negate each choice; and (e) given that the universal and the particular are also interdependent, all (i.e., a and b and c and d and e) are a case of mutual causation. It is also that the synthesis of one case or critical purchase becomes the middle ground for the next critical moment. In itself, synthesis is not middle ground *unless and until it becomes the next thesis*.

The familiar triadic structure of Hegelian thought is, thus, not simply a series of building blocks. Each triad represents a process wherein the synthesis absorbs and completes the two prior terms, following which the entire triad is absorbed into the next higher process. Hegel himself preferred to refer to the dialectic as a system of negations, rather than triads. His purpose was to overcome the static nature of traditional philosophy and capture the dynamics of reflective thought. The essence of the dialectic is this ability to see wholes and the conflict of parts simultaneously. As Adorno (1956/1984, p. 38) expressed it, "Dialectics is the quest to see the new in the old instead of just the old in the new. As it mediates the new, so it also preserves the old as the mediated." Rather than viewing matters in linear cause-and-effect terms, dialectical thinking calls attention to the ongoing reciprocal effects of our social world. By implication, theory building is interdisciplinary and cross-disciplinary across social *and* natural sciences.

It is unfortunate that, in the embrace of the unity of opposites, some writers have misinterpreted the Frankfurt School scholars and their use of the term "dialectics" to be an embrace of oppositional thinking (i.e., dialectics as a simple series of dualisms or binary oppositions). This is certainly not the case and a significant misunderstanding. Adorno noted: "Dialectical thought is the attempt to break through the coercive character of logic with the means of logic itself" (Adorno, cited by Gebhardt, 1997, p. 396). In other words, dialectical thought steps within the framework of an argument to offer its critique. Juxtaposition, static opposition, and simple divisions certainly exist, but these are, by definition, undialectical and simple dualisms, since dialectic thinking requires that the conditions and circumstances of the whole be taken into consideration as well. This is the paradox of becoming. To become critical, which for this paper is to become "ethical," is to understand and experience "uncriticalness." To be something is at the same time, is to not be something else.

Parts of dialectical misunderstandings may stem from a widely adopted characteristic in much of Western philosophy that Irigaray (1991) observed is a principle of seeking out noncontradiction. While two oppositional propositions cannot be true simultaneously (see Whitford, 1991), they are locked into a relationship of contradiction and conflict. This has become so because traditional logic focuses on empirical (i.e., mostly quantitative) representations of reality, and necessarily builds on arbitrarily constructed foundations. At some point, the logic is abstracted from reality and it becomes formalized and centralized. Thus, in this "system" of logic, one proposition must prevail, and the other must accordingly be denied. Contra to such a form of logic, critical theory argues form cannot be separated from content. It must continually reflect the whole of reality, not just a simplification of it. As has been previously noted (see Carr, 1997b, 2000b, 2004, 2005, 2006b; Carr & Zanetti, 2000; Zanetti & Carr, 1998, 1999), dialectical relationships do not express simply existence and nonexistence; they also recognize the other possibilities available in the whole. By way of example, Gebhardt thoughtfully noted: "the dialectical contradiction of 'a' is not simply 'non-a' but 'b', 'c', 'd', and so on—which, in their attempt at self-assertion and self-realization, are all fighting for the same historical space" (1997, p. 398).

To help in understanding our assumptions, Horkheimer (cited in Gebhardt, 1997, p. 399) gave other examples of such dialectic logic and suggested we need to think in terms of substantive (i.e., to include normative) opposites rather than only formal/logical positivist/logical empiricist ones. For instance, the contradiction to "straight," which formal logic might seem to suggest is "nonstraight," but Horkheimer offered other negations: "curved," "interrupted," and "zigzag." Another example might be to recognize that there are multiple negations to power: resistance, powerlessness, and quiescence, all of which have different relationships to power and consequently different dialectical resolutions. Thus, "true logic, as well as true rationalism, must go beyond form to include substantive elements as well" (Jay, 1973/1996, p. 55).

The recognition and, indeed, the search for contradiction provides an opportunity to grasp an alternative "reality" and further recognize the one-sidedness of our gaze. In their examination of the arts and culture, the Frankfurt School scholars were quick to point out the manifestations in which "dialectical contradictions within . . . reality [are] the antitheses which 'negate' the theses" (Gebhardt, 1997, p. 398). In relation to art, some of these scholars argued that it had both a mimetic and enigmatic quality such that art carries both a similarity with reality and, at the same time, differences. Adorno (1970/1997, p. 54) spoke of this in terms of "the nonconceptual affinity of the subjectively produced with its unposited other," while Marcuse (1955, 1964) and Benjamin (1929/1997) found that the body of work by the surrealists offered an exaggerated dialectic that provided an opportunity to see the world anew. The juxtaposition of objects in unfamiliar association was one surrealist "technique" that elicited unforeseen affinities between objects and, perhaps, unexpected emotion and sensations in the observer. Marcuse was to discuss the "shock" of the juxtaposition as a contradiction that produces an "estrangement-effect" (1964, p. 67; see also Carr, 1997a, 2002; Carr & Zanetti, 2000). The estrangement from the familiar was also noted by Benjamin (1929/1997), who argued that surrealism needed to be perceived dialectically in order to appreciate its purpose, contribution, and, in particular, to understand that "we penetrate the mystery only to the degree that we recognize it in the everyday world, by virtue of a *dialectical optic* (italics added) that perceives the everyday as impenetrable, the impenetrable as everyday" (p. 237). In fact, Benjamin came to describe this wondrous revelation carried in surrealism as "profane illumination" (p. 227).

Thus, in the tradition of the first generation of Frankfurt School scholars, to be critical theory, critical theory requires a dialectic optic, as Marcuse (1960/1997) nicely summarized:

> Dialectical logic is critical logic: it reveals modes and contents of thought which transcend the codified pattern of use and validation. Dialectical thought does not invent these contents; they have accrued to the notions in the long tradition of thought and action. Dialectical analysis merely assembles and reactivates them; it recovers tabooed meaning and thus appears almost as a return, or rather a conscious liberation, of the repressed! Since the established universe of discourse is that of an unfree world, dialectical thought is necessarily destructive, and whatever liberation it may bring is a liberation in thought, in theory. However, the divorce of thought from action, of theory from practice, is itself part of the unfree world. No thought and no theory can undo it; but theory may help to prepare the ground for their possible reunion, and the ability of thought to develop a logic and language of contradiction is a prerequisite for this task. (p. 449)

In reading the last citation from the work of Marcuse, my readers may wonder if all critical theory can do is to act as a form of critique and as such is "merely" a negative discourse. For Marcuse (1960/1997) and others including Benjamin (1929/1997), this is not and cannot be the case:

> The liberating function of negation in philosophical thought depends upon the recognition that the negation is a positive act; that-which-is repels that-which is-not and, in doing so, repels its own real possibilities. Consequently, to express and define that-which-is on its own terms is to distort and falsify reality. Reality is other and more than that codified in the logic and language of facts. (Marcuse, 1960/1997, p. 447)

The life-world for Marcuse is one grounded in social change and once again, the concept of emancipatory praxis. The "negativity" in dialectics is in its nonaffirmation and in this critical trajectory the destruction of what passes as common sense is a disrobing act to reveal buried presuppositions. Thus, as Marcuse argued, negation provides an important reflective function through the modality of estrangement—it is destructive, but the destruction reemerges in a positive act. It is this act of disrobing and its critique of traditional theory that critical theory carries an ethical trajectory to which I now turn our attention.

## CRITICAL THEORY AND ITS ETHICAL TRAJECTORY

Earlier, I noted that in his articulation, Horkheimer originally described critical theory as "the emancipation of human beings from the circumstances that enslave them" (1937/1976, p. 219). From the outset, critical theory is clearly about liberation from forms of oppression and enslavement with a goal of more egalitarian social order. Such a stand is both a political statement of intent as well as a declaration of what is considered a "correct" objective for theory—a declaration of one form of its ethical trajectory.

Ethics is a system of moral principles on which critical theory takes a strong, overt stand. In some parlances, this might be considered a little curious, if not paradoxical. While the scholars of the Frankfurt School often looked to Marxism for its methods and inspiration, it needs to be recalled that Marx and orthodox Marxists have been scornful of the notion of ethics and have viewed issues of morality as largely a reflection of bourgeois ideology. Paradoxically, of course Marx and Marxism make value judgments as to the perils and exploitative nature of capitalism and the value system that capitalism reflects and seeks to impart. In a similar vein, at one point it was observed that some of Adorno's work reflected the view that morality, like truth, had in the past been turned into ideology (see Wiggershaus, 1986/1994, p. 475; see also Horkheimer, 1941/1997, p. 36). Adorno came to argue that no ethics are feasible in themselves, inasmuch as we may seek to change the social structure around us, or "try to live in such a way that we can believe ourselves to have been a good animal" (Adorno, 1966/1973, p. 299). The public and private dimensions of ethics are not separated in this discourse. Certainly, Adorno and Horkheimer could be said to have "worn their values on their sleeves" in many of their works—not least of which was in *Dialectic of Enlightenment* (1947/1997) where they tried to come to terms with how fascism could arise and gain a firm footing in a nation that seemed to embody the principles or doctrines of Enlightenment. It was Homer's *The Odyssey* that they saw as providing the clue, and in so doing considered the manner in which culture as an "industry" imparted certain forms of morality to legitimate capitalism. It was these forms of morality they found objectionable and it was the manner in which they carried the messages supportive of, and intertwined with, capitalism that led them to conclude, as Connell nicely captured: "It is the philosophical expression of the dominant, bourgeois subjectivity of modernity to which both capitalism and administration force every other form of subjectivity to submit" (2002, pp. 129–130).

Similarly, their colleague Herbert Marcuse (1955; see also Carr & Lapp, 2006) traced the individual and societal origins of morals and ethics to psychodynamic processes in which forms of social repression were to be understood in terms of a historical context—a context that includes whether forms of repression were required for a civilized society. A judgment needed to be made as to whether the systems of domination and repression exceeded the bounds of what was required for a civilized society (i.e., whether the amount of repression was *surplus*).

While, as I noted in the small number of examples above, the members of the Frankfurt School espoused certain moral principles they did not, however, articulate a moral theory or theory of ethics as such. Like their epistemology, their moral philosophy railed against forms of universalism, absolutes, categorical imperatives, instrumental/positivist version of reason, and forms of determinism. The meta-critique of German idealism, as I previously noted, borrowed heavily from Hegel. And the juxtaposition of Hegel with the moral philosophy of Kant is evident in many of the works of the Frankfurt School scholars. Whereas Kant proposed that there was some kind of "practical rule" that was a categorical imperative, the Frankfurt School scholars were critical of this view as it rests upon a positivist form of reason that is disconnected from an assessment of purpose. They were also very critical of the notion that morals could be reduced to a form of pure reason. Having noted that rationality and reason are prompted by various degrees of emotionality, at one point, Adorno and Horkheimer explored the manner in which fear plays a role in the genesis of identity (see Morgan, 2001, pp. 82–88).

In his work titled "Materialism and Morality" (1933/1986), Horkheimer declared: "That human beings autonomously attempt to decide whether their actions are good or evil appears to be a late historical phenomenon" (p. 85). The significance of the Church in a pronouncement of moral principles waned as matters of Church and State became more separate and "the acquisition of moral principles was important for members of the higher social strata, since their position constantly demanded that they make intervening decisions of which they had earlier been absolved by authority" (Horkheimer, 1933/1986, p. 87). The moral principles were authenticated by invoking a positivist version of reason as their warrant card—a rationally grounded morality. It was assumed that the "judgement of character and actions as good or evil should always be possible, just as judging statements true or false, or objective forms of beautiful or ugly is part of the human essence" (Horkheimer, 1933/1986, p. 88). In many senses, the moral principles should emerge as natural law that should transcend epochs and, just like commandments, guide human actions. For Horkheimer, no such transcending commandments are possible, for morality and ethics need to be read in terms of prevailing economic interests and a sociohistorical context. Moreover, transcending "guides" to human action, or the eternal "oughts" of Kantian moral theory, reflects an *undialectical* and, thus, mistaken vision of human history. For example, he noted that in the modern era, "self-interest would transform itself into morality, or rather the two would merge in a new from of human interest that would accord with the more rational condition" (Horkheimer, 1933/1986, p. 102; see also Jarvis, 1998, p. 186). Even at the level of a broad moral principle, the fingerprint of the prevailing economic interest is to be found in the manner in which that same broad moral principle is to be understood. For example, the moral principle of "equality" (like others such as that of "democracy" and "justice") is a normatively empty category:

> The equality which was to be brought about (and which, in the materialist view, developed with the exchange relationship) has been understood in various ways. From the basic demand that everyone should receive an equal share of the consumer goods produced by society (e.g., in early Christendom) to the proposition that to each should be allotted that share which corresponds to their labor (e.g., Proudhon), to the thought that the most sensitive should be the least burdened (Nietzsche), there is an exceedingly wide range of ideas about the correct state of affairs. (Horkheimer, 1933/1986, p. 110)

By resisting prescriptions of guides to human action and the embrace of instrumental/positivist form of reason from which they were fashioned, scholars of the first-generation Frankfurt School insisted upon recognizing the interests best served by forms of universalism, including moral prescriptions. In the interests of emancipation, the key is to illuminate the prevailing conditions that enslave and repress—conditions that are "amoral" or "immoral" (dialectical alternatives of morals); and, in so doing reveal possible alternative visions of the world. Thus, *one form of ethical "trajectory"* from the scholars of the first-generation Frankfurt School resides in their overt critique of the possibility of universal moral prescriptions separate from prevailing economic interests and social-historical contexts. A *second*, very much intertwined, *ethical trajectory* comes in the original critique of positivist forms of rational thinking as the appropriate basis for choosing between alternative courses of action.

In my view, Roger Foster (2001) correctly noted that Adorno and Horkheimer "criticize the positivist version of the Enlightenment, and *not reason as such*. The purpose (of) this critique is to uncover alternative possibilities of rational thinking, which are suppressed by the positivist definition of reason" (p. 73, emphasis added; see also Carr, 2001, 2004). Indeed, *it is positivist rationality that the scholars of the Frankfurt School saw as suppressing the matter of ethics.* Adorno and Horkheimer found Weber instructive in relation to forms of reason, as Connell observed:

> Weber's reformulation of Nietzsche's genealogy of modernity also influenced Adorno and Horkheimer. . . . Weber's distinction between instrumental reason and substantive reason, which picked up on Kant's delineation of the faculties of theoretical understanding and moral reason, was the basis for Adorno and Horkheimer's critique of the domination of instrumental reason. Weber's analysis of the rise of the state and rationalization of politics and law as bureaucratisation was also central to their picture of the totally administered society. (2002, p. 130)

For Adorno and Horkheimer, positivist thinking had "eclipsed" anything but the factual—a state in which cognition is the functionary of amassing and classifying facts. In his work, *The End of Reason*, Horkheimer argued:

> Reason, in destroying conceptual fetishes, ultimately destroyed itself. . . . None of the categories of rationalism has survived. Modern science looks upon such of them as Mind, Will, Final Cause, Transcendental Creation, Innate Ideas, re extensa and res cogitans as spooks, despising them even more than Galileo did the cobwebs of scholasticism. Reason itself appears as a ghost that has emerged from linguistic usage. . . . The name of such reason is held to be a meaningless symbol, an allegorical figure without a function, and all ideas that transcend the given reality are forced to share its disgrace. (Horkheimer, 1941/1997, pp. 27–28; see also Foster, 2001, p. 80)

The critical potential of reason required the examination of the historical context of the present and, in so doing, allows us to contemplate alternative possibilities. In dialectical fashion, for Adorno and Horkheimer, it is in self-reflection of the tensions/contradictions of the present lived experience that harbor suppressed alternative possibilities and visions—"unfulfilled demands embodying that context-transcendent force which makes possible a critical experience of the social order" (Foster, 2001, p. 74). However, Adorno and Horkheimer highlight that in making choices in relation to alternative possibilities, the difficulty with the use of reason is that, in the positivist world of a fetish with amassing facts, reason becomes a form of rationality "grounded" in the assumptions of the positivistic interpretative framework itself. This argument takes us back to the beginning of this chapter and Horkheimer's (1937/1976) critique of traditional theory and the "creation" or "discovery" of facts. Succinctly expressed, the problem highlighted by Horkheimer is that: "If our theories create the facts that are relevant to them, we can only explore truth within a framework that defines what it is" (Greenfield, 1980/1993a, p. 94). This, of course, has been an issue at the heart of the debate in organization theory over the incommensurability of paradigms. This line of argument, and Horkheimer's reflections on the "ghosting" of reason that were noted above, led to the possible conclusion that "in the absence of a neutral, universally valued or valid form of reason, 'the rational assessment' of conflicting approaches is beyond our reach" (Willmott, 1993, p. 697). It is in such a context that knowledge would appear to be grounded in the subjective experience of the individual; and to invoke a relativism that appears to leave little as a basis upon which to make judgements about competing and/or alternative views. It is in this apparent "void" that one could suggest a normative and moral alternative:

As Kuhn (1970) points out, our theories are not just possible explanations of reality; they are sets of instructions for looking at reality. Thus choice among theories and among approaches to theory building involves normative and — especially in the social sciences—moral questions. (Greenfield, 1977/1993b, p. 11; see also Carr, 2004)

Thus, the assemblage of "facts" needs to be seen as holding a moral vision of the world. As Greenfield (1977/1993b, p. 89) also observed: "In judging theories ... we would therefore recognize that we were involved in a truth-making and an essentially moral tasking within a disciplined process of enquiry into social reality." Echoing Horkheimer's critique of rationality, Greenfield argued that "values lie beyond rationality. Rationality to be rationality must stand upon a value base. Values are asserted, chosen, imposed or believed. They lie beyond quantification, beyond measurement" (1991/1993c, p. 194). To make judgements between the different "moral visions" that might be on offer requires us first to recognize the moral vision contained and projected by the theory and practice. Critical theory and its dialectic logic would assist such a process.

## THE WORLD OF CRITICAL THEORY AND ITS ETHICAL TRAJECTORIES IN THE WORLD OF MANAGEMENT

The discussion of critical theory as a form of self-conscious critique or judgment as well as the manner in which it carries ethical trajectory(ies) has significant implications for management. Clearly, to entertain critical theory is to move away from the fetish with facts and a positivist view of the world. With its dialectic optic on the world, critical theory would suggest that the preparation of managers should emphasize the development of a self-conscious and critical attitude rather than only the technical aspects of the job, such that critical theory and the management function grouping of planning, organizing, leading, and controling could indeed become dialectically interdependent. It is "unfortunate" that much of our organization and management discourse carries a positivism that embraces behaviorist assumptions about human beings and structural-functionalist assumptions about agency. Much of the current faddism for MBA carries, at least as a subtext, the idea that management is to be studied and practiced as though it was a form of science. *Critical theory would suggest that the positivist rationality carried in this discourse and practise suppresses, or pushes into the background, the matter of ethics.* I would argue strongly that critical theory is suggestive of a different vision and orientation—a vision where the world of management is conceived to be more of a moral art (Carr, 2004) with an orientation to the work that is based on an appreciation of dialectics.

As his work in the journal *Administrative Science Quarterly* showed, Kenneth Benson (1977) was an early advocate of the notion that organizations should be viewed through an optic of dialectics. Benson noted that dialectics "because it is essentially a processual perspective, focuses on the dimension currently missing in much organizational thought" (p. 3). It was seen as a way to open up analysis to the processes through which people in organizations "carve out and stabilize a sphere of rationality and those through which such rationalized spheres dissolve" (p. 3). Benson suggested that such dialectical analysis proceeds on the basis of four fundamental premises, or principles. These are that: (1) people are continually in a process of constructing and reconstructing the social context; (2) social phenomena need to be studied as part of a totality or larger whole that has multiple connections; (3) social arrangements are exactly that, social constructions with latent possibilities of transformation that become conscious through inherent contradictions in those social orders; and (4) there is a commitment to praxis, while recognizing the limits and potentials of present social arrangements. The manner in which rationality appears is one of the sources where tensions and contradictions provide a reflective (i.e., reflexive) opportunity to comprehend the ethical trajectory of critical theory.

The manner in which a dialectic orientation to the work of management and administration differs from that of the conventional "technical" orientation is summarized in Table 2.1. Previously I have called attention to this distinction (see, e.g., Carr, 1989, 2005, 2006b) but in a more restrictive manner in that the distinction did not draw attention to the issue of ethics. In this version, I also use perforated lines to symbolize an interjection of the normative and to interconnect the technical and the dialectical—a unity of interdependent opposites that through many critical moments may also serve to negate in both arenas that which is currently contaminated and unethical.

The call to view organizations through the optic of dialectics requires managers to adopt a different orientation to their work. With less focus on control and the rejection of the organization as being a "thing," managers needed to perceive their roles as well as those of others in the organization as being active ones in a broader process of transformation in which they act and are acted upon. This transformation is such that the manager should not simply become aware of dialectical relationships between structures and actors, but become more critical in the appraisal of the options in carrying through their tasks. Part of the role is to de-reify established social patterns and to expect contradiction to arise that will require a *working through* of the strains and tensions that arise. As Wilson argued: "Management … is a dialectical interplay of persons whose roles change from one part of the system to another, and who remain open to dialogue and discussion in their continuing concern for the care of public things" (1985, p. 139).

**TABLE 2.1  Technical and Dialectic Notions in the World of Management**

| Technical notion | Dialectic notion |
|---|---|
| 1. People are passive, optimistic, and cipher-like, with little autonomy. The organization structure is a predetermined "thing," acting independently of the thoughts, desires, and actions of human agents. | 1. People are active and social, and can have autonomy in determining their actions. The degree of autonomy is inversely proportional to the extent of surplus repression. The organizational structure is conceived as being in a process of transformation—a process involving a dialectical relationship with human agency. |
| 2. Organizations are abstractions from their general environment with the administrator primarily responsible for control, fine-tuning and acting on personnel to achieve equilibrium. Changes that take place occur as a result of the demands placed on the organization by factors external to it. | 2. Organizations are not abstractions but are representations of rationality (they may contain the specific reality principle) and the results of previous dialectic processes. The generative force of change is contradictions—contradictions that emerge from the totality of the social world. Stability is not the norm but transient and represents a state of obstructed change. Managers should not be preoccupied with control but with working out tensions and strains arising from contradictions. |
| 3. Social relations are conceived of in a positivistic manner as being "technical problems," thus removing areas of social relations from political debate. Part of the toolkit for "fixing" the technical problems is conventional organizational theory, which itself is embedded in a structural-functionalist perspective of the social world. | 3. Social relations have a time and place dimension that recognizes human agents shape organizational structures while being themselves subject to their own historical chain of experiences. Managers should therefore not only be aware of the dialectic between structure and human agency but, as part of working out the tensions and strains arising from contradictions, should open up analysis of the processes through which the current structures, powers, etc., came into being and how they might transform existing negations. Managerial actions would be examined in terms of the interests that are to be served and the ethical "order" they serve. |
| 4. The end results of managerial action are assessed in terms of technical efficiency. The tenets of scientific management provide an appropriate context in which to conceive administrative action. | 4. Managerial action is part of an ongoing process to detect contradictions and work through existing and/or potential tensions and strains without a fundamental desire to preserve a status quo. A touchstone to guide action is emancipatory interest. |
| 5. Facts are treated in their immediate form as truth and exclude knowledge of everything that is not yet fact. | 5. The form in which something immediately appears is not yet its true form and what one sees is a negative condition and not the real potential. |
| 6. The technical notion draws from the structural-functionalist perspective of society as its conceptual prism, embracing positivism, scientific management, classical organization theory, and behaviorism. | 6. A critical theory view of society is drawn upon as the conceptual prism. |

*See:* Carr, 1989, 2005, 2006b

In the working through of the strains and tensions the clashes of meaning that we note in the form of paradox, contradiction and irony can be used as a reflective opportunity to reveal the values that may otherwise be disguised by language, or in text more generally. Language can make and fake "reality," and as such, we need "tools" to help in the creation of the reflexive moments. An example of this reflexiveness can be noted in the work of William Scott (1985) who identified four contradictions that were inherent in a technocratic style of management science that we have come to know as *managerialism*. Scott argued that: "we should repudiate the orthodoxy of managerialism because it is a value system that encourages the treatment of humans in ways that deprive them of their humanness." In revealing such a value system, Scott identified the following:

1. The exacerbation of the subculture of poverty . . .
2. The widening gap between classes . . .
3. Cultural boredom wherein people are encouraged to pursue debasing titillations supplied by organizations for economic reasons . . .
4. Intellectual dishonesty whereby individuals with public visibility in management teach, research, write, and speak in (sic) behalf of systemically corrupt beliefs. (pp. 151–152)

In the preparation of the manager, a call to an understanding of the value systems could involve a greater emphasis on examining the moral dimensions and the values contained in the works of such theorists as Chester Barnard, Henri Fayol, Henry Gantt, Mary Parker Follett, Rosabeth Moss Kanter, Talcott Parsons, Michael Porter, Philip Selznick, Edgar Schein, Frederick Taylor, and Max Weber. Such an approach has been largely neglected—and obscured—through a reading in favor of the "technicians' messages" in their works.

In a similar vein, we should encourage those who research in our field to consider formulating their research questions in a different manner to those of noncritical-orientated approaches. For example, in her examination of administrative leadership in organizations, Colleen Capper suggested that the following research questions are pertinent to a critical perspective:

- Are the experiences, attitudes, values, and behaviours of persons from different social groups considered? How is what is happening in the situation perpetuating unequal relations among people?
- How is the situation encouraging conformity and the abandonment of critical consciousness?
- Who is benefiting from the situation? Whose interests are (and are not) being served by the situation? Whose knowledge/point of view is privileged?
- To what extent is the situation a dodge or crisis point that serves to distract the people in the setting from working on issues of equity and justice?

- How would people with social perspectives different from your own view the situation (in terms of gender/race, etc.)? (1998, p. 356)

The ethical trajectory carried by a critical theory approach is implied in the very construction of such questions. Ongoing development should enhance the quality and the quantity of ethically aware and reflective managers, thus disconnecting the moral disconnect from which emancipatory praxis would emerge. I expect other chapters in this book will surface other ways in which the ethical trajectory of critical theory is evident. But the challenge for us all is in the translation of that trajectory into the ongoing professional preparation of people and praxis.

## ACKNOWLEDGMENT

This chapter has benefited from a helpful critique by Cheryl Lapp to an earlier draft. This intellectual input is gratefully acknowledged by the author.

## NOTES

1. In the year 2000, the author was a guest editor for a special issue of the *Journal of Organizational Change Management* (Carr, 2000a) on "critical theory and the management of change in organizations." The interest in that particular volume was such that the publisher, Emerald, in what was for them an unprecedented action, had an additional print of 1,500 copies run in response to requests for further copies.

   Recent book volumes that have been commissioned include the Routledge series on the *Collected Papers of Herbert Marcuse*, a six-volume publication edited by Douglas Kellner of which three have, thus far, been published. Further examples are the series of volumes published by Belknap of Harvard University Press on the *Selected Writings of Walter Benjamin*, edited by Marcus Bullock and Michael Jennings, and also a volume by Henri Lonitz entitled *Theodor W. Adorno and Walter Benjamin: The Complete Correspondence 1928–1940* (N. Walker, Trans. Cambridge, MA: Polity). Additionally, a number of publishers have recently reprinted works of the Frankfurt scholars.

2. Previous work (eg., Zanetti & Carr, 1998) did refer to the notion of "ethical impulse," but as time has passed it has become very clear that this latter term is inappropriate, as it may lead, albeit inadvertently, to a factual inaccuracy. Ethical impulse implies the consideration of ethics was in some way a passive, incidental, or subliminal occurrence in the work of the Frankfurt School scholars. This is not the case, quite the contrary. Thus, in this chapter the term "trajectory" is paired with the word "ethical" as the preferred terminol-

ogy to signal the *active* or *deliberate* intention that is carried in the work of these scholars.

3. The material contained in this and the next section of this chapter represents an elaboration of sections from a number of previous journal papers by this author that the reader may also wish to consult (see Carr, 1997b, 2000b, 2004, 2005, 2006b; Carr & Zanetti, 2000; Zanetti & Carr, 1998).

4. The significance of how, in the traditional sense, critical theory to be critical theory presupposes dialectics cannot be overstated. Indeed, some theorists, at one level, no longer regard Habermas as a critical theorist, while much of his work was initially undertaken at the Institute, his work has drawn its inspiration from pragmatism and systems theory rather than the fundamental dialectical orientation that is the infusion of critical theory. Indeed, a recently translated series of letters between Adorno and Horkheimer reveals that Horkheimer was of the view that Habermas's work in the area of philosophy was "betraying philosophy and critical theory" and he would "bring shame to the Institute" (Kellner, 2001, p. 23).

5. The reference here to not only positivism but also pragmatism and phenomenology is an important issue. Horkheimer and his first-generation Frankfurt School colleagues were particularly critical of the early American "brands" of pragmatism. Indeed, at one junction Horkheimer (1947/1974) was to declare that pragmatism and positivism share an identification of philosophy with scientism (p. 45, fn. 29; see also Jay, 1966/1973, p. 83). For first-generation Frankfurt School scholars, pragmatism was too undialectical. Its concentration on "what is" qualified it as simply "a descriptive philosophy" (Marcuse, 1968/1988, p. 59) and was a hallmark of phenomenology that led pragmatism into error.

As far as the many critical theorists were concerned, the phenomenological preoccupation with describing the "what is" was the fundamental error present in most versions of pragmatism. Pragmatism, especially the early versions, assembled, analysed, and confirmed "observations" and "appearances," and allotted the status of "facts" on the basis of reductionist categories that the pragmatists themselves predefined. Horkheimer (1947/1974) argued:

In pragmatism, pluralistic as it may represent itself to be, everything becomes mere subject matter and thus ultimately the same, an element in the chain of means and effects. "Test every concept by the question 'What sensible difference to anybody will its truth make?' and you are in the best possible position for understanding what it means and for discussing its importance." (p. 46)

What is clearly missed by the pragmatist is a recognition and acknowledgment that the processes they engage are a mediated construction—mediated by the sociohistorical context and mediated by language, which itself is a vehicle of and for ideology. With this brand of thinking a kind of social amnesia (Jacoby, 1975) is perpetrated, in that we are left with a "received view" of "social realities" rather than what might be an alternative vision. Without recognition of such a perspective, pragmatism leads us into the trap of conceiving of the present arrangements as permanent (see Zanetti & Carr, 2000, pp. 443–444).

# REFERENCES

Adorno, T. (1967). *Prisms.* London: Spearman.

Adorno, T. (1973). *Negative dialectics.* New York: Seabury. (Original work published 1966)

Adorno, T. (1997). *Aesthetic theory* (R. Hullot-Kentor, Trans.). Minneapolis: University of Minnesota. (Original work published 1970)

Adorno, T. (1984). *Against epistemology: A metacritique* (W. Domingo Trans.). Cambridge, MA: MIT Press. (Original work published 1956)

Adorno, T., & Horkheimer, M. (1997). *Dialectic of enlightenment* (J. Cumming, Trans.). London: Verso. (Original work published 1947)

Agger, B. (1991). *A Critical theory of public life: Knowledge, discourse, and politics in an age of decline.* London: The Falmer Press.

Arato, A., & Gebhardt E. (Eds.). (1997). *The essential Frankfurt School reader.* New York: Continuum.

Benjamin, W. (1997). Surrealism: The Last Snapshot of the European Intelligentsia. In *One-way street* (pp. 225–239). London: Verso. (Original work published 1929)

Benson, K. (1977). Organizations: A dialectic view. *Administrative Science Quarterly, 22*(1), 3–21.

Bohman, J. (1996). Critical theory and democracy. In D. Rasmussen (Ed.), *The handbook of critical theory* (pp. 190–215). Oxford, UK: Blackwell.

Capper, C. (1998). Critically oriented and postmodern perspectives: Sorting out the differences and applications for practice. *Educational Administration Quarterly, 34*(3), 354–379.

Carr, A. N. (1986). The political economy of technological change. In P. Watkins, F. Rizvi, & R. Bates (Eds.), *Theory and practice of educational administration* (pp. 102–120). Geelong, Victoria, Australia: Social and Administrative Studies Research Group, School of Education, Deakin University.

Carr, A. N. (1989). *Organisational psychology: Its origins, assumptions and implications for educational administration.* Geelong, Victoria, Australia: Deakin University.

Carr, A. N. (1994). For self or others?: The quest for narcissism and the ego-ideal in work organisations. *Administrative Theory and Praxis, 16*(2), 208–222.

Carr, A. N. (1996). Putative problematic agency in a postmodern world: Is it implicit in the text: Can it be explicit in organisation analysis? *Administrative Theory and Praxis, 18*(1), 79–86.

Carr, A. N. (1997a). Burrell at play: Countering linearity by entering the land of the "dragons." *Administrative Theory and Praxis, 19*(3), 408–413.

Carr, A. N. (1997b). Responding to paradigm proliferation: Public administration as a moral art? *Leading and Managing, 3*(1), 9–25.

Carr, A. N. (Ed.). (2000a). Critical theory and the management of change in organizations [Special issue]. *Journal of Organizational Change Management, 13*(3), 203–304.

Carr, A. N. (2000b). Critical theory and the management of change in organizations. *Journal of Organizational Change Management, 13*(3), 208–220.

Carr, A. N. (2001). Understanding the "imago" Las Vegas: Taking our lead from Homer's parable of the oarsmen. *M@n@gement, 4*(3), 121–140. http://www.dmsp.dauphine.fr/management/PapersMgmt/43Carr.html

Carr, A. N. (2002). Art as a form of knowledge: The implications for critical management. *Journal of Critical Postmodern Organisation Science* (TAMARA), *2*(1), 8–30.

Carr, A. N. (2004). Management as a moral art: Emerging from the paradigm debate. *Philosophy of Management, 4*(3), 47–62.

Carr, A. N. (2005). The challenge of critical theory for those in organization theory and behaviour: An overview. *International Journal of Organization Theory and Behavior, 8*(4), 466–494.

Carr, A. N. (Ed.). (2006a). What does it mean to be critical in relation to international management? [Special issue]. *Critical Perspectives on International Business, 2*(2).

Carr, A. N. (2006b). What it means to be "critical": A case of the appropriate conceptual lens. *Critical Perspectives on International Business, 2*(2).

Carr, A. N., & Lapp, C. A. (2005). Wanted for breaking and entering organizational systems in complexity: *Eros* and *Thanatos*. *E:CO, 7*(3-4). 43–52.

Carr, A. N., & Lapp, C. A. (2006). *Leadership is a matter of life and death: The psychodynamics of Eros and Thanatos working in organisations.* Hampshire, UK: Palgrave.

Carr, A. N., & Mason, S. (1997). Beyond the detached and textual view of power: The importance of the "construction" of identity. *Proceedings of the British Academy of Management*, pp. 744–745.

Carr, A. N., & Zanetti, L. A. (1999). Metatheorising the dialectics of self and other: The psychodynamics in work organizations. *American Behavioral Scientist, 43*(2), 324–345.

Carr, A. N., & Zanetti, L. A. (2000). The emergence of a surrealist movement and its vital "estrangement-effect" in organisation studies. *Human Relations, 53*(7), 891–921.

Connell, M. F. (2002). Theordor A. Adorno and Max Horkheimer. In J. Simons (Ed.), *From Kant to Lévi-Stauss: The background to contemporary critical theory* (pp. 129–145). Edinburgh, UK: Edinburgh University.

Foster, R. (2001). Dialectic of enlightenment as genealogy critique. *Telos*, pp. 73–94.

Gebhardt, E. (1997). A critique of methodology: Introduction. In A. Arato & E. Gebhardt (Eds.), *The essential Frankfurt School reader* (pp. 371–406). New York: Continuum. (Original work published 1941)

Geuss, R. (1981). *The idea of critical theory: Habermas and the Frankfurt School.* Cambridge, UK: Cambridge University Press.

Greenfield, T. (1993a). The man who comes back through the door in the wall: Discovering truth, discovering self, discovering organizations. In T. Greenfield & P. Ribbons (Eds.), *Greenfield on educational administration* (pp. 92–121). London: Routledge. (Original work published 1980)

Greenfield, T. (1993b). Organization theory as ideology. In T. Greenfield & P. Ribbons (Eds.), *Greenfield on educational administration* (pp. 75–91). London: Routledge. (Original work published 1977)

Greenfield, T. (1993c). Re-forming and re-valuing educational administration: Whence and when cometh the phoenix? In T. Greenfield & P. Ribbons (Eds.), *Greenfield on educational administration* (pp. 169–198). London: Routledge. (Original work published 1991)

Guest, D. A. (1939). *A textbook of dialectical materialism.* London: Lawrence & Wishart Ltd.

Horkheimer, M. (1974). *Eclipse of reason.* New York: Continuum (Original work 1947).

Horkheimer, M. (1976). Traditional and critical theory. In P. Connerton (Ed.), *Critical sociology: Selected readings* (pp. 206–224). Harmondsworth, UK: Penguin. (Original work published in German 1937)

Horkheimer, M. (1986). Materialism and morality. *Telos*, pp. 85–118. (Original work published in German 1933)

Horkheimer, M. (1992). *Critical theory: Selected essays.* New York: Continuum. (Original work published in German 1968)

Horkheimer, M. (1997). The end of reason. In A. Arato & E. Gebhardt (Eds.), *The essential Frankfurt School reader* (pp. 26–48). New York: Continuum. (Original work published 1941)

Irigaray, L. (1991). *The Irigaray reader* (M. Whitford, Ed.). Oxford, UK: Blackwell.

Jacoby, R. (1975). *Social amnesia: A critique of conformist psychology from Adler to Laing.* Boston: Beacon.

Jameson, F. (1984). Foreword. In J.-F. Lyotard *The postmodern condition: A report on knowledge* (pp. vii–xxi) (G. Bennington & B. Massumi, Trans.). Minneapolis: University of Minnesota.

Jarvis, S. (1998). *Adorno: A critical introduction.* New York: Routledge.

Jay, M. (1996). *The dialectical imagination: A history of the Frankfurt School and the Institute of Social Research 1923–1950.* Berkeley: University of California (Original work 1973).

Kellner, D. (2001). Introduction. In D. Kellner (Ed.), *Towards a critical theory of society: Collected papers of Herbert Marcuse* (pp. 1–33). London: Routledge.

Lapp, C. A., & Carr, A. N. (2005b, July). *To have to halve to have: "Being" in the middle in changing time's space.* Paper presented at the 4th International Critical Management Conference, Cambridge University, UK.

Lapp, C. A., & Carr, A. N. (2005a). Escalating *mores:* Eleytherias i Thanatos. In C. Gustafsson, A. Rehn, & D. Sköld (Eds.), *Excess and organization* (pp. 118–138). Stockholm, Sweden: Royal Institute of Technology.

Lapp, C. A., & Carr, A. N. (2006). To have to halve to have: "Being" in the middle in changing time's space. *Journal of Change Management, 19*(5), 655–687.

Lukács, G. (1922/1972). *History and class consciousness: Studies in Marxist dialectics.* Cambridge, MA: MIT Press.

Lyotard, J.-F. (1984). *The postmodern condition: A report on knowledge* (G. Bennington & B. Massumi, Trans.). Minneapolis: University of Minnesota.

Marcuse, H. (1955). *Eros and civilization: A philosophical inquiry into Freud.* Boston: Beacon.

Marcuse, H. (1964). *One dimensional man: Studies in the ideology of advanced industrial society.* London: Routledge & Kegan Paul.

Marcuse, H. (1988). *Negations: Essays in critical theory.* London: Free Association (Original work published 1968)

Marcuse, H. (1993). Some remarks on Aragon: Art and politics in the totalitarian era. *Theory, Culture and Society, 10,* 181–195.

Marcuse, H. (1997). A note on dialectic. In A. Arato & E. Gebhardt (Eds.), *The essential Frankfurt School reader* (pp. 444–451). New York: Continuum. (Original work published 1960)

Mason, S., & Carr, A. N. (1999). Individual identity and organisational power practices: Psychostructure and political language. In Y. Gabriel (Ed.), *Organizations in depth: The psychoanalysis of organizations* (pp. 93–96). London: Sage

Mason, S., & Carr, A. N. (2000). The construction of identity in organizations: Beyond the cognitive lens. In A. Rahim, R. Golembiewski, & K. Mackenzie (Eds.), *Current topics in management* (Vol. 5, pp. 95–116). Stanford, CT: JAI Press.

McTaggart, J. (1896). *Studies in the Hegelian dialectic.* Cambridge, UK: Cambridge University.

Morgan, B. (2001). The project of the Frankfurt School. *Telos, 31*(1), 75–98.

Rasmussen, D. (1996). Critical theory and philosophy. In D. Rasmussen (Ed.), *The handbook of critical theory* (pp. 11–38). Oxford, UK: Blackwell.

Scott, W. (1985). Organisational revolution: An end to managerial orthodoxy. *Administration & Society, 17*(2), 149–170.

Wallace, W. (1975). *The logic of Hegel.* Oxford, UK: Oxford University.

Whitford, M. (1991). *Luce Irigaray: Philosophy in the feminine.* London: Routledge.

Wiggershaus, R. (1994). *The Frankfurt School* (M. Robertson, Trans.). Cambridge, UK: Polity Press. (Original work published 1986)

Willmott, H. (1993). Breaking the paradigm mentality. *Organization Studies, 14*(5), 681–719.

Wilson, H. (1985). *Political management: Redefining the public sphere.* New York: Walter de Gruyter.

Zanetti, L. A., & Carr, A. N. (1998). Exploring the psychodynamics of political change. *Administrative Theory and Praxis, 20*(3), 358–376.

Zanetti, L. A., & Carr, A. N. (1999). Exaggerating the dialectic: Postmodernism's "new individualism" and the detrimental effects on citizenship. *Administrative Theory and Praxis, 21*(2), 205-217.

Zanetti, L. A., & Carr, A. N. (2000). Contemporary pragmatism in public administration: Exploring the limitations of the "third productive reply." *Administration and Society, 32*(4), 433–452.

# CHAPTER 3

# PRACTICING CRITICAL THEORY IN PUBLIC ADMINISTRATION ETHICS

**Lisa A. Zanetti**

Other chapters in this book have addressed the topics of critical theory and business ethics, and, to a lesser degree, the broader social environment and its implications. This chapter takes a different direction in that it addresses the possibility of using critical theory to frame an approach to ethics in the public sector, a quite different task indeed. More specifically, this chapter addresses the behavior of civil (career) servants, as opposed to elected officials. I apologize in advance for the U.S.-centric focus, but that is what I know best. I will leave it to others to suggest a critical framework for civil servants in parliamentary systems.

## CONTEXT AND ASSUMPTIONS

Like much about the field of public administration, there is no universal agreement about what constitutes the proper role and ethic for the public administrator. Trustee, delegate, interpreter, discretionist, administrative

*Critical Theory Ethics for Business and Public Administration,* pages 55–78
Copyright © 2008 by Information Age Publishing
All rights of reproduction in any form reserved.

rationalist, and citizen-administrator are just some of the descriptions of the appropriate roles for administrators. Public service is conducted, and public servants operate, in an environment that is quite different from that of business (the private sector). Most importantly, public service is just that: public. Traditionally, there has been a distinction between politics and administration, although this distinction is often challenged both normatively and in practice. Politicians are elected to articulate and represent the will of the electorate through legislation. Administrators (public servants), by extension, are tasked with implementing the will of the people. This implementation is accomplished through the somewhat byzantine channels of federal, state, and local administrative offices.

Just as there is an extensive body of law and regulations governing the electoral system, so too is there a complex body of law and regulations that applies to the conduct of public service. There are rules and oversight functions, legislative and interest group involvement and citizen input. Concerns for democratic accountability demand that the work of public servants takes place in a fishbowl, with all actions and records open to media scrutiny (with exceptions for national security issues). The relatively short terms of elected officials and the demands of political campaigns mean that elected representatives often want near-term results even for intractable issues that require long-term vision and management. And for many public programs, there is a lack of clear performance measures, leaving public administrators open to charges of incompetence and inefficiency. These issues are all well documented in academic and practitioner literature.

Furthermore, public administration demands a commitment to serve the public interest and fulfill a public trust. Public administrators are often required to exercise discretion in implementing legislative and regulatory authority, which has led to considerable deliberation over the proper dimensions of administrative responsibility. Expansion of bureaucratic power has raised troubling implications for democratic governance, leading to concerns regarding the legitimacy of bureaucratic authority and adequate protection of constitutional values (Nigro & Richardson, 1990; Redford, 1969; Seidman & Gilmour, 1986).[1]

As the administrative state grew to its current proportions, concern about administrative ethics took on increased importance. At various points in its publication history, *Public Administration Review* has revisited the question of administrative ethics. Nigro and Richardson (1990) suggest that the debate as reflected in the pages of PAR has addressed three main themes: (1) the debate over whether internal or external controls most adequately governed administrative discretion; (2) the adequacy and appropriateness of neutral competence and responsiveness as core values; and (3) whether discretionary authority could legitimately be used to advance some conception of the public interest.

Rounding out the focus on ethics in public administration is the relatively new Ethics section of the American Society of Public Administration (ASPA). Founded in 1998, the Ethics section has grown quickly and has been one of the most active sections in ASPA. The section sponsors a journal, *Public Integrity,* and its newsletter *Ethtalk* has won a national award. The section has also been active in building online dialogue through the Ethics Network Community and an active listserv. Clearly, many practitioners and academicians are concerned with the dilemma of ensuring right action in public service.

The various approaches to ethics in public administration discussed above are often viewed as incompatible with one another, and tend to be presented as opposing tendencies on a linear spectrum: internal versus external controls, objectivity versus subjectivity, democratic values versus instrumental values. While the differing positions may at times be incompatible, however, they are not incommensurable. For the most part, these considerations of ethics offer alternatives utilizing a common currency— one that accepts as legitimate some form of the liberal democratic state and the importance of market values. This vision incorporates an emphasis on individual autonomy, a focus on individual rights, a reliance on procedural justice, and a commitment to (or at least a resignation regarding) the market as the economic regulatory mechanism, although there is disagreement on the extent to which redistributive policies should be followed by government. For the most part, a concern for rights and procedural justice precedes a concern for the good.

Increasingly, however, there is discourse within the mainstream discussion of administrative ethics that emphasizes empathy, a responsibility to future generations, and a commitment to do no harm: values cited in the ASPA Code of Ethics. It is within this space that I contend we may find room for a critical theory–based approach to administrative ethics. Critical theory is an alternative that presents a very different view of society, the state, and the political possibilities inherent in these. As originally constructed, critical theory viewed itself as humanity's self-knowledge, a means for helping restore self-reflection and understanding to individuals who had become epistemologically flattened under the influence of instrumental reason. The original goal of critical theory was to have a practical intent—to help reveal the socially constructed nature of the world, to explain that ossified social constructs passing as reality are changeable, and then to work to transform society as the expression of an emancipatory vision. I suggest that critical theory has a distinct moral impulse, as well, as I discuss in the following section.[2]

## THE MORAL IMPULSE OF CRITICAL THEORY

Moral philosophy or moral theory is the attempt to achieve a systematic understanding of the nature of right and wrong (Rachels, 1993). There are many approaches to moral theory—cultural relativism, subjectivism, utilitarianism, consequentialism, virtue ethics, and the Kantian categorical imperative, to name but a few. Nearly all the traditional approaches to moral theory, however, suggest an adherence to reason and impartiality as bedrock principles.[3]

The term ethics is conventionally used to convey three different, but related, ideas: a general pattern or way of life, a set of rules of conduct or a moral code, and inquiry about ways of life and rules of conduct (Hamnett et al., 1984). These principles of conduct are phrased in terms of the rights and obligations of social scientists to the people with whom they deal, involving three main commitments: the principle of respect for persons, the principle of beneficence, and the principle of justice.

Such an approach presupposes that ethical standards can, for the most part, be objectively and impartially applied, rendering judgments by "applying abstract principles to moral problems in an almost computational way, giving a procedure for deducing the morally correct answer in any given circumstances" (Clarke & Simpson, 1989, p. 2).This approach endorses a given definition of rationalism in which individuals can proceed rigorously from some point that is assumed to be true, and be confident that the result is likewise and necessarily true. Individuals are presumed to be autonomous, acting with full and perfect (or nearly perfect) information, unencumbered by their passions, relationships, or the world around them.[4]

However, the epistemological basis of critical theory requires it to take a different approach. In describing the critical perspective, Guba and Lincoln (1994) note that it is informed by historical realism, a position that views reality as shaped by social, political, cultural, economic, ethnic, and gender considerations that have ossified over time and are now, mistakenly, assumed to be fixed and "real." Critical theory contends that these reified structures are instead a kind of virtual reality, and we must seek to identify who, or what, has created such a virtual world, and why.

A critical perspective seeks restitution for historical wrongs and emancipation for individuals that are trapped in, and by, these hardened societal structures. There is a moral tilt toward revelation and the erosion of ignorance, incorporating values of empowerment and altruism and combining them with a stimulus to action. The critical perspective requires a transformative intellectual to act as advocate and activist, and, interestingly, demands a kind of resocialization—the understanding and mastery of quantitative analytical techniques utilized confrontationally for transformative purposes (Guba & Lincoln, 1994).

How can we take a philosophy like critical theory and construct an affiliated ethic? Critical theory's philosophical roots are in Marxism, and Marxism, in any form, has generally not been associated with any systematic approach to ethics. Indeed, Marx is said to have laughed whenever the topic of morality was mentioned (McLellan & Sayers, 1990). The prevailing interpretation is that Marx rejected all morality as a reflection of bourgeois ideology, a conclusion derived from his materialist conception of history (Wood, 1991). In the Communist Manifesto (1848/1983), for example, Marx writes that the task of the communist revolution is to do away with both bourgeois property and bourgeois morality. "Orthodox" Marxists have been openly hostile to the idea of ethics, considering any ethic to be the ideology-laden product of the bourgeoisie and therefore deserving of suspicion and contempt. This stance, unfortunately, has given rise to the perception of Marxism (and Marxists) as amoral, willing to justify almost any means to the end (the "dirty hands" dilemma).

But Marxism is hardly a value-free approach, despite the attempts of some to interpret Marx's remarks as evidence of the "value freedom" of Marxist social science (Wood, 1991). Marxism clearly offers value judgments about the inhumanity of capitalism. Steven Lukes (1985, 1991), for example, undertook the task of constructing from the more humanistic manuscripts of Marx an ethic that links individual self-realization, harmonious social relations, and the reduction of alienation. A large part of the confusion regarding Marxism and morality comes, Lukes suggests, from viewing orthodox Marxism (derived from Marx's later works) as the only interpretation. Lukes looks instead to passages from Marx's earlier, more humanistic work to articulate his approach.

Lukes's argument hinges on the distinction between the morality of *Recht* and the morality of emancipation. What has been interpreted as Marxist hostility toward ethics generally is in fact hostility toward *Recht*,[5] which Marx condemned as a means of justifying and stabilizing bourgeois relations of production by cloaking the interests they serve in the guise of first principles of justice, equality, and fraternity (Soper, 1987).

These principles of *Recht* have been defended by philosophers as varied as Hume, Kant, and Rawls on the basis of providing order and stability in conditions of scarcity, correcting for the weaknesses of human nature (self-interest). In this argument, the presence of differing conceptions of "the good" force society to rely on procedure and rights-based justice as a sort of least common denominator. Correspondingly, the smooth functioning of society requires a separation of public and private morality. *Recht* is therefore presented as objective, fair, and nonpartisan. But these claims are illusory, according to Lukes. This kind of proceduralism is not objective and fair; instead, it serves to perpetuate reified structures of inequality that are presented as procedural (i.e., fair) justice and immutable "fact."

Marxism maintains that the conditions of *Recht* are historically conditioned, specific to the distribution of wealth and the relations of production. Social and moral antagonisms are only part of the human condition because the nature of the economic base creates these. Individuals are largely shaped by the environment. If the environment is changed, so will be the individual. The separation of public and private morality is not a fundamental necessity but rather a practical convenience benefiting the architects and controllers of *Recht.* By providing the means for adjudicating conflicting claims, and designing the rules by which this adjudication is performed, *Recht* is able to delay any substantive societal transformation. Those who control *Recht* are able to co-opt those who seek change by offering compromises that lull the have-nots into believing that their interests are being accommodated. It is for this reason that Marxism has generally been antideontological, maintaining instead a teleological goal for society—the goal of human emancipation. The principles of *Recht,* for a Marxist, therefore can have no rationally compelling force (Lukes, 1985, 1991).

Before considering what a critical theory–based practice of public administration might look like, however, it seems important to review several prominent approaches to critical theory and their views on morality and ethics. An exploration of these issues is offered in the sections below.

## VARIATIONS ON CRITICAL THEORY–BASED ETHICS

Kincheloe and McLaren (1994) suggest that the Marxian tradition generally, and critical theory specifically, are not simply relics of some more naive past, a point emphatically shared by Agger (1993). One of the important functions that Marxism and critical theory serve is that of the "loyal opposition" for the promise of modernity (Jarvis, 1998; Therborn, 1996). In this section I explore the critical theory traditions of Horkheimer, Adorno, Habermas, and Benhabib as important representative thinkers, and then draw some conclusions based on a synthesis of these approaches.

## HORKHEIMER: SYMPATHY, COMPASSION, AND A REJECTION OF CATEGORICAL "OUGHTS"

Max Horkheimer did not elaborate a full moral theory. His lack of systematic attention was primarily due to his interpretation of materialism, which did not separate the theoretical and the practical. Given that his critical theory was, above all, to have a practical intent, there seemed to be little need for a separate theory of action specializing in ethical action (Schnädelbach, 1985–86).

Horkheimer was very much in agreement with Kant's dictate that persons must never be treated as merely means to an end. However, he noted that such a standard was in direct contrast to "that which is the rule in the bourgeois world" (Torpey, 1986, p. 72). Capitalist society contains the seed of emancipatory potential but represses it in the interests of promoting self-preservation and self-interest. Morality is a historical phenomenon, influenced by the prevailing social and economic conditions, and understandable using dialectical logic. Horkheimer's morality therefore rejects categorical imperatives, universalism, and instrumental reason.

Horkheimer's rejection of the categorical imperative is rooted in his commitment to dialectical materialism. Categorical oughts suggest a connection to some absolute consciousness, which Horkheimer does not accept: "Binding moral commandments do not exist" (1937/1982, p. 93). The acceptance of obligations points back to an earlier acceptance of commandments and contracts, and Horkheimer draws on Freud to argue that such consciousness of duty can have a profane origin in the internalization of social compulsion (a point later echoed by Marcuse). Reasoning dialectically, Horkheimer argued that *the specifically Moral lies precisely in what cannot be expected, demanded, or compelled* (Schnädelbach, 1985–86).

Instead of relying exclusively on reason and unconditional "oughts," Horkheimer incorporated aspects of emotivism. Emotivism recognizes that moral language is not fact-stating language. Moral language is used as a means for influencing people's behavior, and to express (not report) one's own attitude (Rachels, 1993). Accordingly, Horkheimer emphasized sympathy, compassion, and love over interest and duty. Sympathy and compassion are especially central to his formulation of morality. In order to counteract the prevailing social emphasis on individualism, individuals must be able to sympathize with the suffering of others. *Sympathy thus constitutes an act of protest, because we dare to take exception to the norms of society.* Likewise, compassion recognizes the self in the suffering of the other. Compassion unites the universal with the individual, and the general with the particular. "The moral feeling has something to do with love...but this love concerns the person not as an economic subject nor as an item in the property of the one who loves, but rather as the potential member of a happy humanity" (Horkheimer, 1937/1982, pp. 94–95).

A critical theory of society that understands its purpose as improving the human situation must emphasize human needs and satisfaction in concrete ways. Similarly, such a theory must privilege neither pure reason nor pure feeling, since morality and ethics cannot survive where reason and emotion are separated. For Horkheimer, morality is a psychic disposition that incorporates morally relevant feeling (sympathy and compassion) and translates it into active form (solidarity and the interest in eliminating social injustice) (Schnädelbach, 1985–86).

## HABERMAS: CRITICAL THEORY AND THE PROJECT
## OF DISCOURSE

Jürgen Habermas, generally considered the most direct intellectual heir to the earlier Frankfurt School, has focused on speech (language) as the key to societal and political consensus. Habermas's project is one of remaking critical theory to revitalize and rehabilitate the project of modernity. To accomplish this goal, he incorporates the social contract theory articulated by Locke and Rousseau with Kant's concept of moral autonomy and the moral development theories of Kohlberg (Benhabib & Dallmayr, 1990). Communicative (or discourse) ethics suggests procedural justice as the universal basis for civil, political, and social rights (Ingram, 1993).

The foundation for communicative ethics is provided by Habermas's conception of communicative rationality, the activity of reflecting upon our background assumptions about the world, and bringing our basic norms to the fore to be questioned and negotiated. Critical theory, for Habermas, is a function of critiquing language as the source of human unfreedom.

The inability to communicate effectively has specific repercussions in the public sphere. As the arena in which various interests in society engage in discourse related to the establishment and development of the normative agenda, the public sphere must be accessible to all interests in society. Societies permeated by inequality cannot engage in authentic discourse. Habermas contends that the public sphere has been narrowed to the point where it reflects mostly a preoccupation with solving technical problems, a construction that has created political apathy and reduced the citizen's role to the passive function of choosing between alternative sets of administrative personnel (Habermas, 1962, 1971, 1979; see also Denhardt, 1981b).

Habermas's solution is to reinvigorate the public sphere through discourse. Citizens can raise issues in the public sphere, assess the universality of the issue, and arrive at consensus regarding the proper public position. Habermas envisions a conception of the public sphere as a space for social learning, criticism, and autonomy—collectively, rather than individually, defined (Bohman, 1990). The goal of Habermas's discourse ethics is to provide a theory of justice within which competing normative claims can be fairly and impartially adjudicated. In Habermas's discourse model, agents are not completely autonomous, as they are in liberal theory. Societal norms must be established in dialogue, with each participant behaving in an actively empathetic fashion. Still, interests that are purely personal or nongeneralizable are not suitable for establishment as societal norms, though they should be respected by the community and accommodated if possible. Minorities must be content to accept conditional compromises until they can convince the majority of the superiority of their argument (Bohman, 1995; Braaten, 1991).

Habermas is closest to the Kantian tradition of moral theory, except that he replaces Kant's categorical imperative with the procedure for argumentation. For Kant, moral subjects are bound by a moral law that human nature dictates. This law tells us to act only in ways that we could rationally agree to have everyone act. Principles that are not universalizable must be rejected, because we cannot accept a principle that does not apply for everyone. There is no situational morality. We must always determine what is right before we can determine what is good (O'Neill, 1993; Schneewind, 1993). It is the opposite of utilitarianism, which dictates that we must first determine what is good, and allow that determination to dictate our actions.

## FEMINIST REFINEMENTS:
## BENHABIB'S GENDERED DISCOURSE

Both the liberal and the Habermasian approaches to ethics require a deontological stance that necessarily separates the public from the private domains. The moral self is conceptualized as disembedded and disembodied (Haas & Deetz, 2000). For women, this separation has had the effect of removing them, their perspectives, and their interests from most of the discussion of politics and philosophy. One of the major contributions of feminist theory in the late 20th century has been to deconstruct the perception of liberal political and philosophical theory as gender-neutral. In fact, the "self-evident truths" of equality, freedom, and reciprocity, historically have stopped at the household door (Benhabib, 1992; Fraser, Hornsby, & Lovibond, 1992). The sphere of justice encompassed only independent, autonomous individuals (generally male) in their transactions with one another; considerations of justice in the domestic–intimate sphere of the household were beyond the pale, excluded from moral and political deliberations (Benhabib, 1987, in Jos & Hines, 1993).

But the relegation of women to the private sphere has more complex ramifications than might otherwise be supposed. The exclusion of women and the female perspective is not simply political incorrectness or a moral blind spot. It represents an epistemological error as well. Women, having been omitted from the discourse, cannot simply be reinserted into the public sphere to "correct" the picture (Benhabib, 1992), for this has the effect of forcing women to fit into a model of life and reason that was constructed without the benefit of women's measurements, so to speak. Accommodating the female form requires a comprehensive overhaul.

Benhabib argues that the task of a feminist critical theory is laid out along several dimensions. First, an analysis of the ways in which gender-sex systems have contributed to the oppression of women in the political realm is necessary. Women have traditionally been viewed as negations—woman is what man happens not to be; just like men, only their opposites (Benhabib, 1992). Second, we must recognize that much, if not most, of contemporary moral theory is based on the dichotomy between conceptions of justice and the good life, and work to overcome that dichotomy by engaging in normative, philosophical reflection that anticipates a utopian goal (Kittay & Meyers, 1987).

Benhabib's greatest argument with Habermas is on his reliance on the work of Kohlberg's six-step hierarchy of moral understanding in building his discourse ethic (Kohlberg, 1981; Meyers & Kittay, 1987). Carol Gilligan's (1992) germinal work effectively destroyed the idea that there is only one acceptable type of moral reasoning. The "ethic of justice" preponderant in the work of Kohlberg and others is markedly different from the "ethic of care" Gilligan proposes that most women employ—an approach distinct from and parallel to that employed by men. The central concern in the care ethic is responsiveness to others. Developing and maintaining a network of connections, sustained by communication, is more often the course of women. In Gilligan's care ethic, the more "advanced" stages of moral reasoning include recognition of the illogic in separating selves from others, in resolving the tension between selves and others (the "morality of nonviolence"), and a universal condemnation of exploitation and hurt (the care ethic). Women's manner of moral reasoning may be incompatible with Kohlberg's approach, but it is commensurable in terms of moral worth (Gilligan, 1982; Meyers & Kittay, 1987).

Benhabib seeks to improve upon the Habermasian discourse model by reconstructing it in a way that both accommodates feminist criticisms and helps articulate alternative conceptions of the public sphere. She develops her argument by building on Gilligan, using the conceptions of generalized and concrete others that have been viewed by contemporary (androcentric) moral theory as incompatible or even antagonistic. The generalized other corresponds to the public persona, the atomized, rational being of social contract theory—each person is like every other person, only separate. The interactions between generalized others are distant and institutionalized. The moral categories that accompany these interactions are those of right, obligation, and entitlement, and individuals are accorded a status worthy of respect, duty, and dignity (Benhabib, 1992).

The concrete other recognizes the unique history, identity, and affective-emotional constitution of each individual. With the concrete other, we can recognize and acknowledge the needs and desires of the other, not just the rights and entitlements. Our interactions tend to be private and noninstitutional (though they do not have to be), operating under the norms of friendship, love, sympathy, solidarity, and care, which accompany concerns for responsibility, bonding, and sharing (Benhabib, 1992).

Benhabib argues that ignoring the standpoint of the concrete other, as Kohlberg does, leads to epistemic incoherence in universalistic moral theories by perpetuating the idea of the static self. She seeks a kind of "interactive universalism," which draws on Habermas and Peirce but provides a greater opportunity for feminist critique to redefine the boundaries of the public sphere. Where Habermas suggests that one first assume the generalized (universalistic) standpoint, followed by an assumption about the standpoint of the concrete other, Benhabib urges one simultaneously to assume the standpoints of both the concrete and generalized other (Benhabib, 1992; Haas & Deetz, 2000).

This may be accomplished by engaging in a "moral conversation" in which the goal is not to reach a rationally motivated consensus but rather to demonstrate the willingness and readiness to seek understanding with the other in an open and reflexive manner. This moral conversation does not even have to be a conversation in the presence of the other:

> To think from the perspective of everyone else is to know how to listen to what the other is saying, or when the voices of others are absent, to imagine to oneself a conversation with the other as dialogue partner. (Benhabib, 1992, p. 137)

Importantly, Benhabib's conceptualization of a moral conversation permits one to transcend the "ethic of justice" and "ethic of care" dichotomy (Haas & Deetz, 2002).

## CHARACTERISTICS OF A CRITICAL THEORY–BASED MORALITY AND ETHICS: A SYNTHESIS

Lukes (1985, 1991) construes a Marxist ethic as a form of long-term consequentialism, in which pursuing the goal of human emancipation is the overriding guide to action. Such a characterization is inextricably linked to Marx's purpose of interpreting the world with a view toward changing it. It is also different from a liberal democratic perspective in that it requires a two-tier approach to morality. Individuals must not only accept certain abstract rights and principles, but must also assume a certain responsibility to do more than simply deplore society's failure to respect these. Such an approach commits actors not only to "being moral," but to political activism as well (Soper, 1987). Morality must be considered deeply rooted in all forms of social life and inseparable from social ideals. It is not a passive or secondary consideration, but integral to all human behavior.

There are problems with this approach, of course—problems that are inherent in consequentialist approaches in general. A frequent criticism of consequentialism is that it could lead an agent to commit horrendous deeds so long as they promised the best consequences (Pettit, 1991; Scheffler, 1988). Deontological approaches widely concede that it is sometimes wrong to produce the best result overall, and right not to do so, when producing such a result violates some bedrock principle. Lukes recognizes that the long-term focus of Marxist consequentialism renders it far less sensitive to respecting the liberties and interests of persons in the present.

To ameliorate this weakness, I suggest that the critical feminist approach of Margaret Urban Walker be considered and incorporated. Like Benhabib, Walker dislikes the theoretical-juridical approach to morality and ethics, an approach that she considers a template rather than a moral theory, one that represents morality as compact, propositionally codifiable, and impersonally action-guiding (Walker, 1998). She proposes an expressive-collaborative approach to morality and ethics that acknowledges the interpersonal and collaborative nature of morality. Individuals learn to understand one another and express their understandings through what she calls "practices of responsibility" (Walker, 1998, p. 9). To arrive at this position, Walker envisions morality as a social negotiation in real time, where members of a community work to refine understanding, extend consensus, and eliminate conflict.

This cannot be accomplished, however, unless a community is in equilibrium—where equilibrium is present among people as well as within them. Such equilibria coordinate beliefs, perceptions, expressions, actions, and responses. They are also reflective, critical, narrative, and grounded in analogy. Reliance on analogy and narrative honors the entrenchment, embodiment, and preservation of the moral trainings, discourses, institutions, judgments, and practices of the community (Walker, 1998, p. 70).

Critical reflection, which tests communal understandings of moral practices, pushes toward transparency, which Walker also values. Ideally, she suggests, "moral accounts must make sense to those by whom, to whom, and . . . about whom they are given" (Walker, 1998, p. 70). Enhancing transparency encourages us as individuals to "see through the haze of habitual assumptions and our comfortable or uncomfortable familiarity with them in order to see what is actually going on" (Walker, 1998, p. 216).

Based on the discussion in the sections above, I suggest that a critical theory–based morality and ethics must contain a synthesis of the following components:

- **Skeptical attitudes toward *Recht*.** An ethical stance grounded in critical theory would need to acknowledge the historical context and social construction of the "rules" governing commonly accepted practices of right and wrong. Rather than subscribing to the cult of the Constitution, a critical-ethical stance would accept that the Constitution and our legal system are products of Enlightenment reason with all its inherent shortcomings. The rules of elections and procedural approaches to justice would be viewed critically, as well. Outcomes of illegitimate processes need not be accepted as binding (see also Zanetti & Carr, 1998). Instead, an administrator practicing critical theory would open (or create) space for what Giroux calls "counter-narratives," and see that these counter-narratives receive more than simply formal attention.

- **Reflective self-consciousness**. An ethical stance grounded in critical theory would likewise need to establish and maintain a certain awareness and purposiveness regarding one's actions in the world. This is not easily done, since societal psychodynamics often inhibit active resistance to the status quo by instilling feelings of guilt regarding nonconformance (see Zanetti & Carr, 1998).
- **Sympathy and compassion**. Following Horkheimer, Benhabib, and Walker, an ethical stance grounded in critical theory would incorporate sensitivity to the concrete other. Sympathy with voices on the margins represents an act of protest. Compassion recognizes the suffering of the self in the suffering of others.
- **Practices of responsibility**. Following Walker, practices of responsibility attempt to place people and responsibilities in context with respect to one another. By pushing toward transparency, unequal, unfair, destructive, and exploitative practices become revealed. Transparency is powerful because it exposes elaborate justifications and causes embarrassment, thus creating opportunities for transformation.

## PRACTICING CRITICAL THEORY IN PUBLIC ADMINISTRATION

Since the early 1980s there has been an ongoing attempt to apply aspects of critical theory to public administration and public policy.[6] The interest in critical theory in public administration grew out of a desire to reconnect theory and practice, reuniting fact and value, politics and administration. Its most clearly stated goals have been to address the conditions of domination and dependence that characterize society; to reconnect theory and practice in enlightened, emancipated action (praxis); to examine the basis of bureaucratic domination and the ideological justifications for it; and to replace the instrumental/technical foundations of public policy formation with one based on consensual decision making (Denhardt, 1981a). Additionally, critical theorists in public administration seek to use the powerful tool offered by critique to challenge the implicit endorsement of the status quo; to place policy questions in a larger historical and normative context; to recognize the emphasis on order and regulation creates conditions of power and dependence that lead to societal conflict and disorder; and to examine and democratize social relationships wherever possible (Denhardt, 1981a).

Missing from the discussion so far has been an examination of the ethical implications of applying critical theory to public administration. The literature on administrative discretion amply illustrates that public servants are not of singular mind or unified action. In many instances, administrators are required to make judgment calls based on their own interpretation of the proper ends (as well as means) of a given administrative action or policy initiative. Acceptance of the legitimacy of administrative discretion, as noted at the beginning of this chapter, provides a foundation for a critical approach to public administration.

But what is the ethical standard most appropriately applied to critical public administration in practice? How can public servants reflect critical theory in their beliefs about the nature of the state, and perhaps more importantly, how can practitioners reflect critical theory in their actions? Of particular relevance for public administration is the fact that challenging Recht may mean abandoning any "regime values" approach to administrative responsibility. An administrator might have an explicit responsibility to reject regime values, if these values conflict with the reflective and emancipatory telos of critical theory, or if reflexive examinations of (social) responsibility reveal moral or ethical hypocrisy.

This last possibility is no small matter, to echo Socrates. Many public servants take an explicit oath to uphold the Constitution, and even those who do not take a formal oath expect—and are expected—to be bound by its values. How, then, can there be any suggestion that a public servant reject regime values? This question, always an issue for those who serve the public, has become even more relevant in the present day as citizens grapple with the dilemma of upholding First Amendment rights—particularly the right of freedom of speech—during a time when many disagree with decisions made by the President, even as they support those men and women who risk their lives to carry out the orders of the Commander-in-Chief. Ultimately, it seems to me, we must distinguish between rejection of certain regime values and rejection of the social community itself—not unlike the Christian admonition to love the sinner even as one hates the sin. Can I honor, and want to serve, my community (writ large), even as I abhor, and seek to change, elements of its values?

## CRITICAL THEORY AS PRACTICE: AMBIVALENCE AND CONTRADICTION

I believe the answer to the question posed above is "yes," although I acknowledge that it is not easily accomplished and will often be misinterpreted and misunderstood. Crafting new understandings of the administrator in a critical-transformative role must be built on an understanding of the functions of critique and the moral impulse of critical theory, as well as in a postmodern understanding of the porous and contextual nature of language—what might be called "micropractices of ethics" (Bennett, 2001, p. 144). Recently I suggested, along with Cheryl Simrell King, that critical theory might best be incorporated into public service as part of a "practice" (King & Zanetti, 2005; see also Zanetti, 1998, 2004).

It might be that those public administrators who seek to incorporate critical theory into their practice might best be called "tempered radicals" (Meyerson & Scully, 1995. p. 586). Tempered radicals are individuals who identify with and are committed to their organizations/institutions, yet who also consider themselves part of, or allied with, some group, cause, or ideology that is fundamentally different from (and possibly at odds with) the dominant culture of their organization/institution. Tempered radicals recognize and experience tensions and contradictions between the status quo and alternatively postulated views. Speaking sociologically, these persons exhibit ambivalence. Ambivalence involves expression of both sides of a dualism, in contrast to compromise, which seeks a middle ground and therefore may lose the essence of both (all) sides. In an ambivalent stance, the clear positions of the oppositions are retained (Meyerson & Scully, 1995).

Ambivalence is not considered a virtue in our goal-oriented society. As Westerners generally, we abhor contradiction. How can something be both a and not-a simultaneously? We feel a push to decide, define, clarify, and categorize. Americans in particular value efficiency and decisiveness, enabled by logocentric, instrumental reasoning and technical expertise. So we sort, we prioritize, and, above all, we act. The process used to resolve a dilemma is often unimportant except to the degree to which the process streamlines and expedites the decision making even further.

Because of their ambivalence, public administrators who function as tempered radicals occupy a marginal position in all their identity groups (i.e., they hold mainstream, middle-class bureaucratic views and also identify with some less mainstream position vis-à-vis race, class, gender, etc.). They are frequently critical of both the status quo and unameliorated radical change. Consequently, they find themselves criticized by both radical and conservative observers.

The primary role of the administrator in a practice of critical theory is to provide spaces for the disillusioned and disenfranchised to speak and be heard. It is not an arrangement in which the administrator presumes to know the final answer. It is not the methodical production of facts; it is the mediation between the "is" and the "ought." Administrators trained primarily in technical approaches may recognize tensions and contradictions but do not know how to respond to them (Zanetti, 1998). If anything, they rush to resolve the contradiction—making decisions to bring "closure" much too soon.

But tempered radicals tap into what Lukes (1974) and Gaventa (1980) have termed the "third dimension" of political power relationships. The first two dimensions refer to what political scientists often call pluralist and elitist theories. In the "third dimension" of political power, the dynamics of hegemony are acknowledged. Lukes (1974) argues that in this conception, "A exercises power over B when A affects B in a manner contrary to B's interests" (p. 34). More importantly, "A may exercise power over B by getting him to do what he does not want to do, but he also exercises power over him by influencing, shaping, or determining his very wants" (p. 23). In other words, A affects B by shaping B's conceptions of the issues altogether— for example, by encouraging the impression that certain structures, laws, or relations of production are in B's interest, when they in fact benefit A. This consideration of political power takes into account the many ways in which potential issues are kept out of the political arena through the operation and influence of social forces and institutional practices (Gaventa, 1980).

Tempered radicals function as what Gramsci called the "mediating group" in society. It is this mediating process that produces what Cornell West (1991) calls a fecund criticism—that is, critique in which the primary aim is to discern possibilities in the existing order. This kind of criticism sets two tasks for itself. The first of these is to avoid the extremes of merely condemning the existing order or endorsing an ideal state of affairs. Instead, a fecund criticism tries to describe, explain, and analyze the present conditions in order to envision what kind of alternative might be realized. Second, this form of criticism does not simply put forward judgments, descriptions, or explanations of the present. Its integrity comes from participation in actual political movements that can help create—give birth to— alternatives rooted in the historical context of the present (West, 1991).

The administrator, of course, is just one element of society that can contribute to change. But, I would argue, the potential transformational role of the administrator has been neglected in maintaining the overall reduction that the bureaucracy equals the state. As a proposal for building a public administration to help overcome the estrangement many citizens now feel from "their" government, a critical practice in public administration is an overall approach that can be relevant in a variety of venues. Such a practice, however, will require administrators to take a very different view of their mission as public servants and to walk a fine line in balancing their critical social visions with their legal–political obligations.

Public administrators practicing critical theory can play a significant and important role in effecting change by creating, encouraging, and publicizing counternarratives. bell hooks reminds us that theory creates liberatory practice, a point echoed by Paulo Freire:

> Recognizing that precisely because we are constantly in the process of becoming and, therefore, are capable of observing, comparing, evaluating, choosing, deciding, intervening, breaking with, and making options, we are ethical beings, capable of transgressing our ethical grounding. (1998, p. 92)

Most importantly, I suggest that public administrators learn and practice the art of ambivalence by refusing to rush the resolution of contradictions, either in the articulation of theory or in the policy implementation process. This is an echo of Benhabib's call to consider both the generalized and concrete other simultaneously. We don't typically perceive ambivalence as a virtue, much less an art, but it can be both of these things to the extent that it allows time for the organic resolution of a perceived dilemma, or permits the transfiguration of opposites into a more powerful whole. Learning to practice ambivalence by holding contradictions[7] is not intuitive for most of us, and it most certainly is not encouraged in most walks of life. We risk appearing indecisive, inefficient, incompetent, or—especially in these times—even treasonous. But to the extent that we, as public servants, and as the teachers of public servants, construct (or allow the expression) of counternarratives that may be contrary to *Recht*, exhibit or experience sympathy, compassion, and reflective self-consciousness as political statements, honor practices of responsibility toward others, and protect (or construct) space for contradiction and transgression, we can indeed practice an ethic of critical theory.

## NOTES

1. Harmon (1995) summarizes three successive "generations" of consideration of administrative responsibility through the representative positions of Friedrich and Finer, Simon and Waldo, and Cooper and Burke.

    The question of the superiority of internal over external control of administrators was initiated by Carl Friedrich (1940), who expressed confidence in the ability of the administrator to execute his/her duties with "the proper regard for existing preferences of the community" (Friedrich, 1940, p. 232 in Harmon, 1995, p. 49). Herbert Finer strongly disagreed, contending that responsible administration in democratic government could only be achieved through subservience to the people through their elected representatives

(Finer, 1940). Friedrich's position, argued Finer, represented a naive faith in the benevolence of human nature; strong external controls (such as sanctions, conflict of interest regulations, and professional codes of conduct) are necessary to prevent bureaucratic tyranny. The debate was fleshed out in the 1940s through the work of others such as Levitan (1943), Leys (1943), and Appleby (1947).

The Simon-Waldo debate, Harmon suggests, added a different normative dimension by examining the core values to be pursued in public administration. Simon (1946,1947/1976, 1952) used the fact/value dichotomy to establish a distinction between administration and policy. Value judgments, particularly controversial ones, were properly the realm the legislative body; fact judgments (the most efficient means for carrying out a given policy) were the realm of the administrator. In practice, Simon recognized that this distinction necessarily blurred; however, he argued that the functional separation of responsibility was to be maintained as much as possible. To the extent that administrative discretion was necessary, it should be conducted in accordance with community values. Waldo (1952a, b) objected to Simon's fact-value/administration-policy distinctions, and sought to infuse the study of administration with a more substantive assessment of the role of democratic theory (Harmon, 1995).

More recently, scholars such as John Burke and Terry Cooper have developed distinctive approaches to administrative responsibility. Burke (1986) endorses a formal-legal definition of responsibility in which administrative discretion must be subordinate to hierarchical control. When administrators perceive contradictions or conflicts between the duties they tasked with performing, they are to refer these conflicts to higher political authorities. Personal beliefs should be secondary to political obligation. Cooper (1982, 1990, 1991) advocates a "responsible administrator" and an "ethic of citizenship," suggesting that the administrator's primary obligation is to some conception of the "public interest" or common good - a responsibility emerging from the fiduciary role of public administration.

Another notable approach to administrative responsibility that has emerged in recent years is affiliated with the "Blacksburg Manifesto," which argues that Public Administration (sic) is legitimate because it stems from the covenental spirit of the Constitution. Public Administration serves as an important link between the people and the institutions of government, and therefore is inherently democratic. It is not inconsistent with democratic principles, therefore, for public administrators to exercise discretion in a manner that reflects "principled autonomy" and regime values (Rohr, 1985, p. 416). Public Administration can serve as a balancing mechanism, and can also add to the representativeness of government (Rohr, 1985,1986). But while Public Administration can serve as an important check on elected representatives, it must also be subject to checks on authority - allowing only "constrained discretion" (Spicer and Terry, 1993, p. 245).

2. For instructive explanations of the distinctive Marxism of the Frankfurt School, see Held, 1980; Gorman, 1982, 1985; Bronner, 1994; and Alway, 1995.

3. Some recent developments in feminist ethics abandon the commitment to impartiality.
4. Clarke & Simpson's (1989) assertion reflects a concern that moral theorists (primarily in the field of philosophy) seek to adhere to a syllogistic approach. Ethicists in public administration, however, generally recognize that determining right action is a much less deterministic proposition.
5. While *Recht* is the German word for "law," as used in this context it has a much broader meaning.
6. See, for example, Denhardt and Denhardt, 1979; Denhardt, 1981a,b, 1987; Ramos, 1981; Forester, 1985, 1989, 1993; Felts, 1992; Scott, 1985; White, 1986, 1987; Box, 1995, 2002; Fox and Miller, 1995.
7. I want to note that the practice of holding contradictions is not the same as accepting double standards, as double standards necessarily imply value judgments.

## REFERENCES

Agger, B. (1991). *A critical theory of public life: Knowledge, discourse, and politics in an age of decline.* New York: The Falmer Press.

Agger, B. (1993). *The discourse of domination.* Evanston, IL: Northwestern University Press.

Alway, J. (1995). *Critical theory and political possibilities: Conceptions of emancipatory politics in the works of Horkheimer, Adomo, Marcuse, and Habermas.* Westport, CT: Greenwood.

Appleby, P. H. (1945). *Big democracy.* New York: Knopf.

Benhabib, S. (1987). The generalized and concrete other: The Kohlberg-Gilligan controversy and feminist theory. In S. Benhabib & D. Cornell (Eds.), *Feminism as critique: On the politics of gender.* Minneapolis: University of Minnesota Press.

Benhabib, S. (1992). *Situating the self.* New York: Routledge.

Benhabib, S., & Dallmayr, F. (Eds.). (1990). *The communicative ethics controversy.* Cambridge, MA: MIT Press.

Bennett, J. (2001). *The enchantment of modern life: Attachments, crossings, and ethics.* Princeton, NJ: Princeton University Press.

Bohman, J. (1990). Communication, ideology, and democratic theory. *American Political Science Review, 84*(1), 93–109.

Bohman, J. (1995). Public reason and cultural pluralism: Political liberalism and the problem of moral conflict. *Political Theory, 23*(2), 253–279.

Box, R. (1995). Critical theory and the paradox of discourse. *American Review of Public Administration, 25,* 1–19.

Braaten, J. (1991). *Habermas' critical theory of society.* Albany: State University of New York Press.

Bronner, S. (1994). *Of critical theory and its theorists.* Oxford, UK: Blackwell.

Burke, J. (1986). *Bureaucratic responsibility.* Baltimore: Johns Hopkins University Press.

Clark, S. G., & Simpson, E., (Eds.) (1989). *Anti-theory in ethics and moral conservatism.* Albany: State University of New York Press.

Cooper, T. (1982). *The responsible administrator: An approach to ethics for the administrative role.* Port Washington, NY: Kennikat Press.

Cooper, T. (1990). *The responsible administrator: An approach to ethics for the administrative role* (3rd ed.). San Francisco: Jossey-Bass.

Cooper, T. (1991). *An ethic of citizenship for public administration.* Englewood Cliffs, NJ: Prentice Hall.

Denhardt, K. (1989). The management of ideals: A political perspective on ethics. *Public Administration Review, 49*(2), 187–192.

Denhardt, R. (1981b). Toward a critical theory of public organization. *Public Administration Review, 41*(6), 628–635.

Denhardt, R. (1981a). *In the shadow of organization.* Lawrence: The Regents Press of Kansas.

Denhardt, R. (1987). Images of death and slavery in organizational life. *Journal of Management, 13*(3), 529–541.

Denhardt, R., & Denhardt, K. (1979). Public administration and the critique of domination. *Administration and Society, 11*(1), 107–120.

Felts, A. (1992). Organizational communication: A critical perspective. *Administration and Society, 23*(4), 495–513.

Finer, H. (1941). Administrative responsiblity in democratic government. *Public Administration Review, 1*, 335.

Forester, J. (1981). Questioning and organizing attention: Toward a critical theory of planning and administrative practice. Administration and Society, 13(2), 161–205.

Forester, J. (Ed.). (1985). *Critical theory and public life.* Cambridge, MA: MIT Press.

Forester, J. (1989). *Planning in the face of power.* Berkeley: University of California Press.

Forester, J. (1993). *Critical theory, public policy, and planning practice: Toward a critical pragmatism.* Albany: State University of New York Press.

Fox, C., & Cochran, C. (1990). Discretion advocacy in public administration theory: Toward a platonic guardian class? *Administration and Society, 22*(3), 249–271.

Fox, C. J., & Miller, H. T. (1995). *Postmodern public administration: Toward discourse.* Thousand Oaks, CA: Sage.

Frazer, E., Hornsby, J. & Lovibond, S. (Eds.). (1992). *Ethics: A feminist reader.* Cambridge, MA: Blackwell.

Frederickson, H. G. (1982). The recovery of civism in public administration. *Public Administration Review, 42*(4), 501–508.

Friedrich, C. (1940). Public policy and the nature of administrative responsibility. In C. J. Friedrich (Ed.), *Public policy.* Cambridge, MA: Harvard University Press.

Freire, P. (1998). *Pedagogy of freedom: Ethics, democracy, and civic courage.* New York: Rowman & Littlefield.

Fromm, E. (1956). *The art of loving.* New York: Harper & Row.

Fromm, E. (1979). *To have or to be?* London: Abacus.

Gaventa, J. (1980). *Power and powerlessness: Quiescence and rebellion in an Appalachian valley.* Chicago: University of Illinois Press.

Gawthrup, L. (1984). Civis, civitas, and civilitas: A new focus for the year 2000. *Public Administration Review, 34*(1), 101–107.

Gilligan, C. (1992). *In a different voice.* Cambridge, MA: Harvard University Press.

Gilligan, C. (1987). Moral orientation and moral development. In E. Kittay & D. T. Meyers (Eds.), *Women and moral theory* (pp. 19–36). Lanham, MD: Rowan & Littlefield.

Gorman, R. A. (1982). *Neo-Marxism: The meanings of modern radicalism.* Westport, CT: Greenwood.

Guba, E., & Lincoln, Y. (1994). Competing paradigms in qualitative research. In N. Denzin & Y. Lincoln (Eds.), *Handbook of qualitative research* (pp. 105–117). Thousand Oaks, CA: Sage.

Haas, T., & Deetz, S. (2000). Between the generalized and the concrete other: Approaching organizational ethics from feminist perspectives. In P. M. Buzzanell (Ed.), *Rethinking organizational and managerial communication from feminist perspectives* (pp. 24–46). Thousand Oaks, CA: Sage.

Habermas, J. (1962/1989). *The structural transformation of the public sphere.* Cambridge, MA: MIT Press.

Habermas, J. (1971/1973). *Theory and practice* (J. Viertel, Trans.). Boston: Beacon Press.

Habermas, J. (1979). *Communication and the evolution of society* (T. J. McCarthy, Trans.). Boston: Beacon Press.

Habermas, J. (1984). *Theory of communicative action: Volume 1. Reason and the rationalization of society* (T. J. McCarthy, Trans.). Boston: Beacon Press.

Habermas, J. (1985). Interview: A philosophico-political profile. *New Left Review, 151*(3), 75–105.

Habermas, J. (1987). *The theory of communicative action: Volume 2. Lifeworld and system: A critique of functional reason* (T. McCarthy, Trans.). Boston: Beacon Press.

Habermas, J. (1990). *Moral consciousness and communicative action* (C. Lenhardt & S. Wever Nicholson, Trans.). Cambridge, MA: MIT Press.

Habermas, J. (1995b). Reconcilation through the public use of reason: Remarks on John Rawls' political liberalism. *Journal of Philosophy, 92*(3), 109–131.

Habermas, J. (1995a). On the internal relation between the rule of law and democracy. *European Journal of Philosophy, 3*(1), 12–20.

Hamnett, M. P., Purter, D. J., Singh, A., & Kumar, K. (1984). *Ethics, politics, and international social science research: From critique to praxis.* East–West Center, HI: University of Hawaii Press.

Harmon, M. (1995). *Responsibility as paradox.* Thousand Oaks, CA: Sage.

Held, D. (1980). *Introduction to critical theory.* Berkeley: University of California Press.

Held, V. (1993). *Feminist morality: Transforming culture, society, and politics.* Chicago: University of Chicago Press.

hooks, b. (1994). *Teaching to transgress: Education as the practice of freedom.* NewYork: Routledge.

Horkheimer, M. (1937/1982). *Critical theory: Selected essays.* New York: Seabury Press.

Horkheimer, M. (1933/1986). Materialism and morality. *Telos, 69,* 85–118.

Howard, D. (1988). *The Marxian legacy.* Minneapolis: University of Minnesota Press.

Hoy, D., & McCarthy, T. (1994). *Critical theory.* Cambridge, MA: Blackwell.

Ingram, D. (1993). The limits and possibilities of communicative ethics for democratic theory. *Political Theory, 21*(2), 294–321.

Jay, M. (1973/1996). The dialectical imagination. Boston: Little, Brown.

Jos, P., & Hines, S. Jr. (1993). Care, justice, and public administration. *Administration and Society, 25*(3), 373–392.

Kincheloe, J. L., & McLaren, P. L. (1994). Rethinking critical theory and qualitative research. In N. Denzin & Y. S. Lincoln (Eds.), *Handbook of qualitative research* (pp. 138–157). Thousand Oaks, CA: Sage.

King, C. S., & Zanetti, L. (2005). *Transformational public service: Portraits of theory in practice.* New York: M.E. Sharpe.

Kittay, E., & Meyers, D. (Eds.). (1987). *Women and moral theory.* Lanham, MD: Rowman & Littlefield.

Kohlberg, L. (1981). *Essays on moral development.* San Francisco: Harper & Row.

Levitan, D. (1943). The neutrality of the public service. *Public Administration Review, 2,* 318.

Leys, W. (1943). Ethics and administrative discretion. *Public Administration Review, 3,* 10.

Lukes, S. (1974). *Power: A radical view.* New York: Macmillan.

Lukes, S. (1985). *Marxism and morality.* Oxford, UK: Clarendon Press.

Lukes, S. (1991). *Moral conflict and politics.* Oxford, UK: Clarendon Press.

McCarthy, T. (1990). Introduction. In J. Habermas, *Moral consciousness and communicative action* (pp. vii–xiii). Cambridge, MA: MIT Press.

McLellan, D. (1979). *Marxism after Marx.* Boston: Houghton Mifflin.

McLellan, D., & Sayers, S. (Eds.). (1990). *Socialism and morality.* London: MacMillan.

Meyers, D., & Kittay, E. (1987). Introduction. In E. Kittay & D. Meyers (Eds.), *Women and moral theory.* Lanham, MD: Rowman & Littlefield.

Meyerson, D., & Scully, M. (1995). Tempered radicalism and the politics of ambivalence and change. *Organization Science, 6,* 585–600.

Moon, D. (1995). Practical discourse and communicative ethics. In S. K. White (Ed.), *The Cambridge companion to Habermas* (pp. 143–166). Cambridge, UK: Cambridge University Press.

Nalbandian, J. (1990). Tenets of contemporary professionalism in local government. *Public Administration Review, 50,* 654–662.

Nigro, L., & Richardson, W. (1990). Between citizen and administrator: Administrative ethics and PAR. *Public Administration Review, 50*(6), 623–635.

O'Neill, O. (1993). Kantian ethics. In P. Singer (Ed.), *A companion to ethics* (pp. 175–185). Cambridge, MA: Blackwell.

Pettit, P. (1991). Consequentialism. In P. Singer (Ed.), *A companion to ethics* (pp. 230–240). Cambridge, MA: Blackwell.

Rachels, J. (1993). *The elements of moral philosophy* (2nd ed.). New York: McGraw-Hill.

Ramos, A. (1981). *The new science of organizations.* Toronto: University of Toronto Press.

Rawls, J. (1971). *A theory of justice.* Cambridge, MA: Harvard University Press.

Rawls, J. (1995). Reply to Habermas. Journal of Philosophy, 92(3), 132–180.

Redford, E. (1969). *Democracy in the administrative state.* New York: Oxford University Press.

Rocco, C. (1994). Between modernity and postmodernity: Reading dialectic of enlightenment against the grain. *Political Theory, 22*(1), 71–97.

Rohr, J. (1995). Professionalism, legitimacy, and the constitution. *Public Affairs Quarterly, 4,* 401–418.

Rohr, J. (1996). *To run a constitution: The legitimacy of the administrative state.* Lawrence: University of Kansas Press.

Rose, G. (1978). *The melancholy science.* London: Macmillan.

Scheffler, S. (Ed.). (1988). *Consequentialism and its critics.* Oxford, UK: Oxford University Press.

Schnädelbach, H. (1985–86). Max Horkheimer and the moral philosophy of German idealism. *Telos, 66,* 81–114.

Schneewind, J. B. (1993). Modern moral philosophy. In P. Singer (Ed.), *A companion to ethics.* Cambridge, MA: Blackwell.

Schroyer, T. (1973). *The critique of domination.* New York: George Braziller.

Schubert, G. (1957). "The public interest" in administrative decision-making: Theorem, theosophy, or theory? *American Political Science Review, 51,* 346–368.

Scott, W. (1985). Organization revolution: An end to managerial orthodoxy. *Administration and Society, 17*(2), 149–170.

Seidman, H., & Gilmour, R. (1986). *Politics, position, and power* (4th ed.). New York: Oxford University Press.

Simon, H. (1946). The proverbs of administration. *Public Administration Review, 6,* 53–67.

Simon, H. (1947/1976). *Administrative behavior: A study of decision-making processes in administrative organization* (3rd ed.). New York: Free Press.

Simon, H. (1952). Development of a theory of democratic administration: Replies and comments. *American Political Science Review, 46,* 494–496.

Singer, P. (Ed.). (1991). *A companion to ethics.* Cambridge, MA: Blackwell.

Soper, K. (1989). Feminism as critique. *New Left Review, 176,* 91–112.

Spicer, M. (1990). A contractarian approach to public administration. *Administration and Society, 22,* 303–316.

Spicer, M., & Terry, L. (1993). Legitimacy, history, and logic: Public administration and the constitution. *Public Administration Review, 53*(3), 239–246.

Steffy, B., & Grimes, A. (1986). A critical theory of organization science. *Academy of Management Review, 11*(2), 322–336.

Stever, J. (1990). The dual image of the administrator in progressive administration theory. *Administration and Society, 22*(1), 39–57.

Stewart, D. (1991). Theoretical foundations of ethics in public administration. *Administration and Society, 23*(3), 357–373.

Stivers, C. (1996). Active citizenship and public administration. In Wamsley et al. (Eds.), *Refounding public administration* (pp. 260–278). Newbury Park, CA: Sage.

Tar, Z. (1977). *The Frankfurt School.* New York: Wiley.

Therborn, G. (1970, September/October). A critique of the Frankfurt School. *New Left Review,* 65–96.

Torpey, J. (1986). Ethics and critical theory: From Horkheimer to Habermas. *Telos, 69,* 68–84.

Waldo, D. (1952a). Development of a theory of democratic administration. *American Political Science Review, 46,* 81–103.

Waldo, D. (1952b). Development of a theory of democratic administration: Replies and comments. *American Political Science Review, 46,* 501–503.

Walker, M. (1998). *Moral understandings: A feminist study in ethics.* New York: Routledge.

West, C. (1991). *The ethical dimensions of Marxist thought.* New York: Monthly Review Press.

White, L. E. (1987–1988). Mobilization on the margins of the lawsuit: Making space for clients to speak. *Review of Law and Social Change, 16,* 535–564.

White, O., & McSwain, C. (1990). The Phoenix project: Raising a new image of public administration from the ashes of the past. *Administration and Society, 22,* 3–8.

Wood, A. (1991). Marx against morality. In P. Singer (Ed.), *A companion to ethics* (pp. 511–524). Cambridge, MA: Blackwell.

Young, I. (1987). Impartiality and the civic public. In S. Benhabib & D. Cornell (Eds.), *Feminism as critique* (pp. 56–74). Minneapolis: University of Minnesota Press.

Zanetti, L. (1997). Advancing praxis: Connecting critical theory with practice in public administration. *American Review of Public Administration, 27*(2), 145–167.

Zanetti, L. (1998). At the nexus of state and civil society: the transformative practice of public administration. In C. S. King, C. Stivers, et al. (Eds.), *Government is us: Public administration in an anti-government era* (pp. 102–121). Thousand Oaks, CA: Sage.

Zanetti, L. (2003). Holding contradictions: Marcuse and the idea of refusal. *Administrative Theory and Praxis, 25*(2).

Zanetti, L. (2004). Repositioning the ethical imperative: Critical theory, *Recht,* and tempered radicals in public service. *American Review of Public Administration, 34*(2).

Zanetti, L., & Carr, A. (1997). Putting critical theory to work: Giving the public administrator the critical edge. *Administrative Theory and Praxis, 19*(2), 208–224.

Zanetti, L., & Carr, A. (1998). Exploring the psychodynamics of political change. *Administrative Theory and Praxis, 20*(3), 358–373.

CHAPTER 4

# BUSINESS ETHICS AND ITS WORLD

### Martin Fuglsang

*Capitalism is not at all territorial, even in its beginnings:*
*its power of deterritorialization consists in taking as its object, not the earth,*
*but the "materialized labour" the commodity. And private property is no longer*
*ownership of the land or the soil, nor even the means of production as such, but of*
*convertible abstract rights. That is why capitalism marks a mutation in worldwide or*
*ecumenical organizations, which now take on a consistency of their own: the world-*
*wide axiomatic, instead of resulting from heterogeneous social formations and their*
*relations, for the most part distributes these formations, determines their relations,*
*while organising an international division of labour.*

—Deleuze & Gauttari (1987, p. 454)

## ITS DOXA

Let us begin by invoking the ambience of common sense, by reconnoitring the terrain of mere opinion, where business ethics most certainly seems to grow and blossom. In this conceptual and to some extent reflective land-scape there is a strong presupposition that business ethics is good business or, more precisely, that in the atmosphere of late capitalism good business

*Critical Theory Ethics for Business and Public Administration*, pages 79–93
Copyright © 2008 by Information Age Publishing
All rights of reproduction in any form reserved.

becomes ethical through a thoughtful and well-mannered management practice. Buzzwords certainly abound, and their affiliated theoretical disciplines, such as corporate social responsibility, aesthetic leadership, value management, multicultural management, diversity management, and coaching in all shapes and forms, are prospering, along with the discipline of business ethics itself. Theoretical reflections and managerial practices are inscribed with clear traces from the humanities, not least from philosophy, indicating that the managerial field in general, and business ethics in particular, is explicitly staged as the production of subjectivity and is organised in a positive signifying regime of moral statements that, by and large, inscribe ideas of empowerment, emancipation and self-development through the conceptualisation of self-management and self-valorization. Business ethics, both as a theoretical discipline and a managerial practice, now becomes a pure actualization of the ever expanding connective synthesis between capitalism and the so-called enlightenment of humanity. Accordingly, we find an overwhelming tendency to define the concept of ethics with regulatory atmospheric moral principles and related honorific epithets, not realizing that morality itself is a specific assemblage of thought, self, and action that must be produced in order to find its productivity and, not least, its functionality.

So we are engaged in a circular problematic. The idea, the concept, and the conceptualization of business ethics is first and foremost produced inside the topography of late capitalism, while business ethics is at the same time portrayed as an enlightened and humane principle of governance of late capitalism itself, organized around a moral assemblage and its derived self-inflicted regulatory actions. It is this circular nature of business ethics that this chapter will try to investigate, not so much in order to portray its ethical logos, but more importantly, to trace its logic of sense and its functionality inside late capitalism, constituting a praxis through which late capitalism continuously expands.[1] By this inquiry we are of course implicitly stating that business ethics is sensible, or to be more precise, we are at the outset claiming that business ethics is a specific logic of sense within late capitalism and that it plays a significant role in the ongoing expansion of capitalism though its organizational principles and its technologies of contemporary management, that is, its micropolitical arrangement of signs, images, and words. In this sense, this exploration unfolds in a zone of imperceptibility between capitalism and humanism: what we could call the humanization of capitalism or, if one prefers, the capitalization of humanism, that is, a passage and zone of imperceptibility in which the managerial discipline of business ethics unfolds and evolves. As such, business ethics, as a discipline in its dual sense of both being a theoretical reflection in the domain of business and a managerial practice that designs modern organizations and their worlds is therefore to be considered a symptom of the transitory forces that drive late capitalism, and not something that stands outside as a reflective category looking in upon the practices that unfold in the world of business. Business ethics is like any other contemporary managerial technology of intimacy, be it a theoretical reflection or the organization of concrete actions, a highly flexible control working directly in and upon the white canvas of our subjectivity, that is, the world in which we think, feel, and act.

In creating this assertion in regard to business ethics as a generalized object[2] inside the reflective managerial practices of contemporary work-life, we are first and foremost focusing on business ethics as statements; not only as imperatives, but to that particularly illocutionary force that is linked to every statement by a social obligation, or in short, to what Deleuze and Guattari (1987), with their inspiration from both Michael Foucault (1972) and J. L. Austin (1965), call order-words. The question is how these order-words actualize into managerial technologies of a biopolitical nature in order to create a continually diversified and receptive body that enables late capitalism to accumulate and expand. We are therefore not concerned with the differentiated and ongoing discussions in the field of business ethics as such, that is, the rigorous debate concerning what kind of conceptual ethics is to be applied in order to govern the working souls of self-valorization, approached as deontology, virtue ethics, or the philosophies of utilitarianism. In this light, and to make our endeavor even more clear, what we seek in this chapter, is a continuation of the line of thought instituted by Jones, Parker and Bos (2005), relating business ethics and its common sense to a critical inquiry that might transform our understanding of business ethics toward problematics, that is, something that "shakes you, jolts you out of your complacent acceptance of 'what is'" (p. 18), rather then solutions that are to be instituted as mechanical rules for action, shaped by the anthropomorphic morality of good taste and upright manners, or what we often refer to as good sense.

As a consequence of this line of inquiry, we have dispensed with any idea that connects business ethics with any philosophy of the sovereign subject and the ideology of an autonomous life. Instead we are approaching business ethics through a concept of production as an ongoing circulation of values, beliefs, and desire through which the subject as a specific and localized individuation becomes a machinic process of self-development, self-management, and self-valorization. Or to say it slightly differently, business ethics, as a gaseous medium of values and derived virtues, actualizes as a common subjectivity that not only becomes a result of the production process of late capitalism, but also constitutes a necessary input to the process of production as such. This presupposes a new idea of capitalist production and, not least, a reconceptualization of the connectivity we find in the multiplicity we could call work–life existence, indicating the nexus of what we are to conceive of as business ethics as a logic of sense and thereby as a central component in the ongoing differentiation of late capitalism. Business ethics as a generalized object is thus composed as a biopolitical technology that modulates, transforms, and reassembles the forces embodied in the flesh and soul of the employee into the organizational dynamism of the corporation.

## ITS WORLD

When we talk of late capitalism, we are emphasizing a transmutation of capitalism as a world that was to some extent prophetically visualized by Karl Marx in the Grundrisse, where he writes:

> Nature builds no machines, no locomotives, railways, electric telegraphs, self-acting mules etc. These are products of human industry; natural material transformed into organs of the human will over nature, or of human participation in nature. They are organs of the human brain, created by the human hand; the power of knowledge, objectified. The development of fixed capital indicates to what degree general social knowledge has become a direct force of production, and to what degree, hence, the conditions of the process of social life itself have come under the control of the general intellect and been transformed in accordance with it. To what degree the powers of social production have been produced, not only in the form of knowledge, but also as immediate organs of social practice, of the real life process. (1973, p. 706)

For Marx, this carried associations of utopia, a state of liberating transmutation where the political economy of capitalism would break down from within because it would decrease labor time in the process of production and thereby dissolve the general measurement of value and wealth, that is, the classical labor theory of value and a production based on exchange value so very dominant in the birth of the self-contained discipline of economics. But, as we can see today, this is not the case; there is no internal breakdown within the capitalistic process of production in the societal actualizations we at present know as the "information society" or the "knowledge economy." On the contrary, what we are witnessing is a general transformation of the valorization of capitalistic production and its constituent forces of production, that is, a transformation of its conceptualization of measurement, its entities known as commodities, and its components for and in the process for production, all in all, expanding the landscape and not least the horizon in which capitalistic production takes place. What we call free time, or, more precisely, the time of nonwork, has in this state of late capitalism become a differentiated commodity of excess and thereby an environment recognized by an endless process of cultural consumption creating a marketplace for desire, dreams, hopes, and delirium. As such, the mode of production has changed the flow of energy from the discipline of hands and the confinement of bodies to the control of human subjectivity, that is, the mode of existence understood as the ontological fabric in which the subject and its worlds become. It is, as Paolo Virno emphasizes, a process of production under the auspices of a post-Fordist materialization, governed by the General Intellect, in which the temporality of late capitalism is no longer reduced to fixed capital as Marx envisioned it, since it does not need a "mechanical body" or an "electronic soul" in order to be directly productive, because

> [i]n so far as it organises the production process and the "life-world," the general intellect is certainly an abstraction, but real with a material and operative function. However, the general intellect comprises knowledge, information and epistemological paradigms, so it also sharply differs from the real abstractions typical of modernity that embodied the principle of equivalence. Whilst money, as the "universal equivalent," in its independent existence embodied the commensurability of products, labours and subjects, the general intellect establishes the analytical premises for any kind of praxis. The models of social knowledge do not turn varied labouring activities into equivalents; rather, they present themselves as "immediately productive force." They are not units of measure; they constitute the immeasurable presupposition of heterogeneous effective possibilities. (Virno, 2001, p. 2)

This is of course an abstraction. But it is a real and certainly manifest one as it actualizes in the transformation of the factory, the workforce, and the technologies of management, to take the most notable examples since World War II. Factories, which have meanwhile been transformed into corporations and enterprises, are no longer primarily producing goods and services to meet preexisting demands; through an exponential growth in advertising and the ever-growing sophistication of branding strategies, they are now producing consumers, more particularly, the worlds in which goods, demands, and desires become interconnected and thereby sensible on the white canvas of subjectivity (Gorz, 1980; Klein, 2001). At the same time, management is no longer primarily about regulation and protocol or about explicit orders and commands, but rather about the technologies of the self, constituted as technologies of intimacy, such as programs of self-development based on the axiomatic of social psychology, motivation techniques, and self-related decision-making procedures. As such it has become a machinery of incorporeal transformation that is actualized in the soul and realized in body of each and every employee: the worker is resurrected as a coworker, the workforce is now conceived of as human resources with infinite and differentiated potentialities, in other words, as an immaterial and affective multiplicity of self-regulated individualities striving for their own

emancipation. This constitutes a conceptual understanding of late capitalism as an ongoing variation of difference and repetition, or maybe more
precisely, a repetition submersed in a demand for an ongoing differentiation that has been so elegantly visualized by the organizational demand for
lifelong learning and an ever-changing individualized competence portfolio. As such, capitalistic appropriation is an open-ended totality of circulation that does not first and foremost produce subjects and objects, but
places the production of subjects and objects in continuous variation along
its series of management technologies. Or, to frame this transformation
in more general terms, we can portray this receptive change of the factory
into the corporation, the worker into the coworker, and the workforce into
human resources, as a transformation from disciplinary societies into societies of control (Deleuze 1995), which has become the hallmark of Empire
(Hardt and Negri 2000); it is a transmutation of the social bios through a
power that regulates life from within by reinvesting itself in life in order to
absorb and rearticulate it through and through. This power does not stem
from a localized authoritarian voice, a voice we know from the school, the
barracks, the asylum, and the old walls of the Fordistic factory and thus a
voice that organizes the receptive body from the outside through its commands and protocols, its schematics of time and its nomination of place,
but a power that only actualizes by its function and its capability to admin-
ister life in its complete expansion, so stunningly exposed in the field of
human resource management and its encapsulating positive conception of
the "whole human being," that is, "life" itself submerged into the new fluid
mechanisms of biopower and its technologies of control. It is a power that

> [w]ould no longer simply be dealing with legal subjects over whom the ulti-
> mate dominion was death, but with living beings, and the mastery it would be
> able to exercise over them would have to be applied at the level of life itself;
> it was taking charge of life, more then the threat of death, that gave power its
> access even to the body. If one can apply the term bio-history to the pressures
> through which the movement of life and the processes of history interfere
> with one another, one would have to speak of bio-power to designate what
> brought life and its mechanisms into the realm of explicit calculations and
> made knowledge-power an agent of transformation of human life. (Foucault,
> 1978, pp. 142–143)

In the transformation from the disciplinary societies to societies of control, we are now completely submerged in the processes and mechanisms of
biopower. Although biopower was also a cornerstone in the manifestation of
capitalism in the area of discipline, life could then still escape between the
hauling and the housing. The change lies in the mechanisms and processes
through which biopower functions in its administration of life, or to formulate it differently, biopower runs through contemporary existence without

friction mediated by the production of late capitalism and is thus no longer in need of expressing itself through an authoritarian voice and an enclosed space. Capitalistic production itself has become biopolitical, and has as such become a production of our social being, that is, the horizon in which our existence is given sense and becomes sensible. It is a transition from formal subsumption to real subsumption, as the "achievement of the subjection by the capitalist mode of production, of the whole society" (Negri, 1989, p. 72), a contemporary state of fluidity, where we are submerged into a permanent production of transient social relations, as a kind of "metaproduction" of services and infinite activities that flows through the modality of work–life existence, constituting zones of imperceptibility by its continuous variation and dissolution of the borders between life, work, and existence (Deleuze, 1995, p. 181). As such, it is a mode of production in which subjectivity becomes both the cause and effect of production and thus becomes directly productive as a machinery of knowledge, power, signs, and desire, and not just as an apparatus for reproduction. Or to clarify this even further, it is a production of social relations that constitutes our social bios as an "ideological" environment in which these social relations live and reproduce; a transition from formal subsumption to real subsumption as a biopolitical production, where the concept of biopower not only designates the biological classifications of life, but in the most elaborated sense of life, designates forms of life. Therefore it is, as Lazzarato perhaps ironically suggests, no longer a question of understanding the mode of production in its classical connotation, but of understanding its incorporeal transformation into the production of modes (2004a, p. 202), preconditioned by the machinic processes defining the social formations, which in their expansion becomes a production of lives. The concept of "immaterial labor," itself a multiplicity of heterogeneous intensities, establishes a very different conception of contemporary life, not just in relation to work, but to the conjunction of work–life existence. This conjunction is a relational modality in which

> [t]he activities of this kind of immaterial labour oblige us to question the classic definitions of "work" and of "workforce," because they are the result of a synthesis of varying types of savoir-faire (those of intellectual activities, as regards the cultural-informational content, those of manual activities for the ability to put together creativity, imagination and technical and manual labour ; and that of entrepreneurial activities for that capacity of management of their social relations and of structuration of the social cooperation of which they are a part). This immaterial labour constitutes itself in forms that are immediately collective, and, so to speak, exists only in the form of network and flow. The organisation of its cycle of production, because this is precisely what we are dealing with, once we abandon our factoryist prejudgments, is not immediately visible because it is not confined by the walls of a factory. (Lazzarato, 2004b, p. 3)

This inevitably transforms the idea of management, or to be more precise, the mechanisms and processes of managerial control through which managerial practices can modulate a differentiated common subjectivity into a subjugated subjectivity that is constantly accessible for the variation of production. In this light, the exponential expansion of human resource management and its derived conceptualizations and techniques should not come as any surprise, as it transforms our understanding of management into the ideological ambience of empowerment and self-development through self-management and self-valorization, that is, a biopolitical machinery of social technologies in which business ethics seems to be the most vibrant and intense insignia, as it inscribes a soul into the flesh of our contemporary corporations, a soul that shines brightly by its moral virtues tattooed on the bodies of its employees by its semantics and schematics of conduct and which is signified outward, toward its stakeholders through its branding strategies and in its immaculate corporate social responsibilities.

## ITS FUNCTIONALITY

Business ethics is in this sense like any other contemporary management apparatus, be it appraisal interviews, coaching, and its therapeutic genealogy or value management, a technology of power and control, but not a control that aims toward predefined models or for that matter, invariant repetitions constituted in the image of predescribed rules and protocols for execution in relation to a given work task. On the contrary, business ethics is a technology that expands each and every employee into an ongoing variation of repetition, by the demand for continuous interpretation and negotiation of the propositions and predicates that define the atmospheric ethos of the organizational arrangement, often portrayed in the vision and mission statements and objectified in the annual appraisal interview. It is a question of interpretation and negotiation in the light of order-words that transversally organize the arrangement of the collective corporation defined as the double circulation of subjectivity, which actualizes as transient social relations; order-words that not only express themselves in the imperatives, but by the illocutionary force that is the exactly expressed in each and every statement, proposition, and predicate, that is, as instantaneousness incorporeal transformations that actualize themselves in the soul and are realized in the body. Order-words are thus

> [n]ot a particular category of explicit statements (for example, in the imperative), but the relation of every word or every statement to implicit presuppositions, in other words, to speech acts that are, and can only be, accomplished in the statement. Order-words do not concern commands only, but every act that is linked to statements by a social obligation [...] The relation between

the statement and the act is internal, immanent, but it is not one of identity. Rather it is the relation of redundancy. The order-word itself is the redundancy of the act and the statement. (Deleuze & Guattari, 1987, p. 79)

As such, business ethics is an arrangement of order-words, or what we could call an assemblage comprised of order-words, that designate the individuation of any given statement or proposition, and which in their turn, designates the subjectification of any given enunciation, and thus transforms the receptive body of the employee in correlation with the horizon of sense constituted by the assemblage of business ethics. As a consequence, order-words as redundancy has thus to be understood as a specific kind of action, one that commands and thereby exercises its control through its incorporeal transformations by changing the composition of the body and thereby its actions and passions, that is, the receptive field of the body. This arrangement of order-words is hence what we are to conceive of as the technological enterprise of business ethics in its preoccupation with the body as corporeal action and incorporeal transformation, expanding our conception of action beyond the logic of intentionality and beyond the consciousness of the subject, and toward acts that are immanent to the statements, propositions, and predicates expressing them; or, in short, toward acts that are incorporeal but nonetheless manifest in bodies, by arranging, organizing, and prescribing the sensible composition of body. This transformation is vividly exposed in the exact moment when the jury announces the verdict guilty upon the accused, since this is not so much a summarizing representation of the linguistic fixture unfolding in the court of law, in which the body of the accused is staged in the center of juridical inflection, as it is an incorporeal transformation that directly intervenes in the arrangement and composition of the body. This transformation, as a noncorporeal attribute of the statement "guilty," is instantaneous in a dual sense, "by the simultaneity of the statement expressing the transformation and the effect the transformations produces" (Deleuze & Gauttari, 1987, p. 91) and changes the qualified and conditional being of the body by transforming it from a state of an accused to that of a convict. It is not only a different phenomenological signification that now covers the body as an exterior emblem and thereby constitutes a new sphere of interpretation, but a qualitative ontological displacement of forces that affects the body and the forces the body can affect in its actualized state of being. The court of law is no longer the free citizen's exit, but the prisoner's entrance to the schematic, planned and institutionalized surveillance; the court of law is no longer the door of freedom, but the gate of confinement.

As such, business ethics, construed as an assemblage of order-words and expressed through, for example, the corporation's vision and mission statements, its strategies and procedures for social responsibility, its codex and prescripts for conduct, and its internal lifelong learning programs, accords with the most powerful and transversally extended order-word in the modulation of late capitalism, that is, the injunction to become a subject. This order-word is not alien to any of us; it is the dominant will ruling the area of humanistic enlightenment as an ambience in which we are told that our freedom not only embraces us, but in which we actualize as free citizens, now transcribed into the freedom of consumerism as an area of infinite and self-contained choices. Capitalism, understood as the materialized form of labor as the "commodity," and as the production of consumers and their worlds, is not at all in any opposition to the ideology of humanism and its quest for liberation. On the contrary, the former expand through the imperatives of the latter, so vividly exemplified by the assemblage of business ethics and the statements and predicates expressing its order-words. It is in this sense that business ethics becomes a technology of biopower, because it enables the managerial practices to create an unmediated and highly flexible control over the subjective processes that both constitute the mode of production, as well as becoming the outcome through production itself. This is the real expansion of late capitalism into all areas of the Socius and where

> [i]t is no longer possible to confine subjectivity merely to tasks of execution, it becomes necessary for the subject's competence in the areas of management, communication and creativity to be made compatible with the conditions of "production for production's own sake." Thus the slogan "become subjects," far from eliminating the antagonism between hierarchy and cooperation, between autonomy and command, actually re-poses the antagonism at a higher level, because it both mobilizes and clashes with the very personality of the individual worker. (Lazzarato, 1996, p. 135)

In which way and to what extent the order-words of business ethics mobilize and clash with the actualized individuality of the employee is always subject to the singular event through which the order-words enter. Consequently, business ethics does not function by predefined codings or by segmented and explicated regulations for expression and execution, but rather as a virtual connectivity between differentiated preindividual flows of intensity through which the employee and his or her executions are materialized as sensible expressions in accordance with the compounded world of the corporation. This, of course, imposes the most extended area of obedience by the indeterminate nature of command, because every fixation and regulation of command becomes a question of an ongoing willingness to commit to the 'abstract' and always negotiable goals for the employee in accordance to the continuous modulation of the signifying regime expressing the corporation and its strategies. By "abstract" we do not necessarily mean unmediated, but rather that any explication of content is open for an ongoing interpretation and negotiation, exactly in the manner that we have become accustomed to the organizational principles for lifelong learning and its self-reflective essence. So we do not necessarily mean obedience introduced by any external forces, but, in accordance with the immanent force of order-words, we are conceptualizing a self-inaugurated obedience constituted by an ongoing commitment and willingness to interpret and negotiate the content of any given goal, exactly in the manner that we have become accustomed to the idea of the annual appraisal interview and its schematics for self-development. There is, in other words, a conception of obedience in the ambience of self-empowerment in agreement with the concept of freedom instituted by the epochal nature of enlightenment, subscribed into the order-word "to become a subject" and distinguished all the way to the micropolitics of management as self-sufficiency, self-determination, and self-reflectivity. It is certainly a highly flexible form of control where the employees in the production of post-Fordism are transformed into what Lazzarato so elegantly portrays as worker-monads expressing their singular and heterogeneous worlds, but all in strict harmony and compossibility with the synthesized world of the corporation, that is, a corporation constituted by a highly divergent and heterogeneous flow of expressions, but all in convergence with one and the same horizon of sense. This may not be the best of all worlds as envisioned by Leibniz (1992, see especially paragraphs 53–65), but it is the most efficient and creative one, as it at once "affirms the workers' autonomy, independence and singularity (individual substance) [and] on the other hand, it requires workers to belong to the organizational world, since this world is internal to the situation and conduct of the subject" (Lazzarato, 2004a, p. 194).

By this, we are of course not proposing any image of business ethics as a subjugation into the enforcement of discipline and it is thus not an image that derives from the classic idea of imprisonment or confinement, which we often see portrayed in critical management discourse, with its emphasis on some form of humanistic liberation from the inhumane order of things (Fuglsang, 2007). On the contrary, what we are conceptualizing is a control that works thoroughly and directly through the liberating imperatives of business ethics, such as empowerment, self-development, and self-management. These imperatives expressing the order-words of business ethics do not work by exclusion, but through an ongoing integration of nonconformed qualities, by producing a consistency for the highly heterogeneous, divergent, and fluctuating expressions that constitute the productive force of the corporation. It is, so to speak, not the body with all its actions and passions that have to be disciplined, as this would be highly unproductive with regard to the demand for a rapid circulation of desire and a highly flexible production of values, tests, commodities, and consumption. On the contrary, these have to be set free in the divine horizon of innovation and creativity, but only to the extent that these actions and passions contribute to the consistency of the assemblage of overcoding, that is, business ethics can be seen as an all-embracing intersection between the semiotic system of signification and the semiotic system of subjectification or what Deleuze and Guattari conceptualize as the machine of faciality, where

> [f]aces are not basically individual; they define zones of frequency or probability, delimit a field that neutralizes in advance any expressions or connections unnameable to the appropriate significations. Similarly, the form of subjectivity, whether consciousness or passion, would remain absolutely empty if faces did not form a loci of resonance that select the sensed or mental reality and make it conform in advance to a dominant reality. The face itself is redundancy. It is itself in redundancy with the redundancies of significance or frequency, and those of resonance or subjectivity. (1987, p. 168)

This machine of faciality is what keeps the heterogeneous, divergent, and highly productive flows of innovation and creativity in control inside the rapid circulation of late capitalism. It is, so to speak, the substance of expression that creates the consistency in which these flows converge, creating the limits and controlling the extension of the processes of deterritorialization by composing the horizon of signification and the receptive field of subjectification in which these flows become sensible and motivate ongoing interpretation. The face is the "icon proper to the signifying regime, the reterritorialization internal to the system" (Deleuze & Gauttari, 1987, p. 115); it is the white wall of the corporation containing the black holes of the employee's subjectification, their senses, their conceptions, and not least their interpretations. As such, business ethics becomes an organization through the spectrum of a divergent process of normalization, not by strict identity and not even by resemblance, but by the extension of sameness in relation to the degrees of variation in accordance to a fluctuating norm, that is, a norm and thereby a normativity that are constituted within and in relation to the individualized programs and schematics of empowerment and self-development of each and every employee. Business ethics is a social production of normalities that determines the degrees of variation and deviance in relation to which everything is acknowledged by exactly their degrees of variation and deviance. It does not operate by exclusion, but by an all-embracing inclusion of arrangements of choices, but only to the level and to the extension of variation and deviance in relation to the overcoding image of sameness, because this is precisely how that which is not given significance and substance by reference to a binary segmentation is continuously and transversally controlled. It is not a question of exclusion, except of course in cases of complete eradication from the white wall of the corporation (the horizon of sense), but a question of an ongoing discussion of the commitment to and application of the fluctuating norms in conjunction with the self-development, the self-management, and the empowerment of the employee, or what we could call the drama of the subjectification of the worker-monad. Business ethics, then, understood as a machine of faciality, overcoding the deterritorialized and highly creative and productive expressions of the employee in strict compossibility with the order-words unfolding as incorporeal transformations, is of course a morality in the ambience of becoming a subject. It composes an image of self-sufficiency, self-regulation, and self-management in correspondence with our willingness to commit, negotiate, and interpret the fluctuating norms constituted as a series of variation and deviance through which we become and evolve. It is a morality that constitutes a self-imposed control established through our own recurrent self-valorization. In this sense, we have to engage ourselves in an ongoing transformative and moral code to become "free" through the demands for flexible production and endless consumption, wherein business ethics, with its emphasis on empowerment, self-development, and self-management, actualizes a double-bind of control by its inherent notion of freedom. As such, business ethics, like any other sophisticated and individualized biopolitical technology, is a contemporary managerial practice that normalizes by degrees of variation and deviance, constituting a plane of consistency populated by an ongoing differentiation of personalized expressions, where each and every one of us has become the subject of a specific regime of enunciation: express yourself, take a stand, have an opinion. Oh yes, go ahead, make our day: make it a "critical" opinion.

This face is the substance of enunciation. It is a white wall, synthesizing the productive forces of capitalism and the emancipatory essences of humanism, populating the black holes of our individualized subjectification; it is a machine of faciality that overcodes the decoded flows of our actions and passions by producing a stigmatic and extremely ideological conception of freedom, into which we are utterly submerged and modulated in accordance to a new area of machinic enslavement (Deleuze & Guattari, 1987, pp. 456–459). But it is also intertwined with the pure ethical quest to reformulate what we mean when we conceptualize our collective emancipations and liberation in the midst of the highly flexible and rapid circulation of late capitalism. It is not a question of asking which regime or which system most forcefully stigmatizes and enslaves us: we find traits of enslavement and liberation in each and every regime and system (Deleuze, 1995). We should ask, instead, which decoded flows are able to follow completely different paths than that of the intersecting face between signification and subjectification; this face of absolute but negative deterritorialization, that reterritorializes in our souls and is realized in our bodies, transforming all of us into intrinsic and self-controlled components in the all-embracing machinery of valorization. But then again, this question of how is always subjected to the singularized events that continuously traverse us before we are composed in our self-indulgent aptitude for saying I; and it is, in any case, always a different story!

## ACKNOWLEDGMENT

The author would like to thank Thomas Basbøl, our resident writing consultant here at the Department of Management, Politics and Philosophy (CBS), for his language-editorial effort. Especially his outstanding sense for the semantics used and thereby the rhythmic composition of text has been highly appreciated.

## NOTES

1. We use the term "late capitalism" as it resonates in Frederic Jameson and especially how it connects to the writings of Maurizio Lazzarato, Paolo Virno, and Antonio Negri; as a pervasive condition of our own age constituted by the indetermination and imperceptibility between economic and cultural processes of production and where the notion of "late" generally convey "the sense that something has changed, that things are different, that we have gone through a transformation of the life world which is somehow decisive but incomparable with the older convulsions of modernization and industrialization, less perceptible and dramatic, somehow, but more permanent precisely because more thoroughgoing and all-pervasive" (Jameson, 1992, p. xxi).
2. It is important to emphasize that business ethics as a generalized object is to be understood as a specific arrangement of our subjectivity, an arrangement that has become a knowledge-power object and thereby has become directly productive inside late capitalism and its managerial practices.

## REFERENCES

Austin, J. L. (1965). *How to do things with words.* Oxford, UK: Oxford University Press.

Deleuze, G. (1995). Postscript on control societies. In *Negotiations* (pp.177–182). New York: Colombia University Press.

Deleuze, G. (1990). *The logic of sense* (M. Lester & C. Stivale, Trans.). New York: Columbia University Press.

Deleuze, G., & Guattari, F. (1983). *Anti-Oedipus: Capitalism and schizophrenia* (R. Hurley, M. Seem, & H. R. Lane, Trans.). Minneapolis: University of Minnesota Press.

Deleuze, G., & Guattari, F. (1987). *A thousand plateaus: Capitalism and schizophrenia* (B. Massumi, Trans.). Minneapolis: University of Minnesota Press.

Foucault, M. (1972). *The archaeology of knowledge and the discourse on language* (A. M. Sheridan Smith, Trans.). New York: Pantheon Books.

Foucault, M. (1978). *The history of sexuality: Volume 1. An introduction.* New York: Vintage Books.

Fuglsang, M. (2007). Critique and resistance—On the necessity of organisational philosophy. In C. Jones & R. ten Bos (Eds.), *Philosophy and organisation.* London: Routledge

Gorz, A. (1980). *Paths to paradise: On the liberation from work.* Cambridge, UK: South End Press.

Hardt, M., & Negri, A. (2000). *Empire.* Cambridge, MA: Harvard University Press.

Jones, C., Parker, M., & Bos R. t. (2005). *For business ethics.* London: Routledge.

Jameson, F. (1992). *Postmodernism: Or, the cultural logic of late capitalism.* Durham, NC: Duke University Press.

Klein, N. (2001). *No logo.* London: Flamingo.

Lazzarato, M. (1996). Immaterial labor. In P. Virno & M. Hardt (Ed.), *Radical thought in Italy* (pp. 133–147). Minneapolis: University of Minnesota Press.

Lazzarato, M. (2004a). From capital-labour to capital-life. *Ephemera: Theory and Politics in Organization, 4*(3), 187–208.

Lazzarato, M. (2004b). General intellect: Towards an inquiry into immaterial labour (E. Emery, Trans.). *Multitudes.* Online at http://multitudes.samizdat.net/article.php3?id_article=1498. Accessed June 18, 2006.

Leibniz, G. W. (1992). *Discourse on metaphysics and the monadology* (G. R. Montgomery, Trans.). New York: Prometheus Books.

Marx, K. (1973). *Grundrisse: Foundations of the critique of political economy* (M. Nicolaus, Trans.). New York: Penguin.

Negri, A. (1989). *The politics of subversion: A manifesto for the twenty-first century* (J. Newell, Trans.). Oxford, UK: Polity Press.

Virno, P. (2001). *General intellect* (A. Bove, Trans.). Online at http://www.generation-online.org/p/fpvirno10.htm. Accessed May 22, 2006.

Virno, P. (2004). *A grammar of the multitude* (I. Bertoletti, J. Cascaito, & A. Casson, Trans.). New York: Semiotext(e).

# PART II

CT ETHICAL ANSWERABILITY AND ACCOUNTABILITY

# CHAPTER 5

# STORY ETHICS

### David M. Boje

By way of introduction, the story ethics I have in mind is to stop fitting a simple linear beginning, middle, and end (hereafter BME) narrative structure onto phenomenal complexity (Boje, 2000; Letiche, 2000). BME is too oversimplifying, does not get at the interweave of your story and my story. We are answerable for our participation in the corporeality of one another's stories because that participation is unique and nonrecurrent. We are answerable when we occupy one-occurent, participation in-the-moment of Being, that is compellent acknowledgment of our unique obligation to do the deed of story listener and storyteller, to act answerably to change the social (Bakhtin, 1993, p. 42). Yet oftentimes, whatever the storytelling, many people do not feel complicit.

I take the perspective that our stories intertwine, yet we know little of where others' stories begin, or how they will unfold, and perhaps move unconnectedly. As we witness our complicity, there is obligative compellentness that nonparticipants do not possess. We may not pay much attention to the weave of stories in which we participate. Or despite awareness of such a weave, we may just deny any ontological culpability. When others' living stories interfere with our own, we can become more aware.

One reason why participating in Being, witnessing or otherwise complicit in oppression, does not bring about compellent obligative answerability

*Critical Theory Ethics for Business and Public Administration*, pages 97–117
Copyright © 2008 by Information Age Publishing
All rights of reproduction in any form reserved.

to act is that we have lost our skills as storytellers and become meaningless narrators. Walter Benjamin (1936/1955, p. 83) begins by proclaiming,
"*The art of storytelling is coming to an end.*" We have lost our "ability to tell a
tale properly" because "experience has fallen in value" (pp. 83–84). His
last line informs the thesis of this chapter: "The storyteller is the figure in
which the righteous man encounters himself" (p. 109). The storyteller is
not just communicating experience of self or others, but engaged in moral
reflexivity. For Benjamin, changes in capitalism took the art of storytelling
away from the craft-arts, from the context of weavers, mariners, and other craft-contexts where there was time to hone listening and telling skills,
where journey-persons traveled, and returned to tell tales. With the novel,
the information age, division of labor, and the managerialist command that
workers no longer story while they work, the ancient orality skills became
just narrative skills of the disinterested reader, the apathetic bystander, the
one not compelled to do anything about anything. In narrative, there is all
that explication, the privileging of textual ways over oral ways, and we are
just text-readers, not complicit in moments of social Being. In the lost art,
listeners provided their own explication, they did not need tellers to fill-in-
between-the-lines, and silence could communicate.

## Complexity of Systemicity and Storytelling

I take a complexity perspective on storytelling and its relation to what I
call "systemicity." Complexity may have clear patterns in simulations (frac-
tals, bifurcations, etc.). In the corporeal world it's not so clear, coherent,
and discernable. We look for completion, for patterns that resolve, but often there are just contradictions, and no happy ending, not even temporary restful patterns in sight. *Systemicity* is what is unfinished, unfinalized,
unmerged, and downright mysterious. Systemicity is not a static idea of
some whole, completed, finalized "system" that has no mystery. Complexity
comes about then systemicity is not absolutely clear. We are not so smart
that we can sort out the complexity of systemicity and its relation to the web
of stories in which we participate, that are also unfinalized, not as full of
BME coherence as narrativists present.

Gabriel's (2000), Czarniawska's (1997, 1998), and my work (Boje, 1995,
2001a, 2006a, 2006b), define story (as well as narrative) quite differently.
Gabriel and Czarniawska take a coherence view (proper story has BME).
For Gabriel there must also be embellishment. For Czarniawska a problem
is resolved. Boje, by contrast, looks at antenarrative, and at emergent stories that are terse, fragmented, socially distributed, and do not meet the
coherence criteria. Yet, it is these incoherent tales, and the lost ability to
make sense of them that Benjamin laments, that is critical to answerabil-

ity. Czarniawska (2004) changed her definition, somewhat, and now allows for fragmented, interrupted, and distributed storytelling. However, she still prefers the more "petrified" narrative (her term).

We enter storytelling mostly often in the middle, and have little clue about any beginning or where its going to end, which it never does. We enter into what is already in motion, and do not stick around to see how it all works out, if it ever does. In this way an organization, be it public or private, is quite mysterious. We listen, "What are they saying?" "Why are they saying it here and now?" We fill in-between-the-lines overlaying structure of BME, just the way we were taught to do in those writing courses we took in high school. It's the way so many movies are presented, and many novels for that matter. In short, there is a narrative expectation for coherence that goes back to Aristotle (350 BCE). Yet, in what I view as storytelling, there are many possibilities, and everything is rarely resolved. I do not experience too many tidy endings in my daily life. There are no guarantees that an ending will happen or some "antenarrative" will attain coherence (Boje, 2001a, pp. 1–5).

In what follows I specify how narrowly narrative ethics has been theorized. Then, I open up a space for story ethics, not as a supplement, but in a dynamic relationship to narrative ethics. I begin by deconstructing narrative ethics.

## NARRATIVE ETHICS

Deconstructing Adam Z. Newton's (1995) award-winning and quite influential book is appropriate. Newton holds deconstruction, particularly the version practiced by de Man, entirely responsible for the hesitation about addressing ethics in the ways of narrative.

Figure 5.1 illustrates the interplay of the eight analytic processes (adapted from Boje, 2001a, p. 21). Derridian deconstruction is a style, not a method. I am aware that making it accessible by positing a map is against the grain. What I propose as "story ethics" traces our participation in one another's stories. I begin by defining how I approach the deconstruction of Newton's narrative ethics.

The idea of the narrative deconstruction analysis is to use the first seven analytic moves to flesh out all the missing stuff (missing duality poles, missing view to what is hierarchical hegemony, missing voices, missing sides to the story, missing counterplots, and missing exceptions to their universalistic principles). The seventh move is critical since it now lets you step back and see the full dynamics in play, that "control narrative" (Boje, 2006a) is leaving out. Step 8, I would argue, is the summation of all the prior steps. It allows one to see not just a new perspective, but to flesh out the dynamic

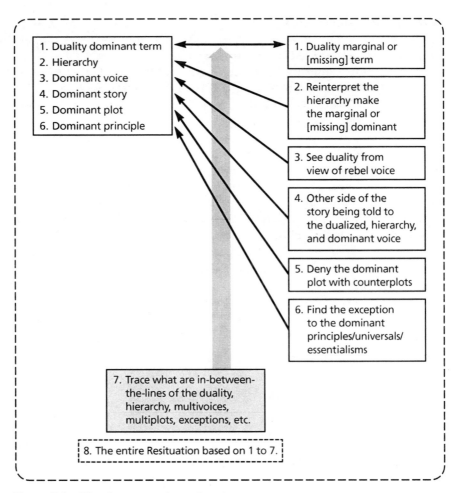

**Figure 5.1**  The deconstructive resituation.

relations in the fuller social field of antenarratives, and more dialogic stories (Boje, 2006a). In fleshing out the resituation we can overcome a key objection to deconstruction, that is, that it is only about destruction.

Deconstruction allows one to extend what Kant (1781) called "architectonics." Kant only looked at the cognitive aspects. Bakhtin (1990, 1993) developed the architectonics into the interanimation of aesthetic, ethical, and cognitive discourses. I have done a brief analysis of architectonics with several students (Boje, Rosile, Durant, & Luhman, 2005). The point of *resituation* is architectonically to get outside the Western dualities, and see the dynamics dialogically. Architectonics then is a dialogism (one of several types, along with polyphonic, stylistic, and chronotopic dialogisms).

The "dialogic manner of story" (see Bakhtin, 1981; specific cites are in Boje, 2006a) is another way to put this. I take the view that while narrative and story overlap, and interpenetrate, there are some occasions where the differences are important. The "control narrative" since Aristotle (350 BCE) has put BME coherence, a sequencing and even causal linking of episodes and characters, as a prison of the more dialogic manner of storying and antenarrating, which have more dynamic architectonic dialogical interplay.

My focus is not to destroy the control narrative, but to see how it is contextualized and embedded in the struggle with storytelling, including counterstories, counterplots, antenarrating, exceptions, etc. Resituation is about moving from either–or duality into "and" relationship; to see, in this instance, how narrative ethics, and story ethics interpenetrate one another, and are dialectic or dialogic with one another in the space and temporality of the social. I turn now to deconstructing narrative ethics.

Newton's 1995 book, *Narrative Ethics*, is exceptionally well written. Newton attacks deconstruction for not tending more specifically to ethics. Yet, I find that what he writes about narrative is tightly constituted around literary writing. His narrative ethics removes oral storytelling from the narrative playing field. More accurately, it imprisons storytelling within narrative writing. Over and over again, storytelling is treated as something writers do inside their texts, and mostly these texts are novels.

## Dualities

There are many dualities. Key among these are written narrative textuality versus orality of traditional storytelling; novel versus other forms of writing; literary stylistics over other stylistics (painting, photos, science writing, corporate writing, and speaking styles such as conversation, speeches, skaz of everyday speech appropriated for corporate use such as "just do it" or "I'm loving it").

The power of narrative is for Newton, in its textual features, its form, and hermeneutic-layering (Newton, 1995, pp. 289–290, 304). But to Benjamin (1936, p. 93), the layering comes from many rounds of telling, listening, and retelling, in a "slow piling on one top of the other of thin, transparent layers which constitutes the most appropriate picture of them and in which the perfect narrative is revealed through the layers of a variety of retellings." Newton seems to truncate storytelling into written narrative forms, structures, and hermeneutic reading, at every turn of the page, but not the king of rounds of listening and telling in a tribe of storytellers, in a community of craftspeople. For example, Newton (1995, p. 290) reads Walter Benjamin as a lament over the loss of "the layering of *storytellings*" and how novel "transacts inner-persuasion across all dimension of text." Newton's layering is also unlike Bakhtin's. Like Benjamin, Bakhtin (1981, pp. 9–10) sees the phenomenon as multilayered in a socially dialogic way. Storytelling is multiplotted, and as a "canonical genre the epic and novel "began to sound in new ways" (p. 6). It is the new ways that Newton focuses on, which have moved away from orality of the social and into textual representation. Newton (1995, p. 28) cites Bakhtin's focus on "the living word" but restricts it to narrative text, and to readers reading texts.

In short, the duality is novel writing over orality. There are other important dualities that come out in the analytic deconstructive moves that follow. A key one is certainly that writers of novels are intellectuals, whereas storytellers (particularly in Benjamin) are craftspeople doing crafts of storyteller, and when they do writing, they do it as the craft of people working in "industrial technology" in communities of tellers and listeners doing maritime travel, and factory jobs in weaving, sewing, wine-making, stonemasonry, printing, etc. The duality is liberal art versus the craft arts.

## Reinterpreting the Hierarchy

If we continue with Newton's (1995, p. 290) reading of Benjamin's (1936/1968) classic essay, The Storyteller, the perspective is about everything that is textual representation. Newton (1995, p. 55) reflectionism self-deconstructs when he asserts narrative texts "reflect states of reality" and "such reflectionism" does not need to be treated as "naive." It self-deconstructs again when Newton (1995, p. 24) says, "I am aware of the dangers of collapsing the difference between the world of the text and the world which this final example of life-turned-into-story raises." Newton's "reflectionism" claim is that the world of novels reflects the wider world of social discourse.

Newton's duality of textuality over community storytelling truncates the search for answerability. We are not asked to look at texts outside the novel nor to social discourses in orality.

If we explore a bit by reversing the hierarchy of writing over orality, what do we discover about Benjamin's essay? Benjamin's (1936/1968, p. 83) reflections on the works of Nikolai Leskov "teaches us that the art of storytelling is coming to an end. Less and less frequently do we encounter people with the ability to tell a tale properly." Storytelling was once "the securest among our possessions," this "ability to exchange experiences" (p. 83) has been taken from us. Like Gertrude Stein (1935), Benjamin does not see newspapers demonstrating the traditional practices of storytelling. Both find nothing remarkable in the narrative style of newspaper writing. It is clear that Benjamin is lamenting the passage of mouth-to-mouth storytelling (p. 84), and sees few instances of it replicated in written narrative versions: "Experience which is passed on from mouth to mouth is the source from which all storytellers have drawn" (p. 84). This supports Gabriel's (2000) claim that proper storytelling is not prevalent in organizations.

The storyteller is not textual, but fully embodied in "corporeality" (p. 84). The storyteller is part of a "tribe of storytellers" and these are more traditional the traveling "trading seaman" and the stay-at-home "resident tiller of the soil" (pp. 84–85). These did produce some storyteller writers, but became archaic types of writing as the trade structure of the Middle Ages gave way to the factory guilds. As a critical theorist (Frankfurt School), Benjamin is tracing how the traveling journeymen and the crafts of the artisan class were no longer the "university" for training the "masters of storytelling" (p. 85). In terms of ethics, "the art of storytelling is reaching its end," says Benjamin (1936/1965, p. 87) "because the epic side of truth, wisdom, is dying out," which is evident in the concomitant transition that "quite gradually removed narrative from the realm of living speech and at the same time is making it possible to see a new beauty in what is vanishing." And in place of living storytelling embedded in the trades of craftspeople, Benjamin sees the emergent novel writers. They do not write in the style of orality, the epic passed from mouth to mouth, until it is penned as epic. Rather, Benjamin sees a different kind of novel writing that is not taking "what he tells from experience—his own or that reported by others" (p. 87). The novel, as Newton (1995, p. 141) stresses, is all about representation in "representational economy" of the novel, the mimetic of what is in human social life, made over into just pure fiction to effect textual catharsis.

In short, reversing the duality, we find that Benjamin is lamenting the passing of oral tradition and the emergence of a style of novel writing that is a move away from ipic forms. Benjamin argues this transition to modern novel emerges because the form of modern capitalism have removed the community where storytellers could practice their telling and their listening competencies, their ability to convey experience. And what is this new form of novel? It is the transition from storytelling to communication as "information" (p. 88) that offers "prompt verifiability." And it is incommensurate, and "incompatible with the spirit of storytelling" and "the art of storytelling has become rare" in the time of the "dissemination of information" (p. 89). "The value of information does not survive the moment in which it was new" (p. 90). Storytelling, on the other hand, "does not expend itself. It preserves and concentrates its strength and is capable of releasing it even after a long time" (p. 90). It was the ancient art of storytelling "to keep a story free from explication" (p. 89). "The storyteller foregoes psychological shading," leaving that to the listener (p. 91). These are three factors that Benjamin (1936/1968, p. 90) says define "their germinative power to this day." In the place of the factors of not expending itself, being free from explication, and not psychologically shading (leaving that to the listener or reader), Newton (1995) substitutes quite different factors.

## Rebel Voices

In Newton, the listener disappears and becomes just a reader, a reader seduced into answerability by the narrative form and structure. In Benjamin's (1936/1968) traditional art of storytelling, the gift of retelling came from the listener listening, being able to recount the story from the place in memory of the listener, by integrating the story heard with one's own experiences, and expecting to be asked to repeat their version in a tribe of storytellers. The rebel voice of the teller who is in the "milieu of work—the rural, the maritime, and the urban" is left at the margin. In its place Newton focuses on the literary writer and the literary critic of the literary writer. He does not sink into the lowly life of the storyteller who is the worker. Newton's storytellers do not begin their story by telling the "circumstances in which they themselves have learned what is to follow" (Benjamin, 1936/1968, p. 92).

I think Bakhtin can be a rebel voice. Bakhtin (1990) is cited throughout Newton as the basis (along with Levinas) for a narrative ethics of answerability. For example, Bakhtin's heteroglossia is translated by Newton (1995, p. 253) to be "ceaseless oscillation between centripetal and centrifugal forces." Yet for Bakhtin (1981) heteroglossia is the forces of language itself, not just writing, but spoken and architectural, and gestural language, such as in stylistic dialogism (the interplay of many written and nonwritten stylistics). For Newton the power of narrative is in quite physical forces. "Narrative ethics in these [text] cases conforms to a strict physics of force and counterforce" (Newton, 1995, p. 114). It would seem that for Newton, dialogism is only in the physics of written language, and only the forms of other stylistics, such as conversation or science-talk embedded in the novel.

My own rebel voice would speak of the ethnographies, to sociology of everyday speech acts, to the ethnomethodology of social class, and political and economic types of writing that are beyond the pages of the novel. Newton's narrative inquiry is too narrow. There are many different kinds of writing that a novel will mimic and many kinds of orality, but there is also a world outside the grasp of the typesetter and graphologist (Newton, 1995, p. 170). There is the authoritarian power of corporations, of publishers, who control what novels are distributed, and on what topics, especially, as Benjamin (1936, pp. 83–84) remarks, in times of war and terror. There are controls on textual production in late modern capitalism.

## Other Side of the Story

The other side of the story of Narrative Ethics is Story Ethics. Story rights, for example, is the side of the story not told by Newton (1995). It is how story rights inhere in the tribe of storytellers, in their very community, in their social rounds of telling, listening, and retelling (as we explored above). Newton closes out his book by writing about Benjamin's (1936/1968) essay The Storyteller. Newton (1995, p. 292) sees only "readers coming ever closer to the story" and drawn like flies into "the gentle flames of his story" and to their death. The other side of this story is Benjamin talking about something entirely different.

For Benjamin (1936/1968, p. 93) "dying was once a public process in the life of the individual" but now we do not make paintings of people on their deathbed, as was done in Medieval times. Like storytelling, dying is being pushed further and further out of the world of the social and the living. To Benjamin, "death is the sanction of everything that the storyteller can tell" (p. 94). It is the storyteller embedding his or her tale deep in natural history where death makes a regular appearance (p. 95). Newton (p. 116) truncates Benjamin's sociology of death, to just being writing about the "ultimate aesthetic act." But what is Benjamin getting at with the "gentle flame"? I think it is another side to the story told by Newton. Benjamin (1936/1968, pp. 108–109) says, "The Storyteller is the man who could let the wick of his life be consumed completely by the gentle flame of his story... The storyteller is the figure in which the righteous man encounters himself." It is where the storyteller has integrated what others told him or her to tell, and what has been integrated form the living story of experience. It is not just the narrative tricks of the writing. Writers and readers and oral tellers participate in the sociological, in social classes, in economic differences, in racial and other diversities.

Finally, Newton (p. 14) cites Coleridge when claiming that "lives turn into stories and stories fold back again into lives." My reinterpretation of the duality is that lives turn into stories and stories fold back into our lives, not only from texts, but from storytelling in our day-to-day conversations.

## Deny the Dominant Plot

The plot in Newton's (1995) Narrative Ethics is that the written narrative affords the structures and forms that implicate the reader in ethical answerability, a responsibility for readers to what they read. The dominant plot is that using writerly tricks of rhetoric, the reader becomes answerable. "And more that we are responsible for knowing" due to the "catharsis of narrative ethics" (Newton, 1995, p. 292). My denial of the plot is that this is a textual ethics, tied to Aristotle's (350 bce) poetic catharsis. The dominant plot is what I call "control narrative" coherence (Boje, 2006a). The control narratives are "texts" that are supposed to "tax readers with ethical duties which increase in proportion to the measure with which they are taken up" (p. 292). I deny the plot that an ethics of reading is more powerful than an ethics of storytelling community. If people, by textual ethics, and the ethics of reading, could relate to "the infinite, the transcendental, the stranger" (p. 292), surely there would be no sweatshops, no exploitation of labor anymore.

Newton (1995) interprets the critical ethics of Thodor Adorno as limited only to "readability" (p. 54). Yet for Adorno, what was important about was how narrative regulated experience. Adorno (1990) looked at how writing with all its punctuation tries to capture orality in the text, but in the end its just text and no one is really speaking (as Newton, 1995, p. 21, notes). In addition, there is indication that Adorno's critical theory moves past the narrative in novel-text into organization storytelling. For example, Adorno (1963/2000, p. 170) ends his series of 1963 lectures by declaring, "There is no ethics... in the administered world."

## Find the Exceptions

There are many exceptions to the principles and universals stated in Newton. The main one is Newton's (1995, p. 101) "essential principles of narrative ethics [are] at work in the novel" and nowhere else. It is the novel that "summons readers" to ethical answerability (p. 101). To Newton the narrative itself has a powerful effect the narrator and reader dare not 'shake off' (p. 289). Stories are nested and embedded in narratives. He reads Benjamin's (1936/1968, p. 90) line about "preserves and concentrates its strength" as something that narrative does, instead of something that was a survival from mouth-to-mouth rounds of telling and retelling. To Benjamin, the survival of the mouth-to-mouth competency to retell experience, to commit it to memory, was only found in a few exceptional writers, who had themselves been craftspeople. Newton (1995, p. 289) refers to what Benjamin (1936, p. 90) calls "germinative" power. It was not the embedding of story inside narrative form, it was how the storyteller left gaps for the listener to fill in, and, as discussed earlier, does not expend itself like information in narrative-explication, or like the modern novel in laying out the psychological shading. Newton (1995, p. 292) says, "Narrative ethics is not merely a property of texts." Yet, when we read his principles of narrative structure and hermeneutics, it's all about textual composition, the writing of novels, and not about the sociality of storytelling, in its many stylistic forms. In short, sociality and corporeality, the political economy of printing and publishing—these are always exceptions for Newton.

Newton does not address the sociological or economic context of writing narratives, and the kinds of narrative ethics that are positing as legitimate under corporate rule. It is ironic that Newton (1995, p. 159) cites Irving Goffman. Goffman is a sociologist; he observes the dramaturgy of social performance, not the senders and receivers of textual material. He is studying the theatrics of image management, the ways in which image is part of the symbolic economy. Goffman is outside the closed system representation of the narrative text, even beyond the intertextual relationships. There is a substitution Newton keeps making for "webs of interlocution" and "webs of exchange" outside the text, for those mimetic ones that novel writers can imprison inside the text (p. 142). For example, Netwon (p. 116) argues, "Because exigency lies behind occasions for storytelling in this novel, the stories... perform a narrative ethics."

The implication is stories and storytelling can only accomplish ethics when imprisoned in the text of a novel or other literary work. In short, ethics of the novel substitutes for any storytelling in the sociology beyond the novel. Each substitution of surface values for experiences of storytelling in community puts what Newton cherishes further out of reach. It only further "mystifies intersubjective encounter" (1995, p. 142). Newton (p. 18) says "intersubjective responsibilities and claims ... follow form acts of storytelling" yet it is only the textual-mirror of storytelling, not the exploration of the act of storytelling in corporeality that Newton is exploring. And Newton has the very concept the "aesthetic slippage" (p. 142) from the countervailing discourses of the embedded sociology of storytelling situated in community, in organization, and in political economy down to "narratives proper" (p. 18). Benjamin (1928), for example, in "One-Way Street," makes the point that "literary activity" is no longer confined to "literary frameworks" in books, but extends to the signs and ads printed all over city streets and shops.

A final exception I want to comment on is the marginalization of turn-taking in ethical behavior. Newton (1995, p. 114) says, "empirical support for ethical behavior in discourse, turn-taking processes, for instance" are in the "metaphysical sense" examples of "pained speech." Newton wants to remove storytelling as a "profane" kind of expression, part of face-to-face turn-taking, part of spoken discourses not tethered to the physics of the novel. Over and over again, Newton finds the sociology of storytelling behaviors as well as "communal narratives" (p. 111) to be not as effective as narrative ethics fashioned in the pages of the novel, and in the minds of the reader turning those pages.

## Trace In-Between-the-Lines

In looking at the dualities, reversing their hierarchy, setting in play the rebel voices, other side of the story, denying the dominant plot, and finding various exceptions allow us now to look more closely at what is in-between-the-lines of all these relationships. Between the author's text and the world of the socioeconomic or corporeality of capitalism stands the reader. "A theory of narrative ethics entails the perhaps peculiar notion that characters' fates take place in the presence of readers." The reader is at a distance between text and character, between reader and character (p. 292).

In-between-the-lines Newton (1995, p. 140) is swept away by narrative ethers, reading for the ethics of intersubjective registers in "the play of forms" in the novel. The author's contempt and pragmatic ethics (p. 139) is supposed to seduce the reader. That is his "ethics of narration" (p. 116). It is inherently textual, in narrative acts that are "compelling formulations" in the text (p. 116).

Newton drives a wedge between written words and spoken words not re-spoken in the text. He depends on the novel to be the sole harbinger of the "transcendental power of language" (p. 109). Stories always become the "private property" of texts. Only talk that is types is part of narrative ethics. In claiming to be doing "Bakhtinian ethics" Newton (p. 47) is not exploring the dull spectrum of non-novel stylistics, for which Bakhtin (1981) is known.

Newton's dislike of de Man's deconstruction focuses on his refusal to impart ethics in the views on agency, and in structures of the text (pp. 37, 54). Newton accuses de Man of "scrupulous [ethical] hesitation" (p. 37), "reified aesthetic formalisms" and "bloodless formalist correctives" (p. 54), and a "nondialogical imperialism" (p. 304). Yet, in-between-the-lines of Netwon's text, one could make those same accusations and ask for answerability. Newton does at least part of what he protests in de Man. Newton does claim ethics as the province of hermeneutic theories of narrative textuality and does not look at the dialectic aspects of textuality and orality stylistics. His deconstruction of de Man's ways of deconstruction concludes that de Man ways "convert readers into its [i.e., text's] jailer-detainees" (Newton, 1995, p. 49). And that de Man "defies the ethical immediacy of human speech" (p. 38). These charges are ironic, since Newton continually jails storytelling in narrative prison, and truncates ethical immediacy of human speech to novel-embedded speech.

## Resituation

Newton (1995, p. 290), in passing, says, "Narrative ethics range across a spectrum. The Bakhtinian addressivity of utterance that would forge for

Newton an intersubjective alliance" (p. 290) is one part of the spectrum. From the above deconstruction, it would appear the sociality of a community of storytellers, who orally tell and retell, and sometimes write, is another important place on the spectrum. To Newton the "force of story" makes the narrator feel he or she knows the characters (p. 290). In the "force of representation" Newton theorized implicit "representational power" (p. 290). This representational power of narrating comes from translating the Other into a character, and even a fictional one, is as Newton (1995, p. 291) "fraught with ethical tensions." Yet the sheer experience of telling, listening, connecting one's experience to a telling (making it a co-telling) is part of the power of the sociality of storytelling, its communal aspects, that is more than just the writing of narrative. In narrative and story there is an arbitrary tyranny imposed by authors and, the imprisoned character, the imposed shaping, the very "despotism of form" (Newton, 1995, p. 291).

My resituation is to look at the question of answerability as interplay of narrative ethics and story ethics. I call for resituation of the narrative ethics project. I call for a story ethics not imprisoned in typeset pages, or in the poetics of text-based hermeneutics.

I want to treat answerability with more ambivalence. I want to question whether reading a text or hearing a storytelling in community imparts ethical answerability. It would seem, in my experience, that people oftentimes eschew answerability, and even when obviously and self-acknowledged complicity, there is denial of answerability.

Instead of truncating narrative discourse to the novel, and its physics of forces, I would like to suggest we look at the more social, psychological, and phenomenal aspects of storytelling in and between organizations. If we open narrative inquiry to multiplex of written and orality stylistics, as well as to the theatrics of gesture, then we get a more thickly described understanding of the relationship of the limits and exigencies of answerability.

Newton (1995, p. 24) notes the danger of his collapse of the differences of the "world of the text" and the world of "life—turned-into-story." He then proceeds to do what he has qualified. Novels reflect upon and mimic everyday and extraordinary life. In short, Newton's project is to compose narrative ethics by reading from great literature (e.g., Dickens's *Great Expectations*, Faulkner's *Absalom Absalom*, Hawthorne's *Scarlet Letter*, etc.) responsible obligations in everyday life from varied narrative forms. I argue for looking at the grounded processes of the social, for storytelling-in-use, in the collective processes of everyday life, where the strictures about narrative coherence and form are more grotesque and carnivalistic. Certainly everyday life mimics fictional patterns, and fiction mimics everyday life. The point I am making is to study the interrelationships of narrative ethics (that would run everyday life as novel) and story ethics (that is more dynamic less coherent than novels, even polyphonic ones). Shifting story ethics into the phenomenal world of everyday life gives ethics and story more ethnographic, sociological, and historical import.

## STORY ETHICS

We do not get a transcript of our own or Others' stories. My observation is that my living story is in fragments, and my encounters with others' living stories are equally fragmented. Furthermore, I have argued that Newton (1995, p. 30) Narrative Ethics needs to be more than "textual engagement" or that novels reflect all as need to know about social discourse.

I would like to question answerability ethics. People I study who purchase shoes from Nike or many of products from Wal-Mart do not seem to feel at all implicated in what goes on in sweatshops of our global economy (Boje, 1999a, 1999b, 2000, 2001a, 2001b, 2006a).

Most agree that many people are hurting, working in horrid conditions, but consumers and most management academics refuse to be implicated. They refuse to be incriminated in anything so onerous as a sweatshop. They are not responsible. Since they are not answerable, their reaction poses an ethics problem. Despite rather abundant storytelling in activist websites, and a sprinkling of press stories, people do not feel the worker's plight on their conscience. When I ask my students about this, about half tell me they do not feel compelled to be concerned by stories of workers in faraway countries.

### Compellent Storytelling

What kinds of stories are compelling? Is an answerable story one that haunts us? Is it one that puzzles us? Is it one that keeps unraveling deep secrets? Is it unmistakable tragedies in which we have some complicity, no matter how minor? Must our complicity be explicitly spelled out in the storytelling?

Answers to these questions are about guilt and blame. Many students in my classes, or colleagues at conferences, do not feel answerable, or evoked to acceptance of complicity in what is out of sight, far away, and keep it out of mind. Guilt is not a simple emotion. Guilt may be something that slowly sinks in, over many tellings about this or that condition. Who is to blame for environmental pollution, sweatshops, the bankruptcy of Enron, and the demise of Arthur Anderson—can remain unanswered in the storytelling. Perhaps there is plenty of blame to go around, and everyone points at others, never themselves.

People psychologically repress and suppress what is disturbing. They defend themselves against claims of answerability. Many corporations committed to unethical practices have no choice but to defend and to vehemently protect the false idea of their lack of complicity because such a narrative, when compelling, has currency in the marketplace. We have so many places and spaces to decide to be answerable or not. Too much remains unanswered. The systemicity keeps moving and rearranging, and whatever compellent narratives are enacted in one context, does not hold for very long. The truth is always a thousand truths. We manipulate our choice of truth by changing perspective, deciding which perspectives to manage as images and which to hide away.

A hint of suspicion enriches the complexity of organization and inter-organizational relations, as well as relations between workers and organizations, and customers and organizations. In the face of suspicion, many corporations play it quite seriously. Others play well with the ambivalence. There's no problem here. Many a corporation hides their secrets. Many executives hide their secrets. Many employees and consumers have secrets. We all have suspicions. We live in a web of suspicions. Denial can be an exchange on different registers of emotion and will. Some are vehement and outraged. Others play it unphased, even nonchalant.

The limitation of answerability ethics is that many people do not accept guilt, blame, or complicity. They, for example, may prefer bold denial, and have no discernable sense of conscience answerability for global practices. Many, even if they could decipher Figure 5.1, do not want to know. Their egoism is quite selfish when it comes to thinking about their relationships to others, especially to others different in gender, ethnicity, race, class, or economic circumstance. Answerability, then, must deal with how people live with guilt, and keep far way from guilt over any kind of complicity, no matter how compellent the storytelling. Its been my experience that some very intelligent people divorce stories of sweatshop working lives from their persona lives as shoppers, and from stories of fellow workers in the brotherhood of workers globally, whatever their plight. This makes it easy for corporations to sweep the dirt under the carpet by crafting rather compellent narratives. In other words, compellent storytelling is not enough. There are psychological reasons why people just will not be answerable.

## Compellent Narrating

A proper narrative is thought to have BME, but unless there is participation, can it be compellent? Corporations hire the best talent to craft narratives to be compellent, but are they? They make sophisticated use of double narration, embedding the narratives of actors and sports stars into the corporately orchestrated narrative. But, is this manipulation of narrative compellent? It's not compellent when people cannot decipher or deconstruct their own complicity. Nike tells many white lies, one after the other, to avoid its own compellentness in workers' conditions. At least Nike does seem to lie, to those of us in the anti-sweatshop movement, to avoid complicity (Boje, 2000, 2001b, 2006a).

Deconstructing narrative compellentness gets us into a genealogy of narrative moves that altogether is fairly complex. That's the problem with Nike's narrative compellentness, to leave a trail of one oversimplistic alibi-narrative after another, and just keep moving and telling defensively. Nike heads down a path, in my view, one spin after another, and all the time defending its practices, while claiming to be transparent in how it is monitoring sweatshop abuses of its subcontract factories. The path gets more and more complex. What is supposedly transparently presented in narrative to spectators is a way of telling from a certain perspective, or just plain trickery, faking transparency.

The fakery is one that Newton (1995, p. 38) clearly identifies, when writers "want readers to hear a polyphony of voices" alongside the author's "orchestration of them." The problem is those of us in the movement deconstruct the feigned polyphony, the lack of actual worker voice, in one spin after another, and Nike skips down the path to tell and sell another spin. When we call Nike on its complicity, the answer is "sorry that way of telling is not us anymore." Yet, there is a problem for Nike in this. Moving down the path means setting out one manipulation scheme after another, each a bit more elaborate than the last. A thousand little choices are swept under the rug, and a few come out from under. And when these collide, there can be emergent effects that spiral out of corporate control.

For example, Ernst and Young audits could find no sweatshops in the 1990s. When the narrative shield unraveled in the exposé press, then former ambassador Andrew Young was sent to tell his compellent narrative that there were none. Challenged by Doonesbury cartoon caricatures, Nike skipped down the path and hired various academics to write glowing ethical reports (Boje, 2000; Landrum, 2000a, 2000b). Landrum and Boje (2000) did an ethnostatistic analysis of the invalidity of academic data gathered, statistics methods and rhetorical embellishments by Amos Tuck professors' MBA students. Nike skipped further along, and caught up with the Wal-Mart and Kathie Lee Gifford scandal, formed the Fair Labor Association (what a misnomer). FLA is paid for by corporate fees, and does monitoring studies, taking over the role of Ernst & Young auditors, the infamous Andrew Young's whistle stop tour of Nike factories, and the various academic empiric whitewashes.[1]

Nike's current strategy: to suspend disbelief, leave a little bit of culpability showing. FLA monitors actually find and report occurrences of subcontractors engaged in blocking organizing, paying below legal wages, hiring underage workers, withholding overtime payment, physical and mental abuse, etc. Nike is in an amazing position. It can claim to be policing and enforcing its ethical code, but the behavior keeps going on in the same frequency and intensity as before. The lawsuit by consumers in California was won in the court. The court judgment upheld that Nike's transparency rhetoric claiming it had used FLA to curtail sweatshops was too much of an exaggeration. Skipping down the path, Nike claimed that it had protection under the First Amendment of the Constitution to free speech, and that includes the right to freely lie in corporate advertising. It was not upheld. Nike did pull most of its Transparency 101 program off its websites. Nike, and many others, still uses FLA reports of sweatshop abuses of its contractors, writing compellent narratives, each time, as to what is being done to uphold ethical standards. It's one choice point after another. At each point is the decision, to lie or to tell the truth, to tell a compellent narrative that tidies up one misstep after another, or engage a more complex storytelling. At each point a gaggle of storytellers try to decipher the trail markers.

## And

I want to reiterate that its about "and" not either/or. We are talking about a dynamic of compellent narrating and compellent storytelling. It is just that alibi narrating has this way of trumping compellent storytelling, particularly the compellent participant-storytelling by workers, who speak out to activists, and a few reporters.

There is defensiveness, the presentation of counternarrative to any damaging storytelling, such as a counternarrative of why sweaty globalization practices is part of economic development, part of the road a developing Third World economy must take to get to the top. The compellent narrative offers the spectator, the consumer, managers, and contractors closure, that there are no sweatshops, and if there are, the corporation is not to blame or in any way answerable for what its contractors do, nor should consumers be at all concerned, or any academics, for that matter. Besides, the road to the top narrative claims that if there are sweatshops, well that's the way it should be, the way it ought to be (an ethical claim). The compellent narratives are oftentimes dominant ways of narrating, and overcome any fledgling storytelling, no matter how compellent. The interplay of compellent narratives and compellent stories is why there can be millions of workers still slaving in sweatshops in the great global economy of late modern capitalism, and very few academics have anything "*critical*" to say on the subject.

## RELEVANCE TO CRITICAL THEORY ETHICS

It's time to deconstruct Newton's Narrative Ethics to make room for Story Ethics. I think it is relevant to critical theory ethics, because Newton keeps referring to Adorno, Bakhtin, Habermas, and to Marx. Newton (1995, p. 14) is skeptical about Habermas's ethical approach to obligation stemming from a universal reason that is self-evident. Newton picks up the gauntlet of answerability from Bakhtin, but restricts it to textuality. He restricts Adorno's concern for authoritarian orders in the "real" to a matter of "readability" when Adorno clearly, as I have shown, is all about ethical failures of administrative ethics, in organizational and capitalism discourses. Newton sprinkles his text with references to Marx, to "ideological constraints" and to the "bourgeois status quo" (p. 55).

In our book on *Critical Theory Ethics* we raise an important moral question for the relation of narrative to story ethics. In the corporeality of global capitalism are we not complicit in the production, distribution, and consumption practices of reading and writing? Complicity in storytelling, as tellers and as listeners, is a complex topic, because social behavior in relationships, be they local or global, it's always a moral question.

There are critical limits to answerability, to the thesis that reading a narrative or listening to a storytelling will persuade one to act. There is an assumption that direct participation in reading a story, or participating in an act that is storyable, will result in obligation to do something to bring something more ethical into being. Adorno and Horkheimer turned increasingly to Nietzsche to critique administrative ethics and the culture industry to explain why workers and consumers, though participants and complicit, were not being *answerable* for changing the system.

I think Friedrich Nietzsche (1844–1900) would call *Business and Public Administration Ethics* forms of "slave ethics" (Nietzsche, 1887/1956, pp. 170–171). Slave ethics, as conscience "in its highest form as behind it a long history of transformations" (p. 192). Ethics is "branded on the memory" of the slave (p. 192). "Whenever man has thought it necessary to create a memory for himself, its effort has been attended with torture, blood, sacrifice" (pp. 192–193). Business and public administration ethics is too often an apologetics for cruelty. The pain of "stoning, ... breaking on the wheel, piercing with stakes, drawing and quartering, trampling to death with horses, boiling in oil or wine (these were still in use in the fourteenth and fifteenth centuries), the popular flaying alive, cutting out of flesh from the chest, smearing the victim with honey and leaving him in the sun, a prey to flies" (Nietzsche, 1887/1956, pp. 193–194). Today's cruelties are less public spectacles of torture, and more the slow torture of excessive performative, slave wages, and lack of freedom to organize. Yet as Newton (1995, p. 55) observes about Hawthorne's novel, *Scarlet Letter*, "allegorical modes of perception can imprison social relations far more effectively than any stocks" or other spectacles of Medieval cruelty. And these allegorical mechanisms transcend the novel, and permeate the social discourses of organization.

I have argued that the answerability thesis is overstated. People avoid the guilt and blame of answerability and addressivity complicity in contemporary cruelty. They engage in denial that they are at all complicit in the cruelty of late modern global capitalism. Nike and Wal-Mart are unashamed of the cruelty of sweatshop life. They tell compellent narratives to counter the marginalized storytelling of cruelty to workers. Sweatshops are characteristics of capitalism's most cruel centuries. With literary fiction's answerability, people do not rebel against suffering of humans in sweatshops, or animals in slaughterhouses, as long as there is a business ethics of sensemaking apologetics. When the cruelty appears egregious in the storytelling done by workers, then the masses rebel only a little. Indeed business ethics narrates sweatshops suffering cruel working conditions in order to effect national economic progress.

Business and public administration ethicists are completely absorbed in "modern" experience of capitalism, with "no knowledge of the past, no desire to understand it... they presume, all the same, to write the history of ethics!" (Nietzsche, 1887/1956, p. 194). Ethics is more about damages suffered, and calculated compensations between creditor and debtor. "And may we not say that ethics has never lost its reek of blood and torture—not even in Kant, whose categorical imperative smacks of cruelty? (Nietzsche, p 197).

## NOTE

1. For a history of monitoring and whitewashing, see Boje's website http://business.nmsu.edu/~dboje/AA/monitors.htm

## REFERENCES

Adorno, T. (1990). Punctuation marks. *Antioch Review, 48*, 300–305.

Adorno, T. W. (1991). *The culture industry: Selected essays on mass culture*. London: Routledge.

Aristotle. (1954). *Rhetoric and Poetics* (Rhetoric translated by W. Rhys Roberts; Poetics translated by Ingram Bywater). New York: The Modern Library (Random House). (Original work written 350 BCE)

Bakhtin, M. (1981). *The dialogic imagination: Four essays* (C. Emerson & Michael Holquist, Trans.). Austin: University of Texas Press.

Bakhtin, M. M. (1990). *Art and answerability* (M. Holquist & V. Liapunov, Trans.). Austin: University of Texas Press.

Bakhtin, M. M. (1993). *Toward a philsophy of the act* (M. Holquist & V. Liapunov, Eds.). Austin: University of Texas Press.

Benjamin, W. (1936/1968). The storyteller: Reflections on the works of Nikolai Leskov. In H. Arendt (Ed.), *Walter Benjamin illuminations* (pp. 83–109). New York: Harcourt, Brace, and World.

Benjamin, W. (1928). *Einbahnstraße* [One Way Street].

Boje, D. M. (1995). Stories of the storytelling organization: A postmodern analysis of Disney as "Tamara-land." *Academy of Management Journal, 38*(4), 997–1035.

Boje, D. M. (1999a). Nike, Greek goddess of victory or cruelty?: Women's stories of Asian factory life. *Journal of Organizational Change Management, 11*(8), 461–480.

Boje, D. M. (1999b). Is Nike Roadrunner or Wile E. Coyote?: A postmodern organization analysis of double logic. *Journal of Business and Entrepreneurship, 2,* 77–109.

Boje, D. M. (2000). Nike corporate writing of academic, business, and cultural practices. *Management Communication Quarterly, 4*(3), 507–516.

Boje, D. M. (2001b). *Narrative methods for organizational and communication research.* London: Sage.

Boje, D.M. (2001a). Carnivalesque resistance to global spectacle: A critical postmodern theory of public administration. *Administrative Theory and Praxis, 23*(3), 431–458.

Boje, D. M. (2006b). *Storytelling organization.* London: Sage.

Boje, D. M. (2006a). Breaking out of narrative's prison: Improper story in storytelling organization. *Storytelling, Self, Society: An Interdisciplinary Journal of Storytelling Studies, 2*(2), 28–49.

Boje, D. M., Rosile, G. A., Durant, R. A., & Luhman, J. T. (2004). Enron spectacles: A critical dramaturgical analysis. *Organization Studies, 25*(5), 751–774.

Cai, Yue. (2006). *Story strategy dialogisms at Motorola Corporation.* Unpublished doctoral dissertation, Management Department, New Mexico State University.

Czarniawska, B. (1997). *Narrating the organization: Dramas of institutional identity.* Chicago: University of Chicago Press.

Czarniawska, B. (1998). *A narrative approach to organization studies.* Thousand Oaks, Ca; Sage.

Czarniawska, B. (2004). *Narratives in social science research.* London: Sage.

Gabriel, Y. A. (2000). *Storytelling in organizations: Facts, fictions, and fantasies.* London: Oxford University Press.

Horkheimer, M., & Adorno, T. W. (1944/1972). Dialectic of enlightenment (J. Cumming, Trans.). New York: Herder and Herder.

Illich, I. (1993). *In the vineyard of the text: A commentary to Hugh's Didascalicon.* Chicago: University of Chicago Press.

Landrum, N. E. (2000b). *A quantitative and qualitative examination of the dynamics of Nike and Reebok storytelling as strategy.* Unpublished doctoral dissertation, New Mexico State University, Management Department.

Landrum, N. E. (2000a, August). *Environmental rhetoric of Nike.* Paper presented at the Academy of Management All Academy Showcase Symposium on "Time and Nike."

Landrum, N., & Boje, D. (2000). An ethnostatistical analysis of Nike's Tuck Report. In J. Biberman & A. Alkhafaji (Eds.), Business Research Yearbook: Global business perspectives, Vol. 7. International Academy of Business Disciplines (pp. 614–618). Saline, MI: McNaughton & Gunn Inc.

Nietzsche, F. W. (1887/1956). *The birth of tragedy, and The genealogy of morals* (F. Golffing, Trans.). New York: Doubleday Dell.

Newton, A. Z. (1995). *Narrative ethics.* Cambridge, MA: Harvard University Press.

Ong, W. J. (1982). *Orality and literacy: The technologizing of the word.* London: Routledge.

CHAPTER 6

# NO ALIBI IN ETHICS

## Bakhtin's Philosophy of the Act and the Question of Answerability in Business

### Olga Belova

## INTRODUCTION

In the film "The Corporation" Sir Mark Moody-Stuart, former CEO of Royal Dutch Shell, tells a story of how Earth First activists arrived on the doorstep of his country home to protest against Shell's involvement in environmental damage and human rights abuses. Contrary to their usual tactic, the activists did not choose to launch a media campaign or march through the streets. The impact they were after was personal, not public. Determined to call Mark Moody-Stuart to personal account, they stretched the banner "murderers" over the roof of his house. Mark had little choice but to engage in a dialogue with protesters and even served them tea on his front lawn to "smooth" the conversation. However, while assuring environmentalists that "he cared about the same things" as they did he steered clear of discussing his involvement in Shell's destructive practices. Protesters' hopes

*Critical Theory Ethics for Business and Public Administration*, pages 119–133
Copyright © 2008 by Information Age Publishing
All rights of reproduction in any form reserved.

to challenge his actual, not professed concerns, were short-lived. For Mark, putting a personal signature under his actions was out of the question.

This chapter grapples with the issues of answerability and its place in current approaches to business ethics. Business ethics have long sought to produce and codify moral norms to encourage corporate citizenship and morally responsible business operations. In practice, however, such norms often turn out to become alibis for evading individual responsibility. Their generalized and abstracted-from-real-life formulations mean that anyone in particular feels hardly obligated by them. This frustrating realization could have been what brought Earth First activists to challenge the Shell CEO in person: while Shell's Business Principles of "respect for people" and "integrity"[1] apply to everyone, they do not call any specific person to account. The purpose of this chapter is to explore these tensions between ethics as responsibility to a norm and ethics as responsibility for *my* acts, or as I will refer to as *personal answerability*, which I develop with reference to Bakhtin's philosophy of the act. The chapter starts by looking at Kant's moral philosophy from which gave rise to the tradition of universalist and prescriptive ethics. Here I query in particular the way in which Kant transforms the status of a moral norm into "law" or "duty," and implications that it has for business practice where ethical codes come to be articulated as universal obligations to be fulfilled. This helps us probe into contradictions inherent in deontology and the paradoxical practices that it leads to in business. In search for alternative ways of approaching the meaning of responsibility, I turn to Bakhtin's philosophy of the act in which he proposes that taking up of responsibility, or "answerability" in his words, cannot be motivated by transcendental ethical norms and can only arise from each specific act for which the moral subject must be answerable. I argue that Bakhtin's grounding of answerability in the act and toward the other makes a contribution to conceptualizing *ethics as a response rather than a statement,* an open-ended and ongoing task rather than a dogma that tends toward reification of conclusion. It develops an ethics based on answerability of one unique living being to another who find themselves inextricably and infinitely bound in moral relations. Importantly, this chapter presses an argument for personal responsibility that is flaringly absent in the corporate world.

## ROOTS AND PARADOXES OF NORMATIVE BUSINESS ETHICS OR "WHY HELL IS PAVED WITH GOOD INTENTIONS"

The limitations of the mainstream theories of business ethics have recently become one of the topics of debate in critical studies (Parker, 1998; Roberts, 1996; ten Bos, 1997). Questions about the purpose, value, and the very philosophical foundations of business ethics revealed that the theoretical, historical, and social undercurrents shaping ethics discourses are far from being politically neutral or value-free (Munro, 1998; Legge, 1998). In fact, they are deeply implicated in the modern structures of political and economic power, and their technical and quantitative focus (Paul, 1987) works to legitimize the instrumental and managerialist position of much of the modern management science. The whole of organizational life is now seen as shot through with moral issues and a wealth of research has emerged to confirm that they are a crucial part of doing management research (Rhodes, 2000; Wray-Bliss, 2003).

Deontology has become one of the particular targets of the recent critique of business ethics discipline. Originating in the moral philosophy of Kant, this theory postulates that moral norms take the form of "categorical imperatives" or laws that are determined though rational and theoretical reasoning. But let us take these points in turn.

In his *Fundamental Principles of the Metaphysic of Morals* (1785) Kant made an argumentative move that determined the meaning of morality for centuries to come. He argued that morality belongs to the realm of pure philosophy (metaphysics) rather than empirical philosophy and that its meaning therefore must be determined by logic and pure reason. Pure reason for Kant is a form of rational reasoning that is free from everything empirical such as practical experience and emotional knowledge as they arguably cloud judgment and clarity of thinking. If moral norms are determined without the interference of people's situational knowledge they will maintain their validity and purity. As Kant (1975) states: "the basis of obligation must not be sought in the nature of man, or in the circumstances in the world in which he is placed, but a priori simply in the conception of pure reason." Deduced through abstraction from any particularities, moral laws will exist *a priori* persons' concrete actions and function as impartial guides in moral decision making.

In according primary importance to the work of pure reason, Kant makes a key assumption about the nature of people as rational beings. He assumes that people we all have the same reason so will accept a moral if it is determined objectively—what is rational for me is by definition rational for you (Legge, 1998, p. 156). This endows a moral norm with obligatory, binding force and makes it applicable universally, across time and space boundaries. To be moral therefore means to act in accordance with the ethical law or as Kant calls it "categorical imperative"; only if performed for the sake of law can an act be truly selfless because in doing good one can still be motivated by self-interest (be it pursuit of happiness or fear of consequences). Setting apart what's good and what's moral is the lever that moves the whole of Kantian ethics: good is not moral unless it is done out of a sense of duty. Only the good postulated by law is absolute and without qualification, and armed with such ethical norms, Kant argues, even the commonest of persons will find it easy to tell the evil from the good and make a sound, moral judgment.

This is of course an oversimplified summary of Kant's arguments but it demonstrates the creation of a link between the notion of good and duty, which I would like to unpick with reference to Bakhtin's work (1990, 1993). Bakhtin was deeply troubled by the reasoning behind the transformation of a norm into "duty." For him the argument that a norm is moral because it is determined through *theoretical rational reasoning* and is binding exactly because of its rationality (Bakhtin, 1993, pp. 25, 29)[2] closes on itself in a loop of internal reference: my acts should be motivated by a system of norms that functions according to its own internal logic and has a binding force precisely because of its abstract and technical nature (Gardiner, 1996). For someone to be moral, then, the question to ask is not how should I act in a given situation but rather, how do I act to fulfill my duty as commanded by a (moral) law?

Perhaps not surprisingly the application of deontological ethics leads to a number of paradoxes as to what it means to be moral. First, it determines the content of a moral norm by separating abstract reasoning from situational knowledge or circumstantial response to a problem. Yet, it claims to guide humans through the complex and far from being clear-cut moral choices of everyday life. Few would deny the fact that our actions take place in an infinitely unpredictable variety of circumstances and are deeply interwoven with actions of others around us. Implicated in this "social fabric" we draw on reason as well as intuition, common sense, and emotions to decide, together with others, the meaning of good and evil. These decisions often have to be made under the pressure of irresistible forces and unavoidable demands that are part and parcel of our everyday experience. Deontology, however, in its abstraction of life events to categories implies that that knowledge comes ahead of the fact (Munro, 1998), that moral choices can be decided in advance and stop being choices as such. In fact, personal choice becomes undesirable as it invalidates the primacy of the rule.

Second, by shifting responsibility from concrete moral actors to supraindividual agencies, deontology corroborates the logic of control by hierarchy and obedience to authorities that have become a pervasive feature of modernity (Bauman, 1995). Yet, when rules fail, it is personal misjudgment that is at fault. This is the quandary in which American soldiers in Iraq found themselves when they were accused of torturing prisoners with the silent agreement of their superiors. The supremacy of the rule meant that individuals could shrug off responsibility by pointing up the hierarchy, and at the same time they could be made sacrificial lambs when the authority of rules came under threat.

Third, in formal ethics moral behavior becomes simply a matter of compliance with the rules, a technical process with individuals acting as ethically neutral, "moral castrati," as it were (Bremer, Logan, & Wokutch, 1987), who should not be concerned with consequences of their actions. As Kant states,

> Finally, there is an imperative which commands a certain conduct immediately. . . . It concerns not the matter of the action, or its intended result, but its form and the principle of which it is itself a result; and what is essentially good in it consists in the mental disposition, let the consequence be what it may. This imperative may be called that of morality. (1785, emphasis added)

Pushing this reasoning further, one might argue, and Morson and Emerson indeed do, that a technically impeccable performance of an action makes it ethical, in which case "a computer could be the most ethical agent. No one would have to think, care, or be responsible from one moment to the next" (Morson & Emerson, 1989, p. 14). Thus, moral behavior can be reduced to a dextrous application of rules unaffected by actual circumstances of moral choice or concerns about its results. Deontology, as Legge (1998) points out, leads to the "alienation problem" by legitimating the distance between motivations and consequences of one's actions.

So when such "objective" moral norms come to regulate the deeply pragmatic and political terrain of business, their collision or collusion seem inevitable. As Jackall (1988) argues in his powerfully exposed ethnography of corporate managers' morality, societal moral norms do not stand the competition with the expediency-ruled, short-term orientation of modern private institutions. Personal values and virtues must be left aside if one wants to survive in the corporate word. As one of the managers in his study explains, "What is right in the corporation is not what is right in a man's home or in his church. *What is right in the corporation is what the guy above you wants from you*" (Jackall, 1988, p. 109). One might suspect that this is a piece of tacit knowledge that cannot be openly declared as the official understanding of what "right" means. Yet, we would not need to look hard to find evidence of the opposite. "The Code of Business Conduct & Ethics" of a large American multinational, a major supplier in the automotive industry, provides a good example.[3] The first entry of its Code, entitled "Conflicts of Interests," states: "Each employee of [X] Corporation is expected to avoid engaging in activities that conflict with, or have the appearance of conflicting with, the best interests of the Company and its stockholders." A few lines down the page we read the entry on "Corporate Opportunities": "Employees owe a duty to [X] to advance the Company's legitimate interests when the opportunity to do so arises."

An immediate question springs to mind: What is the meaning of "duty" and "ethical" in this context? Is it ethics at all? To disobey an instruction can be a costly mistake, as Fox News reporters Jane Akre and Steve Wilson found out when they were fired by their employer, Fox News, for refusing to water down their investigative report on the use of antibiotics in cow's milk production, which harm humans.[4] The report was to inform the public about questionable practices of major milk producers but it failed the test of "rightness" by Fox News, which went to court to defend it. The paradox here is in how easily "ethical" can be conflated with "private interest," and how close formal ethics can come to border enlightened egoism.

Ironically, most of the people most of the time hardly make any use of an ethics document. It might deserve a curious glance from new recruits when browsing through their induction packs; or warrant a more scrutinizing reading in times of enquiry in order to prove that a proper policy is or is not in place, and once the trouble is over, be put back on the shelf, or at best, be given a face-lift to prevent bad press in the future.

The paradoxical ways in which modernity made use of the logic of formal ethics has been argued with much greater insight and sophistication elsewhere (e.g., Bauman, 1995). My point, however, is to just highlight the problematic logic behind normative ethics, which paradoxically binds everyone and no one and to suggest the need for a different approach to moral issues, one where taking responsibility is not induced by an external compulsion, a preexisting "ethical grammar" (Nealon, 2003), but arises from my present relationships with those concrete others whom my decisions and moral choices affect. In Gardiner's words, we need a "feasible ethics," which provides "a close connection to an integral, viable life-world—ethics must emerge organically "from below," rather than be arbitrarily imposed "from above" (1996, p. 122). This, I suggest, is the direction in which Bakhtin's philosophy of the act might take us.

## RESPONSIBILITY AS A "NON-ALIBI IN BEING"

The question that preoccupied Bakhtin throughout his life and that formal ethics failed to address was precisely the connection between morality and a person's life-world, choices that we make and what makes them compelling for each of us. His inquiry was driven by questioning the value of ethics created outside any person, act, or circumstance and by asking, What makes me and my acts morally motivated?

The answer, Bakhtin suggests, lies in recognizing that our moral choices take place in the *concrete world of action and values.* One does not live or act in a theoretical world; in it an individual and her choices do not exist in principle—the very fact of theorizing is owed to thinking "as if I were not there" (Bender, 1998, p. 189). At any particular moment, Bakhtin says:

...he [an individual human being] sees clearly these individual, unique persons whom he loves, this sky and this earth and these trees ... and the time; and what is also given to him simultaneously is the value, the actually and concretely affirmed value of these persons and these objects ... and he understands the ought of his performed act, that is, not the abstract law of his act, but the actual, concrete ought conditioned by his unique place in the given context of the ongoing event. (1993, pp. 33–34, original emphasis)

Our acts, he suggests, take place as unique events of being: at any time we find ourselves in unrepeatable once-occurrent moments of place and time, with a unique perspective on the world from that position. This perspective is characterized by an *emotional-volitional tone* that conveys affective, volitional, and valuative stands that become actualized in the performance of an act. As Bakhtin explicates:

It [the emotional-volitional tone] expresses the entire fullness of a state of being qua event at the given moment, and expresses it as that which is given as well as yet-to-be-determined from within me as an obligatory participant in it. (1993, pp. 38)

So my act only becomes meaningful, nonaccidental, motivated when I acknowledge my ownership of it through its unique "intonation." What I have done could not have been done by anyone else. Bakhtin describes this owning of an act as *personally signing* it, putting *a signature-recognition* under it. And here comes the crucial point: answerability *is always already* in the act, which is the embodiment, the actualization of my "attitude that is morally valid and answerably active" (Bakhtin, 1993, pp. 38). Answerability cannot be "assigned" to my act externally or "contained" only to its content; it arises from the *unity of my act* as an unrepeatable unique taking of position.

This unescapable, *always-already-there* answerability means that my moral position is unique and only I can be answerable for it. It means, in Bakhtin's words, that there is no *"no alibi in Being"* (1993, p. 44), that what I have done could not be replaced with anyone else's moral imperative nor justified by codified abstractions. The "non-alibi in Being" transforms an empty possibility, "an unsigned document which does not obligate anyone to do anything" (Bakhtin, 1993, p. 44) into the actual answerable act. The *personal signature* that one is prepared to leave points to the concrete, not abstract, responsibility that transforms the general into the compelling.

Critics might be quick to argue that if moral value is determined by an individual from her particular perspective, such value is indefensible because it is relative, subjective, even irrational. This is indeed so if we see act as being separable into its objective content and its subjective happening. Yet, Bakhtin argues, this would be an artificial separation. In its performance, act represents *a unity of event*. Not a unity that finalizes, completes, or closes off meaning, but a unity that brings together the emotional-volitional tone, semantic content and my irreducibly unique place in the world, and produces an actively experienced and answerable for whole. In its unity, an act is more than subjective or even rational: it is *answerable for* (Bakhtin, 1993, pp. 32–33). It performs a decision that brings together the hypothetical and the actual, the general and the individual, a decision that transforms possibility into a unique singularity.

## ARCHITECTONICS OF THE ACT

So for Bakhtin a person's act and its spontaneous unity of emotional, cognitive, and moral dimensions becomes a central point of inquiry, which he sets out to analyze, perhaps contrary to one's expectations, in structural terms. His ambition here is to suggest an alternative to the notion of "system" with its formalizing, categorizing, and technical characteristics. For this he borrows the term architectonics from Kantian vocabulary where it means "the art of the system" but brings a new twist to it. While for Kant architectonics implies constructing a system of scientific knowledge where "art" stands for perfection, Bakhtin takes "art" to mean dynamism, transformation, and uniqueness. For him, architectonics embodies an ensemble of cognitive-ethical values that motivate an act rather than a sum of its compositional parts and content. Unlike "system" and its fixed, stable frame, architectonics is an activity rather than a state because "the relations it orders are always . . . in a dynamic tension" (Holquist, 1990, p. xxiii) and because it is rooted in the morally and emotionally active position of a human being. For Bakhtin it then brings together generalized aspects of irreducibly concrete acts and yet makes them concretized and meaningful through their relationship with each other (1993, p. 65).

The notion of *architectonics* is central to Bakhtin's moral philosophy. It implies that our actions are anchored within unique evaluative and affective relationships (affect meaning here any emotion, not just compassion or sympathy) and are only meaningful if not divorced from their author and context of their happening. By describing Bakhtin's ethics as "architectonics of responsibility," Holquist refers precisely to this unity of responsible and responsive human existence in which all values and acts (personal, scientific, political, religious) make sense only in their relationships and as concretely experienced rather than theorized.

## CO-EXPERIENCE AS AN ETHICAL RELATION

To live from one's value-center and to act in accordance with it does not mean, however, to act in one's own interests only. Since actions actualize relationships, they imply answer not only to and for myself but also to and for the other. Indeed, Bakhtin articulates the self–other relationship in dialogical terms in that every emotion, desire, or thought of mine arises as a response and address to the concrete other.

He starts from what might seem an obvious point: as I and others occupy our unique once-occurrent positions, we will necessarily have different horizons and vision: "As we gaze at each other, two different worlds are reflected in the pupils of our eyes."[5] I always see and know what the other person is unable to perceive: the world behind her back, the emotions on her face, the whole range of things and relationships inaccessible from her horizon. So I-for-myself always need the other-for-me and vice versa to make sense of us and the world. The important implication of this argument is that our being is by nature unfinalized and incomplete and without this *surplus* or *excess of vision* we would remain hopelessly solipsist in the perception of ourselves, others, and the world.

*Outsideness* then is what motivates our relations with others. It invites us to engage in the risky, humbling, but mutually enriching practice of *participative thinking* or *co-experience* in which we actively *enter in* or *live into* the other's position. *Co-experience* here does not mean "coinciding" with the other. Trying to live the other person's experience in exactly the same way as she does and being able to fully understand her position is empathy that, as Bakhtin suggests, impoverishes both persons by reducing their differences to sameness. *Co-experience*, by contrast, implies a creative productive process of actively entering the other's consciousness without completely losing the value-producing "surplus" yielded by an external perspective: I do not live the other's experiences as mine but as hers, my reaction to her suffering is not a feeling of pain but a word of consolation. *Co-experience* in the Bakhtinian sense prevents complete absorption of self by the other or drowning of the other in me. Instead, it demands openness in which each party remains a speaking, feeling, and actively answerable subject without compromising its alterity and identity.

Thus, the self–other relation becomes a balancing act between participation and distance, an intense, even conflictual negotiation of the boundary between them. Ethically, Ponzio (1987) suggests, it translates into an internal anxiety, my obsession with the other, my *answerability* to her. I answer, but only "across" a boundary that makes the distance between us tangible yet insuperable. This, Morson and Emerson (1989, p. 11) conclude, is the essential difference between formal ethics, empathy, and *co-experience*: while formal ethics respects no persons, empathy respects one, and only *co-experience* recognises both. As a co-experiencing being, my question then is not: what should I do? but: how should I act towards the other (Nielsen, 1998)? So answerability becomes "born and maintained through the necessity of *response* to the other person, and such a responsiveness . . . comes necessary *before* the solidification of any theoretical rules or political norms of ethical conduct" (Nealon, 2003).

Thus, by bringing the event of act back from the heights of abstraction to its flesh-and-blood sources, to the here-and-now of its happening we do not return to the all-powerful and knowing subject but to the incomplete self who admits a much more imminent obligation, this time coming not from norms that demand compliance but from the other who demands our response.

## ETHICS OF EVERYDAY LIFE?

There are a number of themes emerging from the above discussion that contribute to current debates about the meaning of ethics in general, and business ethics in particular. Broadly, Bakhtin's reader is encouraged to go beyond a narrow-minded view of morality being "contained" inside universally valid judgments (the metaphor of container being symptomatic of modernist thinking) to be extracted only when an action has to be defined as right or wrong. What philosophy of the act forcefully underlines is the responsibility of "authorship and actorship" (Bauman, 1995), which is at the root of a genuinely moral act. Life as a whole becomes a taking up of responsibility, "a single complex act that I perform" (Bakhtin, 1993), in which life choices become moral choices. Bakhtin's insistence on "non-alibi in Being" questions complacency in every sphere of life, working, private, or cultural. It is all too easy, he says, to shrug off moral qualms when an alibi is at hand: in the modern structuring of work and its principle of replaceability (if not me, someone else will do it), in the institutionalized compliance with authority (I only do as I am told), in the accepted separation between different realms of life (the business game has its own rules), etc. A victim of the Stalinist regime himself, he knew only too well how efficient officialdom is in stripping individuals of their unique value systems and how easily it turns them into "pretenders" who speak with alibis rather than from their own responsible positions (Bender, 1998).

The notion of answerability as *always-already-there* gives a cogent answer not only to deontology but also to other forms of normative ethics such as utilitarianism. According to the latter, acts that result in achieving common good or happiness for the greatest number of people are moral. However, to follow Bakhtin's line of thinking, acting by proxy, as a delegate or representative of others is just another alibi for not taking personal responsibility. Representation, he argues, does not abolish answerability; it merely specializes it. In representing others, one is so *personally* and still acts from a unique, only their point in being (Bakhtin, 1993, pp. 50–51). Seeking a safe refuge in the anonymity of others coupled with usurping the power to define what common good is makes utilitarian moral claims untenable. As Bauman (1995) convincingly argued, the most atrocious acts can be committed in the name of order and common good, with perpetrators seeing themselves and others as collectivities from which all trace of personal has been purged, fellow feelings suspended, temporarily pushed out of heart. Less dramatically, but not less productively, seeing other ethical distance from others is an accepted *raison de faire* in today's businesses. As one of the managers from Jackall's study (1988, p. 127) says: "As long as those people [who drink dangerously contaminated water] can't be identified, as long as they are not specific people, it's OK [for the factory to pollute the water]. Isn't that strange?"

By situating the ethical moment within prosaic acts, by positing it as ongoing rather than static, as achieved rather than given, Bakhtin's philosophy urges us to think of everyday actions as moral choices. In this sense, as Bender (1998) suggests, Bakhtin develops an intersubjective, microsociological ethics that can be described as an *ethics of everyday life*. The task of this ethics is to explore architectonics of people's acts, their "morality-in-use" (Durepos & Mills, this volume), which demands descriptive and anthropological research rather than the purely theoretical one. Examples in point could be the already mentioned Jackall's ethnography of American corporate managers, as well as Watson's (1998) study of British managers' moral practices. While reaching quite different conclusions, both authors are interested in managers' thoughts about what morality means to them and whether it is possible to manage morally. The value of such studies is exactly in their specificity since they "can show us different ways in which human beings, in different social settings, both talk about and tackle issues and it can give us some idea of the outcomes and implications of people acting in various ways" (Watson, 1998, p. 254). Such studies makes a significant contribution to critical ethics by showing that organizational life is shot through with moral decision making, that the nature management practice is inherently moral, and that by studying the variety of settings in which moral dilemmas have to be solved we can better understand what we mean by these terms (Morgan, 1998).

## OTHERNESS AND RESPONSIBILITY IN CRITICAL ETHICS

As has been insistently argued by postmodern theorists, the point of ethics is above all to respond, to treat the other as worthy of genuine attention and action. To quote Bauman again, "A postmodern ethics would be one that readmits the Other as a neighbour, . . . An ethics that recasts the Other as the crucial character in the process through which the moral self comes into its own" (cited in Nealon, 2003, p. 138).

This is the invitation that Bakhtin extends in his texts: to acknowledge and engage with others as unique, answerable to subjects. It can be argued that the very concept of personal signature embodies a double bind of commitment. On the one hand, it acknowledges ownership of the act for oneself—it is mine and no one else's, while on the other it acknowledges ownership *for* the other, signing being always directed *toward* someone, having an addressee, calling to be recognized back. The need for the other in order to be oneself is a crucial turn from formal ethics whose only concern was with the individual and her commitment to the rule. In formal ethics, others exist in the form of generalized entities, such as society, community, or public sphere (Gardiner, 1996, p. 122) and are assumed to share and agree to the rules of their being and are interchangeable and predictable in their actions. For Bakhtin, however, abstract otherhood does not respond to and indeed contradicts the realities of being. We engage first and foremost with social others by sharing the lived experience of time, place, and affective and meaningful relations with them: "Man-in-general does not exist; I exist and a particular *other* exists—my intimate, my contemporary (social mankind), the past and future of actual human beings (of actual historical mankind)" (Bakhtin, 1993, p. 47, original emphasis).

So too is the ethical relation. Occurring on the boundary between self and other, it arises from the "real," concrete, and personal self–other engagement, whose richness is conveyed in Bakhtin's seemingly interchangeable but subtly different notions of *participative thinking, living into, feeling into, empathizing*. These, each in their way, reduce the ethical distance, prevent from treating the other as "a case of a general rule" (Bauman, 1995), a thing-like object to be acted upon. It is in the unique, unrepeatable, uncategorizable event of self–other engagement that my moral obligation is born. And with no alibis at hand, it is my call to deal with its ambivalence: where to draw the line, put a limit, intervene, or step aside. Bauman's thinking seems to follow the same line as Bakhtin's when he says that "facing the ambivalence of good and evil (and thus, so to speak, "taking responsibility for one's own responsibility") is the *meaning* (the sole meaning) of being moral" (1995, p. 2, original emphasis).

## CONCLUSION

It has been the argument of this chapter that Bakhtin's philosophy of the act poses a serous challenge to currently prevailing ethical theories. As Gardiner points out, it

> implies an ethics that escapes the inherent limitations of both utilitarianism
> and Kantian-based ethics, the former promised on egoistic self-interest and

essentially an apologia for the unfettered market, and the latter based on a self-validating, absolutist moral code, which is necessarily external to and repressive of everyday social relations. (Gardiner, 1996, p. 123)

But my point is that it does not just stop there. I suggest that it encourages us to look beyond the *content* or *product* of our acts as sole repositories of ethical meaning, to question the comfortable habit of consuming life, including its moral choices. Instead, in our search for post-metaphysical ethics we are invited to look back at ourselves as the only bearers of responsibility. With no alibis available in rules or roles, it is back to ourselves as "social, political and moral human beings working in organizations, rather than as managers or organizational "experts" (Watson, 1998, p. 267) to put a signature under our acts. This is an invitation for answerability for one's life in its entirety, which can become fully meaningful only through the unity of answerability.

So against the ethics of living by a transcendent norm Bakhtin proposes the ethics of being true to oneself. Is it feasible in the business world? Some, as Jackall (1988) would suggest, it is not: the logic of bureaucracy always takes upper hand by turning questions of morality into questions of administration. Others, like Watson (1998), might take a more hopeful view that managers can initiate critical reflection on the moral value of their practices. While being invariably bound with pragmatic concerns, these reflections, he suggests, manifest the potential for taking moral positions thoughtfully and personally. So as well as possibly being a utopian project in which the aims of ethics and the logic of production cancel each other, in our age of "no viable alternatives," Bakhtin's philosophy of the act can encourage us to think what these could be.

## NOTES

1. Shell's Business Principlies, available at http://www.shell.com/home/Framework?siteId=envandsoc-en&FC2=&FC3=/envandsoc-en/html/iwgen/making_it_happen/commitments_standards/business_principles/our_business_principles_30032006.html, accessed on August 28, 2006.
2. Bakhtin's work has presented several problems of translation due to original terminology, which no doubt contributed to the ongoing debate regarding the interpretation of his thought. This double referencing (with first number indicating pages in the English translation of *Philosophy of the Act* and the second pages in the Russian text) enables the reader to follow both texts if needed.
3. The name of the corporation has been omitted as this Code is not a publicly available document.
4. http://www.fair.org/index.php?page=1426, Fairness and Accuracy in Reporting website. Accessed August 17, 2006. See also the movie "The Corporation."

5. The second set of pages refers to the Russian text *Raboty 20-kh godov* where the essay "Author and Hero in Aesthetic Activity" is published.

## REFERENCES

Bakhtin, M. (1986). *Speech genres and other late essays* (V. W. McGee, Trans.). Austin: University of Texas Press.

Bakhtin, M. (1993). *Toward a philosophy of the act* (V. Liapunov, Trans.). Austin: Texas University Press.

Bakhtin, M. M. (1984). *Problems of Dostoevsky's Poetics* (C. Emerson, Trans.). Minneapolis: University of Minnesota Press.

Bakhtin, M. M. (1990). Author and hero in aesthetic activity (V. V. Liapunov, Trans.). In *Art and answerability: Early philosophical essays* (pp. 4–257). Austin: University of Texas Press.

Bauman, Z. (1995). *Life in fragments: Essays in postmodern morality.* Oxford, UK: Blackwell.

Bender, C. (1998). Bakhtinian perspectives in "everyday life" sociology. In M. M. Bell & M. Gardiner (Eds.), *Bakhtin and the human sciences* (pp. 181–195). London: Sage.

Blanchot, M. (1969/1993). *The infinite conversation* (S. Hanson, Trans.). Minneapolis: University of Minnesota Press.

Bremer, O. A., Logan, J. E., & Wokutch, R. E. (1987). Ethics and values in management thought. In K. Paul (Ed.), *Business environment and business ethics: The social, moral, and political dimensions of management* (pp. 61–86). Ballinger.

Buchholz, R. A. (1987). The business/government/society relationship in management thought. In K. Paul (Ed.), *Business environment and business ethics: The social, moral, and political dimensions of management* (pp. 19–37). Ballinger.

de Man, P. (1989). Dialogue and dialogism. In G. S. Morson & C. Emerson (Eds.), *Rethinking Bakhtin: Extensions and challenges* (pp. 105–114). Evanston, IL: Northwestern University Press.

DesJardins, J. R., & McCall, J. J. (2000). *Contemporary issues in business ethics.* Belmont, CA: Wadsworth/Thompson Learning.

Emerson, C. (2003). Bakhtin at 100: Art, ethics, architectonic self. In M. Gardiner (Ed.), *Mikhail Bakhtin* (Vol. 2, pp. 296–314). Thousand Oaks: Sage.

Ferrell, O. C., Fraedrich, J., & Ferrell, L. (2002). *Business ethics: Ethical decision making and cases* (5th ed.). Boston: Houghton Mifflin.

Gardiner, M. (1996). Alterity and ethics: a dialogical perspective. *Theory, Culture and Society, 13*(2), 121–143.

Gardiner, M. (2003). Foucault, ethics and dialogue. In M. Gardiner (Ed.), *Mikhail Bakhtin* (Vol. 4, pp. 61–80). Thousand Oaks, CA: Sage.

Holquist, M. (1990). Introduction: the architectonics of answerability (V. V. Liapunov, Trans.). In *Art and answerability: Early philosophical essay by M.M. Bakhtin* (pp. ix–xlix). London: Routledge.

Jackall, R. (1988). *Moral mazes: The world of corporate managers.* New York: Oxford University Press.

Kant, I. (1785). *Fundamental principles of the metaphysic of morals.* Retrieved August 18, 2006, from http://etext.library.adelaide.edu.au/k/kant/immanuel/k16prm/index.html

Legge, K. (1998). Is HRM ethical? Can HRM be ethical? In M. Parker (Ed.), *Ethics and organizations* (pp. 150–172). London: Sage.

Morgan, G. (1998). Governance and regulation: An institutionalist approach to ethics and organizations. In M. Parker (Ed.), *Ethics and organizations* (pp. 221–237). London: Sage.

Morson, G. S., & Emerson, C. (1989). Introduction: rethinking Bakhtin. In G. S. Morson & C. Emerson (Eds.), *Rethinking Bakhtin: Extensions and challenges* (pp. 1–60). Evanston, IL: Northwestern University Press.

Nealon, J. T. (2003). The ethics of dialogue: Bakhtin and Levinas. In M. Gardiner (Ed.), *Mikhail Bakhtin* (Vol. 4, pp. 136–155). Thousand Oaks, CA: Sage.

Nielsen, G. (1998). The norms of answerability: Bakhtin and the fourth postulate. In M. M. Bell & M. Gardiner (Eds.), *Bakhtin and the human sciences* (pp. 214–230). London: Sage.

Parker, M. (2002). *Against management: Organization in the age of managerialism.* Cambridge, UK: Polity Press.

Parker, M. (Ed.). (1998). *Ethics and organizations.* London: Sage.

Paul, K. (1987). Business environment and business ethics in management thought. In K. Paul (Ed.), *Business environment and business ethics: The social, moral, and political dimensions of management* (pp. 1–17). Ballinger.

Ponzio, A. (1987). The relation of otherness in Bakhtin, Blanchot, Levinas. *Semiotic Inquiry, 7*(1), 1–18.

Rhodes, C. (2000). Reading and writing organisational lives. *Organization, 7*(1).

Roberts, J. (1996). The moral character of management practice. *Journal of Management Studies, 21*(3), 287–302.

ten Bos, R. (1997). Business ethics and Bauman ethics. *Organization Studies, 18*(6), 997–1014.

Watson, T. (1998). Ethical codes and moral communities: the Gunlaw temptation, the Simon solution and the David dilemma. In M. Parker (Ed.), *Ethics and organizations* (pp. 253–268). London: Sage.

Wray-Bliss, E. (2003). Research subjects/research subjections: exploring the ethics and politics of critical research. *Organization, 10*(2), 307–325.

CHAPTER 7

# THE CRITICAL ISSUE OF ACCOUNTABILITY

## Harro M. Höpfl

In recent years corporate, professional, and governmental accountability has elicited a substantial academic literature, as well as a great deal of practical reform and experimentation. Until well into the 1960s "accountability" was an occasionally used variant for "responsibility"; it has since become a favorite term in political and corporate rhetoric. I propose here to locate accountability as a topic for critical social science, to examine the concept itself, and then to consider what difference a critical approach to accountability makes. It emerges that just as critical theory poses fundamental questions about accountability, so accountability in turn raises questions for critical theory. These questions cannot all be addressed here, but they may at least be signaled.

## CRITICAL KNOWLEDGE

The defining concepts of critical theory I take to be emancipation and democratization (Alvesson & Deetz, 2000). These twin premises cannot be explored philosophically here (but see Geuss, 1981). But they are only con-

*Critical Theory Ethics for Business and Public Administration*, pages 135–155
Copyright © 2008 by Information Age Publishing
All rights of reproduction in any form reserved.

tingently connected with each other. Democracy might not be emancipatory, and an emancipatory understanding need not be democratizing: it might be accessible only to a knowledgeable vanguard, and emancipation might be something imposed from above. So unless democratization is to be an elite or gnostic project, social scientific truth must be not only accessible in principle to some relevant *demos*, but must in fact be embraced by it. Actual *demoi* have notoriously "failed" repeatedly in this respect. A critical social science does not, however, become theoretically solvent simply because some populace accepts its findings, or insolvent if it does not (Fay, 1975). Nevertheless, emancipation (originally, freeing slaves) as an objective of science demands the elimination of mystification, ideology, or false consciousness, and its replacement by truth and transparency. A "critical" understanding is not one that replaces one mythology or ideology by another. An emancipatory social science must therefore be able to make sustainable truth-claims about social things, and it cannot simply choose an epistemology because it sustains the kind of claims about the world that it wants to make. Nor can it settle for the "indolent inductivism" (Greenleaf, 1964) customary in indictments of globalization, capitalism, and "Enron, Worldcom, etc." Since at least some postmodernisms write of knowledge in implicit inverted commas, their serviceability for any critical enterprise is therefore questionable; hence the objections of—for example—critical realists (e.g., Benton & Craib, 2001), or critics of postmodernist philosophies of "lack" (Tonder & Thomassen, 2005). This is to say nothing of the challenging task of making postmodernism accessible to ordinary people.

## CRITICAL MORALITY

For critical social science, moreover, emancipation and democracy are moral imperatives: they indeed define the moral high ground. Given its Marxist inheritance, any critical position on morality is, however, bound to be ambivalent. The penchant for Nietzsche and the taken-for-granted truth of moral relativism (*en gros* if not *en detail*) do nothing to reduce the ambiguity (e.g., Jones, Parker, & ten Bos, 2005). Morality in any ordinary sense is also likely to be at odds with the radicalism of the critical approach, since morality arguably presupposes ongoing practice, custom, and tradition. Taking morality seriously may well be socially "conservative" (i.e., not revolutionary) in its practical implications. By contrast, so-called "revolutionary" or "provisional" moralities are radical enough, but they have necessarily been entirely consequentialist and historicist. The genre has proved eminently capable of justifying unspeakable outrages (cf. Camus, *L'homme revolté*, 1951; he of course wrote decades before the Cultural Revolution or the Khmer Rouge). Some critical writers are conspicuously hostile to consequentialist moral theory (e.g., Tinker & Gray, 2003), but they seem to see evil potential only in the supposed consequentialism of their "conventional" opponent. But Hayek (1962, 1976, 1988), for example, is less of a consequentialist than even Aristotle or Aquinas were (Kukathas, 1989). If a moral or ethical[1] position is to underwrite a critical understanding of accountability, then it cannot be a "revolutionary" or "provisional" morality. There are, however, other moralities that do not compromise critical radicalism. Some versions of human rights or social justice are radical enough. The problem here is that human rights are irreconcilable with moral relativism, and "social justice" is itself a human rights theory. An alternative is a moral philosophy that raises the bar of business ethics so high that businesses are bound to fall short: Levinasian ethics or some especially stringent version of Kantian ethics for instance. But such moralities are too exacting or too opaque even for academics to conform to in their professional conduct, so there seems little prospect of applying them to enterprises and activities in less sheltered worlds.

Another alternative is purely internal criticism, where business and the professions are judged by the standards they themselves proclaim. This demands no substantive ethical commitment on the part of the critic. It is, however, merely a polemical stratagem, dependent in part on the rhetorical naivety of business and the professions, and it would lose its force if they were better advised (by Henderson, 2001, for example). Those who have done the most to investigate the relation between corporate and professional self-presentation and conduct in this area (e.g., David Owen, Brendan O'Dwyer, Prem Sicca) certainly do have a substantive moral position.

But even given an appropriate critical morality, it remains the case that neither democracy nor emancipation can possibly count as unconditional moral goods. Suffice it to say for now that democracy is not like, say, health or virtue. The progression "democracy is good, more democracy is better, most democracy is best" cannot survive inspection, not least because of the threat of populism of which critical theorists are only too aware (Laclau, 2005; on the idea of "the people" generally, see Canovan, 2005). As for emancipation, it is another term for being set free, and at this time of day freedom can hardly be regarded as unproblematic as a concept, let alone as a good. We return to both these topics later.

## ACCOUNTABILITY AND CRITICAL THEORY

What then of a democratizing and emancipatory approach to accountability in the world of business, management, and the professions? Here critical theory confronts a topos that it did not itself generate, and that has been dealt with largely in terms of manners of thinking and acting that are uncongenial to it. Accountability has no necessary connection with emancipation or democratization. On the contrary, it takes as its basis the legitimacy of authority and therefore the "asymmetrical power relationships" that critical theory problematizes. Its conception of democracy is liberal/ pluralist and not emancipatory or radical. Nor are critical theorists on their home-ground in considering the pragmatic issues of institutional engineering that are requisite, as I shall argue, for any accountability. The old Marxist and positivist alternative to practical knowledge and prudence, namely the belief that science and historical inevitability can between them dictate policy and strategy (if not, perhaps, tactics), has been comprehensively abandoned as a theoretically defensible position. But nothing about critical social science can guarantee practical wisdom or judgment, the old moral virtue of prudence (Pieper, 1946; Polanyi, 1958; Oakeshott, 1962, 1975); there is not even an obvious door through which the critical tradition can admit it, given its intellectualism.

## THE NATURE OF ACCOUNTABILITY

Since the contours of the linguistic terrain of accountability are still unclear, some prior elucidation is necessary. Accountability and responsibility occupy the same linguistic space. Among European languages both ancient and modern, only English seems to distinguish the two by separate words, as Mulgan (2000) notes. But the distinction is important, because although accountability always implies responsibility, the converse is not the case. Languages that lack a separate word for accountability have to qualify *responsabilità, responsabilité, responsabilidad, Verantwortlichkeit, Verantwoordelijkheid*, etc., adjectivally to make the distinction. Conversely, however, English usage of the term "account" creates its own confusions, as will be seen shortly.

Any relationship of accountability demands that the following questions be answered: *who is accountable? to whom? for what? how, or by what procedure?* and *when?* This relationship postulates an *agent* (the answer to *who* is accountable?) that has been entrusted by some *principal* (i.e., a *superior* in respect of *this* relationship: accountable *to whom?*) with a task. It must, moreover, be a task that requires the exercise of discretion, skill, and judgment in the agent's use of the principal's resources or authority (accountable *for what?*). That is the *point* of employing an agent. "Micro-managed" employees are not agents who can be held to account: their acts are simply their master's. An agent must subsequently render an account to the principal, according to some arrangement previously specified, or presupposed as custom and practice. Accountability must, finally, include the possibility that the account will be rejected, and the agent visited with some sanction or penalty (answering the question accountable *when* and *how, in what way?*).

## ACCOUNTS AND ACCOUNTABILITY

The historically original concept of accountability, on which all others are parasitic, is that of stewardship, which unambiguously connotes a relationship of sub- and superordination.[2] That these are presupposed by accountability is, however, less obvious in English than it might be, because giving and receiving "accounts"—explanations, narratives, stories, justifications, elucidations—is intrinsic to personality, and is a feature of the everyday converse of civil and private association (see Munro & Maurittsen's admirable *Accountability*, 1996, and Judith Butler, 2005, Ch. 1; her foil Nietzsche was using *Verantwortlichkeit*, responsibility, in the context of promising, crime, and punishment). Such accounts commonly do not involve superiors and subordinates. But conflating this kind of accounting with the accounting of accountability is plausible only in English, where "account" (originally a reckoning-up of money or other resources received and expended) has been used metaphorically since at least the 17th century to refer to any kind of explanation, story, relation, report, narrative, or justification. Other European languages at most have occasional metaphors such as "settling accounts" (e.g., "abrechnen," "zur Rechenschaft ziehen," "régler les comptes," "alla fin dei conti"), which trade upon the finality of a financial reckoning and settlement. There is no reason to introduce the concept of accountability to explicate relationships in which "accounts" may indeed be demanded and owed, and may be rejected with unwelcome consequences to the "accountor" (as in a family or friendship, the quasi-contractual relations of tradesperson to client, or the informal relations of neighbors). For here the rejection of an account can in turn be rejected (precisely because there are no agents and principals), producing stalemate, which is what accountability is designed to avoid. Again, people are sometimes said to be "accountable only to themselves," and thus not liable to any sanction by definition. This, however, is plainly because any duty can be construed as answerability to the authority and sanctions of conscience or God, and thus to a higher "external" authority. The conflation of the accounting of accountability and of accounts as explanations thus conduces to misreading two postulates of the accountability relationship as merely contingent or optional features: the existence of an agent and a principal (i.e., a superior) and the liability of the agent to sanctions. Mulgan's (2000) analysis, with which I otherwise largely concur, is therefore right to include a sanction as a component in any accountability arrangement, but not for the reason he suggests.

The concept of accountability, then, is not an "elusive" or "chameleon"-like concept (*pace* Sinclair, 1995, p. 219; see Mulgan, 2000, p. 562), although fashions in usage have muddied the waters; Mulgan, Dubnick (2003), and others offer welcome clarification. In some circumstances individuals may of course be unclear about whom exactly they are supposed to answer to (Sinclair, 1995). But that is the way with fashionable words. What is unclear and contestable is not the *concept*, but rather which kind of theorization will best elucidate the nature of accountability in general and any specific accountability relationship in particular, and the considerations proper to it. This will now be explored.

## ACCOUNTABILITY (A) AS A LEGAL RELATIONSHIP

The most inescapable and least theoretically exigent interpretation relevant to all accountability relationships is a legal understanding. In cultures rooted in the European inheritance or drawing on it, law has here superseded religion and/or the family, which for much of the world and much of human history have been the dominant idioms for specifying all relationships with any degree of formality (such as accountability). Moreover, the concepts that define what is now called accountability have had a specifically legal referent in the West, at least since Roman times: agency, trust (*fides*, whence fidelity, confidence, good faith), account or reckoning (which in Latin was *ratio*, in Greek *logos*), responsibility (from *respondere*, to answer a charge, summons, or court), penalty, sanction, etc. "Accountability" is a late 18th century coinage, and "account" and its European variants *conto, cuenta, compte, Rechnung*, etc., are medieval, as is "responsibility." The most obvious legal concept that accountability can fit, apart from trust, is contract, which demands a court or tribunal as third-party adjudicator. Accountability need, however, not be to a court of law.

## ACCOUNTABILITY AS A MORAL RELATIONSHIP

But the fact that accountability can be construed in legal or quasi-legal terms in no way qualifies its moral character. How legality and morality are related is notably problematic (e.g., Kelsen, 1978; Hart, 1961; Finnis, 1980), but the borders between them are porous. Any legal trust or contract, for instance, also imposes a moral obligation, and accountability precisely involves trusting and being (en)trusted. Moreover, an agent liable to sanctions (i.e., punishments) must be a moral agent, and the only inherently inadequate "accounts" are those that convict him or her of moral derelictions: a culpably low level of competence or application, or failing to respect the terms of the trust; no punishment without guilt, as the familiar legal maxim says. Moral accountability is, moreover, never merely one way. Principals are just as subject to moral norms as agents. This is, however, obscured where accountability is to a "sovereign," including a "democratic" sovereign; the significance of sovereignty for critical democratization will become apparent.

## ACCOUNTABILITY AS A POLITICAL RELATIONSHIP

In addition, accountability is also always "political," in that every exercise or arrangement of accountability is in principle eligible to be modified or superseded by some agency of the state: by a legislature, court, regulator, commission, tribunal, official, even by "the people" or "society", provided they are "personated," in the expressive old word. All these in turn can be superseded by some higher "international" authority (actually inter-state or supra-state authority), such as the EU, NATO, the World Bank, the WTO, international courts, even the UN, were it not generally impotent. I shall argue below that the rhetorical "we," "society," "the community," "the international community," "the oppressed" are spurious actors, and that the various persons, organizations, movements, and concourses purporting to be their voice and agent can have no incontestable authorization, only greater or lesser moral authority.

## ACCOUNTABILITY AS A PRAGMATIC RELATIONSHIP

Last but by no means least, accountability is a matter for pragmatic deliberation. The arrangements it always demands may be evaluated for their efficacy, and changed accordingly. Much of legal and institutional reform of accountability in the last 20 years has been concerned with little else. Pragmatic deliberation is subject to moral considerations as well as to legal and political ones. Equally, moral deliberation cannot dispense with the practical skill, prudence, and judgment required in pragmata: least of all in respect of accountability, which is a relationship entirely dependent on arrangements, and about which nothing sensible can be said that does not issue in or elucidate deliberation about practice.

## CORPORATE AND PROFESSIONAL ACCOUNTABILITY

This discussion will concentrate on corporate social responsibility, or even more tendentiously "corporate citizenship," both of which include corpo-

**142** ◼ H. M. HÖPFL

rate accountability (Crane & Matten, 2004, Ch. 1). But the accountability of the professions must also be considered. The accountancy profession's accountability here occupies a special place, not only because of its historic link with accountability, but because accountancy provides one of the best tools for overviews of the complex relationships involved in the use of entrusted resources, the essence of accountability. Even non-financial and perhaps nonquantifiable overviews of this kind are described as "accounting" or "audit" in oblique tribute to its capacities (Power, 1999; see also Owen, Swift, Humphrey, & Bowerman, 2000).

## STAKEHOLDERS AND SHAREHOLDERS

Critical approaches to corporate social responsibility must address the stakeholder–shareholder controversy, unless they wish to confine themselves to unmasking accountability as a managerialist stratagem. It is preordained that they will in one way or another endorse the widest possible version of stakeholding. The shareholder alternative is in any event passé even in corporate self-presentation (Crane & Matten, 2004). From a critical point of view, moreover, shareholders are at best one of many stakeholder groups with claims on publicly quoted corporations; these in turn are merely one of the economic entities to which "democratic" accountability should apply. But merely taking the stakeholders' side is now widely understood to be not enough from a critical point of view, morally or pragmatically. Stakeholding is plainly predicated on some social democratic doctrine, which is why the further left and right reprobate it equally (as Friedman & Miles, 2006, p. 139, and Stoney & Winstanley, 2001, point out). "Corporate governance" approaches (for the best analysis, see Keasey, Thompson, & Wright, 2005), that is to say devising an institutional architecture (or, to change the metaphor, engaging in institutional engineering) is prima facie even less attractive, except to the very small number of academics of a critical persuasion who take the matter seriously, notably David Owen. It is of little consequence whether corporate governance is in its British form of codes, principles, "voluntarism" and intermittently government regulators, or American traditions of rules, and punitive legal and bureaucratic regulation, most recently illustrated in the Sarbanes–Oxley Act. From a critical perspective neither stakeholding nor corporate governance can get to the root of the matter, namely the ideal of a democratized and emancipated economy, perhaps world.

## STAKEHOLDING

The incoherences inherent in the ideal of stakeholding have been sufficiently articulated, classically by Friedman (1970), but more recently by Sternberg, Henderson, Jensen, and others, and need only a summary here. Proliferating the number of stakeholders to which corporations (i.e., in effect, managements) are accountable makes corporate managements less, not more accountable. It allows and even requires them to arbitrate between these various claimants, as is explicitly acknowledged by proponents of stakeholding (Friedman & Miles, 2006, pp. 4–8). Since the interests and demands of various stakeholder groups are normally inconsistent or mutually contradictory, management can then pursue its own interests, which are bound to coincide with the perceived interests of some stakeholder group or other. Thus, to be accountable to everybody is in effect to be accountable to no one. Furthermore, management under these circumstances is deprived of any operational criterion, any "corporate objective function" for judging success or failure, worthwhile or not worthwhile projects (Jensen, 2000). Again, the category of stakeholder can include anyone you please, including those hostile to the very existence of some or all corporations; it has even been extended to embrace the cosmos, the environment, and the birds and the bees. The road to this conceptual absurdity has been inadvertently paved by the vagueness of the criteria for inclusion offered by stakeholder theorists: "being affected by" or "affecting" the activities of a corporation; or those upon whom the well-being of the corporation depends (Friedman & Miles, 2006, pp. 4–8). Finally, CSR demands that corporations be regarded as agencies of the welfare state, rather than as economic enterprises whose purpose is to survive and prosper by offering goods and services in the marketplace, and whose justification is in terms of either or both of (a) the experience and theories of the functioning of markets and the nonfunctioning of their alternatives; (b) firms being the consequences of the legitimate exercise of rights of association and property, and freedom of action under the rule of law, according to which anything that is not illegal is legal. "Shareholder-only" doctrines of accountability contend that CSR is intentionally or in effect a Trojan horse for collectivist and anti-capitalist projects (see especially Henderson, 2001), which in the hands of some critical theorists it certainly is. The edge can be taken off these criticisms (see the robust if occasionally knockabout piece by Phillips, Freeman, & Wicks, 2003), but they have hardly been entirely neutered.

## THE CRITICAL APPROACH TO STAKEHOLDING

Critical understandings of accountability under the aegis of democratization and emancipation answer the questions "who is accountable, or responsible, to whom, for what, when, and how?" in terms of the accountability of managers, executives, directors, owners, and professionals to some demos (democracy from *demos*, the citizen body—the *populus* in the Roman republic, whence "people"—and *kratein*, to rule), and the demands of emancipation. At this point, however, the concepts of democracy and freedom invoked here call for some examination.

Taking emancipation (or freeing) first: opponents of stakeholding themselves emphatically affirm that the ends and activities of corporations must respect *liberal* freedoms (Friedman, 1970; Hayek, 1988). Corporations themselves also readily acknowledge their subjection to "human rights," even though the concept itself *is* contestable (e.g., MacIntyre, 1985). The subjection of the professions to "natural justice," an altogether different concept, is not questioned by anyone either. But these are negative, framework criteria, side constraints within which corporations and professions must operate. They in no way define their *purposes*, and say nothing whatever about who has a right to determine and implement these purposes authoritatively. They do not define the *identity* of the corporation, nor do they specify its accountability (except to shareholders), or the arrangements to secure that accountability, or the criteria that agents of corporations are to use when there are conflicts between the *moral* duties they owe to different parties: to directors, shareholders, employees, suppliers, customers, local or central government, or "society." The only *demos* acknowledged as authoritative over the corporation on such a construction of their identity and duties is the *demos* personified by agencies of the state, or by supra-state organizations. More precisely, since like "capitalism" itself corporations are predicated on the rule of law, the only state or supra-state organizations that are intrinsically entitled to call them to account are courts, or regulators constituted by law. This is at once their strength and their weakness, and not only from a critical point of view (see J.S.Mill, 1871, Bk V, Chs. 8, 10, 11; Kukathas, 1989; Gray, 1998), but especially from the environmentalist, "market failure" and "mere compliance" perspectives which critical theory has made its own. Evidently much is or may be entirely legal that is also deplorable.

## DEMOCRATIZATION

The force of introducing "democratization" here is evident. According to Thomas Hobbes's classic exposition of the logic of sovereignty (1651), accountability—not of course his term—has to stop somewhere, and it stops with the sovereign. A democratic sovereign, like any other, is therefore able to call everyone else to account, for anything, on any occasion, is not limited by laws or forms, and can regulate, direct, and control everything at its discretion. By parity of reasoning, the sovereign is itself accountable to no one. The implications of this will occupy us in a moment.

Both the strengths and the weaknesses of democracy taken generically are familiar enough. Even those unsympathetic to political democracy have always recognized it as linked to liberty (e.g., Aristotle, *Politics*, Bk. VI, Ch. II). Its rationale has always been some belief that to be subject to an authority without having a right to designate and remove those that exercise it is a violation of self-government, moral autonomy, equality, liberty in the quite unpretentious sense of not being slaves. The objections are equally familiar (see now Graham, 2002). Subjection to political authority is not *per se* a violation of any moral autonomy that can be intelligibly claimed; the only freedom and equality it "violates" is that of the war of all against all, or freedom to do as one pleases. Democracy for its part may mean majority or class tyranny (*Federalist Papers* No. 10, followed by Tocqueville and J. S. Mill), not self-government but the government of each by all the rest (J. S. Mill, *Representative Government*, 1861, Ch. 1); in itself it does little or nothing to protect individuals or minorities, which depend not on democracy, but on constitutionality and the rule of law (Dahl, 1970). It is moreover doubtful that democracy can deliver the "rule" by "the people" that it promises. Being able to take some part in designating or dismissing holders of public office, authorizing, responding to, or legally resisting governmental actions and initiatives, participating in political initiatives oneself, even exercising some judicial function by jury service, all these are symbolically important and may be circumstantially of practical value. But they do not amount to "governing" or "ruling", which presupposes initiating and commanding, not merely responding. But even supposing direct or—stretching language still thinner—indirect citizen participation to be equivalent to ruling, the *demos* remains to be identified.

Democracy postulates some arrangement or symbolization whereby the factual multiplicity of "wills" of a *demos*, a "people," is made a facsimile of the decision ("will") and acting of a natural individual. That arrangement or symbol must be a majoritarian decision procedure, where some part is allowed to stand for the whole. Any requirement approaching unanimity would amount to institutionalizing grid-lock, or would require converting every dissentient into "an enemy of the people," or at best "mistaken" about the common good (Rousseau's General Will), so that their votes might be discounted. The majority must, however, be a majority of some *demos*, and so the decision procedure *presupposes* an already existing *demos*, and therefore an already established institutional order to determine its membership (Dahl, 1989, Ch. 9): no *demos* identifies itself.

What is crucial for the cogency of a critical approach to democratized accountability, then, is to establish the identity of a relevant *demos*, and to determine the scope of its authority with respect to the regulation of corporations and the policing of the professions. Any such *demos* will be sovereign by definition, but this sovereignty does nothing to resolve the question about what limits it ought to recognize to its own authority and competence. All this may of course be ignored by simply insisting on the sovereignty of the *demos*, as when trial by jury is insisted on regardless of the circumstances of cases. Nevertheless, a democratic sovereign is as "arbitrary" as any other, and it is not the point of critical social science to introduce arbitrary government. "Arbitrary" is a word derived from *arbitrium*, meaning will, and hence doing as I please: "this is my will and my command; let my will stand in place of a reason" (the ancient maxim of tyranny). *Arbitrium* also means judgment—as in "arbitrator," who is of course not to act arbitrarily. "Arbitrary government" might thus simply mean government not subject to any *institutional* limits on its authority (as in "parliamentary sovereignty"). But by the 1640s it had already become a term of abuse in Britain; it was used (interchangeably with "will") in the establishment of the "court" to try Charles I in January 1649 for his "wicked design...to introduce an arbitrary and tyrannical government..." (Gardiner, 1962, p. 357). Sovereign arbitrariness or unaccountability does not of course imply immunity from moral compunctions or censure, nor was this ever denied by Hobbes, by his predecessors, or by Carl Schmitt in the 20th century. Nevertheless, such moral responsibility cannot be brought home to the sovereign in the form of *accountability*, least of all when the sovereign is some *demos*: "A perfect [i.e., unlimited] democracy is, therefore, the most shameless thing in the world," to quote Edmund Burke's *Reflections on the Revolution in France*. Only pluralism can avoid the logic of sovereignty, if anything can. But critical theory and practice tolerates pluralism only where it is practically ineliminable or politically congenial, the plurality approved as difference, multiculturalism or moral pluralism, say; in any other respect, little has changed here from the position expressed by Dye and Zeigler in their *Irony of Democracy*.

I cannot here do what has not been done by an entire literature, both critical and not. Certain points about what is *not* a resolution of the issues relating to democratic accountability are, however, clear.

## THE STATE AS AGENT FOR THE DEMOS

In the first place, merely proposing the imposition of a "democratic" sovereignty on corporations and professions is morally and conceptually not nearly enough. In the absence of further articulation, the agent acting for the *demos* is the state, whether it is national or local government or the courts. Calling it "the people," "the community," or "Society" is not to provide an alternative, but to restate the same problem in different words. What can count as an act of a corporation is a familiar philosophical as well as legal problem. The problem with "Society" or "the community," the rhetorical "we," or "the people" as agents is just as acute; with the "international community" or some personified section of the population of a state or the world it is worse still. It would be more than a mere irony if critical theory ended with some boilerplate statism, with the control and management of corporations, and now of the professions as well, vested in the collectivist state redivivus under the label of "democratic accountability." Part, but only part, of the irony here would be that it would be at the expense of both Marxist and liberal traditions of hostility to the state (Wolin, 1961, Ch. 10), a distrust that in Marxist practice has, admittedly, been largely devoid of practical effect.

It is of no consequence in this respect whether such a state acted in accordance with "public opinion" or not. Critical theory does not require to be reminded of the dangers of populism. Indeed, the argument for an emancipatory science is premised on the prevalence of false consciousness. To arm false consciousness with the power of the state would be positively perverse. But neither can an argument for democratization be based on anticipating what might be the conclusions of public reasoning and deliberation under optimal epistemic conditions: uncoerced discourse yielding to nothing except the force of the strongest argument; reflection behind a "veil of ignorance"; "agonal" confrontation; a "truly historical understanding" of one's circumstances and society; or whatever regulative conceptual machinery is to be deployed. The point precisely is that if the conclusions of such deliberation could be anticipated, they would not require political deliberation, and if they do, the ideal conditions postulated precisely do not exist.

## THE LAITY AS JUDGE AND JURY

Again, the rationale of "self-government" or democracy is of no force where urgency or expertise is intrinsic to decision-making. It evidently does not apply: in operating theaters, on flight decks, or in enterprises such as war, policing, diplomacy, civil engineering, the administration of a health service or a disaster relief program, or the production of goods and services under competition, which demands careful coordination, sustained attention to detail, diurnal administration, the discerning and exploiting of opportunities, and rapid response. It does not even apply to the design or delivery of academic courses, or to academic appointments. The argument from sovereignty also has no moral force wherever judging the competence of agents itself requires competence. As has been argued, accountability implies moral rights and duties on both sides. The rights involved here include rights of professions to self-government. The undoubted existence of a power/knowledge relation between members of professions and their clients or even the general public does not alter the fact that accountability demands just judgments of accounts. Incompetents cannot judge justly, nor can those convinced of the guilt of the "accused" a priori. Thus only specialists can judge cases of medical negligence, or the incompetence of lawyers, architects, accountants, etc., or (non)compliance with intricate financial regulations or alleged financial frauds, or the conduct of persons placed in circumstances of which ordinary individuals have no experience. As it has been discussed in the critical literature, democratization is treated as simply a matter of mobilizing power against the professions; the moral issues are taken as resolved (e.g., O'Dwyer, 2003; Owen, 2005, p. 26; Tinker & Gray, 2003). This, I am arguing, is not the case.

## THE PUBLIC INTEREST

There are any number of individuals and groups claiming to act for collective entities such as "Society," "the people," or some "community," or to represent the "public interest." The question is which of these claims can be made good, and how. The "public interest," which corporations and professions are said to ignore, neglect, or spin into their own private interest, is not a given; like any other interest it is constructed. Whose construction, then, is to be definitive? It seems doubtful that critical theory could settle for a pluralist, market, or merely procedural method of constructing it, for (apart from other objections) none of these guarantee desired substantive outcomes, such as social justice. Nevertheless, stakeholders are irreducibly a multiplicity, and there is no automatic moral hierarchy in the strength of their claims on the resources of corporations, or to entitlement to participation in their decision making (which can only mean participation in policymaking). The source of the vulnerability of professional associations to critical assault (e.g., Canning & O'Dwyer, 2001; Sikka & Willmott, 1995) is that they are subject to a conflict of interest: at once trade associations looking after the private interests of the profession, and quasi-judicial and policing organizations responsible for its public standing, good order, and discipline (the "public interest"). Nevertheless, subordinating them to the state, or to cause or interest groups and activists, is not necessarily any improvement. Indeed, to replace professional self-government (or for that matter independent corporate managements) by civil or criminal litigation, the inevitable consequence of progressively more peremptory and detailed legal regulation, is often to make matters worse, except for lawyers. It is in any event nothing to do with democratization or emancipation.

## AFFECTING, AND BEING AFFECTED BY, POWER

It seems to be untenable to continue to maintain that a corporation is "essentially" constituted by its management and shareholders, as agent and principal respectively. The reason, however, is not the directness or seriousness of the "effects" on the latter of the corporation's faring well or badly, despite the consensus of the stakeholding literature that affecting and being affected by are the criteria for establishing a stake, and that the strength of claims on a company is proportionate to the directness of the effect. By itself neither the power of organizations over others nor the converse establishes any right. The rights of professions to exercise coercive authority over their member (with exclusion from practice as the ultima ratio) are strictly correlative to the professional duties that their members have in any event, and are legitimated by that, and not by any "effect." Again, the activities of enterprises may (and often do) have extremely unwelcome or even calamitous consequences for various individuals and groups, for the environment, for sustainability, for employment, etc. This "power" of corporations is taken by critical theory to be a sufficient ground for subjecting them to "democratization." But by itself it generates neither an identification of a relevant *demos* nor any right to be involved in their government, any more than being adversely affected by the activities of (say) environmentalists or trade unions generates a right to be allowed to participate in the government, policymaking, and administration of such associations, or taking an examination generates a right to set and mark the papers, or being subject to the jurisdiction of criminal courts or the police generates a right to participate in judging, or to have a voice in the way a criminal investigation is conducted. The analogy to the polity presupposed by the demand for democratization only works if the "stakeholders" are constitutive of the corporation or profession, in the same way that a *demos* is by definition a constituent component of the polity. Being constitutive of an organization, however, is in no sense the same as affecting or being affected by its activities. The categories of persons and groups identified in the stakeholder literature (employees, shareholders, suppliers, customers, and "communities," sometimes even competitors and notoriously, in one account, terrorists and therefore presumably organized criminals as well) have entirely distinct relationships with corporate bodies, and are by no means all constitutive of them. The strongest case here is plainly employees. But even with them, it is impossible to see how there can be or should be any uniform or equal entitlement. The claims on a university of a long-serving porter, for example, are clearly morally stronger than those of a flighty, ambitious academic who is merely passing through. But in the former case they involve no moral or legal right to participate in the university's government or teaching, whereas in the latter they do.

No one has ever argued that bodies corporate are morally entitled, or should be legally entitled, to do as they please. Indeed it is a strong argument for the independence of corporations and the self-government of professions that they *can* be legally controllable and accountable, unlike state-instruments (consider, for example, crown immunity, or industrial or radioactive pollution by state-enterprises). But what form regulation or constraint of the activities and power of corporations (and professions) should take is in large measure a pragmatic matter of efficaciousness. Those normally identified as stakeholders do indeed have moral claims upon corporations, but these claims might equally be upheld by markets, courts, processes of bargaining if they are contractually related to the entity, or by corporate governance arrangements or direct or arm's-length regulation by government agencies: they do not *entail* participation in their government.

## ACCOUNTABILITY AS A RHETORICAL PRACTICE

Whatever form accountability may take, it cannot be that of converting the conduct of a business or the policing of a profession into a permanent process of negotiation and confrontation with those who have or can impose a claim on the agents of the corporation or profession. The critique of corporate pretensions to social, environmental, and economic responsibility is that they are mere spin, in that there is no "stakeholder dialogue," but at best a willingness of corporate agents to listen to stakeholder concerns. But a corporation or profession that "genuinely" (and a *fortiori* institutionally) involved stakeholders in its decision making would be even more morally and legally unaccountable, since the responsibility for any decision would be diffused. It is (conceptually and legally) difficult enough to assign responsibility to and in corporations as now constituted. If the corporation were identified as not only management and directorate but also the collectivity of its stakeholders, it would be impossible. This no doubt is why the constitutional order of the corporation under stakeholding has been so poorly thought out.

Accountability, as has been argued above, entails a relationship between a principal and an agent. If the agents or organs of stakeholders are to remain independent of management, that leaves two possible candidates: politicians, those "legitimated" by some vote, and activists, acting for themselves or interests or causes, without such a legitimation; the work of both may be a full-time employment. The topic is obviously too vast and contentious to pursue here. But the characterization of activists as animated by public spirit, concern, and altruism is gratuitous. Activists come in many stripes, and their motives, conduct, and purposes may or may not bear inspection. Politicians and officeholders were traditionally linked to activists and a broader public via the medium of political parties. This link was always fragile, and party identification has become so evanescent in many polities that a crisis of legitimacy has been recurrently proclaimed. Whether that is true or not, there is nothing to suggest that the authority of politicians has been, or could be, successfully appropriated by activists. Accountability supposes a principal and an agent, and a continuing, more or less formal arrangement. Resistants and single-cause groups are not possible principals of corporations (or professions), and can be made to appear so only by their claim to be agents of the people and hence the sovereign, a claim that is inherently contestable.

Accountability, again, is not "dialogue." It is in any case difficult to envisage "dialogue" when the good faith of corporate actors with respect to motives, accountability, responsiveness, transparency, materiality is routinely impugned, or even ruled out as impossible in the nature of things. What takes place is rather cause groups and corporate actors attempting to legitimate themselves in the face of an amorphous "public opinion," responding to and trying to set a "public agenda" that has only a media-existence, an evanescent climate of opinion and fashion. This, however, is nothing like accountability. All accountability, as analyzed earlier, is inevitably a "rhetorical" practice: persuading or rebutting persuasions. So of course are proceedings in a court of law, a general meeting of shareholders, the disciplinary boards of a profession, the hearings of a Parliamentary Select Committee, a university disciplinary or ethics committee, or responding to the Public Audit Office or a regulator. The difference between these and the political rhetoric of any "dialogue" between corporations or professions and cause groups and activists is that an accountability arrangement must be premised on standards of just dealing. Here the rhetoric must revolve around whether these standards, themselves not in dispute, have been complied with or not. Although such a "hearing" of accounts is juridically peculiar in that the principal is often also judge and jury, even the principal's verdict is subject to the rule of law, the superior authority of the state, and a sequence of appeals. Not so with stakeholder "dialogue," where there is no agreement even on what supposedly agreed standards mean (Stoney & Winstanley, 2001) and no appeal, and where those demanding accounts may not even concede the right to exist of those from whom they demand accounts, and may have no investment in their survival, let alone flourishing. The strength of the position of, say, Owen or O'Dwyer is that, occasional appearances notwithstanding, theirs is not an anti-capitalist crusade.

## CONCLUSION: THE POTENTIAL OF ACCOUNTABILITY

Accountability, then, can impose only a limited and circumstantial liability on professions and corporations. What critique envisages as a more radical liability generated by democratization and emancipation is not perspicuous, and needs to be articulated more clearly. It is currently specified too often by explicit or disguised negatives: it is not bureaucratic, not marked by asymmetries of power, not hierarchical, not pollutant, not consumerist, not managerial, not exploitative, not perhaps even capitalist. It is, however, to be emancipatory (i.e., none of the above), democratic (i.e., none of the above), to do with sustainability in at least one of its senses, agonal (i.e., not consensual), and so forth. If democratization and emancipation are to be developed into something more than abstract desiderata, they must be "operationalized." I see no critical alternative (and Owen, 2000, for one does not suggest that there is any such alternative) to "institutional engineering," in terms of entirely familiar interpretations of managerial (and popular) motivation, and of the most effectively constructed web of incentives and sanctions that may make managerial conduct predictable and reliable. This cannot be dismissed as managerialism, positivism, or "panoptical" reasoning. Benthamites were certainly conspicuously successful reformers. Their institutional engineering is paradigmatically exhibited in James Mill's 1819 *Encyclopaedia Britannica* entry "Government," or in the reform of the Poor Law, the Northcote-Trevelyan reforms of the British civil service, the Factory Acts, and Fabianism, rather than Bentham's Panopticon. But the manner of reasoning is in fact much older than Bentham. Pocock (1975) and Hirschman (1977), among others, have traced its republican provenance, and the reasoning behind much monarchical absolutism is no different, as the reflections of both Hobbes and Montesquieu illustrate. It is also precisely the manner of reflection Marx and Engels themselves adopted, albeit in a peculiarly optimistic form, in generating their prescriptions for the revolutionary society in the *Manifesto, The Civil War in France,* etc., or in approving, say, the factory inspectorate of Britain. Subjecting managers of enterprises to a miscellaneous demos of activists is not an alternative to institutional engineering, or to having managers and bureaucrats ultimately making decisions.

The critical conceptual equipment of emancipation, domination, and asymmetries of power is here in need of more explication. Power cannot be anything other than asymmetrical, though it is most unlikely to be uniformly or perpetually so, on any of the possible understandings of power (see the critiques of Steven Lukes's theory of power in *Political Studies Review,* May 2006, Vol. 4(2)). Resistance, democratization, and emancipation seek to lessen or reconfigure the asymmetry, but cannot abolish it. There is in any event nothing inherently illegitimate in some persons having power over others. The freedom that such power abridges or eliminates may be an illegitimate freedom. Moreover, there is no incompatibility between being free and acknowledging the authority of someone else: on the contrary, freedom may reside precisely in the *acknowledgment* of authority. Democracy, in every version, then, is not an alternative to "asymmetries of power," in the sense of inequalities of moral and institutionalized authority (I have developed this point in Hopfl, 1999). In essence, it is a procedure for designating and controlling hierarchs. In the classical republican tradition, a virtuous *demos* exhibited its civic virtue precisely by its recognition and choice of its "natural aristocrats," and by the recognition—underpinned by complex arrangements—of the duty to allow them authority to act, and to leave judging them to those likely to judge justly (e.g., Harrington, 1656).

## NOTES

1. There is in my view no viable distinction between these two terms, except that "ethics" is probably best confined to the moral considerations peculiar to some specific occupation.
2. A reviewer supposed my account here to be a version of "agency theory." But agency theory (like any theory of a human activity) is merely an abstraction from a practice, and what I am doing is to characterize the practice from which theories of accountability have been abstracted.

## REFERENCES

Alvesson, M., & Deetz, S. (2000). *Doing critical management research.* London: Sage

Benton, T., & Craib, I. (2001). *Philosophy of social science: The philosophical foundations of social thought.* Basingstoke, UK: Palgrave.

Butler, J. (2005). *Giving an account of oneself.* New York: Fordham Press.

Canning, M., & O'Dwyer, B. (2001). "Professional Accounting Bodies" disciplinary proceedings: Accountable, transparent and in the public interest? *European Accounting Review, 10*(40, 725–749.

Canovan, M. (2005). *Nationhood and political theory.* Cheltenham: Edward Elgar.

Crane, A., & Matten, D. (2004). *Business ethics: A European perspective.* Oxford, UK: Oxford University Press.

Dahl, R. A. (1970). *After the revolution.* New Haven, CT: Yale University Press.

Dahl, R. A. (1989). *Democracy and its critics.* New Haven, CT: Yale University Press.

Dubnick, M. J. (2003). Accountability and ethics: Reconsidering the relationships. *International Journal of Organization Theory and Behavior, 6*(3), 405–441.

Fay, B. (1975). *Social theory and political practice.* London: Allen & Unwin.

Finnis, J. (1980). *Natural law and natural rights.* Oxford, UK: Oxford University Press.

Friedman, A. L., & Miles, S. (2006). *Stakeholders: Theory and practice.* Oxford, UK: Oxford University Press.

Friedman, M. (1970, September 13). The social responsibility of business is to increase its profits. *New York Times Magazine.*

Gardiner, S. E. (1962). *Constitutional documents of the Puritan revolution, 1625–1660* (3rd revised ed.). Oxford, UK: Clarendon Press.

Geuss, R. (1981). *The idea of a critical theory.* Cambridge, UK: Cambridge University Press.

Graham, G. (2002). *The case against the democratic state: An essay in cultural criticis.* Thorverton, UK: Imprint Academic

Gray, J. (1998). *Hayek on liberty* (3rd ed.). London: Routledge.

Greenleaf, W. H. (1964). *Order, empiricism and politics.* Oxford, UK: Oxford University Press.

Harrington, J. (1977). *The commonwealth of Oceana* (J. G. A. Pocock, Ed.). Cambridge, UK: Cambridge University Press.

Hart, H. L. A. (1961). *The concept of law.* Oxford, UK: Clarendon Press.

Hayek, F. A. von. (1962). *Law, legislation and liberty: Volume II. The mirage of social justice.* London: Routledge

Hayek, F. A. von. (1976). *The constitution of liberty.* London: Routledge.

Hayek, F. A. von. (1988). *The fatal conceit* (W.W. Bartley, Ed.). London: Routledge

Henderson, D. (2001). *Misguided virtue: False notions of corporate responsibility.* London: Institute of Economic Affairs.

Hirschman, A. O. (1977). *The passions and the interests: Political arguments for capitalism before its triumph.* Princeton, NJ: Princeton University Press.

Hobbes, T. (1946). *Leviathan* (M. Oakeshott, Ed.). Oxford: Blackwell.

Hopfl, H. M. (1999). Power, authority and legitimacy. *Human Resource Development International, 2*(3), 217–234.

Jensen, M. C. (2005). Value maximization, stakeholder theory and the corporate objective function. *European Financial Management, 7*(3), 297–317.

Jones, C., Parker, M., & ten Bos, R. (2005). *For business ethics.* London: Routledge

Keasey, K., Thompson, S., & Wright, M. (Eds.). (2005). *Corporate governance: Accountability, enterprise and international comparisons,* Chichester, UK: Wiley

Kelsen, H. (1978). *Pure theory of law* (2nd ed.). Berkeley: University of California Press.

Kukathas, C. (1989). *Hayek and modern liberalism.* Oxford, UK: Clarendon Press.

Laclau, E. (2005). *Of populist reason.* London: Verso.

MacIntyre, A. (1985). *After virtue* (2nd ed.). London: Duckworth

Mill, J. S. (1871). *Principles of political economy* (7th ed.). London: Longmans, Green, Reader, and Dyer.

Mulgan, R. (2000). Accountability: an ever-expanding concept? *Public Administration, 78*(3), 555–573.

Munro, R., & Mouritsen, J. (Eds.). (1996). *Accountability: power, ethos and the technologies of managing.* London: International Thomson Business Press.

Oakeshott, M. (1975). *On human conduct.* Oxford, UK: Oxford University Press.

Oakeshott, M. (1962). Rationalism in politics. In *Rationalism in politics and other essays.* London: Methuen.

O'Dwyer, B. (2003). Conceptions of corporate social responsibility: The nature of managerial capture. *Accounting, Auditing, and Accountability Journal, 16*(4), 523–557.

Owen, D., Swift, T., Humphrey, C., & Bowerman, M. (2000). The new social audits: Accountability, managerial capture or the agenda of social champions. *European Accounting Review, 9*(1), 81–98.

Owen, D. L. (2005). *Corporate social reporting and stakeholder accountability: The missing link* (No.32-2005 ICCSR Research Paper Series). Nottingham, UK: Nottingham University Business School.

Pieper, J. (1965). *Traktat über die Klugheit* (7th ed.). München, Germany: Kosel Verlag.

Phillips, R., Freeman, R. E. & Wicks, A. C. (2003). What stakeholder theory is not. *Business Ethics Quarterly,* 13(4), 479–502.

Pocock, J. G. A. (1975). *The Machiavellian moment.* Princeton, NJ: Princeton University Press.

Polanyi, M. (1962). *Personal knowledge: Towards a post critical philosophy.* London: Routledge.

Power, M. (1999). *The audit society: Rituals of verification.* Oxford, UK: Oxford University Press.

Sinclair, A. (1995). The chameleon of accountability: Forms and discourses. *Accounting, Organizations and Society,* 20(2/3), 219–237.

Sikka P., & Willmott, H. (1995). The power of "independence": Defending and extending the jurisdiction of accounting in the United Kingdom. *Accounting, Organizations and Society, 20*(6), 547–581.

Sternberg, E. (2004). *Corporate governance: Accountability in the* marketplace (2nd ed.). London: Institute of Economic Affairs.

Stoney, C., & Winstanley, D. (2001). Stakeholding: Confusion or utopia?: Mapping the conceptual terrain. *Journal of Management Studies,* 38(5), 603–626.

Tinker, T., & Gray, R. (2003). Beyond a critique of pure reason: From policy to politics to praxis in environmental and social research. *Accounting, Auditing and Accountability Journal,* 16(5), 727–761.

Tønder, L., & Thomassen, L. (Eds.). (2005). *Radical democracy: Politics between abundance and lack.* Manchester, UK: Manchester University Press.

Wolin, S. S. (1961). *Politics and vision.* London: Allen & Unwin.

# PART III

CT ETHICS FOR ORGANIZATIONAL CONTEXTS

CHAPTER 8

# LEGAL FICTIONS

## Critical Theory Criticality and the State of Economics and Management

**Robin Matthews**

### INTRODUCTION

Possibly crisis is the natural state of affairs. We are faced now as usual with major crises—social, economic, political, and personal. Perhaps change itself is the crisis, opening up desire, opportunity, aspiration that we try to direct and limit through inventing legal fictions, property rights, for example, designed to bring the illusion of permanence, to channel desire and opportunity into social and organizational evolution and to veil entropy, decay, and impermanence, the other face of change. In some traditions desires, aspirations, and change are associated with progress, in others with sorrow (Kalansuriya, 1987). If the definition of law is broadened out to include the effects of conventions, culture, routines, personality, and history, as well as rules and regulations, then law acts as a kind of grammar (call this organizational grammar), that governs events and activities (the morphology of organizational grammar), permissible relationships and linkages between them (the syntax of organizational grammar), and interpretation of them.

*Critical Theory Ethics for Business and Public Administration*, pages 159–183
Copyright © 2008 by Information Age Publishing
**159**

Equally important, law in the sense of organizational grammar is an invisible veil, a mask such that, though it is merely one of many masks, can appear to be the only mask: a mask that can be confused with reality or even become reality itself.

This chapter sets out versions of property rights, all legal fictions; one strong version is a foundation of economic and business analysis (of globalization, in particular), in which organizational grammar is concealed; another, a poem, Legal Fiction by William Empson, which reveals it through an extended conceit. A legal fiction is a "facetious euphemism for an untruth" (Simon, 1960; Haffenden, 2000). Change on all scales, large or small, is always possible, and the balance of probability, in the global economy, appears to be shifting toward the former, a point of criticality, defined as a situation (Bak & Chen, 1991; Bak, 1997; Jensen, 1998) where single events have the widest possible range of effects and new ways of thinking are required particularly in business and compounded in business and management education. Empathy, in the sense of being able to identify with the *Other* in nature and in society is an important element of ethical behavior and this is a function of consciousness of (a) the grammar adopted in making choices and (b) awareness that alternative grammars exist. Beneath the ostensible crises are issues of consciousness, of revealing, (unveiling) the grammar, the legal fictions of private property rights govern economic and business policy and analysis, especially of globalization.

The development of consciousness is at a critical point. There are two root propositions in the chapter; the first concerns the evolution of organizations and the second, consciousness. The first proposition is that the evolution of societies and organizations is driven by Darwinian processes, emergent properties of a system that includes outer and inner dynamics, and organizational grammar: an interaction of complex adaptive systems. The second is that new levels of consciousness are required, subtle consciousness, that involves awareness of the inner grammar that conditions thinking, policy, and the interpretation of history, and ultimately the emergent properties of the brain. The study of the brain as an organic machine, a network of neuronal processes (that perhaps can be simulated by a computer) conditioned by the internal personal and social components of organizational grammar, are the subject matter of cognitive science. Subtle consciousness, the awareness of organizational grammar generally that conditions thinking, policy, and interpretations is the subject matter of the critical theory as discussed in this chapter. Organization is defined in the broadest terms, ranging hierarchically from the public to the private and from individual activities or businesses to big corporations or entire societies. A general model is presented in the next section. A key element is organizational grammar.

Organizational grammar is defined more extensively than Wittgenstein's notion. He thought of grammar as *rules for the use of a word* or rules that *determine meaning*. Organizational grammar includes (a) surface rules permitting some moves and interpretations and forbidding others, that are expressions of (b) subsurface rules that govern ways of thinking about and interpreting society. Surface rules include explicit laws, regulations, treaties, and so on as well as implicit cultures, values, mores that serve as standards for judging quality and success or failure. Organizational grammar includes representations such as rules, laws, regulations, cultures, programmed modes of ways of thinking, however complex such neuronal processes are. It also encompasses deeper elements or structures, beneath the level of awareness, that determine prevailing discourse of a situation.

Organizational grammar itself is a CAS and its elements (nodes) interact with one another, conflicting with, reinforcing or dampening one another, while still retaining an internal cohesion. There is no general agreement about the exact meaning of a complex system but there is about their characteristic features, as outlined in the next section. A common feature of CAS is that they acquire information about the environment, identify regularities in the information, and condense regularities into a kind of schema or models that they can adopt to handle the world. Complexity can signify chaotic dynamics, or refer to cellular automata, neural networks, adaptive algorithms, disordered many body systems, pattern forming systems (Kauffman, 1993; Pettersson, 1996; Simon, 1996).

Organizational grammar as used here has many correspondences; to Wittgenstein's notion of grammar, for example, as part of a language game permitting some and forbidding others, serving as a standard for judging success or failure; to Foucault's archaeological method as in *The Archaeology of Knowledge* that exposed systems of thought and knowledge (epistemes) and genealogy as in *Discipline and Punish intended to show that systems of thought and behavior, including ethics (as in* Nietzsche's *genealogy of morals) emerged out of history, in a manner that I describe as evolutionary.*

The representations of grammar may evolve spontaneously, gradually, or in a punctuated fashion. Evolution and emergence in the case of grammar is akin to Darwinian processes in which evolution takes the form of increasing fitness to a given organizational environment, itself the product of interacting complex, adaptive systems in a manner described by the meta model below. In the process evolution described by the meta model, new organizations and organizational structures result from natural selection, or in a Schumpeterian sense, competitive dynamics, perhaps through small changes over long periods of time (Darwinian gradualism), or from punctuated equilibrium (Eldridge & Gould, 1971) in which selection, or competition, triggered by technological change operates on species (in this case, entire industries).

Organizational grammar has two roles in Figure 8.1. First, it is itself a complex adaptive system that interacts with three other complex adaptive systems: (1) factors external to organizations, that is the environment of organizations; (2) organizational assets, tangible and intangible; and (3) the organizational payoffs to their stakeholders. Second, organizational grammar governs the elements that are included within each of the other three categories of Figure 8.1, and the relationships between them.

The notion of organizational grammar leads to a definition of consciousness. The definition in this chapter differs from that of cognitive sciences and philosophy, which are mainly concerned with the mechanics of consciousness that consists of "technical problems of studying a system of a hundred billion or so neurons stuffed into the skull.... Consciousness consists of states of awareness or sentience or feeling" (Searle, 2005); the mystery of how the brain functions; neuronal processes or circuitry that correlate with consciousness (Koch, 1998; Pinker, 2000). Consciousness here is defined as awareness of the grammar that governs the mechanics of consciousness close to the Buddhist or Sufic notions of subtle consciousness (Izutsu, 1960; Suzuki, 2000; Matthews, 1998). The idea is that there are many levels of consciousness, each having its own grammar. This chapter is concerned with the grammar underlying the mechanics of consciousness, especially with respect to private property rights. Returning to the idea of complex adaptive systems (CAS), considering CAS in terms of networks (as in Figure 8.2), consisting of nodes and connections between them: both of these are determined by organizational grammar. Mostly it is implicit and we are unconscious of it. Possibility of consciousness in the sense used here arises only with awareness of the extent to which grammar conditions and determines the perception of things.

Critical theory has two different origins and histories; one in economic and social theory, the other in literary criticism. In literary criticism it focuses primarily on the analysis of texts. The chapter adopts both approach-

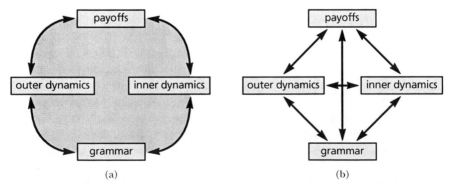

(a)  (b)

**Figure 8.1**  Alternative pictures of the meta model of strategic analysis.

es, placing property rights as they appear in current economic and social thinking against their poetic version. The arbitrariness of the underlying grammar of PRP is shown up in contrast to that explored in an extended conceit in Empson's poem.

Legal Fiction, according to Empson's notes on the poem, "explores the pragmatic, moral and eschatelogical ramifications of private property rights in land, taking its inspiration from the medieval Latin maxim…[that]: the owner of the soil has a prima ownership of everything reaching up to the heavens and down to the depths of the earth" (Haffenden, 2000, p. 229). This view of private property rights, Haffenden goes on to say, "has always been a legal fiction," exposed paradoxically by the extended conceit in the poem, "Your rights extend under and above your claim/Without bound; you own land in Heaven and Hell…."

The purpose of this chapter is to point out arbitrariness in the underlying grammar and the existence of alternative grammars by deconstructing the grammar of various versions of PRP. It is no accident that Derrida refused to define deconstruction. Paradoxically deconstruction as a technique is to shed technique just as a caterpillar sheds its form as it transforms itself into a butterfly, a kind of deconstruction. Deconstruction is not a technique precisely because if it is allowed to become a technique it becomes a construction, an architecture, itself part of the organizational grammar that conditions or programs activity and thinking on the surface and subsurface. Deconstruction is like successively unpeeling of infinite layers, like the Sufi process of *kashf* or unveiling. Poetic language makes this clearer. Whereas the language of analytical work appears precise, it merely conceals the grammar that underpins it; poetic language is ambiguous, rich, at the same time explicit about the many layers of meaning it contains. A poetic version of property is discussed alongside the PRP effecting a kind of deconstruction, a *kashf.* Globalization, a late stage of global capitalism, provides a convenient context in which to develop these ideas.

## GLOBALIZATION COMPLEXITY AND THE PROPERTY RIGHTS PARADIGM (PRP)

The aims of this chapter are (1) to expose a specific grammar, the grammar underlying the economic and social theory that is based on the notion of private property rights, and (2) to point out that this grammar is to a great extent arbitrary. Three conceptions of property rights are outlined: Schumpeterian form, weak form, and strong form private property rights.

Each has distinctive elements of organizational grammar, embodied in a set of assumptions. The first was identified by Schumpeter as the existence of private property and debt market to align savings and investment.

The next two forms are referred to as the property rights paradigm (PRP) in the literature. What I term weak form PRP, based on the same foundations as the Schumpeterian version, is differentiated by its concentration on efficiency rather than growth, insistence upon not just the existence of markets, but the existence of efficient markets. Together with Schumpeterian dynamics underlies the discourse of competitive advantage. The third, strong form PRP, is based on a much tighter grammar. Strong form PRP has increasingly driven economic policy and lies at the root of the interpretation of the global economy.

Under PRP individual owners exclusively have the rights over the services of the assets or property they own; to consume, delegate, rent, gift or sell any portion of them as they like. Fundamental assumptions that underlie the grammar of the three modes of PRP are set out in Table 8.1.

Private property rights reflect market values and market values, that is, values determined by supply and demand, reflect the preferences and values of society. If A1 holds, no matter who the owner is, he or she has to consider opportunity cost, the most valuable alternative in disposing of them in a particular way. If A2 holds as well, owners will seek the highest-valued use for their property. Thus, given A1 and A2, private decisions are based on public, or social, evaluation because they are based on opportunity cost calculations. On these assumptions, if property is privatized (allotted exclusively to individuals) and if a market system is established globally, every individual has the incentive to put it to the highest valued use. Hence we have a set of policies established internationally through institutions like the Internation-

**TABLE 8.1   The Grammar of PRP**

| Private property rights in Schumpeter | Weak form PRP | Strong form PRP |
|---|---|---|
| S1. Existence of a debt market | W1. Existence of efficient markets | A1*: The existence of efficient markets |
| S2. Profit maximizing by firms | W2. Individual rationality | A2: Individually rational behavior |
| | | A3: A restricted definition of efficiency |
| | | A4: The separation of issues of efficiency and distribution |
| | | A5: The individual is the appropriate judges of how resources should be allocated |
| | | A6. Time reversibility |
| | | A7. Monetization of payoffs |

al Monetary Fund (IMF), the World Bank, the World Trade Organization (WTO), and the European Union (EU) in the Maastricht Treaty, through privatization policies and policies of deregulation worldwide. These policies are designed to maximize growth and wealth worldwide.

## The Global Economy as a CAS

Complex adaptive systems (CAS) are sometimes described as interdependent networks—telecommunications networks, networks of neurons in the brain, computer networks ecologies, ant colonies, immune systems. Interdependence is an important characteristic of CAS, sometimes described as nonlinearity or a feedback system. The adaptive element captures the role of agents in a CAS: they are active, they react to circumstances, they make plans and revise their plans; in other words, they are not passive with respect to change but they attempt to adapt.

The global economy (Figure 8.2(a)) arose from the interaction of three phenomena, each a complex adaptive system; the financial and technological revolutions and their interaction with demand that led to the current phase of global capitalism. The financial revolution had two aspects: the institution of market-determined exchange rates (that gave rise to the possibility of cross-country transfers of funds and foreign direct investment) and the creation of new forms of debt, new types of bonds and derivatives. The technological revolution beginning in the 1970s in communications information and biotechnologies, led to increased competition, shorter product cycles, and the need to seek global markets to reduce costs and to increase demand. Thus technology fed the need to globalize, globalization increased competition and accelerated technical change, which in turn increased the need for finance, which itself was a global phenomenon as financial institutions merged across national boundaries.

Along with these developments, private property was instituted, through privatization, as part of programs of shock therapy in the former Soviet bloc, Reaganeconomics, Thatcherism, and so on, in all but a few states that have become part of global wealth creation. Elsewhere we have the Other; states marginalized in the wealth creation process, designated variously as failed or rogue states; individuals and within states everywhere; the universal criminal economy; and networks of terrorism.

## Characteristics of CAS

Figure 8.1 gives alternative descriptions of the analytics of a meta model of organizational development as an interaction of four complex adaptive systems. There are many definitions of complexity and complex adaptive systems, but for the purpose of this chapter four are representative of their essence: interdependence, adaptation, emergence, and ambiguity.

*Interdependence.* Interdependence comes in two forms, first across space, second across time. Across space we have interdependence in the form of complementarity (or superadditivity, both economic terms) or synergy (the favored managerial term). Putting together the components of a complex adaptive system results in quantitative changes (the whole is somehow greater than the sum of the individual parts) and qualitative changes (the whole is different from the individual parts, as water differs from its components hydrogen and oxygen). Across time, complex adaptive systems contain feedback effects, one part of the system interacts with another across time.

Figure 8.2 presents the global economy emerged as an interacting network, a CAS with finance technology and global demand interacting as a positive feedback system capable of producing upswings and downswings or, as Schumpeter described them, as Kondratieff waves, alternating cycles of prosperity and depression triggered by technological and other outer dynamic shocks.

*Adaptation.* A second aspect of complex adaptive systems is also illustrated by the globalization example: agents or decision makers adapt. New financial instruments are created in response to the need to fund technology, technology adapts in response to competitive pressures, from which emerges the need to find new markets and cheaper resources; that is the development of global capitalism.

*Emergence.* The third defining aspect of complexity and complex adaptive systems is emergence. New phenomena emerge; in the globalization example new technologies, new financial instruments, new markets. The world becomes quantitatively and qualitatively different. Rather than the scientific process taking the form of a nexus of cause, scientific laws, predictions, and perhaps the possibility of control, the scientific process under complexity

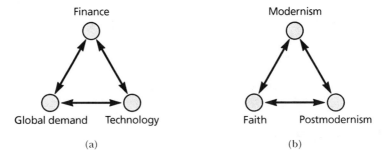

**Figure 8.2** Figure 8.2. Globalization (a) as positive feedback and (b) as potentially chaotic.

has a historic property. What happens now and in the future is determined by how the past unfolds and we have an unending dependence of the present and future on the past. Surprise becomes the rule rather than the precise prediction and the rise of emergent economies are part of this.

*Ambiguity.* The fourth aspect of CAS, ambiguity, shows up in a number of ways. Primarily this chapter focuses on ambiguity in the sense that many different grammars rule at any one time: exemplified by the coexistence of the grammar associated with PRP and the quite different grammar of the poetic conceit in Legal Fiction. Another important source of ambiguity arises out of the many different types of behavior that are possible in CAS; equilibrium and disequilibrium, cyclical or point attractors, randomness and chaos are all possible. Furthermore, CAS are characterized by diversity of pattern; the emergence of niches and segments that are exceptions and challenges to mainstream trends and most markedly, the absence of a global super competitor, characteristics that we see in Figure 8.2(b).

## Conflicting Grammars in the Global Economy

Figure 8.2(b) presents a different CAS perspective of the global economy than Figure 8.2(a): again, it is illustrated as a simple three-component network. Using Ernest Gellner's classification, the global economy can be seen as an interaction of three conceptual frameworks: modernism, postmodernism, and fundamentalism. Modernism in Gellner, as in Habermas, is identified with the Renaissance project, the belief in progress based on scientific and technological achievement, a Popperian process of conjecture and refutation, that systematically hones down scientific hypotheses about the world until essential truths are discovered. Gellner conflates postmodernism with the kind of relativism that he sees as permitting many different interpretations; a kind of anything-goes approach. Faith, he conflates with fundamentalism, according to which eternal truths are to be found in scriptures of one kind or another.

The real issue is that we have three alternative organizational grammars, an example of what Wittgenstein called the diversity principle of grammar. Each serves a purpose. Part of the purpose of the modernist discourse is to construct a grammar that enables the laws of nature to be harnessed by technology into work, first mainly manual work, then increasingly into cognitive work that previously had to be performed by human beings. Postmodernism recognizes that alternative organizational grammars exist. Faith, which Gellner conflates wrongly with fundamentalism, has a number of possible bases, including (1) *knowledge by presence*, in which there is no separation, is posited between the observer and the observed: *knowledge by presence* implies that they have become part of the same unity; (2) belief that truths are to be found in the scriptures of one kind or another or for that matter in art or poetry. Gellner interprets the ideas represented in Figure 8.2(b) as contradictory. They represent three alternative grammars and sources of ambiguity since in fact all three hold (even in the individual mind) and govern perception of the world and their interaction is a potential source of chaos, particularly if the relatively simple three-component networks in Figure 8.2(a) and (b) are connected in the larger network pictured in (see the emphasized linkages) in Figure 8.3.

## A Meta Model of Organizational Evolution

Briefly, the elements of a meta model of organizational evolution can be explained an interaction between four CAS: outer dynamics, inner dynamics, payoffs, and organizational grammar. Each of the categories can be considered as a network of interacting elements or nodes, as in Figure 8.3.

*Outer dynamics.* Outer dynamics (*the context of business*) contain factors more or less outside an organization's control: they effect organization but are more or less unaffected by the organization.

*Inner dynamics.* Inner dynamics, sometimes described as *core capabilities, core competencies,* or *dynamic capabilities,* describe the ability of organizations to adapt to outer dynamics. Inner dynamics are made up of an organization's (1) tangible and intangible assets together with (2) managerial dimensions, concerned primarily with decision making.

*Payoffs.* Payoffs are the outcomes produced by organizations for their stakeholders. They include quantitative outcomes, sales, profits, market shares, and rates of return on different assets that relate fundamentally to their owners (shareholders). Though they include qualitative as well as quantitative outcomes and relate to many different stakeholders, the grammar of PRP interprets them in money terms and focuses on shareholder returns.

*Organizational Grammar.* Organizational grammar describes the rules, laws, treaties, agreements, culture, traditions, and conventions that govern the other three components of the meta model: payoffs, outer dynamics,

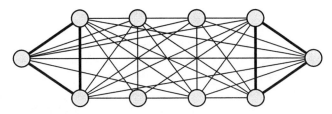

**Figure 8.3**   A complex adaptive system (CAS) as a network.

and inner dynamics. Organizational grammar originates partly from the outside of organizations (determining outer dynamics) and partly inside organizations (inner dynamics). Organizational grammar determines which payoffs the organization focuses on and which stakeholders are considered most important. Most important organizational grammar describes the mindsets of the people who formulate the rules, who make decisions and adapt them afterward. The way people approach problems is partly habitual (conditioned by experience); in other words, they learn ways of adapting to their environment.

As a category in itself, organizational grammar has its own morphology consisting of nodes (formal/informal, social/personal, implicit/explicit rules) and a connecting syntax that binds them. It determines which elements or nodes (morphology) are considered significant in the other three CAS and their connectivity (syntax).

## Global Capitalism in the Meta Model

The primary outer dynamics of global capitalism as described in Figure 8.2(a) are macro economic pressures and technological change. Macro economic pressures induced the United States under the Nixon administration to abandon the system of fixed exchange rates that had ruled since the end of World War II, altering the grammar of international capitalism in favor of market-determined rates. Technological change in the Schumpeterian tradition, changing the competitive landscape, was a further element of outer dynamics. Inner dynamics are represented by the responses of firms and organizations to the change in outer dynamics, searching for new and increased sources of finance, new markets, cheaper materials, and lower cost methods of production. Payoffs from globalized capital are lionized in terms of accelerated economic growth and wealth worldwide and the emergence of the (so-called) new economy in which, unlike the picture of decades previous to the 1990s, rapid growth became consistent with low inflation, which was largely attributable to productivity increases in new economy industries (information, communication, and biotechnologies).

## PROPERTY RIGHTS IN ECONOMIC, SOCIAL, AND POETIC LIFE

Organizational grammar ranges over a number of spectrums, formal/informal, internal external, and individual/social, and can, using Eco's terms, be open or closed in the extent to which it determines outcomes and interpretations. In this section, the grammar of PRP is contrasted with that of the poem Legal Fictions. Two traditions of PRP are outlined, the Schumpeterian and what I term weak form PRP. The terminology is quite loose and the two traditions are not entirely distinct. Thinking about business incorporates elements of both, with the qualification that the current discourse of business and management texts is less likely to emphasize Schumpeterian instability in a capitalist system. PRP discussions, illustrated in Table 8.1, focus on the characteristics of interdependence and adaptation, whereas ambiguity is an essential element of poetry. A third tradition of PRP, which I term strong form PRP, has a much tighter grammar than either the Schumpeterian or the weaker form discussed in this section. Strong form PRP dominates discussions about globalization.

In both versions of PRP, performativity, value for money, and wealth creation are the dominant payoffs. The Schumpeterian version is essentially concerned with growth and instability in capitalism in contrast to PRP versions that are concerned primarily with efficiency and optimality in a more static sense. Technology is emphasized in the Schumpeterialn tradition as an outer dynamic. PRP puts more emphasis upon the importance of the consumer and of choice. In both, competitive dynamics, together with the two fundamental assumptions of weak form PRP, outlined above (A1, the existence of markets, and A2, individually rational behavior) underlie the connectivity (syntax) of capitalism. In the Schumpeterian version, outer dynamics are dominant. PRP weak and strong give more credence to the ability of capitalist firms to adapt, stressing notions of core and dynamic capabilities and generally the possibility of creating self-adaptive inner dynamics, based on certain aspects of grammar, especially routines, architectures, and corporate culture.

## Property Rights in Schumpeter

In the dynamics of Schumpeter, the two distinguishing features are private property ownership and the existence of a debt market enabling savings to be channeled into investment. Private ownership furnishes incentives to accumulate wealth and accumulation is the result of technological change (new processes, products markets) by an innovating class of entrepreneurs. The drive to innovation and accumulation together with competition are the outer dynamics of capitalism. Inner dynamics are reflected in the organization's positioning with respect to demand and resources and the variability and adaptability of its asset base. Processes are Darwinian: adaptation to outer dynamics is the result of random variation within inner dynamics; access to valuable assets and entrepreneurial management. Grammar is reflected in the selection processes that are described in Figure 8.4. In fact, the figure can be seen as summarizing much of the content of a modern text in corporate strategy. Firms seek competitive advantage, a concept attributed to Michael Porter that has a Schumpeterian heritage. Other firms copy their activities, rivalry sets in and competitive advantage and survival are threatened. Entry barriers, especially advantages of large-scale production can delay the forces of competition only temporarily and the organization can only survive in the long term through innovation. Those who innovate successfully survive and achieve competitive advantage, but are exposed to the same competitive processes again and again. Those who fail to innovate sooner or later are selected out, eliminated, and their resources are freed up for more productive use.

Hence we have the restless creative destruction of capitalism. In modern terminology Schumpeter saw capitalism itself as a complex adaptive system, but the capabilities of adaptation at the organizational level were seen by Schumpeter to be limited by the capacity to innovate. Eventually Schumpeter saw capitalism as collapsing in on itself largely as a result of intellectuals' disillusion with the system. Underlying Schumpeter's analysis was (1) a theory of growth dependent on innovation and entrepreneurship and (2) a theory of instability, resulting from bunching of technological change, which gave rise to long waves of prosperity and depression. Payoffs in the Schumpeterian system take a monetary form of accumulated wealth and profit and a stream of new products. As each wave became exhausted the rate accumulation of wealth and profit and therefore consumption tended to fall, only to be rejuvenated at some later date by a fresh bout of technological change and innovation.

## Property Rights in Weak Form PRP

This version of property rights is concerned with the static properties of an economic and social system: in Lyotard's terms concerned with *performativity*. Although it is not often recognized, the approach of mainstream economics has always been evolutionary. In modern terminology we could describe the various neoclassical approaches as versions of CAS. However, the evolutionary properties of capitalism have been disguised by the assumption that markets are efficient and clear rapidly (demand and supply close up rapidly in response to price signals) so things are basically in equilibrium. Following Alfred Marshall, conventional (but not Keynesian) economics has followed a comparative static approach according to which shifts in outer dynamics (income, taste, technological change, government policy, and so on) result in adjustments of demand and supply the inner dynamics. Payoffs are basically monetary, through prices, wages, and profits: if they accrue to individuals with private property rights then an incentive exists to put resources to their highest valued use. The incentive mechanism provided by PRP provides the grammar of the system.

Both weak and strong form PRP draw on Ricardian rent theory. In Ricardo, rent is a surplus accruing to scarce fertile land. The most fertile land earns the most rent and a gradation of rental values exists corresponding to gradations of fertility down to marginal land, which just covers costs of production. Ricardian rent has been generalized to a return to any scarce resource, or more precisely the firm's ability to link resources and create the quality of self-adaptation out of interdependence, emergent properties that enable the firm to sustain its competitive advantage: The notion of capability replaces fertility in a set of theories that are generally classified under the heading of resource-based theories, but which actually form a subset of a more general theory, that of CAS. In turn, theories stressing the importance of capabilities and self-adaptation can be broken down into three groups that probably overlap: (1) those that stress the importance of the ownership of scarce assets tangible or intangible: natural resources, proprietary resources from patents, or special relationships with customers (governments or private), brands and reputation; (2) those emphasizing knowledge; and (3) those emphasizing the ability of a firm to learn. All three fit into the general class of CAS, in which linkages (synergies or complementarities) between assets tangible or intangible, physical or human give the capacity to adapt inner dynamics to ever-changing outer dynamics.

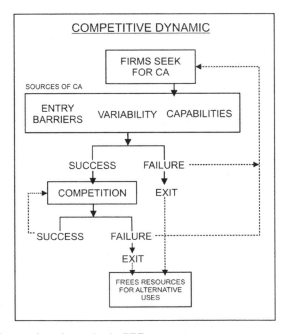

**Figure 8.4**  Competitve dynamics in PRP.

## EMPSON'S POEM

Legal Fiction

Law makes long spokes of short stakes of men.
Your well fenced out real estate of mind
No high flat of the nomad citizen
Looks over, or train leaves behind.

Your rights extend under and above your claim
Without bound; you own land in Heaven and Hell;
Your part is of earth's surface and mass the same,
Of all cosmos' volume, and all stars as well.

Your rights reach down where all owners meet, in Hell's
Pointed exclusive conclave, at earth's centre
(Your spun farm's root still on that axis dwells);
And up, through galaxies, a growing sector.

You are nomad yet; the lighthouse beam you own
Flashes, like Lucifer, through the firmament.
Earth's axis varies; your dark central cone
Wavers, a candle's shadow, at the end.

In the poem, which is reproduced below the property rights, conceit is pushed to absurdity. The image is of the earth's surface as the face of a cone and private property ownership being defined not only at the surface but stretching the throughout the cone to the ("still on that axis. . .") point of the cone at the center of the earth ("Hells/Pointed exclusive conclave. . .") and upward infinitely in an expanding cone ("through galaxies, a growing sector") into the stars and the heavens. Inner and outer dynamics merge in the poem. The grammar is partly that of geometry.

Geometrically, property cannot be overlooked ("no high flat. . . . Looks over"; see a in Figure 8.5) and in the shadow of an expanding cone it cannot be left behind (by "no train. . ."; see b in Figure 8.5). And as in the global economy the citizen is a "nomad." The text is open, stretching over time and space, rational and irrational. In the conceit, private property rights range over the conscious, rational world ("well fenced out real estate of mind. . ."), to the dreamlike Dantesque underworld of the unconscious ("where all owners meet") in Hell or Paradise at the end of time. In the lighthouse image the cone is first transformed into a lighthouse beam, wavering at the still point of the spinning cone at earth's core (ironically the image puts the earth and the temporary owner at the center of the universe), then into shadow candlelight (echoing Macbeth's "out brief candle, life is but a walking shadow, a poor player that struts and frets his hour upon

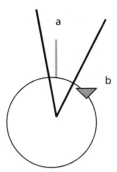

**Figure 8.5**  The geometry of legal fictions.

the stage and then is heard no more. . .") that is extinguished along with the legal fiction of property ownership "at the end": the ultimate payoff in the currency of "Heaven and Hell" and yet of light ("the lighthouse beam you own").

The poem is playful. Empson notes that General Pit-Rivers, a great archaeologist with a large estate in Wilshire in the early part of the 20th century, shot down a plane with an elephant gun, killing the pilot, but was acquitted of murder at Winchester Assizes on the grounds it was trespassing. So the law had to be changed.

The organizational grammar in the poem is loose and open. In that it is sensitively dependent upon reader responses, it is chaotic. In Figure 8.6 the morphology (nodes) are linked through metaphor and the map of connectivity is to a great extent arbitrary. Figure 8.6 presents only one of many interpretative maps, and even to assets as it does, that this is the territory, is to invite contradiction.

## STRONG FORM PRP

The current discourse of modern globalization is based on a strong form of PRP. According to this, private property ownership, free and efficient markets globally in labour, capital, goods and finance results in an optimal situation with respect (1) to the allocation of resources for income and wealth creation and (2) to the growth of income and wealth. The narrative is as follows. Differences in wealth and income internationally are eliminated by free movement of physical capital (FDI) to areas of relatively low wages and resource prices. This process is augmented under universal free markets by free movement of cheap labor and resources in the other direction to high wage price areas. Movements in both directions reduce wages and prices where they are relatively high and raise them where they are relatively low.

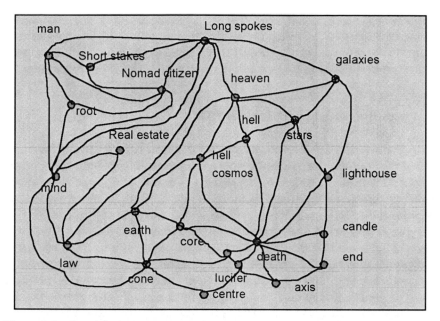

**Figure 8.6** Legal fictions as a network.

Similarly, free movement of financial capital enables investment funds to be channeled to those areas where rates of return on investment are highest. Thus not only is the allocation of resources for income and wealth optimal in a static sense but the growth of income and wealth is maximized.

Even leaving aside the potential for chaos in CAS, illustrated in Figure 8.2(b), this narrative of globalization has many gaps even within its own discourse; issues of fairness, distribution, future generations, ecological issues (entropy, social costs, pollution, emissions), principal agent problems, exploitation of monopoly power.

## Efficient Markets

An assumption in management texts, especially in finance, is that stock markets give accurate information (immediately in the case of strong form efficiency, or in the medium to longer term in the case of strong form efficiency), about the capabilities of organizations (their assets and management) and their fitness to adapt. Information efficiency is carried over to prices on all markets; wages and other resource prices reflect (marginal) productivity, product prices reflect opportunity costs (plus perhaps a markup, the rationale for monopoly regulation), stock prices follow a random walk dictated by outer dynamics, the cost of debt on the market reflects the opportunity cost of capital. The efficiency properties of PRP are contingent on market efficiency. The legitimacy of the assumption is deeply questionable. It constitutes a legal fiction in itself (Soros, Buffett). As Mandelbrot points out, movements in stock prices do not look as if they are random.

## Fairness Inequality and Strong PRP

In the argument for private property based on A3, an efficient or optimal allocation of resources is one where it is impossible to make one person better off without making another worse off in material terms (Pareto optimality). Efficiency is defined in terms of the need to get more for less, or *performativity*. The question as to whether the allocation of property rights was just or not, or whether some are favored above others, is by A4 a separate ethical issue best decided by individuals according to A5. That some individuals may be unable to bid for the use of a resource simply through lack of funds and hence are disadvantaged itself is considered a question partly of chance and choice and partly something that can be remedied by investment in education. Underlying the entire argument is A5, that individuals exercising their private property rights on the market should be the ultimate judges, free to exploit resources, conserving them or not.

## Future Generations and Strong PRP

Will one generation provide for another? The individual is the best judge, A5. With respect to future generations, consider any given time horizon. Divide the future time horizons into discrete periods. It is elementary that optimization over the entire time horizon requires optimization within the discrete periods. If income and wealth generation is suboptimal in period 1 with respect to period 2, because, for example, there is too much consumption in period 1 relative to saving and investment for period 2, According to A1 and A2, investment will be increased (and consumption reduced) in period 1 and investment will be reduced in period 2 (and consumption increased). A6 permits this to happen. So provided the propositions hold, the situation is optimal in every period.

The problem faced by current generations is to maximize present value, A1. This means discounting future income streams. The higher the discount rate, the less we value the future. But discount rates reflect the evaluation of risks and the time preferences of individual decision makers,. They may turn out to be wrong, to miscalculate, but does an agency exist (governmental, intergovernmental) capable of making better guesses than current private property owner? The answer, according to A5, is no.

## Distribution and Strong PRP

Many distributions of income and wealth between individuals and between generations are optimal. Issues of distribution, justice, and efficiency issues are separated by A4. A3 as a definition of optimality simply requires that it is impossible to make one individual better off without making another worse off: there are no gains to be made from trade using A1 and A2. There may be infinitely many such distributions, but given the universality of markets differences and wages and prices for a given quality of labor and resources will tend to be eliminated by free movements of labor, goods, and financial and physical capital.

## Sunk Costs of Investment and Strong PRP

Similarly, some resources do not lend themselves to pricing in an ordinary way. Here we are speaking of a problem akin to that of public goods. Once they are in existence, use of the flow of services from them does not deplete them, and the variable cost associated with using them may be negligible or even zero; assets such as capital goods, reputation, an educated workforce fits into this category equally well as traditional public goods, education, knowledge, communication networks, a sustainable environment. Hence they should be free or at least provided at low (marginal) cost. But is there a cost of creating them in the first place and how are the creators to be recompensed? How are people to be motivated to provide them? If they are not then the existence of such public goods, however necessary,

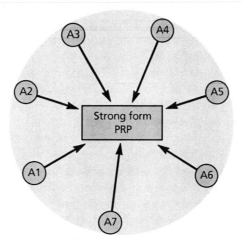

**Figure 8.7** PRP as a legal fiction.

is threatened. Governments traditionally take over such responsibilities, paying for the creation of public or merit goods by taxes, and providing through government provision through subsidized private provision. For this weak link in PRP we must look to the Coase theorem below.

## Entropy and Strong PRP

Essentially transactions with the environment involve not only and not even primarily exchanges of private property rights between individuals as envisaged by A2, but transactions with nature in which low entropy is withdrawn from nature in exchange for high entropy (pollution and waste). A5 rules this consideration out. Instead markets between individuals for environmental resources can be arranged by, for example, transferable licenses: a proposal being considered internationally as a solution to environmental issues. In such a system, as environmental resources become increasingly scarce, so licenses become increasingly valuable providing an incentive under A1 and A2 to conserve the license and hence the environment to which it relates. Perhaps national governments may license private agencies market such licenses. As to those resources that must remain common property, the oceans, national parks, the firmament, they are considered part of human rights. Again we must look to the Coase theorem set out below.

## The Coase Theorem and Strong PRP

Private property rights envisage exclusive rights over the use of a resource. And exclusivity is difficult to achieve in an interdependent world. Many actions by one set of individuals affect others; the exercise of private property rights often treats the private property of others as if it were free when it is not, thus failing to take into account true values. This is the essence of the externality problem.

To deal with such issues within the PRP framework, Ronald Coase (1960) extended the lPRP grammar: the Coase theorem. We can divide the theorem into two parts; reciprocity and efficiency.

Consider reciprocity first. If individual 1's activity harms individual 2, so preventing individual 1's activity harms individual 1. Using examples from Coase and Pigou, landering cattle, sparks from steam engines, noise from laundries and (if their papers had been written later) carbon emissions harms others farmers, households near laundries, and the community generally, preventing cattle from using open ranges, curbing railroads, or carbon emissions, shutting laundries, also creates harm to cattle owners, railroad or laundry users, and consumers of goods and services whose production needs carbon. The important thing for Coase was the creation of property rights, not their apportionment to individuals: A3, A4, A5.

On efficiency, Pigou suggested tax and subsidy solutions to such problems: tax the polluter or pay a subsidy to reduce pollution. Coase pointed to the incentives to create markets if the benefits of so doing exceed the costs (transaction costs). The incentive is contingent on the existence of private property rights: all that matters is that someone possesses them. So whether the property rights are held by the farmer or the rancher, the farmer or the railroad, the laundry or its neighbor is immaterial. So long as they were held as private property, the incentive exists to set up markets to deal with the problem. Property rights can be traded and opportunity costs considered. The theorem can be extended almost indefinitely; to the problems of wandering cattle, railroads operating near wheat land, pollution problems generally.

## Transaction Costs, Coase, and Strong PRP

If property rights can be can be bought and sold, the price at which they are bought and sold will reflect the competing valuations of the parties concerned. If the value of the herd is increased more by cattle feeding on crops than the market value of the crops, then cattle will be permitted to wander and graze: if the value of the products produced with the use of hydro carbons exceeds the perceived damage to the community, than firms will be allowed to pollute. Alternatives to markets do exist and these will be considered. Fences can be built, alternative fuels can be used by railroads or corporations, fuel-efficient production methods can be invented and there is an incentive to take up these alternatives, provided they can be adopted more cheaply than (the cost of) the damage they are designed to prevent. In other words, given PRP individuals have the incentive to provide the cheapest solutions. All solutions may involve as part of their cost transactions costs (including information, policing, and implementation costs associated with alternative solutions). Thus given private property, market solutions will be adopted A1 if they are the cheapest; if not, other solutions will be adopted. If the pollution (externality) persists under PRP, this is because the costs of eliminating it exceeds the damage it does. In any case, the PRP provides an optimal solution.

## Ownership, Control, and Monopoly Power under Strong PRP

The principal agent problem are disposed of in the same way. Managers (agents) may have an incentive not to put the resources they control to their highest valued uses from the owners' or stockholders' (principals) point of view. Managers may carry out policies that maximize their own utility rather than that of the owners, or workers who take too much leisure during their work time, a problem quaintly called shirking. Again the Coase theorem as set out in the previous section can be applied. In this case it involves apportioning ownership rights to managers, to workers, and to owners, in such a way that their income and wealth increases alongside that of the organization they manage. Again if the problem persists under PRP, the costs of eliminating it must exceed the damage. Essentially issues of the exploitation of monopoly power and sunk costs can be dealt with in the same way.

## Monetization

As noted in an earlier section, payoffs can take many forms and strictly A2 requires maximization of utility. Utility is a common denominator reducing different payoffs to a commensurable quantity. Unfortunately, what people exchange on markets is not utility (or payoffs) but money in exchange for goods, services, or payoffs. These may be reducible to utility but not to money. Hence to assume the possibility of A1 we must assume that everything can be expressed in money; this is what is meant by monetization. Incentives systems of all kinds referred to in previous paragraphs and thus the efficiency aspects of strong PRP depends on this assumption. To some extent monetization can be handled through the Coase theorem. Things will be monetized, provided the expected benefits exceed the costs of doing so. However, monetization is perhaps the weakest link in the PRP edifice.

## Strong PRP Creates Long Spokes from the Short Stakes of Man

We have an imposing grammar: a closed text illustrated in Figure 8.6. If markets exist, things are optimal. If markets don't exist, then provided the freedom to create private property rights exist, things are optimal too, since the fact that they don't exist means that the (transaction) costs of setting them up must exceed the benefits of so doing. In the case of public goods provide governments have the obligation to create private property rights, intellectual property rights, patents, for example, then the sunk costs associated with investments can be recouped. On exactly the same principle as that of externalities, the problem is reciprocal and the issue is one of the existence of property rights not their distribution to one individual or another. In cases where private property rights don't exist, then A1 ensures the obligation of the government to create them and offer them on the market by A2, then provided the anticipated benefits exceed the costs they will be bought and sold and their nonexistence implies that the costs of creating and enforcing them, transaction costs exceed the anticipated benefits.

## CONCLUDING REMARKS

This chapter relates ideas from several disciplines using concepts of organizational grammar, consciousness, complex adaptive systems, and openness. The degree of openness is related directly to the degree of complexity: the greater the complexity, the greater the openness and the greater the degree of connectivity in the organizational grammar. In terms of the meta model or framework outlined in the chapter, openness is associated with a relatively loose organizational grammar with connectivity between categories of the model inner dynamics outer dynamics, and payoffs being as marked as connectivity within them. It determines the categories that are considered, accepting some and neglecting others. Organizational grammar imposes a pattern. A loose grammar permits multiple interpretations, ambiguity, high degrees of information, and surprise: the meaning it imposes is emergent, contingent upon the response, the essential outer dynamic being the reader him- or herself. In that it contains information,

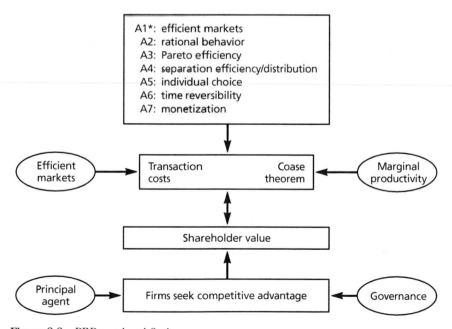

**Figure 8.8** PRP as a legal fiction.

the pattern of a loose organizational grammar is chaotic, not random; every part of the pattern has a meaning in itself. Many different grammars are capable of organizing the same data and it is tempting to say that there is no data unless there is organizational grammar. It acts like a map that determines an entire landscape in a territory that consists of many landscapes; rather than being a map of a landscape, it is a map that is the landscape. In the sense that alternative organizational grammars exist, a particular grammar veils the territory. Consciousness is defined in the chapter as awareness of the organizational grammar. Consciousness is a process of unveiling, in Sufic terms *kashf*.

Property rights are central to the definition and interpretation of globalization. Four legal fictions with different degrees of openness have been discussed. The most open is the poem Legal Fiction itself, with immense scope for interpretation and categorization of its elements in terms of the meta model as a set of discrete categories would shackle its interpretation unacceptably. Of the legal fiction, property rights appear in the literature, the Schumpeterian version is the most open and complex. According to the model capitalism is driven mostly by outer dynamics of technology and competition, and essentially the grammar of this version of property rights consists of A1 and A2, the existence of markets and rational behavior.

The Schumpeterian version of property rights is distinguished from weak and strong form PRP. Weak form PRP allows for the self-adaptation of organizations within the capitalism (inner dynamics may be self-adaptive), rather than as in the Schumpeterian version, permitting self-adaptation at the level of the system as a whole. The focus of weak and strong form PRP is on efficiency, rather than on growth and instability emphasized by Schumpeter.

Strong form PRP underlies the current interpretation of globalization, as it does the discourse of management, both in business itself and in business schools. Unconsciously it imposes a tight organizational grammar upon business policy and analysis. The theoretical apparatus of management is based upon the relationships discussed in the previous section and illustrated in Figure 8.8. The chapter has been concerned with deconstructing the organizational grammar of strong form PRP.

## REFERENCES

Bak, P. (1997). *How nature works: The science of self organized criticality.* Oxford, UK: Oxford University Press.

Bak, P., & Chen, K. (1991, January). Self organized criticality. *Scientific American*, pp. 26–33.

Coase, R. (1960, October). The problem of social costs. *Journal of Law and Economics*, 1–44.

Eldridge, N., & Gould, S. J. (1971). Punctuated equilibrium: An alternative to phyletic gradualism. In T. J. M. Schopf (Ed.), *Models of Paleobiology* (pp. 82–115), New York: Freeman and Cooper.

Haffenden J. (2000). *The complete poems of William Empson.* London: Penguin.

Izutsu, T. (1960). *Sufism and Taoism.* Berkeley: University of California Press.

Jensen, H. J. (1998). *Self organized criticality.* Cambridge: Cambridge University Press.

Kalansuriya, A. D. P. (1987). *A philosophical analysis of Buddhist notions: The Buddha and Wittgenstein.* Delhi: Sru Satguru.

Kauffman, S. (1993). *The origins of order: Self organization and selection in evolution.* New York: Oxford University Press.

Koch C. (1998). *The quest for consciousness.* New York: Roberts and Company.

Matthews, R. (1998). The myth of global competition and the nature of work. *Journal of Change Management, 11*(5) 378–398.

Pettersson, M. (1996). *Complexity and evolution.* Cambridge: Cambridge University Press.

Pinker, S. (2000). *Words and rules: The ingredients of language.* New York: Basic Books.

Searle, J. R. (1995). The mystery of consciousness. *New York Review of Books, 42*(17).

Simon, H. A. (1996). *The sciences of the artificial.* Cambridge, MA: MIT Press.

Suzuki, D. (1934). *Essays in Zen Buddhism: Third series.* York Beach, ME: Samuel Weiser, Inc. 1953. Edited by Christmas Humphreys.

CHAPTER 9

# MONSTERS OF ACCOUNTING

## An Ante-Ethics Approach

**Alexis A. Downs**
**Rita A. Durant**
**William L. Smith**

## INTRODUCTION

Ours is a story of ante-ethics, a place before competence got split off from emotion and logic. With ante-ethics, we try to imagine an anterior condition. We imagine a time before Aristotle, a time before he split apart the triad of competence, reason, and emotion. For Aristotle, Ethos described how well the speaker convinced the audience that he or she was qualified to speak on the particular subject; Pathos was an appeal to the audience's emotions; and Logos was the logical appeal. The logical appeal relied on facts and figures, on data which would be difficult to manipulate, especially if from a trusted source. Logos enhanced ethos. However, a logical appeal could mislead and could be inaccurate. Use of facts and figures to confuse and/or convince the audience disturbs the otherwise clear relationship between what is and what is represented.

*Critical Theory Ethics for Business and Public Administration*, pages 185–209
Copyright © 2008 by Information Age Publishing
**185**

Maybe Aristotle caused our "issues" in accounting and ethics when he split ethos from logos. Accountants are positioned to (or pretend to, if you are critical) guard the true order. On the other hand, accountants earn their fees through their efforts to construct and forge the distinctions that help us identify and account for ourselves and others. Therefore, in order to imagine a time before Aristotle and effectively locate authority in relatedness, we look at what happens when an accountant faces blurred boundaries: contradiction, separation, and transformation. Unification of ethos (ethics) with logos (categories of facts and figures) depends on being *both* separate *and* unified in a greater whole, and the abjection that accompanies this dialectic. As we look to the reintegration of logos and ethos, we find the need to include pathos. We call this trinitarian communion ante-ethics.

In our story, we hope to undermine the myth of clear distinctions in order to highlight the gray area as a place of meeting and honoring *both* the light of consciousness and language and health *and* the darkness of incompetence, lack, and isolation. In the Volunteer Income Tax Assistance (VITA) site, foreigners transgress boundaries. Order is elusive. Using critical theory's charge to look inward, we turn to Kristeva's (1982, 1991) counsel to find the stranger within. We begin with a story about an accountant who is trying to do the right thing.

## THE STORY: TRYING TO DO THE RIGHT THING

On a Tuesday evening between 5:00 and 8:00 p.m., Alexis and student volunteers carried five laptops to a church across the street from the university and assembled a Volunteer Income Tax Assistance (VITA) clinic, which is a U.S. Internal Revenue Service (IRS)–sponsored program designed to provide free tax preparation services to low-income taxpayers, including those who require assistance in applying for an earned income tax credit (EITC). Taxpayers who seek the credit face the daunting task of tackling the 58-page IRS Publication 596, "Earned Income Credit, for use in preparing their 2005 federal income tax returns." The incentive for figuring out how to file for the refundable credit is the potential of up to $4,400 available to a family with two or more children, amounts lauded as "successful in lifting millions of persons out of poverty" (http://www.maldef.org/publications/pdf/EITC.pdf). In addition, some states, including Kansas, offer a state EITC as well.

As clients appeared with their documents—Forms W-2, 1098, 1099, etc.—student volunteers began to chorus: "Alexis, Alexis, could you look at this?" The students expected prompt, clear, cogent responses, responses she didn't always have. For example, some time in late February, two Romanian students arrived at the VITA clinic. Alexis was not familiar with the filing

requirements for nonresident aliens, nor had she addressed those requirements in any class she taught or had taken. She had never prepared a Form
1040NR, which is the appropriate form to report the taxable income of
nonresident aliens. Furthermore, although the student volunteers received
the IRS-provided manuals and successfully completed an online test, they
didn't learn about the form and the myriad, related requirements. Alexis's
ethical obligations to serve those who came to her for help clashed with
her ethical obligations to provide clear answers. She was in a conundrum,
and part of the problem was that she was dealing with boundary-crossing
issues.

Insofar as the VITA program is aimed at low-income taxpayers, these
students as low-income taxpayers qualified for assistance. Insofar as they
were non-resident aliens, assistance was problematic. Like countless other
foreign students, they received relatively small stipends from the university
and, thus, had received their Forms W-2, which report wages earned. In addition, some foreign students also received Forms 1042-S, which appeared
to report income that was not taxable due to a tax treaty between the U.S.
and a foreign country. However, some Forms 1042-S indicated that taxes
had been withheld.

If the income was not taxable, Alexis wondered, why were taxes withheld? Lacking Internet access on her laptops, she acquired permission to
borrow the church office computer to look up the tax treaty on the U.S.
Internal Revenue Service website. Based on the instructions found there
for completing the Form 1040NR, she directed the student volunteer to
prepare Form 1040NR. A few weeks later, after completing more Forms
1040NR in the same way, Alexis "googled" Form 1040NR and found that
several universities had posted relatively simple, Form 1040NR instructions.
When another Romanian student appeared, Alexis instructed the student
volunteer to follow the procedures indicated on the other universities' websites. The student left, but returned an hour later, saying that she didn't get
as great a refund as her fellow Romanian students. Alexis replied that she
would look into it, though she felt inadequate to the task of solving "the
Romanian problem." In addition, she felt irritated. Six years of public accounting experience as a tax preparer as well as a half dozen university tax
classes and continuing education didn't seem to have prepared her for the
Romanian students and their relatively miniscule refund amounts.

Alexis is a CPA and an Associate Professor in Accounting and embodies the rights and duties of station, as explicated in the published rules
and principles that regulate the behavior of CPAs (Cooper, 2004). In addition, Alexis follows requirements of the state, Oklahoma, in which she
is licensed. (See https://www.ok.gov/oab/docs/admin_code_clean.pdf.)
Furthermore, the Code of Professional Conduct of the American Institute
of Certified Public Accountants (AICPA) consists of two sections: Princi-

ples and Rules. (See http://www.aicpa.org/about/code/index.html.) The Principles include the following articles: (1) In carrying out their responsibilities as professionals, members should exercise sensitive professional and moral judgments in all their activities; (2) Members should accept the obligation to act in a way that will serve the *public interest* [italics ours], honor the *public trust*, and demonstrate commitment to professionalism; (3) To maintain and broaden public confidence, members should perform all professional responsibilities with the highest sense of integrity; (4) A member should maintain objectivity and be free of conflicts of interest in discharging professional responsibilities. A member in public practice should be independent in fact and appearance when providing auditing and other attestation services; (5) A member should observe the profession's technical and ethical standards, strive continually to improve competence and the quality of services, and discharge professional responsibility to the best of the member's ability; (6) A member in public practice should observe the Principles of the Code of Professional Conduct in determining the scope and nature of services to be provided.

As she supervised the VITA clinic, Alexis attempted to carry out her responsibilities to the public interest. In the enactment of the clinic, her mediatory tools—such as laptops, Internet, instructions, assistants, forms, training, feedback, and ethical rules—created their own sets of problems. One tool in particular, the Internet, widely touted as the way to simplify filing, required numerous mediatory tools for its successful use. For example, the clients had to sign hard copies of Form 8453, U.S. Individual Income Tax Declaration for an IRS e-file Return, which Alexis then mailed to the IRS. Unfortunately, email notification of any errors arrived days later, when the clients were long gone, causing Alexis to spend additional time attempting to contact the clients either by phone or letter as most clients did not have or did not provide e-mail addresses. If the tax refund or balance due changed, the client had to return to the clinic to sign another Form 8453. Also, because each Form 8453 submitted needed to include the clinic's electronic filing identification number (EFIN) and a unique taxpayer document control number (DCN), Alexis could only get the DCNs from the DCN reports, which were generated only after the returns had been electronically transmitted. In lieu of Form 8453, some clinics used client PINS; however, in order to use a PIN, the client must have the prior year's adjusted gross income (AGI), which most clients did not have or provide. Unlike paid preparers, a VITA clinic is not authorized to retain client records, so during the 2005 tax season, Alexis's clinic did not have any prior year client tax information.

Alexis's lived experience is the antithesis of order insofar as she was unable to obtain and, therefore, provide clear and unambiguous answers to facilitate proper representation and reporting of individuals' income. Like

Bateson's (1972) double bind, her situation was one in which no matter what she did, she would violate an ethical trust: to her clients and students when she didn't have the answer easily at hand; to the students in her accounting classes when she spent the inordinate amount of time required to track down VITA solutions and less on class preparation; to the clinic when she accepted clients she was unprepared to help; and to herself as she grew increasingly anxious about how to conduct the research upon which her university tenure depended. She couldn't win.

Although VITA was designed to help low-income taxpayers who qualify for EITC, Alexis suspected that many of her potential clients went to RAL (refund anticipation loan) providers to obtain instant refunds—although at usurious rates. Such RAL providers include H&R Block (Maull, 2006) and certain auto dealers who encourage taxpayers to use RALs as down payments for car purchases (MacDonald, 2006). In addition, banks provide checking accounts to taxpayers who previously did not have accounts and who now need accounts for direct deposits of refunds. Banks, while ostensibly acquainting taxpayers with the world of finance, will benefit from any mistakes made by these unsophisticated taxpayers: fees for overdraft protection and for insufficient funds are profitable (Berenson, 2003). She felt overwhelmed and anxious, caught in the double bind of being responsible for successful client outcomes but lacking the resources available to paid preparers.

According to Bateson (1972), the general characteristics of a double bind are the following: (1) The individual is in a situation in which she feels it is vitally important to respond appropriately; (2) the individual's correspondent is expressing two orders of messages, and the one message denies the other; (3) the individual feels unable to comment on the messages. Paradoxically, resolution of double binds accompanies learning. So, in Alexis's case, she acknowledged the importance of competent tax preparation and the importance of serving the public interest; she experienced a Code of Ethics that seemed to offer two different messages: competence and service. However, the injunction to serve was at odds with competency. And the dilemma seemed inexpressible because to express it was to admit failure.

Although VITA's processes differ in important ways from those typical of accounting, such as retaining client records, its ethical tools and constraints are similar. As a public servant, Alexis's role was to commit herself to the needs of others, while, as an objective member with integrity, she was required to stand apart from the public. Alexis's story, therefore, provides a lens through which to critically examine broader issues of accounting and ethics. In order to proceed, we touch briefly on observations about the dual imperatives of ethics, and then we use activity theory (e.g., Engestrom, 1987) as a model for understanding how the individual is embedded in larger social systems. Finally, we examine the issues of accounting and ethics in terms of the "foreign" as explicated by Douglas (1966) and Kristeva (1982).

## (AT LEAST) TWO PLACES AT ONCE:
## ETHICS AND ACTIVITY SYSTEMS

Confronted with the ambiguities of the VITA site, Alexis experienced the weakness of an ethical code of conduct that places primary emphasis on individual agency (Yuthas, Dillard, & Rogers, 2004). The AICPA Code of Ethics charges the individual to be responsible for enforcing and maintaining ethics. This position is consistent with Western moral philosophy, which examines the choices of a rational human being. Accordingly, most business ethics texts charge the individual with making the best possible decision in accordance with the professional code of ethics. Nevertheless, as Yuthas et al. (2004) observe, structural forces and power asymmetry of the larger community constrain individual action.

Reilly and Kyj (1994) point out that ethics requires both (1) that the individual economic man rationally maximizes his individual self-interest and (2) that affective normative bonds can be fostered and maintained in accordance with social responsibility. As Alexis encountered the world of volunteer tax preparation, she was expected to be both a separate agent with objectivity and integrity and an obedient servant to collectives, such as associations and the public interest. In addition to principles, the ethical code specifies institutional rules, which "tell us in an immediate, concrete way what we ought to believe in a local situation and how we ought to behave" (Cooper, 2004, p. 21). In a problematic situation, the accountant turns to the rules for specific guidance; furthermore, the rules—not the principles—are enforced. The rules of the AICPA Code of Ethics, described above, first call for a metaphorical ontological boundary between self and others: for example, Independence (Rule 101) and Integrity and Objectivity (Rule 102). Boundaries that locate the accountant on the same side as the client are only provided by Rule 201's additional call to provide Professional Competence and Due Professional Care and Rule 301's protection of Confidential Client Information.

Therefore, for Alexis, while Principle 2 required her to serve the public, the rules asked her to set herself apart from the community. In addition to the AICPA Code of Professional Conduct, Alexis was particularly challenged by the Statements on Standards for Tax Services (SSTS) 6, an enforceable standard issued by the AICPA for tax practitioners: "The member must advise the taxpayer promptly, regardless of whether the member prepared or signed the return in question, when he or she learns of an error in a previously filed tax return" (Raabe, Whittenburg, & Sanders, 2006, p. 21); she is not to notify the IRS of any error without the consent of the client. Given the constraints of the VITA situation, Alexis would have difficulty locating and notifying a client if she found that a previously filed return contained an error.

The principles and rules may be well intentioned, but in effect they put Alexis in a double bind: to serve the public and, as an individual CPA, to separate herself from the public. The problem she faced was that of boundaries: not only where to draw the line concerning which forms, signatures, and errors, but also more fundamentally, whether her identity lay "with or against" the collective. Additionally, ethics is nearly always expressed in terms of the agency of the individual, particularly "given the absence of consideration of what is normally termed 'politics'" (Parker, 2003, p. 201). This is a legacy of the individualistic values inherent in both positivism and structuralism: To know something is to stand outside it; the boundaries separating inside from outside simultaneously demarcate better from worse. Furthermore, the resultant rationalism eschews any emotions (pathos). One who is an agent is responsible for maintaining separation from and superiority over the environment and its social and worldly contents, while serving the "Other," who must therefore be kept *both* at bay *and* ready to contribute to the needs of the "Self." Further, the self–other boundary is complicated by the multiple ways of defining oneself. One theory that considers the multiple levels of identity is that of activity systems. We turn to Engestrom's (1987) model of activity systems in order to locate the individual within larger systems and to examine the contradictions that propel movements and the tools that mediate relationships between and among individuals and systems.

## ACTIVITY SYSTEMS MODEL

Yrjo Engestrom and the Center for Activity Theory and Developmental Work Research at the University of Helsinki developed the activity system model from Soviet activity theory, which focused on the multilevel interaction of embedded individual psychological systems; economic and cultural, historical and institutional contexts; and the tools that emerge to mediate the interactions. The concept of an activity expands learning beyond narrow, individualistic, cognitive development. According to early theorists, such as Vygotsky and Leont'ev, "activities" are (1) mediated, (2) collective, and (3) driven by contradictions (Engestrom, 1987). Language is a mediatory tool, as are any systems created to bridge the individual and the collective: electronic and ethical systems, job roles, etc.

Any task, including ethical accounting practice, can only be understood in the context of its activity system—the interconnected system of tools, individual psychological and cognitive traits, voice and speech genres, culture, and society. Such activity systems experience the systemic contradictions and disturbances among its different entities, which trigger—according to Engestrom (1987)—unpredictable emotional and cognitive disturbances, which, in turn, give rise to more tools. Tools are, in part, solutions to problems of the need to account for ourselves in a collective, but, once implemented, the tools become entities that change the original systems, which then require further mediation. The inference that the tools, therefore, are perfectly rational, self-evident, and independent is flawed. It is exactly because the tools are disconnected from the context, as a number system is independent of the items that are counted, that the tool itself requires mediation.

In the case of VITA, computers and e-filing have changed tax preparation. For example, preparers no longer need to understand the whole form; they just transfer numbers from one form, a W-2, to another form, a 1040. Computer software prompts the preparer, such that the preparer retrieves a number from a given box on the W-2 and enters it appropriately in the computer. However, preparation of the Form 1040NR is not seamless. In our story about the international students, complications arose because some forms, such as the Form 1042-S, were unfamiliar to students and to Alexis. Although the software accommodated the preparation of Form 1040NR, the software did not clearly prompt the preparer. When Alexis looked at the Form 1040NR instructions that were provided by the universities' website, she was in effect seeking instructions for instructions, or tools upon tools. In addition, Forms 1040NR cannot be e-filed. Consequently, Alexis needed different processes for preparation of Forms 1040NR.

Forms and instructions are tools; instructions for instructions become tools upon tools. Tools mediate, but like bridges, they not only connect—they also separate. One day, an international client came in to the VITA clinic looking for help in amending her just-filed 2005 tax return. The return had been e-filed as a Form 1040 by another tax service, so Alexis hesitated to take on the problem. The client was reluctant to return to the tax service that had originally prepared the return. In response, Alexis handed the client sets of instructions for Forms 1040, 1040NR, and 1040X (to amend the original Form 1040). Overwhelmed, the client gaped at the thick set of instructions, which she clearly could not read, interpret, and implement. Thus, the tools necessary to "connect" the rules for filing also served to create impediments.

No tool is ever able to connect systems that are considered to be fundamentally divided, and so contradictions multiply. Any new tool is split off from the situated contexts that created the need for it, resulting in the

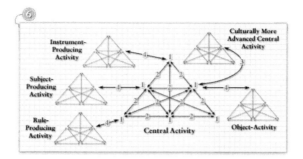

**Figure 9.1**

appearance of external, objective, and *structural* characteristics. The structures in turn constrain the interactions that gave rise to them. Figure 9.1 is taken from the Helsinki website illustrating the relationships among different systems and tools that in turn require mediatory tools to bridge them. (http://www.edu.helsinki.fi/activity/pages/chatanddwr/activitysystem):

The Internal Revenue Code and the IRS forms and related instructions, such as Form 1040 and Form 1040NR, are quasi-objects (Latour, 1993; Serres, 1982) that create quasi-subjects in the categories of persons of resident and nonresident aliens, respectively. The categories take on structural characteristics, and the mediatory tools, rather than bridging, have become borders that separate systems. The nonresident alien anomaly has been born, and with it, the 1040NR anomaly. An estimated 628,200 forms 1040NR were filed in 2005 (Hussain, 2005), not even half of 1 percent of the estimated 132,022,400 Forms 1040, 1040A, and 1040EZ filed in 2005 (Hussain, 2005). The anomaly that is the 1040NR highlights one of the boundary conditions of any activity system and its mediatory tools: they do not contain full information because they have been extracted in order to be context free. Activity systems, therefore, create ethical dilemmas with their conditions of multiple boundaries, anomalies, and decontextualization. At the boundary conditions, the "gray area" of ethics emerges in a shadowy meeting of competence and incompetence; abundance and lack; embeddedness and isolation.

Alexis expected a "black" and "white" environment at the VITA clinic, where she planned to prepare returns for lower income individuals with immaterial amounts of income and relatively simple tax issues. In practice, however, the situation called for her to address systematically blurred or transgressed boundaries: between nations, between the IRS and the U.S. Citizenship and Immigration Services (USCIS), and between student and worker status, to name just a few. All the exceptions and differences that could not be managed by the mediatory tools and rationality of the larger systems entered into Alexis's system and contributed to the enormous anxiety that she felt in managing the VITA clinic. In the following paragraphs, we explore the anxiety produced by anomalies and ambiguities. Because conventional codes of ethics are bound to rational, agency theory and identificatory thinking (Kristeva, 1996, p. 259), reliance on "pure" boundaries is relatively ineffective in the "gray area" of double binds.

Double binds are concerned with the rules and premises of habit. Double binds arise, in part, as a result of an economy of thought processes that are used for problem solving and, in part, in contexts where certain assumptions are automatic. For example, at the VITA clinic, which psychologists might call a "frame," Alexis perceived certain results as right or wrong (i.e., the prepared Form 1040NR is right or wrong). The double bind arose because she thought that the "Romanian" problem could only be resolved by finding the right answer. However, Bateson would likely argue that her framing of the problem was overly concrete. Following Bateson, Engestrom and other activity system theorists would suggest that Alexis expand the frame—that is, learn—in order to resolve the ethical dilemma. Our process of deconstructing and/or reconfiguring frames is the process of ante-ethics.

The activity systems model, which includes double binds and mediating tools, is very helpful in moving beyond an ethics dependent upon the rational individual. Our ante-ethics, which we explicate in the following paragraphs, are proposed as possible resolutions of double binds. Furthermore, our ante-ethics depend on Mary Douglas's (1966) notions of purity and dirt and upon Julia Kristeva's (1982, 1991) notions of abjection and the "stranger" within. Unlike conventional Codes of Ethics, such as the AICPA code, our ante-ethics admits the double binds and contradictions of a subject-in-process.

## BEFORE AND BEYOND ETHICS

According to Douglas, an anomaly is an element that doesn't fit a given set (1966, rpt. 2004, p. 47) and thus implies a set of ordered relations and a "contravention" of that order (1966, rpt. 2004, p. 44). Anomalies are dirt, and dirt provokes anxiety, as in Alexis's case (Douglas, 1966, rpt. 2004, p. 46). How does a society manage anomalies? Douglas (1966, rpt. 2004, p. 49) observes that naming an anomaly as a member of a different class of phenomena solves the potential dilemma. For example, the Nuer designate anomalous, "monstrous" newborns as baby hippopotamuses accidentally born to humans. In other words, the interpretation of the anomaly provides a solution: return it to the river. More generally, societies manage anomalies by means of "pollution rules" (Douglas, 1966, rpt. 2004). Pollution rules are specific and enforceable; they identify what the subject can eat, who she can marry, or, in short, what she can or cannot do with impunity. There may be more than one view of what action is right, but pollution rules are "unequivocal" (Douglas, 1966, rpt. 2004, p.162). According to Douglas, pollution rules work in certain identifiable ways. They uphold the moral code, as follows:

(1) When a situation is morally ill-defined, a pollution belief can provide a rule for determining post hoc whether infraction has taken place, or not.

(2) When moral principles come into conflict, a pollution rule can reduce confusion by giving a simple focus for concern.

(3) When action that is held to be morally wrong does not provoke moral indignation, belief in the harmful consequences of a pollution can have the effect of aggravating the seriousness of the offence, and so of marshalling public opinion on the side of the right.

(4) When moral indignation is not reinforced by practical sanctions, pollution beliefs can provide a deterrent to wrongdoers. (1966, rpt. 2004, p. 165)

According to Douglas (1966, rpt. 2004), pollution codes can work *post hoc* to define anomalous behavior. As the VITA story illustrates, judgments made after the fact about how to complete the forms are easier than judgments *in media res*, when Alexis was surrounded by students and clients.

Pollution rules support the righteous, closed community. "A community would not survive if its members were not committed to it," explains Douglas, "Taboos depend on a form of community-wide complicity.... Taboo is a spontaneous coding practice which sets up vocabulary of spatial limits and physical and verbal signals to hedge around vulnerable relations. It threatens specific dangers if the code is not respected" (Douglas, 1966, rpt. 2004, pp. xii–xiii).We are reminded of the Enron scandal and of the way that the behavior of accountants at Arthur Andersen was singled out—identified as an anomaly—so that the categories of "normal" accounting were not threatened. In addition, the focus on accounting infractions in the Enron scandal reduced confusion and provided a focus for concern. The Andersen accountants were the culprits, rather than—perhaps—the American political economy. More generally, the boundaries can be drawn around "accountants" as "monstrous" so that a preferred category such as "business" is not threatened.

What could Alexis do with her "dirty" anomalies? If she defined preparation of Forms 1040NR as outside the scope of the VITA services, she could throw them out (into the river!). Looking for answers in the "ethics as pollution-rules," she sees enforcement of boundaries, rather than navigation within their gray areas. For example, "Educational services are . . . subject to Rule 102-5 [which] . . . provides that the member shall maintain objectivity and integrity, shall be free of conflicts of interest, and shall not knowingly misrepresent facts or subordinate his or her judgment to others" (AICPA). In other words, the ethical rules require her to banish transgressions and anomalies, but doing so by refusing to serve those with special problems violates her ethical mandate to serve the public.

Enforcement of pollution rules relies on threats and taboos; therefore, such rules are meant to be fear provoking. The proverb "Nothing is certain but death and taxes" links our story with death itself: the greatest of all categorical imperatives. Accounting and accountants are charged with creating and protecting our ability to rationally measure and communicate value. Accountants are, in effect, mediatory tools and so suffer the same paradoxes as all tools: they both bridge and divide; they both interpret and create categories and enable taboos for transgression and contamination. As tools, they become quasi-objects that require further mediation, such as a Code of Ethics. "It would seem that if control of complex modern societies is to be secured, then ever more elaborate forms of economic calculation are required, of which accounting is a dominant instance. ... In particular, its role as a steering medium and its potential for enabling or distorting communication is considered [by Powers et al.]" (Alvesson & Wilmott, 2003, p. 6). Because mediation is recursive, the solution for accounting and ethics is unlikely to be a mediatory element, such as the Sarbanes-Oxley Act of 2002. Instead, it will take the help of "broader based transformations of economic reason" (Power, Laughlin, & Cooper, 2003, p. 151). Such a broader transformation is the purpose of ante-ethics, whose domain is a fictional time before the categories and codes, before we relied on threats and taboos as the way to reconcile two, therefore incommensurable, systems: economic man as a self-interest maximizer and the need of the collective to manage its resources for sustainability. Excavating the fear and longing that are key to, yet denied by, rational ethical systems, we suggest the usefulness of an ante-ethics schema, an *ethos* that admits its integral relations with *pathos* and *logos*.

## BOUNDARY CONDITIONS FOR ETHICAL SYSTEMS

Ante-ethics are proposed to function best when boundaries and clear distinctions get to be a problem. When we, like Alexis, find ourselves facing an anomaly, in a gray area or in a double bind, we return to ante-ethics. As we imagine, ante-ethics inhabit a time outside the social, removed from the cultural values and rules embodied in an association's ethical code. Such cultural values are intended to be introjected; thus, subjects internalize values that originated externally (Cooper, 2004, p. 19). Similarly institutions, defined as rule-governed relationships (Cooper, 2004, p. 21), bear a significant part of the responsibility for creating the rewards and taboos that support introjection of the appropriate values. In such cases, "basic moral beliefs can function like a system of taboos. In a taboo system fundamental moral beliefs are treated as so sacred that ordinary citizens are prohibited from evaluating or judging them.... The main virtue a moral agent needs is blind loyalty to the rules of the tribe" (Cooper, 2004, p. 19).

However, in complex systems, we as moral agents are prone to find ourselves torn among our various obligations to our different systems. Cooper (2004) cites Angeles's (1981, p. 64) definition of a moral dilemma as "a situation in which mutually exclusive moral actions or choices are equally binding." So, when Alexis was bound by a principle that promotes the public interest and rules that requires independence and integrity, she potentially faced mutually exclusive moral actions at the VITA clinic. As noted earlier in our discussion of activity systems, such dilemmas are not only possible but in fact they are highly likely, given the multitude of institutions and cultures in modern society. For example, Alexis felt torn between providing timely and accurate information to her VITA clients and spending time preparing her lectures. By preparing Forms 1040NR, she served the public interest, but she lacked experience that she didn't even know she needed. Such double binds are, in effect, moral dilemmas, in which Alexis's capacity to act intentionally, as required of moral agents, was put at risk.

"We say an act is intentional when someone has the conscious ability to conceive of a goal and to make a choice" (Cooper, 2004, p. 46). Cooper points out that because *ought implies can*, "it is not logical to tell people they ought to do something if, because they lack knowledge and capacity or are externally constrained, they can't do it" (p. 46). Alexis faced limitations on her ability to act when she had incomplete or inadequate information, when she was pulled in two directions at once, and when she encountered situations in which the usual categories didn't seem to fit. When the information was complete, the categorical applications were evident, and the resources were adequate, Alexis was pleased to be able to do the right thing while being efficient and effective.

In complex systems, it is a challenge to access and process all of the relevant information, particularly given the increased likelihood for encountering incommensurable demands among the systems, leading to the paralysis of double binds. When ethical systems have reached their boundary conditions, we suggest it may be useful to imagine a poetic construct before Aristotle's rhetorical division of reputation, emotion, and figures. In such a place, we give up trying to convince others of our values, but rather we attend to theirs. We experience our emotions and are sensitive to the feelings of others, but we make conscious cognitive choices about how we can still trust amidst uncertainty. Accordingly, we allow our numbers to represent not only value, but values. Just for fun, and because we are very fond of

David Boje, we call our poly-logic ante-ethics, and thereby we offer some of our own and others' contributions to features of such a discourse.

Allow us to suggest considering Ashby's discussion of complex systems, particularly his observation that it can be difficult to determine the boundaries of a complex system. The decision is ultimately made by the observer (http://en.wikipedia.org/wiki/Complex_systems). Also, Ashby (1956) proposes a law of requisite variety in which "only variety [in the information, including noise and uncertainty] in R [the regulator system charged with coding and controlling environmental elements] can force down the variety in D [the disturbance] (p. 207). Furthermore, "*R's capacity as a regulator cannot exceed R's capacity as a channel of communication*" (p. 211). How can an accountant, such as Alexis, successfully code the anomalies? How can she perform ethically, while maintaining her dual and often contradictory imperative to be *both* separate from the D, the disturbing anomaly, and include it safely into the larger social system she serves? We propose that she can perform ethically only by admitting variety and uncertainty. Therefore, we suggest that an ante-ethics might be a resource when one needs to increase variety in order to account for anomalies. An ante-ethics is an imaginary construct in which the regulations inherent in regular ethics are temporarily suspended.

Still, while we see a need to open the door to a wider variety of the possible, we do not advocate "L" words: such as licentiousness, larceny, lackadaisicality, or lasciviousness. Instead, we suggest the usefulness of approaches (defined as "movements") that allow variety when we need to deal with anomalies (e.g., with foreigners, with threats of being overwhelmed, when we find ourselves in a double bind, and when we face a moral dilemma). Below, we offer our own perspective on what the approaches might look like. The list is not exhaustive, nor is it authoritative. It is not meant to be considered in any particular order, as the approaches imply and implicate each other and our own perspectives. Our enumerated categories implicate and enfold one another: the numbers are merely nominal and meant to assist in referencing the ideas.

As we open ourselves up to possibilities, we acknowledge Rommetveit (1991): "To deprive one's conversational partner of epistemic co-responsibility is thus to disregard and exclude her or his concern from a shared directed openness toward future possibilities" (p. 14). By including more voices, we increase the amount and complexity of information, and so ultimately enhance R's capacity as a regulator. We call these *approaches* because we intend to suggest a poetic logic of moving toward ambiguities and those persons who bring them.

### Approach 1. Let Go of Certainty
"Knowing . . . is an ongoing, communicative interpretive process. It can never be fixed or complete . . . but must be fixed enough to permit ref-

erence to and ongoing relationships with 'this person'" (Code, 1991, p. 38). Alexis will never "know" the VITA clients. Furthermore, Alexis and the other volunteers can expect the unexpected anomalies, and not just anomalies in the persons of nonresident aliens. If they expect the unexpected, they may be pleasantly surprised. Similarly, as Bakhtin noted, a "dialogical communication constitutes a community of different and often conflicting voices that may not be resolved into one comprehensive self" (cited in Min, 2001, p. 7).

### Approach 2. Present Our Perspective, Admitting it is Partial, and Ask for Input

Presenting ourselves as partial, we explicitly acknowledge our "mutual dependency on one another to become ourselves" (Hagtvet & Wold, 2003, p. 201). When we receive input from others, we open ourselves up to accept what is offered. "To properly react to offering, rhetors [regulators] and listeners . . . engage each other's beliefs and let go of some of their own [beliefs] in the desire to move toward mutual understanding" (Ryan & Natalle, 2001, p. 71). A story from the VITA clinic illustrates this approach.

One evening at the VITA clinic, a woman carrying a booklet about the Kansas Homestead exemption arrived and said, "I want the homestead refund." Alexis asked whether she owned a home. Because she did not, Alexis did not instruct the volunteer to prepare a homestead refund, only federal and state tax returns, and the woman left. Before long, she returned with a companion, who told Alexis, "She should get the homestead refund." Alexis examined again the instructions on the state website and realized that as a disabled taxpayer, the woman qualified for a refund based on rent paid! When Alexis apologized, the companion responded, "That's OK. I had to tell them last year, too."

### Approach 3. Blur the Boundary between Self and Other

We might see ourselves in the Other; we might see ourselves created by the tools we use. Serres's (1982) quasi-object is the object that creates subjects, just as technology creates the cybernetic "human" being. We can look for ourselves in the mediatory tool:

> In a culture like ours, long accustomed to splitting and dividing all things as a means of control, it is sometimes a bit of a shock to be reminded that, in operational and practical fact, the medium is the message. This is merely to say that the personal and social consequences of any medium—that is, of any extension of ourselves—result from the new scale that is introduced into our affairs by each extension of ourselves, or by any new technology. (McLuhan, 1964, p. 7)

We also see one another in ourselves. According to Bakhtin, we look "into the eyes of another or with the eyes of another" (Emerson, 1984, p. 287). "There is no subject prior to infinitely shifting and contingent relations of belonging . . . so that 'being' is constituted not first through the 'Self,' but through its own longings to be with, . . . 'Subjectivity' may be thought of as an *effect* of belonging (Carrillo Rowe, 2005, pp. 17–18, original emphasis). Our ante-ethical principles are loosely based on Foss and Griffin's (1995) feminist principles of equality, immanent value, and self-determination, and Treblicot's (1988) three: (1) I speak only for myself. (2) I do not try to get others to accept my beliefs in place of their own. (3) There is no "given" (pp. 3–6). Reality is, we affirm, ultimately interconnected. If you asked Alexis to identify herself, she most likely would say that she is a tax professor at a small Midwestern university and that she is a wife and a mother. The point is that "Alexis" *is* because she belongs. She acknowledges that she is her individual self, but also a guide to students, a representative of the university, and a person involved with clients at the VITA clinic.

### Approach 4. Stay in the Present

As Jung (1969) observed, by holding two conflicting ideas in suspension, a third emerges. In a dialogical interaction, the "third" emerges between people as a mediational tool, so it contains or at least references more of the context than does a distanciated, commodified tool. The new mediational object tool is a creation with a life of its own, and so it, too, invites a relationship. Ricoeur (1981) explains the phenomenon in terms of a relationship with the text:

> The power of the text to open a dimension of reality implies in principle a recourse against any given reality and thereby the possibility of a critique of the real. It is in poetic discourse that this subversive power is most alive. The strategy of this discourse involves holding two moments in equilibrium, suspending the reference of ordinary language and releasing a second order reference. (Ricoeur, 1981, p. 93)

In addition to being a professor, mother, and wife, Alexis is a sometime equestrienne, and she remembers learning how to canter by looking at the horizon. Before she learned to look at the horizon, she would concentrate on the horse's movement, her seat in the saddle, and the position of her leg by the girth, but what really made the difference was looking at the horizon and the cedar tree on the hill. Similarly, at the VITA clinic, Alexis probably better served the public interest by paying attention to a new mediational tool, the "horizon," rather than to the forms and computers. Attention to the "horizon" is attention to the present.

*Approach 5. Manage Emotions through Detachment*

Ante-ethics are a form of moral sensemaking, and sensemaking is triggered by "disruptive events occurring at the interface between the 'business as usual' of routine situations and the conscious awareness of problem-solving activities. While solutions are still pending, operators are faced with equivocality... and emotions play an important role" (Patriotta, 2003, p. 369). As previously discussed, anomalies experienced as dirt provoke anxiety. Attempting to dispel anxiety through denying it, we are tempted to resort to an ethics of pollution rules, in which we reinforce established categories and eradicate the offending disturbance. Ironically, the more we attempt to pull away from the danger, the more we are caught in the "Chinese handcuffs" of the double bind. We take a stand that communication is intrinsically enjoyable regardless of its results (nonattachment) (Stroud, 2005, pp. 155–156). As we are able to release our fears, we turn to C words: creativity, compassion, curiosity, comfort, care, conversation, and conscious cognition. To mitigate anxiety we choose our beliefs (Beck & Emery, 1985), which we ground in the form of principles and ontological orientations that embrace uncertainty without the anxiety, even in the face of potential loss. Another VITA story is illustrative.

At one VITA session, Alexis reluctantly refused to prepare a return because the taxpayer needed to obtain either Individual Taxpayer Identification Numbers (ITINs) or Taxpayer Identification Number for Pending U.S. Adoptions (ATINs) for his dependents. Alexis's reluctance and the accompanying emotions were triggered by the taxpayer's limited English-speaking ability, by the taxpayer's obvious sincerity and distress, and by the student volunteer's need for a solution, an answer, a result. Much to her surprise, the taxpayer returned some weeks later with sufficient documentation for preparation of Forms W-7, IRS Application for Individual Taxpayer Identification Number, and his return. Because she managed her anxiety, she was able to communicate with the taxpayer, who then could obtain the documents needed.

*Approach 6. Play*

As we move into play, we lose ourselves; we lose our sense of ourselves as a subject, as apart from the object. We become submerged in the activity, and we come out different. Paradoxically, in play as in terror, we engage the unconscious "dirt" within. The "dirt" within is what Kristeva calls the abject. Kristeva explains, "The abject is not an object facing me, which I name or imagine. . . . The abject has only one quality of the object—that of being opposed to the *I*" (Kristeva, 1982, p. 1). The abject is the stranger within and opposed to the rational *I*: "Henceforth the foreigner is neither a race nor a nation. . . . Uncanny, foreignness is within us" (Kristeva, 1991, p. 181).

Ultimately, then, the abundance of foreigners, foreignness, and anxiety means that rules limited to creating boundaries will be broken—as at the VITA clinic. Alexis herself is a new faculty member, a new VITA site coordinator, and a "foreigner" at the university. The rational *I* succumbs. As explained by Ricoeur, "play shatters the seriousness of a utilitarian preoccupation. In play, subjectivity forgets itself; in seriousness, subjectivity is regained" (p. 186). Play is *bricolage,* and the *bricoleur* is someone who adapts tools at hand, changing them as necessary (Derrida, 2000):

> The bricoleur, says Levi-Strauss, is someone who uses the "means at hand," that is, the instruments he finds at his disposition around him, those which are already there, which had not been especially conceived with an eye to the operation for which they are to be used and to which one tries by trial and error to adapt them, not hesitating to change them whenever it appears necessary, or to try several of them at once, even if their form and their origin are heterogeneous, and so forth. There is therefore a critique of language, and an implication that bricologue is the critical language itself. (p. 501)

"Bricoleurs approach problem-solving by entering into a relationship with their work materials that has more the flavor of a conversation than a monologue" (Turkle, 2006, p. 568).

To the extent that the VITA volunteers could adapt the tools at hand—the computers, the forms, the physical space available to them—they managed the anomalies. When the clinic ran out of pens with which clients could sign Forms 8453, the students offered use of their own pens. When clients needed to phone home to obtain additional information, students offered use of their own cell phones.

### Approach 7. Let Go of the Ideal in Order to Immerse Ourselves in the Real

As Mills and Durepos (this volume) suggest, ethics requires a wholehearted acceptance of difference. As Hayakawa (1939) put it, "COW$_1$ IS NOT COW$_2$ IS NOT COW$_3$ . . . The word 'cow' calls up in our minds the features that this 'cow' has *in common* with other 'cows.' The index number, however, reminds us that this one is *different*; it reminds us that 'cow' does not tell us 'all about' the event; it reminds us of the *characteristics left out* in the process of abstracting" (pp. 254–255, original emphasis).

A popular tax research textbook (Raabe et al., 2006) defines the tax research process as the application of law to a particular case: "The researcher must find authority, evaluate the usefulness of that authority, and apply the results of the research to a specific situation . . . to arrive at a truly novel conclusion" (Raabe et al., 2006, p. 46). In effect, everything is an anomaly, and so attention and resources must be given to the particulars at hand in order to find the best solution to each individual case. Such attention can take the form of dialogue. For Bakhtin (1984), dialogue is the starting point for understanding: "The life of the word is contained in its transfer from one mouth to another, from one context to another, from one social collective to another, from one generation to another" (1984, p. 202). As Cooper (2004) explains, we become willing to consider all things, to learn all we can about local contingencies, in order to develop an appropriate "application discourse, *which tries to figure out how to intelligently apply background ideals to diverse concrete situations* (Cooper, 2004, p. 38, original emphasis).

Although Alexis focused on the anomaly presented by Form 1040NR, she could and would admit that each return, no matter which Form was used, was unique and thereby reflected each individual history and context.

### *Approach 8. Listen*

Listening and values are intertwined. We make judgments about the amount of listening owed to each person (Eadie, 1990). In what Gendlin (1978) calls "absolute listening" (p. 116), unique identities are honored when listeners do not "interrupt, comfort, or insert anything of their own as others tell of their experiences" (Foss & Griffin, 1995, p. 11). Our well-intentioned framing of others' experiences interfere with our ability to honor their uniqueness. Additionally, because we listen most carefully to what we think is important (Eadie, 1990), and shared values underlie trust (Hosmer, 1995), careful listening to the other demonstrates a shared value of the point of view and life of the speaker. Opportunities to improve understanding and collaboration, including collaboration in filling out tax forms at the VITA clinic, result from listening.

On one Tuesday evening at the church, a Spanish-speaking couple arrived. Fortunately, a Spanish–English translator was available that evening. At one point, the translator asked Alexis whether the couple could claim their grandson, who lived with them and whom they fully supported, as a dependent. They were obviously pleased when the translator conveyed Alexis's "Yes." However, Alexis received an email informing her that the IRS had rejected the couple's return because another taxpayer (probably the child's parent) had already claimed the child as his dependent. Alexis contacted the translator, who contacted the couple, who then came to the next VITA clinic and signed a revised Form 8453, U.S. Individual Income Tax Declaration for Electronic Filing, with a smaller refund. They were amazingly uncomplaining and polite.

Alexis may not have listened carefully enough in the original dialogue; she only heard that the grandson resided with the couple, who supported the grandson. Eadie (1990) observed that there is only a certain amount of truth that each of us can take (p. 4). Categorizing others' experiences according to our own historical framework is sure to omit key information. In Alexis's experience, parents do not abandon a child and, later, claim that child as a dependent. The experience with that couple taught Alexis a few lessons, which are best explained by Eadie (1990). First, we need to listen to those with whom we might disagree. Second, listening is good; we do good and behave ethically by listening. We must put aside what we want to hear in order to hear what we need to hear (Eadie, 1990, pp. 2–3).

### *Approach 9. Build Relationships*

Confronted with disputes at the borders, one can close the borders or establish cross-border relationships. Openness and closedness of boundaries are both required for relationships (Duck, 1994): "The complex of relational interdependencies arises, in part, through the transaction of shared meanings based on the two original sets of mental foundations provided by the two individual minds" (p. 21). The question becomes one of balancing integration and differentiation (Katz & Kahn, 1978). Systems require boundaries in order to survive, yet these boundaries need to be sufficiently open to engage with the life-sustaining others in the environment (Scott, 1992), at any and all levels of interactions.

For 2006 the tax season, conducted during spring 2007, Alexis hoped to establish relationships with several other university groups. Specifically, she contacted the local Tax Counseling for the Elderly (TCE) group, which is also an IRS-sponsored program that prepares tax returns for the elderly and whose staff of retired tax preparers may offer pertinent expertise. Additionally, she contacted the university's Students in Free Enterprise (SIFE) group to ask for help the following year. Working in partnership with business and higher education, SIFE student teams develop community outreach projects. Crossing boundaries to these other groups, Alexis imagines the value of their help and skills in marketing the VITA program, setting up additional technology, and organizing the clinics. Finally, Alexis started communicating with the university's advisor for Beta Alpha Psi (BAP), an honorary Financial Information organization whose chapters are evaluated annually on their service to members, campus, community, and profession. She hopes to recruit additional VITA volunteers from the BAP group.

### *Approach 10. Celebrate Process*

Vygotsky defined development in terms of the emergence or transformation of forms of mediation (Wertsch, 1985, p. 15). Kristeva (2004), in her Holberg Prize acceptance speech, said that transformation as opposed to adaptation is a feminine capacity. Specifically, she suggests that such transformation is only possible if the individual calls into question her own internal frontiers, and, furthermore, Kristeva understands such renewal processes as journeys. The journeys are dialogic and intrapsychic; therefore, the self-in-flux may be the appropriate site for attention to boundaries. "Critical self-reflection and associated transformation" (Alvesson & Wilmott, 1992,

p. 434) supports a care for the self: "If you care for yourself correctly . . . if you know of what you are capable . . . if you know finally that you should not fear death, well, then, you cannot abuse your power over others" (Foucault, 1988, p. 8). Ethical processes are journeys, in which "people develop their power to perceive critically *the way they* exist in the world *with which* and *in which* they find themselves; they come to see the world not as a static reality, but as a reality in process, in transformation" (Freire, 1993, p. 64, original emphasis).

When Alexis reflected upon the 2006 VITA experience and the unfolding of the ethical dilemma presented here, she experienced some relief and some pleasure. Kristeva (2004) says that transformation is only possible if one is willing to cross borders, especially the "internal frontiers." Kristeva says, "I travel myself," meaning that she crosses internal frontiers. What Alexis realized is that she must and can admit uncertainty, but to do so, she must relinquish the anxiety and cross the internal frontiers. That anxiety is the stranger within: "Uncanny, foreignness is within us" (Kristeva, 1991, p. 181). Just as Kristeva (2004) argues that the semiotic gives meaning to the symbolic, we argue that Ethos cannot be separated from Logos and Pathos. The ethical cannot be reduced to a logical system; Pathos gives meaning to Ethos. Then, with the students, she can celebrate the process of learning. Alexis's feelings of uncertainty gave rise to her consideration of ethics, and mixed feelings indicated a need for ante-ethics.

In their written reflections, the student volunteers expressed appreciation for the VITA experience. One international student, whose return Alexis personally prepared on the evening of the final day for filing, smiled when she met Alexis at the university. Alexis cultivated friendships with three other university employees, whose returns were prepared at the VITA clinic. With the assistance of others, such as Tax Counseling for the Elderly, Students In Free Enterprise, and Beta Alpha Psi, as well as her own learning about VITA, she anticipates a better season next year.

When we are overly constrained, we are not able to make any choices at all, much less ethical choices. Therefore, to the extent that our approaches outlined in our paper on ante-ethics create ways in which we can get out of the double bind, they create the possibilities for us to behave ethically. As we engage in the above approaches, which we liken to movements, we potentially loosen the double bind: We reframe, play, detach, celebrate, learn, and welcome the complexity of our shared and lived experiences. Through dialogue, we double create: both new mediational tools to facilitate our interaction and loving relationships that embrace the uncertainty and blurred boundaries that constrain and contain us. Our solution is always already partial. It is part of us and so we use it and we offer it to you, the readers, to take what you like and leave the rest.

## EPILOGUE: THE MONSTERS OF ACCOUNTING

According to Panozzo (1997), who refers to Latour, modernity is distinguished by two distinct practices: (1) translations that create hybrids of nature and culture and (2) purifications that partition science and society. Purifying rules address not only ethical norms, as discussed above, but also norms and expectations regarding scholarly research. Both the positivistic, empirical approaches emphasized in the U.S. academies and the primarily sociocultural approaches of European academies reflect the will to purify. Accounting research that blends econometric techniques with cultural frameworks are hybrids, or "monsters." Monsters happen when boundaries are set. Our ante-ethics proposes that we go back to the earth, the semiotic, the embodied, to find sources of relatedness that both underpin and reconfigure boundaries. The legality approach to ethics, the purification discourse, isn't helpful in the truly gray areas. In such cases we look for an ante-ethics, a monstrous discourse with Cerberus as its patron, to create new frameworks for understanding and experience.

Accountants, who have the job of clarifying and protecting borders, are archetypal monsters who stand at the border of Hades, where ethical dilemmas threaten. Such accountants exist as monstrous gatekeepers. To them, we offer the ante-ethics of a mythical pre-time in which undifferentiated co-life hummed in the cosmos: one, whole, together, complete.

## REFERENCES

AICPA Code of Professional Conduct. Retrieved June 21, 2006, at http://www.aicpa.org/about/code

Alvesson, M., & Willmott, H. (2003). Introduction. In M. Alvesson & H. Willmot (Eds.), *Studying management critically* (pp. 1–22). London: Sage.

Alvesson, M., & Willmott, H. (1992). On the idea of emancipation in management and organization studies. *Academy of Management Review, 17*(3), 432–464.

Ashby, W. R. (1956). *An introduction to cybernetics.* London: Chapman & Hall.

Bakhtin, M. (1984). *Problems of Dostoevsky's poetics* (C. Emerson, Ed. & Trans.). Minneapolis: University of Minnesota Press.

Bateson, G. (1972). *Steps to an ecology of mind: Collected essays in anthropology, psychiatry, evolution, and epistemology.* Chicago: University of Chicago Press.

Beck, A. T., & Emery, G. (1985). *Anxiety disorders and phobias: A cognitive perspective.* New York: Basic Books.

Berenson, A. (2003). Banks encourage overdrafts, reaping profit. *New York Times.* Retrieved June 21, 2006, from http://select.nytimes.com/gst/abstract.html?res=F50F10F83B540C718EDDA80894DB404482

Carrillo Rowe, A. (2005). Be longing: Toward a feminist politics of relation. *NWSA Journal, 17*(2), 15–46.

Code, L. (1991). *What can she know?: Feminist theory and the construction of knowledge.* Ithaca, NY: Cornell University Press.

Cooper, D. E. (2004). *Ethics for professionals in a multi-cultural world.* Upper Saddle River, NJ: Pearson.

Derrida, J. (2000). Structure, sign, and play in the discourse of the human sciences In C. Kaplan & W. D. Anderson (Eds.), *Criticism: Major statements* (4th ed., pp. 493–510). Boston: Bedford/St. Martin's Press.

Douglas, M. (1966/2002). *Purity and danger: An analysis of the concept of pollution and taboo.* London: Routledge & Kegan Paul.

Duck, S. (1994). *Meaningful relationships: Talking, sense, and relating.* Thousand Oaks, CA: Sage.

Eadie, W. F. (1990). Guest editorial: Hearing what we ought to. *International Journal of Listening, 4,* 1–4.

Emerson, C. (1984). *Problems of Dostoevsky's poetics* (C. Emerson, Ed. & Trans.). Minneapolis: University of Minnesota Press.

Engestrom, Y. (1987). *Learning by expanding: An activity-theoretical approach to developmental research.* Helsinki: Orienta-Konsultit.

Foss, S. K., & Griffin, C. L. (1995). Beyond persuasion: A proposal for an invitational rhetoric. *Communication Monographs, 62,* 2–18.

Foucault, M. (1988). The ethic of care for the self as a practice of freedom: An interview with Michel Foucault on January 20, 1984. In J. Bernauer & D. Rasmussen (Eds.), *The final Foucault* (pp. 1–20). Cambridge, MA: MIT Press.

Freire, P. (1993). *Pedagogy of the oppressed.* New York: Continuum.

Gendlin, E. T. (1978). *Focusing.* New York: Everest.

Hagtvet, B. E., & Wold, A. H. (2003). On the dialogical basis of meaning: Inquiries into Ragnar Rommetveit's writings on language, thought, and communication. *Mind Culture, and Activity, 10*(3). 186–204.

Hayakawa, S. I. (1939). *Language in action.* New York: Harcourt Brace and Co.

Hesiod. *Theogony.* Literature Resource Center. Retrieved July 5, 2006, at http://0-galenet.galegroup.com.www.whitelib.emporia.edu/servlet/LitRC;jsessionid=A876DEE76181D78BD5B7FAA4B3CD1853?locID=empsu_main

Hosmer, L. T. (1995). Trust: The missing link between organizational theory and philosophical ethics. *Academy of Management Review, 20*(2), 379–403.

Hussain, T. (2005). *Projections of federal tax return filings: 2005–2012.* Retrieved June 12, 2006, at http://www.irs.gov/pub/irs-soi/12proj.pdf

Jung, C. G. (1969). On psychic energy. In H. Read, M. Fordham, G. Adler, & W. McGuire (Eds.), *The collected works of C.G. Jung: Vol. 8. The structure and dynamics of the psyche.* Princeton, NJ: Princeton University Press.

Katz, D., & Kahn, R. L. (1978). *The social psychology of organizations.* New York: Wiley.

Kristeva, J. (1977). *About Chinese women* (A.Barrows, Trans.). London: M. Boyars.

Kristeva, J. (1996). *Interviews* (R. M. Guberman, Ed.). New York: Columbia University Press.

Kristeva, J. (1982). *The powers of horror: An essay on abjection* (L.S. Roudiez, Trans.). New York: Columbia University Press.

Kristeva, J. (1991). *Strangers to ourselves* (L.S. Roudiez, Trans.). New York: Columbia University Press.

**208** ■ A. A. DOWNS, R. A. DURANT, and W. L. SMITH

Kristeva, J. (2004). *Thinking about liberty in dark times: The Holberg Prize Seminar.* Retrieved June 14, 2006, at http://72.14.203.104/search?q=cache:PTNk-ukhWvkJ:www.holbergprisen.no/downloads/kristeva_publikasjon_english.pdf+Holberg+Prize+2004+Julia+Kristeva+Oliver&hl=en&gl=us&ct=clnk&cd=4

Lakoff, G., & Johnson, M. (2003). *Metaphors we live by.* Chicago: University of Chicago Press.

Latour, B. (1993). *We have never been modern.* Cambridge, MA: Harvard University Press.

Leach, E. (1976). *Culture and communication: The logic by which symbols are connected. An introduction to the use of structuralist analysis in social anthropology.* London: Cambridge University Press.

MacDonald, J. (2006). *Refund-anticipation loans can carry a high price.* Retrieved June 21, 2006, at http://www.bankrate.com/brm/itax/news/20030127a1.asp?caret=6

Maull, S. (2006). *NY files $250M fraud suit vs. H&R Block.* Retrieved June 21, 2006, at http://www.exisle.net/mb/index.php?showtopic=36928

McLuhan, M. (1964). *Understanding media: The extensions of man.* Corte Madera, CA: Gingko Press.

Min, E. (2001). Bakhtinian perspectives for the study of intercultural communication. *Journal of Intercultural Studies, 22*(1), 5–18.

Panozzo, F. (1997). *Mainstreams, monsters and global accounting.* Retrieved July 5, 2006, at http://les.man.ac.uk/IPA97/papers/panozz11.html

Parker, M. (2003). Business, ethics and business ethics: Critical theory and negative dialectics. In M. Alvesson & H. Willmot (Eds.), *Studying management critically* (pp. 197–219). London: Sage.

Patriotta, G. (2003). Sensemaking on the shop floor: Narratives of knowledge in organizations. *Journal of Management Studies, 40*(2), 349–375.

Power, M., Laughlin, R., & Cooper, D. J. (2003). Accounting and critical theory. In M. Alvesson & H. Willmot (Eds.), *Studying management critically* (pp. 132–156). London: Sage.

Raabe, W. A., Whittenburg, G. E., & Sanders, D. L. (2006). *Federal tax research* (7th ed.). Mason, OH: Thomson South-western.

Reilly, B. J., & Kyj, M. J. (1994). Meta-ethical reasoning: Applied to economics and business principles. *American Journal of Economics and Sociology, 53*(2), 147–162.

Ricoeur, P. (1981). Hermeneutics and the human sciences: Essays on language, action, and interpretation (J. B. Thompson, Ed. & Trans.). Cambridge, UK: Cambridge University Press.

Rommetveit, R. (1991). On epistemic responsibility in human communication. In H. Ronning & K. Lundby (Eds.), *Media and communication: Readings in methodology, history, and culture* (pp. 13–27). Oslo, Norway: Norwegian University Press.

Ryan, K. J. & Natalle, E. J. (2001). Fusing horizons: Standpoint hermeneutics and invitational rhetoric. *RSQ: Rhetoric Society Quarterly, 31*(2), 69–90.

Scott, W. R. (1992). *Organizations: Rational, natural, and open systems.* Upper Saddle River, NJ: Prentice Hall.

Serres, M. (1982). *The parasite* (L.R. Schehr, Trans.). Baltimore: Johns Hopkins Press.

Stroud, S. R. (2005). Ontological orientation and the practice of rhetoric: A perspective from the *Bhagavid Gita. Southern Communication Journal, 70*(2), 146–160.

Treblicot, J. (1988). Dyke methods *or* principles for the discovery/creation of the withstanding. *Hypatia, 3*(2), 1–13.

Turkle, S. (2006). The triumph of tinkering. In B. Coleman, R. Brittenham, S. Campbell, & S. Girard (Eds.), *Making sense: Essays on art, science, and culture* (2nd ed., pp. 566–581). Boston: Houghton Mifflin.

Wertsch, J. V. (1985). *Vygotsky and the social formation of mind.* Cambridge, MA: Harvard University Press.

Yuthas, K., Dillard, J., & Rogers, R. (2004). Beyond agency and structure: Triple loop learning, *Journal of Business Ethics, 51*(2), 229–244.

# CHAPTER 10

# STRATEGY AND CRITICAL THEORY ETHICS

### David M. Boje and Usha C. V. Haley

Critical theory (CT) provides a way to critique the instrumental ethics of strategy (used synonymously with strategic management). This instrumental ethics of strategy comes from a long history of managerialism. Managerialist strategy ideology, discourse, and material practices have sometimes served to instill a top-down, elite participation that reproduces a hierarchy of domination within the organization. Asymmetrical participation in decisions of strategy formulation and implementation appears to keep non-managerialist viewpoints at bay. The instrumental ethics often employed in strategy, in particular, have significant ramifications for broader societal and environmental issues. This chapter summarizes the growing accumulation of CT critique of strategy, and suggests some ways forward. For example, we note that as strategy theory pervaded practice, it has diffused to the point that every discipline from human resources management (HRM) to operations management claims to be strategic. With this widespread mimicry, and simultaneous globalization, comes the possibility that strategy may make every kind of organization from business, government, university, etc. "strategic" with a top-down elite cadre of strategists in charge. Yet, excessive detachment may cause the distortion of effective strategy as with detach-

*Critical Theory Ethics for Business and Public Administration*, pages 211–228
Copyright © 2008 by Information Age Publishing
All rights of reproduction in any form reserved.

ment, strategists become out of touch with the distributed nature of processes and tasks. Some recent work in complexity and emergence strongly corroborates that centered approaches tend to be counterproductive for more effective strategizing. We suggest that an ethics of answerability in wider forms of polyphonic strategy making and strategy governance provides a way to proceed in this increasingly globalized and interconnected world. In short, we call for a pendulumic swing in our understandings of the strategic management of the organization and a beginning of polyphonic strategy from an ethics of answerability.

## THE RISE AND RISE OF STRATEGY

Strategic management, often called policy or "strategy," deals with the direction of organizations and most often of business firms. It includes subjects of primary concern to senior managers or anyone seeking reasons for organizational success or failure. Firms make choices to survive and to prosper. Strategic choices include selecting goals, products, and services; designing policies on how to compete in product markets; choosing the appropriate levels of scope and diversity; and designing organizational structures, administrative systems, and policies to define and to coordinate work. These choices critically influence firms' successes or failures of the enterprise and managers strive to integrate them into a coherent whole. Managerial integration and reinforcement of patterns among the choices marks the set as strategy.

In this chapter we survey the historical trajectory of strategy and discuss some of the weaknesses that have emerged through adoption of its "more scientific" approach. In the first section, we provide a brief history of the development of strategy. In the next section, we highlight some of the enormous influence that strategy has exercised in academic and business environments. In the ensuing sections, we reevaluate strategy and delineate some contributions that CT may make to an ethical and holistic understanding of strategy in a globalized economy.

## HISTORY OF STRATEGY

We would like to tell you the story of the recorded history of strategy. Homer, Euripides, and several early Greek writers discussed strategy. Indeed, our word "strategy" comes from the Greek noun "strategos," with associated root meanings in "army" and "lead." The Greek verb "stratego" means "to plan the destruction of one's enemies through effective use of resources" (Bracker, 1980). Prominent writers throughout history and across cultures have discussed effective strategizing in military and political contexts including Socrates, Kautilya, Sun Tzu, Shakespeare, Montesquieu, Mill, Hegel, Calusewitz, and Tolstoy. In more modern times, Von Neumann and Morgenstern (1944) related the concept of strategy to business with their theory of games.

Strategy has sought from its beginnings to answer the question: "How do firms (or organizations) achieve sustainable competitive advantage?" Researchers have generally portrayed senior managers as engaging in the following steps for business strategy: First, analyzing environments and situations to determine firms' postures; and second, analyzing and using resources to attain major goals. Researchers have often portrayed these two steps as interactive for effective strategizing (Hermann, 2005). Researchers have also divided strategy into content and process. Content researchers study outcomes, positions, scope of firms, and ways of competing; process researchers study how systems and processes lead to outcomes.

Strategy originally developed through case studies and ideas of contingent design over universalistic principles of administration (Rumelt, Schendel, & Teece, 1994). The works of Chandler (1962), Learned, Christensen, Andrews, and Guth (1965/1969), and Ansoff (1965) provided the first definitions of strategy and laid the foundations of the field. Chandler (1962), for example, defined strategy as planning and executing companies' growth, including deciding on the enterprises' long-term objectives and adopting appropriate courses of action. Andrews (1971) added the ideas of distinct competence, company mission, and business definition. He also developed the SWOT analysis in which uncertain environments present Threats and Opportunities to which firms should adapt their Strengths and Weaknesses. Drawing on his experiences, Ansoff (1965) noted that firms' objectives include maximizing economic returns. Except for Andrew's SWOT analysis, consulting firms provided most of the contributions to practice such as the multidivisional structures for diversified firms and Boston Consulting Group's (BCG) growth/share matrix as a tool for portfolio planning (Collis & Montgomery, 1997).

In the 1970s, the strategy process research stream arose partially because of managerial dissatisfaction with strategic planning, which had failed to predict environmental contingencies. As a result, strategic planning often became goal-setting exercises devoid of understandings of the competitive advantages of firms. The more sophisticated the planning became, the more difficult the implementation became (Rumelt et al., 1994). Researchers consequently tried to understand those processes that led to an implicit formulation of strategy and provided various interpretations of strategy creation. Mintzberg and Waters (1978) argued for strategy's emergent nature, which stemmed from different participants' activities within firms, rather than from strategic planning. Similarly, Quinn (1980) introduced the idea of logical incrementalism, showing how organizations refine their general strategic course incrementally as new information emerges from the environment.

Doctoral dissertations from Harvard and Purdue Universities propelled the divergent research stream on strategy content. The dissertations at Harvard elaborated on Chandler (1962) and examined relationships between corporate diversification strategy, organizational structure, and firms' performance. Rumelt's (1974) categorization of diversification strategy emerged as one of the most influential studies of this genre. Rumelt found that relatedness among different businesses positively affected financial performance. Other doctoral dissertations from Purdue revealed the importance of firm heterogeneity (e.g., Hatten, 1974), and concluded that strategy as well as the environment mattered. These studies challenged the previous assumption of homogeneity within industries and provided a foundation for research on strategic groups.

Simultaneously, Schendel and Hatten (1972) fostered the beginning of the empirical swing of the pendulum in strategy, arguing that research should seek cause-and-effect relationships, empirical data, and scientific testing. This redirection from case methodologies and managerial practice became obvious after an influential conference in Pittsburgh in 1977. As a direct result of this conference, researchers changed the name of the field from business policy to strategic management to signal its move to an empirically oriented discipline. Researchers concurred that strategic management or strategy needed to focus more on firms, to borrow from other areas such as marketing and organization theory (Jemison, 1981) and to integrate with economics.

Michael Porter (1980) provided the first template for the new strategy with his book, *Competitive strategy*, which many researchers consider the most influential contribution to the field (Barney, 2002; Hoskisson, Hitt, Wan, & Yiu, 1999). Porter imported ideas from industrial organization economics to build a framework of generic strategies and industry analysis, his Five Forces model: threat of entry, intensity of rivalry among existing competitors, pressure from substitute products, bargaining power of buyers, and bargaining power of suppliers. Intense forces result in low performance, and moderate forces result in high performance, so Porter stated that effective strategy included managing these forces. Porter identified three generic strategies to propel superior performance: overall cost leadership, differentiation, and focus. Following Porter's work, several researchers empirically tested related ideas including entry and exit barriers (Harrigan, 1981), the competitive effects of the learning curve (Lieberman, 1984), and the relationship of market share to performance (Rumelt & Wensley, 1981). Another stream of research integrated environmental determinism and strategic choice (Child, 1972) according to which firms and executives exercised their strategic options. Miller and Friesen (1984) examined how firms obtained a fit between their strategic choices and their environments, combining organizational characteristics such as structure and performance with managers' individual characteristics. Subsequently, Hambrick and Mason's (1984) research on upper echelons and Finkelstein and Hambrick's (1996) on strategic leadership initiated a large stream that stressed the influence of CEOs and top management on strategic decisions.

Williamson's (1975) research cemented the influence of economic concepts and methodologies on the new strategy. Williamson propounded transaction-cost theory, which argues that the appropriate governance structure for a given transaction is not necessarily the most equitable, efficient, or ethical, but one that minimizes total transaction and production costs imposed by bounded rationality and opportunism. Williamson's work influenced research on multidivisional forms, hybrid forms of organization, and international strategy.

To examine relationships between strategy, organizational structure and performance, researchers migrated from the case studies of the 1960s and 1970s to large sample studies containing secondary data, especially PIMS and COMPUSTAT. Standard multiple regression emerged as the dominant statistical technique.

The resource-based view (RBV) of the firm provided the second template for strategy, with the dissertations of Prahalad (1975), Doz (1976), Bartlett (1979), and Ghoshal (1986). The RBV rests on the idea that firms create sustainable competitive advantage by developing and applying idiosyncratic firm-specific resources. Costly, rare, and nonreplicable firm-specific resources contribute to sustainable competitive advantage. Socially complex resources have more value, implying that resources that resist imitation such as culture and reputation stem from complex and often opaque social interactions (Barney, 1991). Researchers have had particular difficulty measuring intangible resources, the primary sources of competitive advantages, and so have often substituted coarse measures such as R&D intensity, advertising intensity, and patents (Hoskisson et al., 1999).

Theoretically, the recent rise of the RBV (e.g., Wernerfelt, 1984)—together with the two closely related content areas, the knowledge-based view (e.g., Kogut & Zander, 1992) and strategic leadership (e.g., Finkelstein & Hambrick, 1996)—have returned attention to the internal aspects of the firm, drawing on early classics such as Barnard (1938), Selznick (1957), and Penrose (1959). Researchers in this stream share an interest in exploring the inner growth engines of the firm, hereto black boxed. These researchers have argued that firms' continued success stems primarily from internal, unique, and often immeasurable competitive resources (Hoskisson et al., 1999).

Methodologically, the pendulum appears to have swung back toward the use of more qualitative approaches. In its early history, researchers made little attempt to generalize case findings to strategy, except for problem-solving skills. Largely because of this, many regarded strategy as unscientific and unworthy of academic study. As the field embraced industrial organization (IO) economics, it began to emphasize scientific generalizations based on study of broader sets of firms. Strategy researchers increasingly employed multivariate statistical tools, with large data samples primarily collected from secondary sources to test theory. However, the development of RBV poses major methodological problems. The study of RBV requires a multiplicity of methods to identify, to measure, and to understand firms' resources. Firms should have distinctive resources that contribute to competitive advantage. Large data sets, secondary data sources, and econometric analyses appear inadequate to understand firms' intangible resources such as corporate culture, tacit knowledge, or stakeholder participation.

## INFLUENCE OF STRATEGY

As we discussed in the previous section, strategy remains firmly grounded in practice, and researchers, governmental policymakers, and managers have started noting gaps in existing theories. The new strategy seems unable to provide answers for the mounting ethical dilemmas that it has so far black-boxed or ignored.

Income inequality and executive compensation have become bellwether issues (Herbert, 2007). Among Americans, wealth is distributed unequally, as it is around the globe. The latest data from the Federal Reserve's Survey of Consumer Finances found that the richest 1 percent of Americans held 32 percent of the nation's wealth in 2001. (This statistic excludes the billionaires in the Forbes list, who control roughly another 2 percent of the nation's wealth.) Inequity in the United States topped every country but Switzerland, among the 20 nations that measure this wealth.

U.S. corporations provide a microcosm of this income inequality with issues of executive compensation and the social concerns that they raise. In December 2006, Morgan Stanley, the second largest U.S. investment house, gave Chief Executive John Mack $40 million in stock and options for 2006, reflecting the largest bonus afforded to a Wall Street CEO so far. Later in that month, Lloyd Blankfein at Goldman Sachs did even better—getting $53.4 million. Data compiled by the Center for Labor Market Studies at Northeastern University in Boston offers a startling look at the numbers behind executive compensation, which remains a key issue in strategy. According to the Center's director, Andrew Sum, the top five Wall Street firms (Bear Stearns, Goldman Sachs, Lehman Brothers, Merrill Lynch, and Morgan Stanley) were expected to have awarded an estimated $36–44 billion worth of bonuses to their 173,000 employees in 2006, an average of between $208,000 and $254,000, "with the bulk of the gains accruing to the top 1,000 or so highest-paid managers" (Herbert, 2007). Conversely, in the United States, between 2000 and 2006, labor productivity in the nonfarm sector of the economy rose by 18 percent. But during that period, the inflation-adjusted weekly wages of workers increased by just 1 percent or about $3.20 a week. The U.S. has 93 million production and nonsupervisory workers (exclusive of farm workers). Their combined real annual earnings from 2000 to 2006 rose by $15.4 billion, or less than half of the combined bonuses awarded by the five Wall Street firms for just 1 year. The once-strong link between productivity gains and real wage increases has been severed.

Despite social rumblings, strategy, and the influence of scientific, top-down normative models, have greatly influenced not just managers, but university education. First, with the rise of strategy in business schools, a capstone course, strategy theories began to have a grip on business education. A capstone is the top stone of a structure or wall. The 'wall' is the whole world of business that must pass through the filter of the capstone strategy course. Soon strategy, by its curriculum placement, began to exercise power over every other discipline. Every business discipline began to mimic strategy, and to align with the capstone, so that every discipline claims to be strategic: strategic leadership, strategic HRM, strategic finance, strategic management information systems (MIS), etc.

Strategy also achieved often uncritical dissemination to nonbusiness disciplines. Hospitals, churches, temples, universities, and political parties began to be run like businesses, to hire cadres of strategists to schematize everyone and everything and to run top-down organizations where none existed. For example, five centuries ago, universities were run by faculty and students, without administrative officials. Century by century, as the division of labor took place between professional administrators and faculty, academic freedom for self-governance began eroding. Deans and presidents run their colleges and university as they feel senior executives would. Some parliamentary faculty and student senates exist, but these bodies tend to be advisory, and restricted to particular issues. These developments led to union movements, but unions have not been effective in reversing the trend. Presidents of universities often portray themselves as CEOs and universities are experiencing the same concerns as corporations on executive compensation. The 2006 survey conducted by the *Chronicle of Higher Education* of 853 colleges, universities, and specialized schools for subjects like medicine found that 112 paid their presidents at least $500,000. This upward spiral of compensation occurred in public as well as private institutions, with 42 presidents of public colleges earning $500,000 or more compared with 23 in 2005. The survey also found that in 2006, seven presidents of private colleges, universities, and medical schools received more than $1 million annually in compensation. Roger Bowen, general secretary of the American Association of University Professors, said academic institutions were coming to resemble corporations. "Presidents now are CEOs. You no longer have treasurers, you have chief financial officers; you no longer have deans, you have chief academic officers. Faculty play the role of labor, students play the role of customer" (quoted in Glater, 2006). Critical of the change, Bowen said that presidential pay increases had outstripped faculty raises and that the widening gap could signal a shift in emphasis from educational achievement to financial management.

The new formulas for strategy are delivering stagnation. We can feel their demise in the post-Enron world, and a refusal to accept strategy as the reason for doing anything and everything. Strategy discourse and ideology invades all domains of social life. However, logically, if every discipline imitates strategy, it ceases to exist as the enclave of the central or top administrators, or the capstone discipline of disciplines. If strategy offers a ready-made formula, to be handed off to other disciplines, then strategy offers no more than illusion. The formula has become quite seductive. In response to stakeholders' protests, and often to pre-empt them, strategy also offers ready-made clichés to be inserted into the formula, such as "We are all responsible for strategy," "We are all knowledge workers," "We are all strategy-entrepreneurs," "We are all empowered by our strategy," and "We all are members of the strategy team." These ready-made phrases can be slotted anywhere in the overall strategic plan. The strategy formulas, be it SWOT, five-forces, RBV, configuration, or learning organization—give the impression of people other than the strategy-elite being in command and control.

Deceit and facades permeate the new strategy, for although managers realize that stakeholders have power, they often deliberately erect facades and screens to obfuscate their control. For example (Haley, 2001) found that customers' boycotts, governmental sanctions and stockholders' divestitures, indicating that stakeholders' strongly disapproved of U.S. multinationals' investing in South Africa during apartheid, did not have the desired effect. Most multinationals did not leave South Africa, although they stated they did. Most continued operations; some erected leaving facades by selling their subsidiaries to wholly owned trusts, which were out of the reach of U.S. stakeholders' protests. Indeed, stakeholders' protests against the support of apartheid appear to have reduced their power to influence the system.

The fall of strategy as we know it is inherent in the spread of superficial formulas, ready-made catch phrases, superficial debate over differences in "organization learning vs. learning organization" or what becomes "resource" with each new generation of RBV strategy researchers. Forcing strategy into every academic discipline, every public agency, every nook and cranny of every organization, makes everyone "instruments without a purpose of their own," to just fit into some strategist's schematization (Horkheimer, 1974, p. 151).

If strategy offers differentiation of similar products and services, then strategy becomes primarily the management of illusion. Differentiation of cheap and expensive models of computers or cars, or fast food and office supplies steadily diminishes. strategy then becomes a reproduction process, inevitable, necessary to effective organization, yet strategic consciousness turns stakeholders into listeners, who accept strategic direction from above.

## REEVALUATING STRATEGY

CT can help to identify several solutions to the effects of the new strategy. First, research within strategy suggests firms rarely implement the grand theories of strategic planning or their successors. Nevertheless, CT claims an impact on strategy theory as discourse and ideology upon material practices. Chief among these is an imposition upon practice of the general premise that strategy makers should be detached, aloof, and separate from operational personnel.

Second, strategy historians acknowledge that strategy has become synonymous with top-down activities of hegemonic blocs or elite cadres. Yet, CT's discourse and ideology specifies effective strategy practice as rooted in wider democratic participation. CT objects to a strategy elite, using top-down, sectionalist governance that circumvents wider forms of participation in strategy making.

A third critique of strategy by CT revolves around grand strategy theories that support an instrumentalist ethics in practice advice. RBV, and the Five Forces model, for example, focus attention on treating people instrumentally, attaining monopolistic control over markets, positioning predatory competitive practices, and have evolved into short-term, exploitative views of environments as instrumental resources. As Horkheimer and Adorno (1944/1972, p. 121) put it, "the people at the top are no longer so interested in concealing monopoly: as its violence becomes more open, so its power grows."

Finally, strategy researchers acknowledge that business strategy imported military command and control models. Since increasingly strategy has assumed position as the capstone course in business schools, students and faculty learn from the new strategy formulas. That means they often learn to adopt an instrumentalist ethics. As business strategy colonized disciplines outside the business college, a command-and-control as well as instrumentalist ethics strategy practice spread to public administration. In these ways, strategy advanced myths of perfect competition, advocated that an elite core of administrators address strategic concerns with not only an instrumental ethics, but also with supposedly rational, logical, linear methods to ensure monopolistic competition. This resulted in governments and universities not only operating as businesses, but administrators becoming typified as strategists, who increasingly operate with instrumental ethics, detachment, and top-down, elite governance.

## INSIGHTS OF CT FOR STRATEGY

What specific insights does the Frankfurt School of CT bring to strategy? The focus of early writing was on the ideology of strategy, and strategy-as-discourse. Paul Shrivastava (1986) applied work by Habermas and Giddens to show the ideological nature of strategy. Shrivastava applied Giddens's concern with factual underdetermination of action norms, universalized sectional interests, denial of conflict and contradiction, normative idealization of sectional goals, and naturalization of status quo power (see Levy, Alvesson, & Willmot, 2003, p. 97). Shrivastava used CT work by Habermas to recommend more "communicative competence" for all stakeholders so they could more readily participate in strategy discourse, and find some liberation from it.

Postmodern perspectives have widely critiqued communicative competence and its univeral aims. Knights and Morgan (1991) have critiqued corporate strategy as allowing managers to impose stratagems on unwitting workers. They questioned the universality of strategy interests, and revealed ways it promotes hierarchy. Strategy sometimes degenerates into a discourse that defines the problems for which strategy claims to be the solution. Smirchich and Stubbart (1985) have argued that strategic discourse impacts broader economic and power relations. The 1998 special issue of *EJROT–Electronic Journal of Radical Organization Theory*, with articles by Booth, Harfield, Stoney, and Thomas, provided CT critiques of strategy. For example, Thomas (1998) argued that strategy discourse is not reflexive about its discursive and ideological positions.

Levy, Alvesson, and Willmott (2001) were critical of the early CT reviews of strategy for being too focused on strategy as ideology and discourse, and missing ways that strategy influences material practices. They attributed this flaw to a lack of attention by CT pioneers—such as Adorno, Horkheimer, Benjamin, and Marcuse (see Boje's introduction in this book)—to the material practices of strategy. Strategy discourses can promote "instrumental" ethics rationality and "reproduce hierarchical relations of power" while privileging "interests and viewpoints of particular groups" (Levy, et al.,

2001, p. 1). CT can provide "an emancipatory agenda, which seeks to probe taken-for-granted assumptions for their ideological underpinnings and restore meaningful participation in arenas subject to systematic distortion of communication" (Levy et al., 2003, p. 93). The instrumental ethics perspective of strategy privileges sectional organization interests while silencing broader social and political standpoints (Alvesson & Willmott, 1996). The main insight CT offers strategy is a path to liberation from top-down sectional decision making, which can enact more polyphonic stakeholder governance as well as alternatives to instrumental ethics.

In our post-Enron world, strategy ideology, discourse, and certainly its practices are engendering more critique than ever. Strategy can create impersonal institutions. Strategic theory and practices are also being changed by globalization (Haley, Haley, & Tan, 2004; Løwendahl & Revang, 1998, p. 755). First, new practices of monitoring supplier firms in countries such as China have changed the reliability of information exchange between multinationals, supplier firms, and other stakeholders. Second, the monitoring practices in global supply chains have altered the relationship between suppliers and their workers. Strategy is characterized by an amazing diversity of theories and practices that have arisen in the last 50 years. Each school of strategy makes legitimate claims on the ability of stakeholders to be confident in the strategy espoused by firms as addressing significant problems.

## WHAT WOULD A CT STRATEGY APPROACH LOOK LIKE?

There have been very few attempts to write a CT perspective on strategy schools, their thinking and practices. One approach to addressing the variety of strategy schools is to look at complementary frameworks that result in stylistic orchestration of images that create significant gaps between espoused and enacted strategy. A second approach would be to use a CT perspective on "discordant pluralism" to show how conflicting perspectives on such a gap can resituate a more effective constellation (Gregory, 1996, p. 605). The approach would be to review how various schools of strategy adopt the complementarism approach, and what a discordant pluralism theory and practice would mean. One result could be to improve the answerability of multinational corporations and their globally distributed suppliers for their ethical practices.

Yet, legitimate concern for making corporate strategy transparent with ethical answerability is subverted by the actual use of consultants by contractors to deceive monitors retained by the corporation (or by its agents, such as the Fair Labor Association). The use of these consultants by contractors, and monitors by corporations, turns the discourse of ethical answerability into image management. Haley (2001) in her empirical longitudinal study also showed how managers in South Africa used adherence to the Sullivan Principles as a symbol of reassurance to opposing stakeholders and an instrument to deflect opposition to investing in that country; and, how Nike has similarly used symbolic adherence to Codes of Conduct to portray itself as a good corporate global citizen that does not run sweatshops.

Both public administrators (agents of the State) who are supposed to regulate wage and hours practices (for example) and business strategists (agents of capital) who are supposed to align espoused strategy told to stakeholders (investors, labor, regulators, etc.) with enacted strategy can claim to be victims of the subverted monitoring that is producing reports testifying about a falsified picture of what is going on. For instance, the use of peer groups to calculate executive pay has become ubiquitous in recent years partly in response to the Securities and Exchange Commission's requirement that companies compare their stock performance with peer groups in tables in the section of their proxy filings devoted to shareholder returns. Theoretically, these tables allow investors to compare their companies' performances against objective benchmarks. But, worries continued that executives, consultants, and directors cherry-picked peer-group members, thereby pumping up packages. The new disclosure rules that went into effect on December 15, 2006, require that corporations reveal which companies they use in their peer groups and provide extensive descriptions of their compensation philosophies.

Without a new understanding of strategy, it is likely that smarter mousetraps will result in smarter mice. For example, China's factories this year are expected to ship goods to America worth over $280 million. Roberts and Engardio (2006) found that despite codes of conduct and elaborate on-site monitoring, over 90 percent of the factories in China engage in fraud of documents and time sheets and pay their workers significantly less than minimum wage, violating overtime rules. Indeed, an entire industry and support structure has arisen to help Chinese factories to defraud audits and surveillance by stakeholders. A compliance manager for a major multinational company who had overseen many factory audits said that the percentage of Chinese suppliers caught submitting false payroll records had risen from 46% to 75% in the past 4 years. This manager estimated that only 20% of Chinese suppliers complied with wage rules, while just 5% obeyed hour limitations (Roberts & Engardio, 2006). The average Chinese worker on a factory floor probably earned around 40 cents an hour—a wage against which no American company with domestic operations could compete, and one which could not sustain a poverty-free life in China.

Global issues such as these raise CT questions about corporate strategy, its stylistic-image orchestration to stakeholders, and ethical-answerability and accountability guarantees that multinational corporations are making globally about meeting published codes of governance, ethical conduct, and local labor, health, safety, and environmental laws. In terms of public administration, stylistic strategy and image management often communicate that things are improving or even under multinationals' control. Yet, if the monitoring process is rife with subterfuge, then the game unravels.

From a CT perspective (see book introductory chapters), to have ethical answerability means that those who directly participate in production and consumption can organize to make their voices heard throughout society and the global order. Workers, for example, are not passive, disinterested nonparticipants. Investors, on the other hand, cannot claim to be passive, to not know any more than they read in the annual reports, business press, or TV news. When corporate strategy is replete with image orchestration, the process of improving labor standards, union organizing, and environmental protection breaks down. There is a crisis of ethical answerability because people do not have reliable information. They do not hear the direct stories and the statistics generated in monitoring are invalid and unreliable.

Meanwhile, the stylistic image-orchestration strategy of subcontractors hiring consultants to produce bogus reporting and multinational corporations affiliating with monitoring arms (such as FLA) that report on the bogus tales and numbers—allows everyone an umbrella of transparency. Nike as well as Wal-Mart can claim that sweatshop abuses of its China suppliers are being monitored, and when a contractor is caught falsifying data, they are punished.

The breakdown of stop-gap strategy solutions appears starkly evident in China, which has embraced the engines of capitalism, including multinationals' investments, with exuberance as paths to development. World Bank studies have found that China's poor grew poorer at a time when the country was growing substantially wealthier (McGregor, 2006). The real income of the poorest 10 percent of China's 1.3 billion people fell by 2.4 percent in the 2 years to 2003, the World Bank studies showed, at a time when the economy was growing by nearly 10 percent a year. Over the same period, the income of China's richest 10 percent rose by more than 16 percent. The findings challenge the basis of government policies aimed at narrowing the country's politically sensitive wealth gap (McGregor, 2006). China, which had relatively even income distribution in 1980 when it embarked on market reforms, is now "less equal" than the U.S. and Russia, using the Gini coefficient, a standard measure of income disparities. The way to close this gap has been the subject of an intense and highly politicized debate in China, with many arguing that economic growth alone provides the best way of addressing poverty, even with uneven results. Yet, the Bank's findings showed the error in the argument that a rising tide lifts all boats. Declining farm incomes cannot explain the fall in income for the poor, as food prices were rising at a faster rate than urban prices in December 2003. Over the period that the study covers, inflation was low and in 1 year, 2002, negative. Indeed, poverty in China could be even worse than the World Bank studies indicated. The Chinese defined poverty at a level that understated the size of the problem, at about Rmb650 ($83) a year in income, equal to about 5 percent of average per capita income, compared with the U.S. benchmark of 12 percent. Rural residents were also forced to buy services, such as health and education, in the cities where they were much more expensive. China's present success story seems unsustainable both for multinational companies and the government, and strategy provides few answers to the dilemma, portending, among other things, a need for the swing of the pendulum.

## STAKEHOLDER CAPITALISM

Increased paces of globalization, interconnectedness, and quantum change suggest that for more effective organizations, a top-down instrumental approach may no longer be effective. It's time for the pendulum to swing again for strategy, and CT provides many insights for a more pluralistic approach.

*Business Week* covered one aspect of this swing of the pendulum in its story on "Karma Capitalism" (Engardio & McGregor, 2006). Some researchers and large companies are exploring that executives should be motivated by a broader purpose than money as these broader motivations lead to more well-adjusted and effective companies. Some researchers are also accepting that companies should take a more holistic approach to business—one that takes into account the needs of shareholders, employees, customers, society, and the environment. Other researchers can foresee the development of theory that replaces the shareholder-driven agenda with a more stakeholder-focused approach or "inclusive capitalism...the idea that corporations can simultaneously create value and social justice" (C. K. Prahalad, quoted in Engardio & McGregor, 2006). For some researchers and senior managers, corporate philanthropy and good behavior provides a competitive advantage for attracting and retaining top talent. While corporations used to do most of their manufacturing, product development, and administrative work in-house, most now use outsiders and outsource these functions. Terms such as "extended enterprise," "innovation networks," and "co-creation" accept that effective and highly functional corporations draw on and nurture various external stakeholders.

In his best-selling book, *The Fortune at the Bottom of the Pyramid*, Prahalad detailed how companies can co-create products with consumers and succeed by tailoring technologies and products to the poor, influencing companies such as Nokia and Cargill. The ultimate goal for an effective firm would be to promote a strategy where stakeholder capitalism replaces shareholder capitalism. The late Sumantra Ghoshal was working on a book, *A Good Theory of Management,* when he died. Ghoshal saw the corporate debacles of Enron and its ilk as the inevitable outgrowth of theories developed by economists and absorbed at business schools. Corporations are not merely profit machines reacting to market forces, he noted; they are run by and for humans and have a symbiotic relationship with the world around them. "There is no inherent conflict between the economic well-being of companies and their serving as a force for good in societies," wrote Ghoshal. According to Prahalad, the quest for strategy is "to develop a capitalism that puts the individual at the center of the universe," placing employees and customers first so that they can benefit shareholders.

Indeed, the seemingly ethereal world of CT, rather than the clinical world of IO, seems surprising well attuned to the down-to-earth needs of companies trying to survive in an increasingly global, interconnected business ecosystem.

## REFERENCES

Alvesson, M., & Willmott, H. (1996). *Making sense of management: A critical introduction.* Thousand Oaks, CA: Sage.

Andrews, K. R. (1971). *The concept of corporate strategy.* Homewood, IL: Irwin.

Ansoff, H. (1965). *Corporate strategy.* New York: McGraw Hill.

Barnard, C. I. (1938). *The functions of the executive.* Cambridge, MA: Harvard University Press.

Barney, J. B. (1991). Firm resources and sustained competitive advantage. *Journal of Management, 17,* 99–120.

Barney, J. B. (2002). Strategic management: From informed conversation to academic discipline. *Academy of Management Executive, 16*(2), 53–57.

Bartlett, C. A. (1979). *Multinational structural evolution: The changing decision environment in international divisions.* Unpublished doctoral dissertation. Harvard Business School, Cambridge, MA.

Booth, C. (1998). The problems and possibilities of reflexivity in strategy. *Electronic Journal of Radical Organization, 4*(1), Available at http://www.mngt.waikato.ac.nz/ejrot/.

Bracker, J. (1980). The historical development of the strategic management concept. *Academy of Management Review, 5*(2), 219–224.

Chandler, A. D. (1962). *Strategy and structure.* Cambridge, MA: MIT Press.

Child, J. (1972) Organization structure, environment and performance: The role of strategic choice. *Sociology, 6,* 1–22.

Collis, D. J., & Montgomery, C. A. (1997). *Corporate strategy, resources and the scope of the firm.* Boston, MA: Irwin.

Doz, Y. L. (1976). *National policies and multinational management.* Unpublished doctoral dissertation. Harvard Business School, Cambridge, MA.

Engardio, P., & McGregor, J. (2006, October 30). Karma capitalism. *Business Week.*

Finkelstein, S., & Hambrick, D. C. (1996). *Strategic leadership.* St. Paul, MN: West Educational.

Ghoshal, S. (1986). *The innovative multinational: A differentiated network of organizational roles and management processes.* Unpublished doctoral dissertation. Harvard Business School, Cambridge, MA.

Glater, J. D. (2006, November 20). Pay packages for presidents are rising at public colleges. *New York Times.*

Gregory, W. J. (1996). Discordant pluralism: A new strategy for critical systems thinking. *Systemic Practice and Action Research, 9*(6), 605–625.

Haley, G. T., Haley, U. C. V., & Tan, C. T. (2004). *The Chinese Tao of business: The logic of successful business strategy.* Singapore: John Wiley & Sons.

Haley, U. C. V. (2001). *Multinational corporations in political environments: Ethics, values and strategies.* Singapore: World Scientific.

Hambrick, D. C., & Mason, P. A. (1984). Upper echelons: The organization as a reflection of its top managers. *Academy of Management Review, 9,* 193–206.

Harfield, T. (1998). Strategic management and Michael Porter: A post-modern reading. *Electronic Journal of Radical Organization Theory, 4*(1).

Harrigan, K. R. (1981). Barriers to entry and competitive strategies. *Strategic Management Journal, 2,* 395–412.

Hatten, K. J. (1974). *Strategic models in the brewing industry.* Unpublished doctoral dissertation. Purdue University, West Lafayette, Indiana.

Herbert, B. (2007, January 7). Working harder for the man. *New York Times.*

Hermann, P. (2005). Evolution of strategic management: The need for new dominant designs. *International Journal of Management Reviews, 7*(2), 111–130.

Horkheimer, M. (1974). *Critique of instrumental reason.* Translated by M. J. O'Connell et al. New York: The Seabury Press (A Continuum Book). First published in German in 1967.

Horkheimer, M., & Adorno, T. (1972). *Dialectic of enlightenment.* Translated by J. Cumming. New York: Herder and Herder. Original edition, 1944, *Dielektik der Aufklarung* by New York: Social Studies Association, Inc

Hoskisson, R. E., Hitt, M. A., Wan, W. P., & Yiu, D. (1999). Theory and research in strategic management: Swings of a pendulum. *Journal of Management, 25*(3), 417–456.

Jemison, D. B. (1981). The importance of an integrative approach to strategic management research. *Academy of Management Review, 6,* 633–642.

Keegan, A., & Boselle, P. (2006). The lack of impact of dissensus inspired analysis on developments in the field of human resource management. *Journal of Management Studies, 43*(7), 1491.

Knights, D., & Morgan, G. (1991). Corporate strategy, organizations, and subjectivity: A critique. *Organization Studies, 12*(2), 251–273.

Kogut, B., & Zander, U. (1992) Knowledge of the firm, combinative capabilities, and the replication of technology. *Organization Science, 3,* 383–397.

Learned, E. P., Christensen, C. R., Andrews, K. R., & Guth, W. D. (1965/1969). *Business policy: Text and case.* Homewood, IL: Richard D. Irwin.

Levy, D. L., Alvesson, M., & WIllmott, H. (2003). Critical approaches to strategic management. In M. Alvesson & H. Willmott (Eds.), *Studying management criti-*

*cally* (pp. 92–110). Newbury Park, CA: Sage. Available at http://www.faculty. umb.edu/david_levy/critstrat2003.pdf

Levy, D. L., Alvesson, M., & WIllmott, H. (2001). *Critical approaches to strategic management.* Paper presented at the Critical Management Studies Conference. http://www.mngt.waikato.ac.nz/ejrot/cmsconference/2001/Papers/ strategy/Levy.pdf

Lieberman, M. (1984). The learning curve and pricing in the chemical processing industries. *Rand Journal of Economics, 15,* 213–228.

Løwendahl, B., & Revang, Ø. (1998). Challenges to existing strategy theory in a postindustrial society. *Strategic Management Journal, 19*(8) , 755–773.

McGregor, R. (2006, November 21). China's poorest worse off after boom. *Financial Times.*

Miller, D., & Friesen, P. H. (1984). *Organizations: A quantum view.* Englewood Cliffs, NJ: Prentice-Hall.

Mintzberg, H., & Waters, J. A. (1978). Patterns in strategy formation. *Management Science, 24,* 934–948.

Penrose, E. T. (1959). *The theory of the growth of the firm.* New York: John Wiley & Sons.

Porter, M. E. (1980). *Competitive strategy.* New York: Free Press.

Prahalad, C. K. (1975). *The strategic process in a multinational corporation.* Unpublished doctoral dissertation. Harvard Business School, Cambridge, MA.

Prahalad, C. K. (2006). *The fortune at the bottom of the pyramid: Eradicating poverty through profits.* Upper Saddle River, NJ: Wharton School.

Quinn, J. B. (1980). *Strategies for change: Logical incrementalism.* Homewood, IL: Dow Jones-Irwin.

Roberts, D., & Engardio, P. (2006). Secrets, lies, and sweatshops. *Business Week On Line.* Available at http://www.businessweek.com/print/magazine/content/06_48/b4011001.htm

Rumelt, R. P. (1974). *Strategy, structure and economic performance.* Boston, MA: Harvard Business School Press.

Rumelt, R. P., Schendel, D., & Teece, D. J. (1991). Strategic management and economics. *Strategic Management Journal, 12,* 5–29.

Rumelt, R. P, Schendel, D. E., & Teece, D. J. (Eds.). (1994). *Fundamental issues in strategy.* Cambridge, MA: Harvard Business School Press.

Rumelt, R. P., & Wensley, R. (1981). *In search of the market share effect.* Proceedings of the Academy of Management, pp. 1–5.

Schendel, D. E., & Hatten, K. J. (1972). *Business policy or strategic management: A broader view for an emerging discipline.* Proceedings of the Academy of Management, pp. 99–102.

Selznick, P. (1957). *Leadership in administration: A sociological interpretation.* New York: Harper & Row.

Shrivastava, P. (1986). Is strategic management ideological? *Journal of Management, 12,* 363–377.

Smircich, L., & Stubbart, C. (1985). Strategic management in an enacted world. *Academy of Management Review, 10*(4), 724–736.

Stoney, C. (1998). Lifting the lid on strategic management: A sociological narrative, *Electronic Journal of Radical Organization Theory, 4*(1).

Thomas, P. (1998). Ideology and the discourse of strategic management: A critical research framework. *Electronic Journal of Radical Organization Theory, 4*(1).

Von Neumann, J., & Morgenstern, O. (1944). *The theory of games and economic behavior.* New York: John Wiley & Sons.

Wernerfelt, B. (1984). A resource-based view of the firm. *Strategic Management Journal, 5,* 171–180.

Williamson, O. E. (1975). *Markets and hierarchies.* New York: Free Press.

# CHAPTER 11

# INTERNATIONAL BUSINESS AND CRITICAL ETHICS

## George Cairns and Martyna Sliwa

### INTRODUCTION

In this chapter, we engage with various aspects of international business (IB) and their ethical dimensions. In addressing contemporary issues of ethics in the field of international business, we take as our starting point its historical development. From our contemplations of its evolution and its contemporary status, we identify a number of tensions inherent in attempts to capture and give credence to ethical underpinnings and consequences of IB. Broadly, we see these as falling under three themes. The first of these is constituted by the standpoint from which IB is viewed, that is, the state, the firm, or the stakeholder.[1] The second arises from consideration of two key aspects of IB, namely the internationalization and globalization of markets and of industries, respectively. Finally, interpretation of the ethical dimensions of IB may be underpinned by either a deontological or a utilitarian paradigm; that is to say, directed toward thinking on duties and intentions, or toward action and its outcomes and consequences.

Following our discussion of the historical context of IB and the early role of the nation-state, we consider its contemporary status, and the shift of focus from the state to the firm as the central player. We outline our un-

*Critical Theory Ethics for Business and Public Administration*, pages 229–257

derstanding of the contemporary sociopolitical, economic, and regulatory frameworks within which IB operates, and consider the impact of these in enabling or limiting the activities of IB. We contemplate the significance of business and government in determining the direction in which these frameworks develop, for what purpose, and to what ends, along with the role and effectiveness of countermovements that stand against the interests of powerful actors. We posit that while, at the present time, there are conspicuous attempts to address the perceived need for ethics in IB, these have a limited influence and cannot in themselves result in the embedding of ethics at the core of organizational purpose, in the sense of pursuit of a "common good" for humanity in general.

We illustrate our argumentation by reference to a range of academic and nonacademic literature on aspects of IB, presenting both mainstream and critical perspectives. We provide illustrations of international business practices and consequences, relating to different geographical and organizational contexts, and seen from the perspectives of different actors.[2] In discussing the multiple and seemingly contradictory and incompatible accounts presented, we seek to surface questions in the reader's mind about what "ethics" means in the field of IB, and whether answers can be provided to these questions that might respond to the array of concerns of all involved stakeholders. In bringing the lens of "critical ethics" to bear on IB, we concur with Jones, Parker, and ten Bos (2005), that much of what constitutes the field of "business ethics" remains bounded by the rationality of managerialism and the "common sense" of day-to-day business practice (c.f. Hartman, 2005; Mellahi & Wood, 2003). We acknowledge that theoretical dimensions of critical ethics are addressed in other chapters of this book and elsewhere (c.f. Jones et al., 2005; Parker, 1998). We approach IB not as a theoretical domain, but rather as a field of human activity, and as such, we do not lead a theoretical discussion of the ethics of IB, but instead we explore the possibilities of a new ethics of IB informed by critical reflection on practice. We do so by reference to Aristotelian philosophy, in particular the concept of *phronēsis*, generally translated as "prudence" or "practical wisdom."[3]

Unlike other of the Aristotelian virtues (e.g., *epistēmē* and *technē*), the Greek term *phronēsis* has not been carried forward into contemporary Anglo-Saxon language usage, but it has aroused recent interest in the fields of philosophy (e.g., Dunne, 1993; Gadamer, 1975; Peters, 1970), medical education (Hilton & Slotnick, 2005), teacher training (Eisner, 2002), fisheries management (Jentoft, in press), political theory (Ruderman, 1997), and management and organization studies (e.g., Birmingham, 2003; Clegg, in press; Clegg & Ross-Smith, 2003; Flyvbjerg, 2001, 2003).[4] However, it is not, to our knowledge, represented in the field of IB. We find one reference in the field of business ethics (Hartog & Frame, 2004), but in it, *phronēsis* is presented as an instrument for dealing with interpersonal issues within the context of "business as usual" organizational activity. Here, we seek to question the institutional framework of contemporary IB, and we contemplate the possibilities for application of a phronetic approach. In proposing to ground the discussion of IB ethics in the concept of *phronēsis*, we believe that the possible theoretical frames that could be employed do not differ fundamentally from those pertaining to the broader area of business ethics. Where we see the need for specific consideration of the international aspects is in relation to "the new rules of eligibility, engagement and wealth creation, which are now defining the global economic game by which individuals, companies and nations must earn a living and make profits in the future" (Brown & Lauder, 2001, p. 100). The first of these three types of rules refers to the declining power of national governments; the second outlines the mechanisms through which organizations compete on a global playing field and in so doing "transfer the risks involved in making a profit in volatile market conditions onto their employees who can no longer assume long term job tenure" (Brown & Lauder, 2001, p. 108). The third set of rules, of wealth creation, gives priority to knowledge, information and human capability within the value-adding process—although not everyone is given the opportunity to participate, since "it is still possible for companies to 'profit' from low-skill, low-wage operations, even if this means a significant deterioration in pay and working conditions of a large section of the workforce" (Brown & Lauder, 2001, p. 121).

Considering the implications of these new rules in relation to profit-oriented ethics leads us to contemplate the nature of governance within the institutions of IB. However, we start our discussion by consideration of the historical antecedents of contemporary IB practice, and their ethical underpinnings and consequences.

## IB AND THE ETHICAL IMPERATIVE IN EARLY APPROACHES TO INTERNATIONAL TRADE

The generic term "international business" is commonly used to describe any form of business transaction, carried out by individuals and/or organizations and involving parties from more than one country. Contemporarily, IB transactions include trade in raw materials, finished goods, and services, as well as investment and financial transactions, collaborations, joint ventures, and relocation of business units to capitalize on lower costs of doing business.

The activity of international business has been undertaken since national boundaries were first established, from the days of the Phoenician Empire to the present. Czinkota, Ronkainen, and Moffett (2005) describe ways in which IB has been used as a tool of governmental policy throughout history; whether as an enabler of development or as an instrument of coercion and control. Whilst IB has a long history, recent developments in the fields of industrialization and globalization, advances in transportation, and the growth of multinational enterprises (MNEs) have led to an increase in its economic, social, and political significance. According to Buckley (2003), contemporary theories of IB embrace elements of fields as diverse as applied economics, finance, business policy and corporate strategy, management, and organization theory. However, our search for aspects of ethics in IB begins from consideration of early developments and their underlying rationales.

A common feature of classical theories of IB was the assumption of imbalanced power relationships between nations, with regard to the distribution of physical and financial resources. Since these theories were built around the concept of the nation-state as the main actor in trade exchanges, the underlying notion of "good" was that of benefit to the individual nation-state. This was reflected in the ideas of the mercantilists (c.f. Vaggi & Groenewegen, 2002), who considered the main objective of international transactions to be in contributing to the prosperity of a nation, defined through the amount of its reserves of precious metals. The key tenet of this approach was that countries should seek to increase these reserves through generating high exports and reducing imports. Since the mercantilists held the assumption of the economy being a "zero-sum game," it was taken for granted that efforts to increase the prosperity of one nation would result in consequential losses for others. This was achieved through the application of selective tariffs to promote exports and minimize imports, whereby the state fulfilled an active protectionist role within the mercantile system. Moreover, the application of mercantile thinking in practice resulted in conflict between competing nation-states, seeking to gain control over land and resources and to secure the greatest share of what was considered a finite volume of trade in the world. In this way, one of the earliest theoretical developments in relation to IB was a key factor behind the spread of European Imperialism and the outbreak of European wars between the 16th and 18th centuries.

The limitations of the regulated and self-interested nature of mercantilism were identified and criticized by 18th-century economist Adam Smith (1776), in his book *The Wealth of Nations*. Smith argued that the key to sustainable economic development lay not in protectionism but in free trade and open competition. While Smith's discussion of international trade remained underpinned by the notion of the "good" defined from the point of view of the nation-state, he saw the possibility of all states gaining some form of advantage as a result of exporting goods, which they could produce more efficiently than any other, while at the same time, importing those for which another country held "absolute advantage" through its own production efficiency. He also believed that replacing the restrictive mercantile system with free international exchange would lead to a reduction in levels of poverty and would stimulate social and moral improvement in all countries engaging in exchange. Drawing upon empirical examples from across the world, Smith provided a new understanding of the wealth-creating process and paved the way for an era of free trade and economic expansion in the 19th century. Smith believed that if all individuals pursued their own best interests in seeking to maximize their own prosperity, the best outcome for society at large would emerge; based on the principle of a social mechanism he referred to as "invisible hand" (Smith, 1776), whereby an individual acting for his own good was seen as also promoting the good of his community. However, while he promoted free trade and open competition, Smith also considered that governments should undertake to provide educational, judicial, military, and other institutional frameworks that would not be profitable for private enterprise. Like Smith, Torrens (1815) and Ricardo (1817) argued for the need for nations to engage in free trade with one another, even where one held absolute advantage over the other in relation to the production of all goods. Behind their theory of "comparative advantage," there remains a similar assumption that, in overall terms, free exchange will benefit all nation-states involved in it.

These classic theories of international trade were concerned with the competitiveness of countries rather than companies and, as such, sought to explain how they could achieve and maintain a positive balance of trade. This would be achieved through every country being able to assume an advantageous position in relation to some others, which were identified as offering suitable targets for its exports. However, while the notion of the good underpinning these theories was that of the broadly defined nation, as entity, and of social and moral improvements for groups relative to their own previous state, they did not see as problematic any notion of inequality of wealth distribution across groups and between nations, inasmuch as they addressed only the issue of improvement relative to the subject's own previous situation and not comparative differentials between subjects.

## CONTEMPORARY THEORIES OF IB

During the second half of the 20th century, the central focus of IB moved from products to services and from country- to firm-based theories. The period was exemplified by the growth of multinational enterprises, which in literature was reflected by a preoccupation with consideration of topics of industries and markets. Accordingly, the definition of "good" as viewed from the perspective of the nation-state has been replaced by one that is centered on the firm as the main actor in IB transactions.

A brief overview of some of the key firm-based theories of IB gives an indication of the ethical rationale that underpins them. For example, Linder's (1961) country similarity theory suggests that trade in manufactured products should take place between countries with similar per capita incomes, and should be directed primarily at exchange of differentiated goods; those for which brand name and reputation play a crucial marketing role. This will ensure the maximization of revenues from sales of these goods within targeted market sectors, clustered based upon the criterion of possession of necessary purchasing power. In support of sales maximization within selected markets, Vernon's (1966) product life cycle theory describes three stages of the cycle, from new product development, into maturity, and from there to standardization. At the same time, in support of overall profit maximization over the life cycle of the product, the theory outlines parallel developments in the relocation of production, from domestic production, to export, and finally to net import by the innovating firm's home country as production is moved to take advantage of lower costs. Again, the main tenet of the theory relates to what a firm should do in order to achieve the highest possible returns for its financial shareholders, rather than to contribute to any general good of humanity.

More complex accounts of the nature of contemporary IB are presented through theories that address issues of interorganizational competition and the possibilities of achieving competitive advantage at a global level. For example, global strategic rivalry theory (e.g., Krugman, 1981; Lancaster, 1980) outlines a variety of ways in which MNEs can seek to gain such advantage over their competitors, including through ownership of intellectual property rights, strong investment in research and development, achievement of global economies of scale or scope, and the successful exploitation of the "experience curve." The ethical imperative here again lies in the paradigm of profit maximization for the global players, and any negative impact on societies is not addressed. This, however, does not mean that the occurrence of such negative social outcomes is not acknowledged by the authors of these theories. For example, in his theory of national competitive advantage, Porter (1990) recognizes the existence of inequalities between and within nations and sees them not as a problem to be addressed but as a potential source of competitive advantage and a necessary condition of industry globalization. Within his "diamond" framework, Porter (1985) identifies both value-adding elements, such as knowledge and technology, and cost-reducing elements, such as the availability of cheap labor and other resources.

Within mainstream strategy literature, it is taken for granted that for industries to globalize, there must be differences in production costs between countries, with a primary element of the difference being reduced costs of labor. This literature not only explicitly recognizes the existence of countries and regions offering cheap labor, but treats them as an essential element of industry globalization. The logic of this line of argument, in support of the drive to lower the costs of production, explicitly requires that many of those who are wanted and used as labor by global companies will, by definition, attract a low level of earnings. This will, in turn, translate into them having a relatively low level of purchasing power and, as a result, they will lack the ability to buy those products and services that they might wish to. Rapley (2004, p. 81) summarizes the paradoxical nature of the relationship between production and consumption, stating that "what people do to advance their interests as consumers can undermine their interest as producers." We would extend this to state that what some people do to advance their own interests as consumers will, of necessity, undermine the interests of others, both as prospective consumers and as adequately rewarded producers.

At this point, we would posit that any consideration of ethics in IB as it is currently constituted requires us to recognize and address the "necessity" of consumption in contemporary society. Within mainstream managerialist IB texts—as in strategy, marketing, etc., texts—the consumer and consumption society is taken for granted (e.g., Rugman & Hodgetts, 2003; Tung, 1998; Wild, Wild, & Han, 2006; Woods, 2001), and any image of a problematic "other" that may presented (e.g., Griffin & Pustay, 2005) is directed at ensuring that it does not interfere with the primary task of "how to" promote efficient and effective production/consumption. While we acknowledge that, at present, the vast majority of the world's people do not participate in such "conspicuous consumption," we point to the power of MNEs and their marketing in achieving successful acculturation of populations into the consumption project in most arenas where it has been introduced. At the same time, however, we note that fulfillment of the imperative of maximizing shareholder return will, of necessity, result in a drive to minimize employee or contractor earnings, and hence to reduce some people's ability to join the consumption project. We return to this paradoxical relationship between production and consumption later.

While trade of goods and services is the most obvious form of IB, notions of the desirability of seeking competitive advantage through identification and exploitation of inequalities at an international and global level are also present within theories of international investment. For example, in his exposition of "eclectic theory," Dunning (1993) argues that successful foreign direct investment (FDI) by the firm is based on the combination of three conditions: ownership advantage, location advantage, and internalization advantage. These three types of advantage are achieved through the possession of an asset that will generate value beyond the domestic market, the exploitation of lower costs in a foreign country, and the ability to control operations within this country. The second of these, in particular, points to the need for the continued existence of economic inequalities between home and host countries as preconditions of the success of FDI ventures.

The firm-based theories of international trade and investment are concerned with explaining and enabling profit maximization within international and global industries through exploitation of identified differences in local factors, including that of costs of production. This exploitation is seen as necessary to support the good of the firm and its shareholders. Any impact upon the situation within lower cost zones of production is seen as either unproblematic, through remaining unstated, or beneficial, in offering new opportunities for employment and development. The ethical dimension of IB exemplified here might best be summarized in the words of economist Milton Friedman (1962, p. 133), who stated that, "(t)here is one and only one social responsibility of business—to use its resources and engage in activities designed to increase its profits so long as it stays within the rules of the game, which is to say, engages in open and free competition, without deception or fraud... for corporate officials to make as much money for their stockholders as possible."[5]

Our brief and, necessarily, selective overview of the chronological and thematic evolution of theories leads us to the conclusion that, neither at its roots nor in more recent conceptualizations, has an ethical dimension been embedded in notions of IB. Consideration of contemporary responses to the narrow focus of ethical concerns within the theories has given rise to more complex discussions of the social and ethical aspects of IB across various fields of inquiry. These move us beyond engagement with the interests of nations and of firms and their shareholders, to include a broad range of stakeholders, all of those who can affect or can be affected by firms and their activities.

At this point, we turn to consideration of the link between theory and practice of IB, and center our discussion on the contemporary context of increasing globalization of business, products, and consumer markets.

## FROM THEORY TO PRACTICE: CONTEMPORARY ISSUES IN IB

We have shown that early theories of IB related primarily to nation-states and products, and that those of the 21st century are, to a large extent, grounded in consideration of the firm, and of cross-border facilitation of services and investment. As such, neither allows an ethical imperative to take precedence; in the first case, over political ambitions, and in the second, over economic considerations. Contemporary literature presents a range of viewpoints on whether or not the activities of MNEs, the policies of governments, and the actions of supranational agencies are seen to be supportive of some wider good, through stimulating economic growth and development (e.g., Legrain, 2002), or contributing to an ever-greater socioeconomic divide between a super-rich global elite and an impoverished multitude (e.g., Kingsnorth, 2003).

Central to any contemporary discussion of the effects of IB is the concept of globalization, and consideration of the impacts of the globalization of markets and of industries, respectively. Theories of the effective globalization of markets rely upon the notion of economic convergence, and hence of consumer buying power and buying behavior. On the other hand, those of the globalization of industries depend on continuing variance in factors of production between countries, enabling economies of scale to be achieved through country selection in order to drive down the costs of doing business.

In the flourishing field of services delivery, competitive advantage is based on a country's access both to suitably skilled labor and to necessary capital. At the present time, developing countries, such as China, India, and Mexico, bring together the combination of a skilled workforce, lower costs than in developed countries, along with high levels of technological capability. In comparison to services in the field of production—particularly of items with low technical specifications—competitive advantage is derived primarily from low labor costs and how and why these are maintained is the subject of critical debate. The literature points to a number of different explanations. Mainstream IB textbooks may provide passing reference to issues of "slave labor," environmental change, and political corruption (e.g. Hill, 2005). However, the predominant discourse is one of offering models and "recipes" for managers and organizations seeking to engage in international business while "managing ethical behavior across borders" (Griffin & Pustay, 2005). Within these texts, there is an implicit assumption that the growth and development of IB are both necessary and inevitable. At the same time, the concept of economic integration underpinned by the neoliberal free market economics of the Thatcher and Reagan era continues to be presented, by and large, as the only possible way forward. However, the concept of free trade has been subject to growing criticism in recent decades and alternatives have been put forward, including Tobin Tax, fair trade, balanced trade, and international barter (c.f. Michalos, 1997), proposals that seek to redress social and economic disparities through various degrees of positive discrimination. In addition, a body of writings now exists that challenges the fundamental principles of unconstrained growth and development.

Naomi Klein (2000) identifies the problematic nature of the tension between the unifying effects of global markets and the social fragmentation of global production, due to their different impacts on socioeconomic structures. However, for some, globalization offers the only solution to the problems of social and economic exclusion and impoverishment. Philippe Legrain (2002) considers that, subject to supranational constraints to eliminate the excesses of corporate and individual greed and exploitation, a totally free market is the only course for future development. For Klein, however, fundamental problems of inequality cannot be addressed by the free market approach.

In order to develop critical discussion of the different perspectives on IB that are apparent across different literature sets, we now elaborate our consideration of the paradox inherent in the simultaneous drives to promote the most effective means of global production, while seeking to provide the ideal global market in which to sell the outputs of this production.

## ORGANIZATIONAL AND MANAGERIAL DISCOURSE: THE PARADOX OF GLOBALIZATION

In this section, we first discuss the rationale behind the internationalization and globalization of business operations as portrayed in the mainstream business strategy and marketing literature. We point to the ways in which issues of ethics and social responsibility are masked and remain unexplicated in the terminology of corporate and marketing strategies and in the language of "advantages" and "opportunities." As we have outlined above, at the present time international business-related theories focus on firms as the main participants in IB transactions. Consequently, in business strategy literature, there is an emphasis on the international and global markets and industries within which firms compete.

The issue of firms' involvement in the development of "global markets" can be traced back to North American marketing literature of the 1960s (e.g., Buzzell, 1968; Elinder, 1965; Roostal, 1963). However, debate on the nature of the globalization of markets is usually grounded in Levitt's (1983) seminal article, in which he refers to the "new commercial reality," whereby national and regional preferences are subsumed into a world of "irrevocably homogenized" customer needs and desires, in which there is convergence of product offerings, prices, and other elements of the marketing mix (Yip, Loewe, & Yoshino, 1988). Levitt's concept of a universalism of consumer wants and preferences has been challenged on a number of bases. One of the major critics of the notion of global homogenization is George Ritzer (1996), most famously in his McDonaldization thesis, in which he presents an image of global market penetration by products and services defined by price rather than quality, and based on universal standards of efficiency, control, and predictability in delivery to the consumer across all outlets in every market. Ritzer challenges the legitimacy and the social desirability of such mass consumption and its dematerialization. At the same time, others (e.g., De Mooij, 2000; Jain & Ryans, 1991; Keillor, D'Amico, & Horton, 2001; Khor, 2001; McAuley, 2004) point to continued differences in consumer tastes and requirements, both across the world and within national markets. Within counterarguments to global convergence, there is an underlying assumption that consumers (i.e., members of the market) have a decisive role in determining the types of goods and services that will be delivered by firms. In focusing on the extent to which they display similar product preferences, this discourse disregards those who are excluded from participation in international and global markets due to their low purchasing power. As Banerjee and Linstead (2001, p. 702) point out, while "TVs, cars, computers, washing machines, refrigerators, air conditioners, processed foods and colas are symbols of the new India... little more than 1 per cent of Indian households own cars and only 6 per cent of households own a refrigerator."

Within the mainstream discourse on global markets, there is a concentration on the ways in which international business can attract the purchasing power of these minorities, and can create and fulfill their consumer needs through development and delivery of services and products. While Bauman (1998, p. 72) refers to this economic stratification of society in presenting the view that "the new rich do not need the poor any more," we would argue that, as far as the interests of firms operating within IB are concerned, maintaining economic inequalities is essential. That is to say, the very essence of being rich requires that there be those who are poor. To explain this line of argumentation, we now turn our attention to the assumptions and rationale that underpin mainstream discussion on the nature of internationalization and globalization of industries.

Mainstream business strategy literature sees the aim of firms in developing their scale of activity beyond national boundaries within a transnational or global arena. Here, the types of operations involve not only selling goods and services to geographically dispersed markets, but also decoupling the processes of production from specific locations and reconstituting them on a global scale (e.g., Howells & Wood, 1993). Within the international business environment, firms implement cost- or differentiation-based strategies (Porter, 1985) in order to achieve competitive advantage, and to maximize ownership, internalization, and location advantages (Buckley & Casson, 1998; Dunning, 1993) through configuring their value chains internationally or globally. The possibility of attaining high profits is linked to exploitation of opportunities for lowering the costs of production, and nowadays this is frequently achieved through selective discrimination in relation to geographical location, governed by differential factors of production, land, capital, labor, and through the existence of a global logistics and transportation infrastructure. Within this model, a necessary condition of the maximization of profit is the ongoing existence of structural discrepancies across nations and regions (Jones, 2002). There is a distinction between the value-adding elements, such as knowledge and technology, and cost-reducing factors, like access to cheap labor, and local tax and tariff regimes (e.g., Porter, 1990). The majority of consumer goods and services in the contemporary world rely upon these cost-reducing factors, in particular cheap labor, in order to support profit maximization. This has resulted in the emergence of new models of supply, such as export processing zones (EPZs) (e.g., Cairns, 2005; Palley, 2002; Young, 1991) and globally networked call centers (e.g., Taylor & Bain, 2005), which take advantage of and seek to maintain differences between local conditions of production and global norms. For some (e.g., Palley, 2002), rather than promoting growth in an ever more competitive global industry context, these developments can lead to a "race to the bottom" as countries—or even regions within one country—attempt to gain competitive advantage. By default, those who serve international and global business as cheap labor attract a level of earnings that prevents them from participating in global markets for many of the products and services to which they themselves contribute.

The mainstream marketing and business strategy literature recognizes the existence of earning differentials between populations and acknowledges this exclusion for sectors of societies. However, extant inequalities are viewed as "opportunities" for achievement of competitive advantage by firms that exploit them through becoming "transnational" (Bartlett & Ghoshal, 1995) or "heterarchical" (Hedlund, 1986). In this way, issues of poverty and economic inequality are not addressed from the perspective of ethics and social responsibility, but are masked by the terminology of marketing and corporate strategies. Thus, in the overall discourse, "(t)he low-paid are not central, but neither are they marginal. It is they whose labour keeps the system up and running. And on a global scale, the low-paid means an enormous mass of people" (Eagleton, 2004, p. 20). Through setting the prices for products and services and through controlling the conditions of employment, including wage levels, MNEs exercise power over members of societies within which they conduct their operations in pursuit of their goal of profit maximization. Thus, international and global businesses have parallel interests in the development and maintenance of both global markets, which consist of those with high purchasing power, and industries that rely on the continuing existence of supplies of low-cost labor (cf. Brown & Lauder, 2001).

Considering the ethical aspects of the IB practices that we identify, first from a deontological perspective, we can see that any universal maxim that addresses the paradoxical nature of the simultaneous drives for convergence of markets and differentiation of industries and centers of production in the contemporary world can only be directed at seeing a duty toward a select group of stakeholders, and an intention to maximize their good at the expense of others. Similarly, consideration of the utilitarian imperative leads us to see it as centered on a desired outcome of maximizing shareholder value through drawing earnings from a select group of satisfied consumers, again serving the best interests of some stakeholders, but to the detriment of others. At a basic level of interpretation of appearances, this discussion of the conceptual underpinnings of internationalization and globalization of firms suggests that international business is a project inherently devoid of ethical considerations beyond the ethics of shareholder return, in that it is dependent upon and reinforces global inequalities. It is in response to this narrow view of ethics in international business that criticisms such as those of so-called "anti-capitalist" and "anti-globalization" movements have emerged.

However, before we consider the nature and impact of contemporary institutional frameworks, we see it as necessary to point to the complexity and ambiguity involved in determining what is "ethical" in business, and what contributes to an ethical outcome in terms of the activities of international and global firms and the choices made by the consumers who constitute their target markets. In the following section, we draw upon a range of illustrations of international business practice.

## (UN)ETHICAL INTERNATIONAL BUSINESS?

From the perspective of those in the "developed" world, questions are raised about the ethicality of working practices, for example, in "sweatshop" EPZ factories (e.g., Palley, 2002; Young, 1991); the global marketplace's "dirty little secret" (Klein, 2000, p. 347), where "(f)ear pervades... (and) governments are afraid of losing their foreign factories; the factories are afraid of losing their brand-name buyers; and the workers are afraid of losing their unstable jobs" (p. 206). However, in relation to some production practices in Pakistan, Kristof (2002) points out that, "sweatshops are the only hope of kids like Ahmed Zia, a 14-year-old boy here in Attock, a gritty center for carpet weaving... (who) earns $2 a day hunched over the loom, laboring over a rug that will adorn some American's living room... the American campaign against sweatshops could make his life much more wretched by inadvertently encouraging mechanization that could cost him his job. 'Carpet-making is much better than farm work,' Ahmed said, mulling alternatives if he loses his job as hundreds have over the last year. 'This makes much more money and is more comfortable.'"

Referring to critiques of life in EPZs "from the comfort of a first class university in Europe," Kenyan journalist Wycliffe Muga (cited in Cairns, 2005, pp. 49–51) comments that

Here… we consider anything that provides employment for our millions of school-leavers as pure and undoubted manna from heaven…all that counts is that thousands of young Kenyans who would otherwise be despairing and turning to prostitution and crime, are now making the same sort of money as most clerical and other such lower-level white collar jobs pay, here in Kenya.… (U)nless your militant do-gooders were going to go to the extent of examining and influencing working conditions in both the cotton fields, and the sisal fields, it would be pointless for them to try and influence conditions in the EPZ factories. For the EPZ workers…come at the end of a long production chain and have a much easier time than the agricultural workers.

While the sustainability of such jobs may be questioned "from the comfort of a first class university," these examples show that what might be seen by Western commentators as illustrations of unethical business practices at an international level, may evoke very different responses in those directly affected by these practices, facing very different choices about work and life in general.

Contemporary international business activities also provide examples of initiatives that are underpinned by widespread Western notions of ethicality and social responsibility. These may be undertaken by MNEs in response to some of the problems that are arguably caused by the operations of these same international businesses. For example, in early 2006, pop star and campaigner against world poverty, Bono, has persuaded four MNEs—Nike-owned Converse, Gap, Armani, and Amex—to participate in the launch of a range of products under the brand name Product Red (Elliott, 2006). On average, involved firms have pledged 40 percent of the profits generated from sales of these products to be donated to the Global Fund to Fight Aids, Tuberculosis and Malaria (Webster, 2006). Supporters of this action see the role of the Product Red campaign in contributing to raising awareness about and reducing levels of world poverty. Global Fund director Richard Feachem commented that, while at present only $5 million of the $4.7 billion raised to fight endemic disease has come from corporate donors, the success of Product Red could lead to an "innovative, large and sustainable income stream." Amex chief marketing officer John Hayes points out that, while "traditional philanthropic models simply cannot solve this problem," it can be addressed by "conscientious commerce that will reward both (its) shareholders and the global community," in a world where corporate marketing budgets are much larger than those of philanthropic organizations. While those who support Product Red point to its positive impact on global problems of health and poverty, critics question the motives behind the campaign and highlight its potential adverse affects. The press release of Red's launch on January 26, 2006, provoked immediate responses on Guardian Unlimited's website (Elliott, 2006), including that of Mahoney Balonie, saying, "Right, so the world gets saved by marketing and selling more junk. personally, I don't buy it. These companies are trying to sell more. If they are worried about global disease, why not just donate the money without the hoopla?" Another respondent, Alex, questioned whether "AIDS (i.e., malnutrition—remember that word?) is going to be faced this way—with a fake advertising campaign for financial services and groovy sunglasses. Are they completely mad?" Here, we would point out that while our presentation of the various examples above may be read as implying that we consider them either "right and moral" or "wrong and immoral," this is certainly not our claim. We present them only to raise questions in the reader's own mind.

Up to now, in considering the nature of contemporary production and consumption at a global level, we have focused on firms and enterprises and consumers and society. However, present-day businesses do not undertake IB free of other institutional constraints; therefore, in the following section, we discuss the frameworks within which IB takes place in contemporary society, along with their sociopolitical, economic, and regulatory implications. We also highlight the role and impact of a range of supranational agencies, mostly established in the aftermath of World War II with the aim of ensuring that trade and international economics did not present a basis for future conflict between nations. We then address the emergence of countermovements that challenge the roles and practices of supranational agencies, and the implications of the conflict between concern for producers and/or consumers, and between the deontological and utilitarian ethical perspectives that may drive them.

## INSTITUTIONAL FRAMEWORKS
## AND COUNTERMOVEMENTS

Within the contemporary domain of IB, individual nation-states retain certain rights and responsibilities in relation to how business is conducted both within their boundaries and by their home-registered firms in other countries. However, since the mid-20th century transnational frameworks that control or influence the nature of IB have been developed. These are administered at a global level by supranational agencies like the International Monetary Fund (IMF), the World Trade Organization (WTO), and the World Bank, and at a regional level through various modes of economic integration, ranging from free trade agreements (e.g., NAFTA), through trading blocs (e.g., Mercosur and the Economic Community of West African States [ECOWAS]), to more complex forms, involving not only economic, but also political integration (e.g., the EU).

Some of these agencies, blocs, and agreements influence the nature of IB by direct intervention in the establishment of legal frameworks under which trade is conducted, while others exert power and influence over the financial and economic environment of IB. The WTO brings together the world's major trading nations in order to develop rules for trade, to undertake the administration of trade agreements, to act as a forum for negotiation in addressing disputes between members, and to monitor the national policies of members. Through these aims, the WTO seeks to ensure that "(c)onsumers and producers know that they can enjoy secure supplies and greater choice of the finished products, components, raw materials and services that they use," with a resultant impact in "improv(ing) the welfare of the peoples of the member countries" (WTO, n.d.). Meanwhile, the EU defines the rules of free trade within the European community of member nations, while globally, it aims to be "a leading player in efforts to liberalise world trade for the mutual benefit of rich and poor countries alike" (European Union, n.d.).

The IMF and the World Bank influence the nature of IB through their activities in relation to the economic and financial environment. Both agencies trace their origins to the 1940s, when they were set up as vehicles for implementation of the Bretton Woods system, which set out rules for management of the commercial and financial relationships between the leading industrialized nations. Today, the World Bank operates as an agency of the United Nations and has as its main purpose the funding of development projects around the world, with a "mission of global poverty reduction and the improvement of living standards" (World Bank, n.d.). The IMF "is an international organization of 184 member countries. It was established to promote international monetary cooperation, exchange stability, and orderly exchange arrangements; to foster economic growth and high levels of employment; and to provide temporary financial assistance to countries to help ease balance of payments adjustment" (IMF, n.d.).

A further grouping that impacts the nature of contemporary IB is the G-8 group of nations, comprising Canada, France, Germany, Italy, Japan, Russia, the United Kingdom, and the United States. The G8 has as its purpose the review of economic developments within the member states and across the global economy, and initiation of international economic and financial policies. In 2005, the stated aims of the group were to "secure political commitment to action on key global issues…in bringing together the key like-minded players from Asia, Europe and North America." The group considers itself "capable of setting the agenda thanks to the economic and political weight of its members and their shared commitment to global security and prosperity" (G8, 2005).

Central to many of the supranational agencies involved in IB is the concept of economic integration, a process aimed at reducing barriers to trade between national markets. The public statements of aims and objectives of most of such agencies, and the principles upon which they were originally founded, are generally indicative of an intent to promote economic integration through an inclusive and developmental intervention in IB, seeking to benefit both producers and consumers through establishment of rules and frameworks for international trade. However, since the 1980s the major driving force behind the WTO, IMF, and the World Bank has been that of neoliberal free market economics.

Critics of these organizations (e.g., Klein, 2000) point out that the contemporary "free market" is anything but free, and show that they have acted over the past two decades to reinforce developed world hegemony through enabling expansion of the activities of MNEs while, at the same time, failing to address structural problems of unequal access to and restricted practices within global markets. Referring to the dominance of the "free market ideology of Ronald Reagan and Margaret Thatcher" in the 1980s, Stiglitz (2002, p. 13) points out that the "IMF and World Bank became the new missionary institutions, through which these ideas were pushed on the reluctant poor countries that often badly needed their loans and grants." He goes on to highlight the ever-greater power of these institutions from the 1980s to the present time, such that developing countries that wish to "better access international capital markets must follow their economic prescriptions, prescriptions which reflect their free market ideologies and theories." He then states that "(t)he result for many people has been poverty and for many countries social and political chaos" (2002, p. 18).

In recent times, the actions of some of the supranational agencies have been challenged in publication and through direct action, whereby they have been accused of supporting the hegemony of "first-world" politics and economics and the drive for market dominance by "developed-world" MNEs. In 1999, opposition to the policies and practices of the major supranational agencies gained a broader public awareness, first with a series of protests in cities across the world, then more significantly in violent clashes at the WTO meeting in Seattle in November. Subsequent actions have taken place at meetings of the G8 and WTO. While the media tend to group these protestors together under the banner "anti-globalization," there is no single universal cause that brings them together. A number of issues, including environmentalism, labor rights, third-world poverty, and anti-war movements, are subsumed within a broad generalization. While some of the protests appear to be more anti-American—anti-Bush, anti-McDonald's or anti-Starbucks—than anti-globalization, there is a general concern within the various movements for the current status quo of the world order, along with a call for a redistribution of political and economic power and for action to address social and environmental problems that are seen as being of critical importance.

In our consideration of the current status of the supranational agencies and their role in IB, we recognize that it can be seen either from the perspective of deontology, focusing on the rights of others and their duties toward them, or of utilitarianism, seeking the maximum good for the greatest number. However, we would posit that the agencies face a dilemma in that, on the one hand, they must respond to the ethical imperative set out in their own aims and mission statements that call upon them to address the needs of society at large at a global level, while on the other, they must take account of the financial imperative of firms—which are necessary participants in and beneficiaries of the agencies' activities, in providing the products and services that will enable the desired economic growth—seeking to promote the maximization of profit and return to their shareholders.

In this text, we have thus far highlighted differences between how the most effective global markets and industries are conceptualized, how new forms of production may be viewed as dehumanizing or as enabling development, and how the gap between the rhetoric and actions of supranational agencies is perceived by many. We recognize that there have been attempts to reconcile the different driving forces and priorities that characterize these variations through development of the concept of business ethics (e.g., Mellahi & Wood, 2003; Michalos, 1995) and the drive for a new "corporate social responsibility" (CSR) (e.g., Gurney & Humphreys, 2006; Whitehouse, 2006). However, some remain sceptical both of the implementation of CSR (e.g., Frynas, 2005; Roberts, 2003); seeing it as being about "managing perceptions and making people...feel good about themselves" (Frynas, 2005, p. 582), and of prescriptive approaches to development of something called business ethics (e.g., Jones et al., 2005; Parker, 1998).

In the final sections of this chapter—seeking to challenge the hegemony of current institutional frameworks, while avoiding both a call for revolution and collapse into nihilism—we draw upon Aristotelian philosophy and its relevance to the issues of "governance." In seeing IB as a domain of practice, we offer our views on the possibilities for a broader ethical decision-making agenda in IB, grounded in the concept of *phronēsis*, or practical wisdom.

## BEYOND CONTEMPORARY IB PRACTICE: CHANGE OR REVOLUTION?

Based on our considerations of the different perspectives on IB, their historical antecedents, and the various interpretations that can be placed upon any particular set of circumstances, we see that the area of ethics and IB represents contested territory. Like others (e.g., Jones et al., 2005), we identify dichotomous views on how the activities of MNEs and supranational agencies are legitimated or challenged when seen through different ethical lenses, on the ways in which various stakeholder groups are represented or excluded from the considerations, and on whether contemporary concerns for development of concepts like business ethics and corporate social responsibility represent catalysts for change, or for reinforcement of the status quo and "business as usual." We posit that the current economic model of global production and markets leads firms to see the search for ever-lower costs of production as a prime driver. When the work process can be physically detached from the market, jobs will be moved across the world in search of the most efficient operational base. In both the manu-facturing and service sectors—in cases where the work requires little or no skill—lowest cost will prevail, often assisted by packages of low or no rent, tax holidays, and curtailment of labor union activity. When the work does require some skill input, growing economies with a pool of educated labor—such as India and China—will dominate. As forms of decision mak-ing on global workplace location develop that are based on recognition and maintenance of economic differentials, we would disagree with Baumann's (1998) notion that the rich no longer need the poor, and would posit that they need them as much as ever, but can detach themselves from them much more readily in terms of geographic proximity and registration in the conscience.

As we have pointed out, there are numerous critics of the prevailing busi-ness logic, and we might consider authors like Ritzer and Klein, along with protests in Seattle, Geneva, and Gleneagles as pointers toward a new world order based on drivers other than short-term financial gain. However, we suggest that these movements lack a critical mass of members and activities at this time and that the drive for conspicuous consumption overshadows such countermovements. As developing economies achieve growth, mem-bers aspire to a lifestyle modeled on that of the Anglo-Saxon first world. De-sires for luxury goods and a more "mobile" lifestyle are translated into basic needs, fueled by and providing the fuel for the "consumption project." We consider that the moral order of this process of development is neither de-ontological nor utilitarian. If there is any dominant "moral imperative," we suggest that it is based on an Anglo-Saxon, masculine-oriented rationale, in which "power *defines* what counts as rationality and knowledge and thereby what counts as reality" (Flyvbjerg, 1998, p. 227, original emphasis). If there is any utilitarian morality, seeking some greater good for all, we posit that this is based on a "bounded rationality" that determines both the terms of opportunity for participation as part of the "all," and also of what the "greater good" is. In the contemporary world, we see international business as an all-pervasive process with little or no opportunity for any member of humanity—or any other species—to escape its influence and impact. We also consider that all forms of government and governance that prevail, whether democratic or authoritarian, exclude some "other" and that the extent of exclusion is purely a matter of degree.

In applying institutional theory to consideration of governance and how contemporary business is constituted, Morgan (1998, p. 224) highlights that "economic relations are embedded in social institutions." He explains that, over history, this economic relationship has been grounded in the concept of property rights, but with the notion of collective ownership rather than private ownership being the norm. However, as Morgan points out, recent decades have seen a trend toward privatization of property. This change has been manifest particularly in the United Kingdom and the United States, but is now built into the neoliberal ideology of institutions like the World Bank and IMF and is a required "structural adjustment" by countries that seek capital funding from them. Any move toward private ownership, and the need for organizations to turn themselves in the first instance to the interests of financial stakeholders, will, as Friedman (1962) points out, drive them to seek to maximize their profits at the expense of other considerations. While Friedman's definition of the aim of business as being to generate profit is balanced by his consideration of the questions "Who protects the consumer?" and "Who protects the worker?" (Friedman & Friedman, 1980), the drive of neoliberal governments and agencies to privatize public services and to minimize interference in the market leads us to ponder the answer to these questions at the present time. Beyond the aim of profit maximization within "the rules of the game," Ladd (1970, p. 499) considers that, "for logical reasons it is improper to expect organisational conduct to conform to the ordinary principles of morality. We cannot and must not expect formal organisations, or their representatives acting in their official capacities, to be honest, courageous, considerate, sympathetic, or to have any kind of moral integrity. Such concepts are not in the vocabulary, so to speak, of the organisational language game." This approach to business has recently been exemplified in the contemporary business world in the case of the executives of Enron (BBC, 2006).

Let us now ponder the possibilities of change to the social and moral order of IB. This, we would suggest, requires a move away from the hegemony of profit orientation. We have challenged the notion that change is currently possible through the (albeit high-profile) activities of ephemeral minority protest groups and a few writers. However, we consider that events such as the emergence of new and undisputed evidence of climate change and its possibilities for cataclysmic impact, the conflict between dwindling supplies of fossil fuel energy sources and ever-greater demand for these, and the failure of neoliberal and neoconservative policies to facilitate the construction of sustainable and secure communities for *homo oeconomicus* hold the possibility for generating a more widespread climate for change. But, we would posit that the key to this lies in a necessary realization of the need to move beyond the short-termism of financial expediency and immediate gain, to genuine concern for long-term sustainability and security. In relation to the implications of such change for IB, this requires concerted action by a broad coalition of involved and concerned stakeholders, and reconsideration of the nature of governance of the institutions of international business.

## SEEKING A NEW EVOLUTION: INSPIRATION FROM ARISTOTLE

Like Jones et al. (2005), we consider the current status of business ethics as a subject; its idealized drive toward instrumental methods for development of the "ethical business" (cf. Mellahi & Wood, 2003); to be a chimera, but again like them, we do not see a critical reaction to this as representing a state of being "against ethics" or of lapsing into nihilism. In line with Jones et al. (2005), as well as such diverse supporters and critics of globalization as ex-WTO advisor Philippe Legrain (2002), former World Bank economist Joseph Stiglitz (2002), and critical journalists Paul Kingsnorth (2003) and Naomi Klein (2000), we posit that a new ethics will require, at a minimum, some reconstitution of the existing frameworks and institutions of IB. Jones et al. (2005) offer ideas for development of a critical business ethics that is challenging to the "common sense" approach—seeking to "stick a spanner in the works" (p. 134)—and we now draw upon the Aristotelian concept of phronēsis in order to offer an additional—not alternative—option for such ethics. In contemplating a phronetic approach to IB, we must first consider the possibility of a rehumanizing of organization, such that the proper purpose of business is seen as serving the ends of humanity rather than of itself, and that of management as being to ensure the success of organization in achieving this end. If we assume this, then we would argue that the Aristotelian virtue of phronēsis is the most important intellectual virtue of the manager.

In his Nicomachean ethics, Aristotle outlines five "intellectual virtues"; *epistēmē, technē, phronēsis, nous,* and *sophia.* In the space of this chapter on IB we cannot address them all, other than to affirm that for Aristotle *phronēsis*—the ability of "man[6] to be able to deliberate about what is good and advantageous for himself," and to be "capable of action with regard to things that are good or bad for man" (2004, p. 150)—represented the most important of the five, "for the possession of the single virtue of prudence[7] will carry with it the possession of them all" (p. 166). For Aristotle, "the full performance of man's function depends upon a combination of prudence and moral virtue; virtue ensures the correctness of the end at which we aim, and prudence that of the means towards it" (p. 163). Thus, Aristotelian *phronēsis* brings together consideration of both means and ends, and of the self and the wider community of "man."

At this point, we must emphasize that *phronēsis* is a form of value-rational knowledge that takes account of context and of the different values and beliefs of those involved, and is oriented toward informing action. It differs from pure scientific knowledge, which Aristotle sees as context-free and unchanging over time, and from technical knowledge of how to make something. *Phronēsis* is oriented toward informing action, not production. Being contextual and value-rational, phronetic knowledge about any matter can be very different between individuals even within one small group. However, it must be stressed that the phronetic project is not one of moral relativism, in that it requires that deliberation be undertaken about options for action and that informed choices be made between alternative, possibly competing rationalities. Also, although *phronēsis* is context dependent it also carries with it the obligation to seek out general inferences about how to act in other related circumstances.

In the contemporary world of social science and organization studies, the concept of *phronēsis* has been subject to discussion and development (e.g., Birmingham, 2003; Clegg, in press; Clegg & Ross-Smith, 2003), most notably by Danish academic Bent Flyvbjerg (2001, 2003). Based on his longitudinal study of urban planning and sustainable development in the Danish city of Aalborg, Flyvbjerg (1998, 2001) challenges the notion that democracy is transparent, inclusive, and conducive to the realization of a "common good." He posits that, rather than applying objective rationality, those in organizations faced with complex problems and policymaking decisions approach them in a way in which "power *defines* what counts as rationality and knowledge and thereby what counts as reality" (Flyvbjerg, 1998, p. 227, original emphasis). Here, the exercise of power determines not only what problems are brought forward for consideration, but also how they are conceived and presented. He argues that the "democratic" process may be one of exclusion and the pursuit of self-interest by powerful individuals and bodies. In his book, *Making Social Science Matter*, Flyvbjerg (2001) posits that complex social issues, of the type that are often simplified and subject to premature closure in the world of "market managerialism," might be explicated by the application of a phronetic approach where the following value-rational questions are addressed at the outset:

Where are we going?

Is this development desirable?

What, if anything, should we do about it?

Who gains and who loses, and by which mechanisms of power? (2001, p. 60)

Flyvbjerg considers that any transition from the form of democracy practiced in the Aalborg context to one intended to serve a broader good requires genuine transparency and accountability, and development of dialogical communication that draws upon all relevant and effective media. This dialogue must acknowledge the mediating processes of power and rationality. Flyvbjerg's writing lays the ground for consideration of what types of social institutions we require in order to move toward a new democracy.

Drawing upon Flyvbjerg's conceptual framework, Jentoft (in press) moves thinking on the role of management, in relation to complex societal issues, beyond consideration of it being either a scientific and/or technological endeavor. He sees it as requiring that political and policy decisions are taken into account along with their implications in the broader realm of community and society. Jentoft brings attention to bear on the political dimension, stating that "the concerns, principles and goals of the management process are matters of preference and choice, and hence political struggle" and that "the name of the game is changing, as 'management' is increasingly being replaced by the broader concept of 'governance.'" It is in seeking ways of enacting a new form of management that involves consideration of a broad range of social values and ethical stances that Jentoft calls for a phronetic approach.

In Jentoft's (in press) text, we find a resonance with the Aristotelian concern for what is "good or bad for man." In relation to complex and possibly ambiguous problems, that involve deliberation on social, economic, ecological, and other implications of their resolution, Jentoft sees the answer to what is "good" as a matter for negotiation within the framework of a democratic society. He calls upon Flyvbjerg's value-rational questions in order to open up thinking on the issue of fisheries management, drawing upon the scientific knowledge of marine scientists, the technical knowledge of the fishing community, and the economic, social, and environmental concerns of broader society. Jentoft's governance perspective "emphasizes the interaction between the state, the market and civil society, recognizing the strengths and weaknesses of each and the need to draw on their respective capacities." He sees the concept of governance as "inviting a more reflexive, deliberative and value-rational methodology than the instrumental, means-end oriented management concept." Jentoft recognizes that problems are not always what they appear to be, often stemming from outside the context that they are made visible within, and he urges the approach of "scouting outwards," in terms of geographical, disciplinary, and chronological contexts. In relation to the third context, and to Flyvbjerg's (2001) fourth question above, he asks, "Are future generations sacrificed for the benefit of the present one?"

Taking a lead from Jentoft, we propose the possibility of a governance-based approach to IB, whereby the institutions that are involved in it—firms, governments, supranational agencies, and countermovements—each bring the views, the knowledge, the (scientific, technical, value-based) rationalities of their constituencies to the table, and commit to the development of a truly democratic discussion in which the role of power is explicitly acknowledged. Such an approach may appear fanciful in the current climate—we ourselves have indicated our pessimism above. However, maybe there are enough people willing to follow the call of Kingsnorth (2003, p. 331) and others and to act on the belief that it

> is our job: to be bold. Not to tinker at the margins, "greening" corporations, waffling about "sustainability", proposing voluntary targets, issuing policy papers, settling for better-than-nothing, politely gathering the crumbs from the table. Our job, now, is to call for everything we want, as loudly as we can—and to keep calling until we get it.

Then, we might find meaningful answers to Flyvbjerg's question, "Who gains and who loses, and by which mechanisms of power?"

## FINAL REMARKS

In this chapter, we have outlined the historical antecedents of contemporary international business and shown that the field is grounded in notions of competition, self-interest, and exploitation. We have illustrated how this philosophy underpins much of the present-day mainstream literature and theories of IB. In challenging these mainstream approaches and introducing more critical approaches, we have also sought to indicate that there is still no easy answer to what is "ethical" or "unethical" in IB. Rather, we posit that consideration of any question of ethicality requires an understanding of context, of the different values and rationalities of the range of involved stakeholders, and some means of taking account to these.

While we offer a fairly pessimistic prognosis on the current state of IB and its countermovements, we draw upon Aristotle's concept of *phronēsis* and its contemporary development in the works of Flyvbjerg (2001, 2003) and Jentoft (in press), to illustrate the theoretical possibilities of a more humanistic IB project based on emergence of a new form of democratic governance that either changes the practices and institutions of IB or, at the very least, leads to radical restructuring of the existing institutions.

## NOTES

1. The term "stakeholder" is read in a variety of ways by different authors. Some consider a fairly narrow constituency, selected for instrumental reasons within the rhetoric of managerialism. We define a stakeholder as any party who can affect, or can be affected by the activities of the organization. This takes us, in

the context of IB, into possible consideration of every living entity, and even future generations.

2. We acknowledge that, as authors, we hold a privileged position of power over the content and style of presentation of these different accounts.

3. In their book *For Business Ethics,* Jones et al. (2005, p. 65) say that, in seeking to break away from rules-based business ethics, "what we need... is practical wisdom." However, they do not develop this line of argumentation, and do not call upon Aristotle's concept of *phronēsis* to elaborate the form of practical wisdom.

4. For a more detailed discussion of our own interpretation and application of *phronēsis* in the field of organization studies, see Cairns and Śliwa (forthcoming).

5. We acknowledge Jones et al.'s (2005) critique of selective use of this quotation from Friedman, in which they point out that he goes on to challenge business's ability to engage successfully with projects that should rightly be initiated by democratic governments, and the legitimacy of any such involvement. However, we would suggest that this presents a "copout" for business, and that there is no reason why businesses should not be capable of determining what is socially desirable.

6. Aristotle, of course, lived in a male-dominated society, but contemporary discussion of *phronēsis* moves us beyond such a discriminatory consideration.

7. In the edition of *The Nicomachean Ethics* used here, the term *phronēsis* is consistently translated as "prudence."

## REFERENCES

Aristotle (350 B.C./2004). *The Nicomachean ethics* (J.A.K. Thomson, Trans.). London: Penguin.

Banerjee, B., & Linstead, S. (2001). Globalization, multiculturalism and other fictions: Colonialism for the new millennium? *Organization, 84,* 683–722.

Bauman, Z. (1998). *Globalization: The human consequences.* Cambridge, UK: Polity Press.

BBC. (2006, May 25). QandA: The Enron case. BBC News Online. Retrieved June 9, 2006, at http://news.bbc.co.uk/1/hi/business/3398913.stm

Birmingham, C. (2004). Phronesis: A model for pedagogical reflection. *Journal of Teacher Education, 554,* 313–324.

Brown, P., & Lauder, H. (2001). *Capitalism and social progress.* Basingstoke, UK: Palgrave.

Buckley, P. J. (Ed.). (2003). *International business.* Aldershot, Uk: Ashgate/Dartmouth.

Buckley, P., & Casson, M. (1998). Models of the multinational enterprise. *Journal of International Business Studies, 291,* 21–44.

Buzzell, R. D. (1968, November-December). Can you standardize multinational marketing? *Harvard Business Review,* pp. 102–113.

Cairns, G. (2005). Perspectives on a personal critique of international business. *Critical Perspectives on International Business, 1*(1), 43–55.

Cairns, G., & Sliwa, M. (forthcoming). The implications of Aristotle's phronēsis for organizational inquiry. In D. Barry & H. Hansen (Eds.), *Handbook of the new and emerging in management and organization.* London: Sage.

Clegg, S. R. (in press). The bounds of rationality: Power/history/imagination. *Critical Perspectives on Accounting.*

Clegg, S. R., & Ross-Smith, A. (2003). Revising the boundaries: management education and learning in a postpositivist world. *Academy of Management Learning and Education, 21,* 85–98.

Czinkota, M. R., Ronkainen, I. A., & Moffett, M. H. (2005). *International business* (7th ed.). Mason, OH: South-Western.

De Mooij, M. (2000). The future is predictable for international marketers. *International Marketing Review, 172,* 103–113.

Dunne, J. (1993). *Back to the rough ground: Practical judgment and the lure of technique.* Notre Dame, IN: University of Notre Dame Press.

Dunning, J. (1993). *The globalization of business.* London: Routledge.

Eagleton, T. (2004). *After theory.* London: Penguin.

Eisner, E. (2002). From episteme to phronesis to artistry in the study and improvement of teaching. *Teaching and Teacher Education, 18,* 375–385.

Elinder, E. (1965). How international can European advertising be? Journal of Marketing, 29, 7–11.

Elliott, L. (2006, January 26). How much of this is down to philanthropy and idealism... *Guardian Unlimited.* Retrieved March 3, 2006, at http://www.guardian.co.uk

European Union. (n.d.). *Activities of the European Union: External trade.* Retrieved May 31, 2006, at http://europa.eu/pol/comm/index_en.htm

Flyvbjerg, B. (1998). *Rationality and power: Democracy in practice.* Chicago: University of Chicago Press.

Flyvbjerg, B. (2001). *Making social science matter: Why social inquiry fails and how it can succeed again.* Cambridge, UK: Cambridge University Press.

Flyvbjerg, B. (2003). Making organization research matter: Power values and phronesis. In B. Czarniawska & G. Sevón (Eds.), *The Northern Lights: Organization theory in Scandinavia* (pp. 357–382). Copenhagen: Copenhagen Business School Press.

Friedman, M. (1962). *Capitalism and freedom.* Chicago: University of Chicago Press.

Friedman, M., & Friedman, R. (1980). *Free to choose: A personal statement.* London: Secker & Warburg.

Frynas, J. G. (2005). The false developmental promise of corporate social responsibility: Evidence from multinational oil companies. *International Affairs, 813,* 581–598.

G8. (2005). *What is the G8 summit?* Retrieved May 31, 2006, at http://www.g8.gov.uk/servlet/Front?pagename=OpenMarket/Xcelerate/ShowPageandc=Page andcid=1078995913300

Gadamer, H.-G. (1975). *Truth and method.* London: Sheid & Ward.

Griffin, R. W., & Pustay, M. W. (2005). *International business: A managerial perspective* (4th ed.). Upper Saddle River, NJ: Pearson Prentice Hall.

Gurney, P. M., & Humphreys, P. (2006). Consuming responsibility: The search for value at Laskarina Holidays. *Journal of Business Ethics, 64,* 83–100.

Hartman, L. P. (2005). *Perspectives in business ethics* (3rd ed.). New York: McGraw-Hill.

Hartog, M., & Frame, P. (2004). Business ethics in the curriculum: Integrating ethics through work experience. *Journal of Business Ethics, 54*, 399–409.

Hedlund, G. (1986). The hypermodern MNC—a heterarchy? *Human Resource Management, 25*, 9–35.

Hill, C. W. L. (2005). *International business: Competing in the global marketplace* (5th ed.). New York: McGraw-Hill/Irwin.

Hilton, S. P., & Slotnick, H. B. (2005). Protprofessionalism: How professionalisation occurs across the continuum of medical education. *Medical Education, 39*, 58–65.

Howells, J., & Wood, M. (1993). *The globalisation of production and technology*. London: Belhaven Press.

IMF. (n.d.). *About the IMF*. Retrieved May 31, 2006, at http://www.imf.org/external/about.htm

Jain, S. C., & Ryans, J. K. (1991). A normative framework for assessing marketing strategy implications of Europe 1992. *Journal of Euromarketing, 11*(2), 189–212.

Jentoft, S. (in press). Beyond fisheries management: The phronetic dimension. *Marine Policy*.

Jones, C., Parker, M., & ten Bos, R. (2005). *For business ethics*. London: Routledge.

Jones, M. T. (2002). Globalization and organizational restructuring: A strategic perspective, *Thunderbird International Business Review, 443*, 325–351.

Keillor, B., D'Amico, M., & Horton, V. (2001). Global consumer tendencies. *Psychology and Marketing, 181*, 1–19.

Khor, M. (2001). *Rethinking globalization*. London: Zed Books.

Kingsnorth, P. (2003). *One no, many yeses*. London: The Free Press.

Klein, N. (2000). *No space/no choice/no jobs—No logo*. London: Flamingo.

Kristof, N. D. (2002, June 25). Let them sweat. *New York Times*.

Krugman, P. (1981). Intraindustry specialization and the gains from trade. *Journal of Political Economy, 89*, 959–973.

Ladd, J. (1970, October). Morality and the ideal of rationality in formal organizations. *The Monist, 54*, pp. 488–516.

Lancaster, K. (1980). Intra-industry trade under perfect monopolistic competition. *Journal of International Economics, 10*, 151–175.

Legrain, P. (2002). *Open world: The truth about globalisation*. London: Abacus.

Levitt, T. (1983, May/June). The globalization of markets. *Harvard Business Review*, pp. 92–102.

Linder, S. B. (1961). *An essay on trade and transformation*. New York: Wiley.

McAuley, A. (2004). Seeking marketing virtue in globalization. *Marketing Review, 4*, 253–266.

Mellahi, K., & Wood, G. (2003). *The ethical business: Challenges and controversies*. Basingstoke, UK: Palgrave Macmillan.

Michalos, A. C. (1997). *Good taxes: The case for taxing foreign currency exchange and other financial transactions*. New York: Duncan Press.

Morgan, G. (1998). Governance and regulation: an institutionalist approach to ethics and organizations. In M. Parker (Ed.), *Ethics and organizations*. London: Sage.

Palley, T. I. (2002). The child labor problem and the need for international labor standards. *Journal of Economic Issues, 363,* 601–615.

Parker, M. (Ed.). (1998). *Ethics and organizations*. London: Sage.

Peters, F. E. (1970). *Greek philosophical terms: A historical lexicon*. New York: New York University Press.

Porter, M. (1985). *Competitive advantage*. New York: Free Press.

Porter, M. (1990). *The competitive advantage of nations*. New York: Free Press.

Rapley, J. (2004). *Globalization and inequality: Neoliberalism's downward spiral*. London: Lynne Rienner.

Ricardo, D. (1817.) *On the principles of political economy and taxation*. London: John Murray.

Ritzer, B. (1996). *The McDonaldization of society* (rev. ed). Thousand Oaks, CA: Pine Forge.

Ritzer, G. (2001). *Explorations in the sociology of consumption*. London: Sage.

Roberts, J. (2003). The manufacture of corporate social responsibility: Constructing corporate sensibility. *Organization, 102,* 249–265.

Roostal, I. (1963, October). Standardization of advertising for Western Europe. Journal of Marketing, pp. 15–20.

Ruderman, R. S. (1997). Aristotle and the recovery of political judgment. *American Political Science Review, 912,* 409–420.

Rugman, A. M., & Hodgetts, R. M. (2003). *International business* (3rd ed.). Harlow, UK: Prentice Hall.

Stiglitz, J. (2002). *Globalization and its discontents*. London: Allen Lane/Penguin.

Taylor, P., & Bain, P. (2005). "India calling to the far away towns": The call centre labour process and globalization. *Work, Employment and Society, 19*(2), 261–282.

Torrens, D. (1815). *Essay on the external corn trade*. London: J. Hatchard.

Tung, R. L. (Ed.). (1998). *The IEBM handbook of international business*. London: Thompson.

Vaggi, G., & Groenewegen, P. (2002). *A concise history of economic thought: From mercantilism to monetarism*. New York: Palgrave Macmillan.

Vernon, R. (1966). International investment and international trade in the product life cycle. *Quarterly Journal of Economics, 80.*

Webster, T. (2006, January 26). Bono bets on Red to battle aids. *BBC News Online*. Retrieved March 3, 2006, at http://news.bbc.co.uk/1/hi/business/4650024.stm

Whitehouse, L. (2006). Corporate social responsibility: Views from the frontline. *Journal of Business Ethics, 63,* 279–296.

Wild, J. J., Wild, K. L., & Han, J. C. Y. (2006). *International business: The challenges of globalization* (3rd ed.). Upper Saddle River, NJ: Pearson Prentice Hall.

Woods, M. (2001). *International business: An introduction*. Basingstoke, UK: Palgrave.

World Bank. (n.d.). *About us*. Retrieved may 31, 2006, from http://web.worldbank.org/WBSITE/EXTERNAL/EXTABOUTUS/0,,pagePK:50004410~piPK:36602~theSitePK:29708,00.html

World Trade Organization. (n.d.). *The WTO...in brief*. Retrieved May 31, 2006, from http://www.wto.org/english/thewto_e/whatis_e/inbrief_e/inbr00_e.htm

Yip, G., Loewe, P., & Yoshino, M. (1988, Winter). How to take your company to the global market. *Columbia Journal of World Business*, pp. 37–48.

Young, L. (1991). Unemployment and the optimal export-processing zone. *Journal of Development Economics, 371–2*, 369–385.

CHAPTER 12

# TECHNO-FUTURIST ETHICS

**Stewart Clegg**
**Nelson Phillips**

## INTRODUCTION

What makes contemporary globalization possible and possible techno-futures imaginable, in part, are the virtual capillaries of instantaneous communication and trade embedded in the Internet. By the 1990s much of organization theories' focus had shifted to the emancipatory possibilities of new virtual technologies potentially rendering hierarchy and bureaucracy redundant (see Clarke & Clegg, 1998). Two scenarios present themselves; one that is ethically oppressive and one that is ethically democratic. The axis of each account is their reckoning of organizational power relations. We consider each account in turn before drawing some conclusions.

## ETHICAL OPPRESSION

### Old Habits Die Hard . . .

People are strange. They can become addicted or phobic to almost anything. Or, put another way, they can become habituated. One thing most members of many organizations seem habituated to are the facts of hierar-

*Critical Theory Ethics for Business and Public Administration*, pages 259–279
Copyright © 2008 by Information Age Publishing

chy. Hierarchy is often seen as a functional necessity of organization premised on rules: where there are rules there has to be command and control, discipline, disciplining and the disciplined, as well as those whose deviance exemplifies the rule and whose conformance is defined by overseers, scrutineers, and auditors. The classic statement of organizations as houses of bondage belongs to Max Weber. According to Weber, the modern world increasingly strips social actors of their ability to freely choose the means and ends of their actions, particularly as it organizes through bureaucracy. In modernity institutions rationalize and organize affairs, cutting down on individual choices, replacing them with standardized procedures and rules. Rational calculation becomes a monstrous discipline. Everything and everyone seemingly had to be put through a calculus, irrespective of other values or pleasures. It was a necessary and unavoidable feature of organizing in the modern world.

Weber was pessimistic about the long-term impact of bureaucracy. On the one hand. bureaucracies would free people from arbitrary rule by powerful patrimonial leaders, those who personally owned the instruments and offices of rule. They would do this because they were based on rational legality as the rule of law contained in the files that defined practice in the bureau. On the other hand, they would create an "iron cage of bondage" (or more literally as translated directly from the original German, a house of hardened steel). The frame was fashioned from the "care for external goods" (Weber, 1976, p. 181), by which Weber meant if these goods were to come into one's grasp in a market economy then one could gain them only by mortgaging one's life to a career in a hierarchy of offices that interlocked and intermeshed, through whose intricacies one might seek to move, with the best hope for one's future being that one would shift from being a small cog in the machine to one that was slightly bigger, in a slow but steady progression.

The iron cage would be fabricated increasingly from the materialization of abstract nouns such as calculability, predictability, and control, to which one must bend one's will. Thus, power concerned less the direct imposition of another's will on one and more the ways in which the conditions of one's existence were increasingly inscribed in a rationalized frame, which one's will had to accommodate as a part of its assent to normalcy. Weber's example is bureaucracy, characterized by rules and regulations, hierarchy of authority, careers, and specialization of roles. The bureaucracy operates in a predictable manner, seeks to quantify, and emphasizes control over people and products through standardized and formalized routines, such as those that Taylor advocated. Recast this way, Taylor had a very specific role to play, materializing the will to power.

If power were never resisted there would be no politics. For Weber, economic action based on the best technically possible practice of quantitative calculation or accounting would be the most formally rational display of the form of rationality. By contrast, substantive rationality would denote concepts of goal-oriented action that will vary according to context and hence be indivisible from the real substance of specific settings. The second chapter of Max Weber's (1978) *Economy and Society* deals with the relationship between formal and substantive rationality (see the excellent account of the different conceptions of rationality in Kalberg [1980]), where substantive rationality is the basis from which resistance springs as a menace to power, at least where it entails a project for humanity instead of a project for private individuals.

Where an individual has so internalized commitment to a rational institution, such as the Civil Service, or Science, or Academia, that the commitment shapes their dispositions in such a way that their will knows little or no resistance to its formal rationality, then this represents obedience to an institutionalized will to power. Power, at its most powerful, is a relation that institutes itself in the psyche of the individual. Simmel (1964, p. 413) explored this when he examined how personality accommodates to the requirements of contemporary urban environments, emphasizing that punctuality, calculability, and exactness become part of modern personalities to the exclusion of "those irrational, instinctive, sovereign traits and impulses which aim at determining the mode of life from within."

Increasing self-discipline, meshing with intensified bureaucratization, rationalization and individualization marked modernity in the social world. External constraint (sovereign power, traditional power) increasingly is replaced by internalization of constraint (disciplinary power, rational domination), assisted by the new technologies of power that figures such as Taylor were developing. As Robert van Krieken (1990, p. 353) puts it, "being modern means being disciplined, by the state [and other organizational forms], by each other and by ourselves; that the soul, both ones own and that of others, became organized into the self, an object of reflection and analysis, and, above all, transformable in the service of ideals such as productivity, virtue and strength." More recent writers such as Elias (1982) and Foucault (1977) are wholly in accord with Simmel (1971) and Weber (1978) in these respects.

The modern, rationalized person was increasingly disciplined in the discourse on power that Simmel and Weber jointly orchestrated. Simmel also saw domination as in part a function of the symbolic content of widely held ideas embedded in everyday practices of life and discourse. These are conceptualized as "precepts," a term derived from the Latin *praeceptum*, meaning instruction, tutelage, injunction, or command. The relevance to Taylorism thus becomes evident as a specific program of instruction and tutelage in domination, in the making of certain precepts obligatory and exemplary, of framing a wholly rationalized way of organizational life. It prepares the social and cultural foundations of a domination already secured economically by relations of production, ownership, and control. As Simmel (1971, p. 119) puts it, one becomes "habituated" to the "compulsory character" of these precepts "until the cruder and subtler means of compulsion are no longer necessary," indeed, until one's "nature" is so "formed or reformed" by these precepts that one "acts … as if on impulse." When this occurs:

> [T]he individual represents society to himself. The external confrontation, with its suppressions, liberations, changing accents, has become an interplay between his social impulses, in the stricter sense of the word; and both are included by the ego in the larger sense. … At a certain higher stage of morality, the motivation of action lies no longer in a real-human, even though super-individual power; at this stage, the spring of moral necessities flows beyond the contrast between individual and totality. For, as little as these necessities derive from society, as little do they derive from the singular reality of individual life. In the free conscience of the actor, in individual reason, they only have their bearer, the locus of their efficacy. Their power of obligation stems from these necessities themselves, from their inner, super-personal validity, from an objective identity which we must recognize whether or not we want to.… The content, however, which fills these forms is (not necessarily but often) the societal requirement. But this requirement no longer operates by means of its social impetus, as it were, but rather as if it had undergone a metempsychosis into a norm which must be satisfied for its own sake, not for my sake nor for yours. (Simmel, 1971, p. 11)

The individual in a situation of formal domination increasingly comes to be subordinated to "objective principles," which they experience as a "concrete object" whose necessity takes the form of a "social requirement …which must be satisfied for its own sake." Foucault (1977) did not put it better or clearer.

## The Individual Subordinated to Objective Principles

Despite the possibilities that now exist for embedding rules in things and thus, relatively, freeing people from their sway and domination, most people seem to be strangely addicted to hierarchy and phobic about any alternatives that might be posited to it:

> Talk about organizations usually centers on who should be in charge. We're used to hierarchy and know how it works. It's a familiar and comfortable habit, the obvious fallback, the default option. When it works, feels precise and clear—we know Bloggs is the boss, he tells us what to do. When it doesn't work we blame Bloggs. We accept that hierarchy has its faults, but we think it's

inevitable. We may try to ameliorate its bad effects, but we never question the basic idea. (Fairtlough, 2005, p. 7)[1]

We may note that this lack of questioning is both practical and theoretical. Practically, from our earliest experiences in school, organized by a "Principal" or "Head Teacher," we spend all our formative years in a hierarchical organization. For those who attended really elite schools, the sense of hierarchy was probably much more pronounced, which means that, given dominant models of social reproduction whereby elite groups tend to reproduce themselves, the experience of most elites who actually run organizations is imprinted in terms of hierarchy. And if practical experience were not sufficient, in management and organization theory the normalcy of hierarchy has been a constituent aspect of almost all English-language thinking about power in organizations, which, revoking domination, placed authority at center stage and deviation from it as power, a resistant and insubordinate property of hierarchical systems.

As discourse about power and organizations was institutionalized in the latter half of the 20th century, the concern with authority and hierarchy was normalized. Power was conceived not as reproducing normal authority and hierarchy but as undermining it, never more famously than in Crozier's (1964) maintenance workers, lowly individuals in the pecking order, who were supposed to have organizational power because of their control over uncertainty! In retrospect, it seems errant nonsense and it is hard to believe that one ever could have taken seriously the implication that the oilcan keepers were more involved in relations of power than were top management teams or the leaders of organizations. Of course, if the discourse on leadership had filled in for the deficiencies of that of power then the situation might have been different, but it didn't, as Gordon (2002) argued; consequently, given that leadership appeared not to be concerned with power, perhaps it was not surprising to find power in the most unlikely places, down among the oilcans.

The functionalist theory of organizations preserves one aspect of the hidden history of power that started with Taylor in the 19th century. Taylor explicitly sought to redesign the human body in its accommodation with the material and social environment that he created, in terms of one necessary way of being. Latter-day functionalists believe, just as strongly, that organization will be as it is because, when it is in fit with those contingencies that it has to deal with, it will have evolved to the one best way of dealing with them. And an unquestioned aspect of that being, in any normal organization, will be for hierarchy to divide tasks, set rules, and design structures. All of these divisions, rules, and designs are necessary for organizations to exist; thus, it is extrapolated, hierarchy must be a necessity. Hierarchy is a necessary bulwark against disorder, against lower order members exerting their agency and using power to mess up the rules, task divisions, and structural designs. Hierarchy is the necessary prerequisite for lower order members to have sufficient fear and loathing of authority and its strict discipline, so that, similar to the poor subjects of the panopticon, what members of organizations know about the conditions of their existence as members holds them submissively in thrall to the necessity of power's devices.

Fairtlough (2005, p. 18) suggests that "hierarchies tend to learn slowly, especially because a lot of effort goes into preserving the superior status of those at the top, inevitably an anti-learning activity." The alternative to hierarchy is not chaos or anarchy. Only our powerful addiction to hierarchy, bred in habit, leads us to believe it to be so. And it is a "powerful" addiction in a double sense; first, it is strong, and second, it is obfuscatory, because, where power is concerned, it creates blind spots, absences, and silences where critical reflection should be. In the absence of critical reflection, alternatives are not thinkable; where there is critical reflection, then alternatives become visible. Hierarchical rights, interpreted through a traditional conception, presume an established order of domination in which is vested a *repressive* right to exercise power over subjects.

Hierarchy has useful functions. It can be used to settle dispute unilaterally as disparate views are rejected in favor of hierarchically preferred options. But the risk is that it will produce stifling cultures of orthodoxy; structures that cannot easily learn from the diversity of their component strengths and voices; leaders who believe their own rhetoric rather than trust that wisdom might possibly reside in the views of those that they seek to rule, sell to, supply, and employ, and power that can only understand resistance to it in terms of illegitimate choices of illegitimate ways to express being an organization member. In shorthand, being a member, it is assumed, means being someone who accepts that the terms of trade for receipt of a wage or salary are that one keeps one's opinions to oneself where they conflict with those of authorities; that one's daily bread buys one's daily acquiescence to whatever authorities choose to do.

Hierarchy has many celebrated advantages, not least being familiarity, unity of powers, and a theory of sovereignty that few would criticize openly. After all, we all know that what bosses do is rule. And the whole legal framework of common law, derived from Masters and Servants Acts, assumes definite powers distributed differentially in terms of relations embedded in the hierarchy. Little wonder that hierarchy is so normalized, so hegemonic, so deeply embedded legally. Within the limits of legal frameworks, those in dominant relations of hierarchy can do drastically bad things to the immediate life chances of those of us who are not, such as making us redundant. That is why in analysis of any system of power relations one should never stop at the organization door, looking only at what goes on inside the organization. One also needs to consider the changing balance of forces in the industrial relations arena, as political parties of differing ideological persuasions use government to shift the balance of power between labor and capital over the legal definitions of what constitutes a contract of employment and its breaches. Often, the balance of power intraorganizationally changes dramatically as a result of changes registered in the political arena. Rights—to strike, to dismiss, to parental leave, to statutory entitlements—ebb and flow with shifts of the political current, as does resistance to their creation, preservation, extension or erosion. Moving in one direction they embolden employers; shifting to another they create anxiety when they offer succor to employees, at what seems to employers to be their expense.

Of course, the law is always an imperfect instrument. Confining resistance to power within its limits sometimes only serves to foster resistance to it, creating confrontation and conflict over its meaning and implementation where it had previously not existed. Recall that even after 25 years of legal imprisonment of Nelson Mandela as an enemy of the state this power did not preserve the state that imprisoned him, and its legality, against the resistance of a people and a movement committed to their own freedom and liberation. The law provides obligatory passage points through which, using its monopoly over the means of violence, the state can seek to channel freedoms and repressions, define rights and obligations, and corral consent as legitimate and exclude dissidence as illegitimate. But history is replete with laws being challenged and overthrown by subjects empowered with the moral necessity of their convictions. In the recent past one thinks of the repeal of the Poll Tax in the United Kingdom; the Orange Revolution in the Ukraine; the defeat of segregation in the United States by the civil rights struggle; and of apartheid in South Africa. Legitimacy does not always equal right; even when the most entrenched hierarchies are backed by might, courageous people can dislodge them.

The paradigm of a sovereign master and commander is almost second nature. It provides an implicit and pervasive model of sovereignty for all strong, macho business leaders. However, there are alternative definitions of sovereignty, significantly different from the paradigm of master and commander, as traced by Kalyvas (2005) in terms of a model of constitutive power. "It erupted on the political scene with the invention of modern constitutionalism," in the form of "an original constituting power," which founds and grounds "a constitutional order while remaining irreducible to and heterogeneous from that order" (Kalyvas, 2005, p. 226). In the constitutive alternative, the emphasis is on the creation of a new order in which power is *productive.* "The sovereign constituent subject is not a repressive force, but a productive agency" (Kalyvas, 2005, p. 227). Instead of "stressing the discretionary power of a superior command emanating from the *top*, the notion of the constituent sovereign redirects our attention to the underlying sources of the instituted reality located at the *bottom*" (Kalyvas,

2005, p. 227). In short, modern notions of sovereignty acknowledge *demos* and *poly*—democracy and *polyarchy*—as well as *hierarchy* and *bureaucracy*.[2]

Fairtlough (2005, p. 9) suggests that we simply do not know how desirable hierarchy is in particular situations, "because it never gets tested against anything other than anarchy or chaos." What is should be tested against, Fairtlough suggests, are contemporary models of polyarchy, including heterarchy and responsible autonomy. Heterarchy means the separation of powers; it builds sovereignty into practice rather than the precedent of domination. It sets up, at best, internal systems for the exercise of voice, the calling to account, and the checking of power and encourages coevolutionary learning because each party has to pay close attention to the cues and signals that the others are attending to; it cannot simply impose "one best way" or "my way or the highway" on members. It works from a team basis, enabling cooperation, fostering coevolution, learning, and innovation, and is committed to pluralism. In diversity it sees strength rather than division. Contemporary forms of virtual communication make the provision of transparent information easier, immediate and cheap. Whereas in the past the slow transmission of information, its necessary archiving and storing in written files, the high costs of reproduction, and limited literacy may all have conspired to make hierarchy more effective, because control was premised on institutionalized routines, that is no longer the case today. The conditions exist in which organizations can empower their members to be more responsibly autonomous, where members can be autonomous but responsible subjects with clear modes of accountability.

Malone (2004) argues that the emergence of virtual immediacy and instantaneity is driving hitherto hierarchical organizations to become increasingly either more heterarchical or responsibly autonomous, or both. Decisions can be made by secret ballot in virtual labs, where arguments for and against actions can be made anonymously on a shared screen. Here the power of good argument will prevail rather than the power of hierarchy, which presumes enlightenment and wisdom reside in domination, a very dubious proposition (if one with a long historical pedigree emanating from the Age of Reason). Organizations can move from command-and-control to coordinate-and-cultivate models, suggests Malone. In this shift management ceases to direct and instead starts to facilitate organization processes for goal setting, standard setting, and value articulation. One corollary is that the cultural ties that bind will flourish and grow stronger in a climate of genuine responsibility and respect rather than in an inauthentic parroting of what are presumed, on the rule of anticipated reaction, to be views that will accord with those who are positions of dominance.

Social scientists have rarely felt it necessary to explain why it is that power should be hierarchical (Hardy & Clegg 1996). It is because of this that hierarchy is reinforced. It is so strongly held that, as Hardy and Clegg (1996) explained, contemporary theory could only imagine that power was what "bad guys" used to try and get their (illegitimate) way while good guys could just rely on the hegemony of authority and hierarchy as a "second nature," a culture that was so acculturated that for most people who lived its everyday life nothing other than it could be imagined (Bauman, 1976). Thus, power served the hegemony of hierarchy and this hegemony deepened its service by simultaneously obscuring those relations of powers that it served, making them feasible, visible, and accountable only as authority.

Both *heterarchy* and *responsible autonomy* are specifications of different forms of rule by many, *polyarchy*. It was Ogilvy (1977) who introduced the concept of heterarchy, meaning multiple rulers, a balance of power rather than a single rule, as in hierarchy. There are many examples of heterarchy that one can identify, such as partnerships in professional organizations, including law or accounting firms or alliance relationships between separate firms. Responsible autonomy is a concept that we first encountered in the work of Andrew Friedman (1977). Responsible autonomy means getting things done not through hierarchical control—which Friedman called direct control—but through the autonomy of a group or individual to decide how they will do what they will do, where what they will do means that they are accountable to some others; hence, the notion of *responsible* autonomy. Earlier, something very similar seemed to have been captured by David Hickson (1966) in terms of the contrasting specificity of role prescription in different organization theories. He identified a convergence around the centrality of the issue of the degree of role prescription but a sharp cleavage between those researchers who thought it desirable and efficient and those who did not. It was a cleavage that broke down, roughly, on the lines of the formal theorists of administration and classical management theory favoring higher prescription, while lower specificity of prescription was favored by the more humanistic researchers.

Many organizational examples of low prescription/high responsible autonomy come to mind and Fairtlough (2005, p. 30) gives as an instance one that is especially dear to our hearts:

> Basic scientific research, in academe and in research institutes, is largely conducted by autonomous groups, which are led by principal investigators. These groups develop their reputations by publishing reports in peer-reviewed journals. Principal investigators apply for research grants from various funding bodies. Grants are given subject to the novelty and significance of the group. The principal investigator's freedom to choose research topics and to recruit people provides autonomy. The group's continued existence depends on it continuing to publish good science—this provides accountability.

Another example is that of investment fund management, where, if a fund does well, the manager may be given more funds to invest and earn more accordingly from fees and commissions; here, autonomy is provided by the internal policies of the financial institution where accountability is evident in the way that the fund performs in a competitive market. Fairtlough (2005, pp. 31–33) sees responsible autonomy as flourishing best where it is encapsulated within rules that are widely understood, transparent, legitimated, and shared, and where action is open to critique, such as regular audit, or being held in some way accountable for the actions taken as a responsibly autonomous subject or unit. Many forms of audit are increasingly institutionalized to deal with conditions of power at a distance—holding people accountable at a distance—such as the growth of standards (Brunsson & Jacobson, 2000). The essence of responsible autonomy is that there is audit and disputed determination by some independent and third party held in good standing, and institutionalized as such.

In heterarchy, as Fairtlough explains it, through rotation of office, and reward schemes related to risk and innovation rather than position, tendencies to domination can be reduced. Heterarchy builds democratic skills and capabilities in what has the potential to be a virtuous circle; it encourages more sophisticated general skills for interpersonal processes, dialogical relations, teamwork, mutual respect, and openness (see the "Alliance Culture" reported in Pitsis, Clegg, Marosszeky, & Rura-Polley, 2003). Admittedly, as Fairtlough (2005) suggests, heterarchies work best when the size of the organization is small, below about 150 people, he recommends. Heterarchy cannot be extended indefinitely as it is impossible to work in what are highly direct democracies once the number of participants rises beyond the circle of people who can know each other reasonably well. However, responsible autonomy within forms of heterarchic organization enables encapsulated boundedness to be created—with devices and agents for boundary spanning—thus extending functional capabilities. Of course, the establishment of efficient responsible autonomy means critique must be in place from the start; the rules and accountabilities need to be clear, and a dispute resolution mechanism must be in place.

Hierarchy is premised principally on "power over" others while the polyarchic alternatives are principally premised on "power to" get things done. What distinguishes heterarchy from responsible autonomy is that in the former there is a constant and continuous interaction between entities and agents in deciding what and how to do something. In many instances, this means that for heterarchy to be successful the alliance that is building it needs to develop an identity for instances of it that is separate from whatever organizational bodies comprise and host the constituent parts (Clegg, Pitsis, Marosszeky, & Rura-Polley, 2002). Responsible autonomy means that there can be a lot more distance between agencies. Both differ from hierarchy in not being subject to arbitrary power vested only in relations of domination. No pure versions of these types will be found in reality; they are abstracted "ideal" types, in the Weberian sense. Most organizations will comprise different mixes of hierarchy, or direct control, heterarchy, and responsible autonomy. The benefits and costs of each will differ in differ contexts.

## ETHICAL DEMOCRACY

### *Technology Makes Us Free . . .*

Weber greatly admired the achievements of bureaucracy, as he saw them at the outset of modernity. In many respects these achievements were quite limited. Twentieth-century bureaucracy (that specifically modern form of organization that Weber saw) never achieved its full realization. We are confronting at the beginning of the 21st century its full realization in what has been named paradoxically "post-bureaucracy," a more flexible and subtle form of organization that embodies bureaucracy in technological devices such as computers, cell phones, PDAs, etc. In other words, Weber saw an initial version of bureaucracy but not its full realization in modernity as the expression of the iron cage. One potential promise of these new techno-futures is that rules can be embedded in the technologies in use, thus freeing the individual subjects to be more autonomous, creative, and innovative. Fairtlough (2005, p. 79) echoes a general view in seeing the development of knowledge-based organizations as major drivers of a shift away from hierarchy toward heterarchy and responsible autonomy. A knowledge economy's virtual communications replace the need for rules, precedents, and files to record them, and greater knowledge means increased scrutiny, awareness, and possibility of audit or whistleblowing.

Neither heterarchy nor responsible autonomy, as distinct forms of polyarchy, are an alternative to power but they are alternative to hierarchy, and they do configure power relations quite differently, around polyphonic rather than hegemonic principles, less concerned with imperative coordination from a single and superior point of view and narration and more concerned with deconstructions and translation of alternative accounts (see Kornberger, Clegg, & Carter, 2005). Optimistically, there is good reason to think that, however slowly, imperative coordination may be giving way to responsible autonomy and heterarchy. There are now technologies available that can handle more distributed authority relations, through the use of digital and virtual communication. The Internet allows for far less centralized modes of organization—and, indeed, in the present state of anxiety in society about terrorist attacks, we are likely to see many organizations adopting more distributed and network structures, with responsible autonomy in each of their nodal points—if only to be sure that the organization can survive a cataclysmic event such as 9/11. It is evident that organizations that have distributed systems and networked leadership will better survive catastrophe. After all, that is precisely what the Internet was designed to do.[3]

While the optimistic scenarios envisage a world in which small and local business, offering unique products, will be globally connected by the Internet, there are more pessimistic aspects of globalization to contend with that are likely to have an impact on organizational power relations. Pessimistically, the times in which we live have grown more troubled in many respects and the necessity of imperative coordination are seemingly ever more pressing. As a result of digital capabilities Western postmodern society not only surrounds those who live within its borders; its global media project images of it to the rest of the world, intensifying the powers of the market enormously.

## Resisting Globally?

In the past the major challenge to market power was the state (Clegg, Boreham, & Dow, 1983) or the organized labor movement. After the failure of Euro-Communism in the 1970s, and the rapprochement of social democracy with the neoliberal agenda from the 1980s, challenge from the state declined. The decline in left politics was paralleled in the industrial sphere as well. Today, the *international* organization of capital confronts *national* labor movements. When one considers the new global conditions of production it is evident that trade unions face a new reality.

Organized labor has had to match the learning trajectory of that capital in whose employ it is globally arraigned. The literature addressing the use of IT in business and administration, and its consequences for social and industrial organization (e.g., Dunlop & Kling, 1991; Zuboff, 1988; Sprague & McNurlin, 1997), provide an archive of the learning process involved in these changes as organizations better manage the supply and value change in an increasingly complex business environment (Sprague & McNurlin, 1997).

Significant global campaigns have emerged from within the trade union movement and from the critics of globalization to confront the new global realities (Hogan & Greene, 2002). However, trade unions remain, for the present, largely nationally institutionalized, and they do not afford much of a threat to existing organization of the relations of production, especially as their recruitment and penetration of the post-industrial services economy is far lower than was the case in the era of industrial labor and society. Also, they are increasingly irrelevant because their leadership is largely male and the domain of their traditional membership female. Thus, the biggest issues that unions face today on the membership front are low female and ethnic minority participation rates such that the people doing the representing rarely share either gender or ethnicity.

Interunion coordination in response to the globalization of value chains was taken forward by the UK Liverpool dock dispute, which took place between 1995 and 1998. Extensive mobilization of support from within and beyond the labor movement was achieved through the use of the Web in concert with more traditional forms of mobilization (Carter, Clegg, Hogan, & Kornberger, 2003). Following the defeat of the union, the skills developed in the struggle have been carried forward to archive the dispute and to develop a sustainable skill base within the community.[4] Within 48 hours of the settlement of the UK dispute an identical dispute broke out in Australia, a locus of support for the Liverpool workers and, at that time, a regulated labor environment (Clegg, 1999).[5] Of critical significance was the role of the Federal Australian government in planning the dispute, involving overseas training of serving members of the Australian armed services.[6]

Clearly learning and countercoordination is taking place globally on all sides, unions, employers, and governments, and new forms of power and resistance can be expected (Little & Clegg, 2005). The emerging global system is far from complete and far from determined, but it is having a profound impact on social and working life in the regions included within and excluded from it. Of course, the speed of change in markets, competition, and technology means that there is a socioinstitutional lag, something that occurs when any new techno-economic paradigm emerges (Perez, 1983). It is information and communication technologies that are driving the distributed processes of globalization and provide new forms of cultural and political indexicality, as well as new forms of countercoordination for excluded constituencies (Little & Clegg, 2005).

## ANTICIPATING RESISTANCE? SIMULATION AND IDENTITY IN THE ELECTRONIC PANOPTICON

U.S. federal legislation, which predates 9/11, requires GPS transmitters to be fitted to all U.S. cell phones.[7] Organizations, not just in government, are increasingly making use of available surveillance technologies to seek enhanced supervision and control. The electronic panopticon is going global in an increasingly insecure world, offering opportunities not only for hypersurveillance but also a new kind of organizational simulation, that is hyperreal, a world where we can "*simulate* a space of control, project an indefinite number of courses of action, train for each possibility, and react immediately with preprogrammed responses to the 'actual' course of events (which is already over and through a simulacrum)" (Bogard, 1996, p. 76). Organizations increasingly neither need a political economy of bodies to *handle* power nor to embed it in a moral economy of the soul through extensive *surveillance*. Instead, they project information in a mode that has been described as "the purest form of anticipation" (Bogard, 1996, p. 76).

Almost all large-scale organizations of any sophistication are increasingly premised on work whose doing is simultaneously subject to hypersurveillance of its being done, characteristic of both managerial work and work more generally. The traces of data that all information-laden actions leave automatically as they are enacted become the objects for analysis, for the speeding-up of processes, of eradicating porosity through which some effort, time, or work might seep, eradicating the gap between the action and its accounts, the work and its record, the deed and the sign. The loop between being, doing, and becoming tightens irrevocably on the terms of those elites that can channel and funnel information, closing down the unaccountable moments in the programmed loop between employees and technologies reporting data that managers have to act on.

Ideally, managers become adjuncts of expert systems, which will instill operational definitions of shareholder value as the highest ethic imaginable. In short, ordinary organizations have capabilities for power that would have been but a dream for a Honecker or a Ford, running a state or a production plant. The trajectory of power has spiraled out from a political economy of the body, has transcended the moral economy of the soul, and now is lodged everywhere and nowhere in a multiplicity of scanning and simulation.

Hundreds of thousands of workers in both government and private industry are subjected to drug tests, have their prior work records scanned, are diagnosed for general health, intelligence, loyalty, family values, economic and psychological stability (through matches generated in searches of other databases), fitted to job profiles, placed on career tracks—or unemployment tracks—all in addition to routine, rigorous monitoring on the job. The virtual scene of work is one where the end of work—who the worker *will have been*, what the worker *will have produced*, what path his or her career *will have taken*—governs the entire process before it begins (Bogard, 1996, p. 117).

Such information is not confined to the gathering of data from the physical spaces that they control, nor is it premised on the crude forms of spying characteristic of the Ford Sociological Department and the Stasi. "Increasingly virtual realities, artificial intelligence, expert systems, sever us from older forms of control and project that control—refashioned, smoothed and streamlined—onto the plane of simulation. . . . The god of surveillance is a virtual reality technician's cyborg dream" (Bogard, 1996, pp. 57, 77).

It is not only the security apparatuses and the legislative assemblies that multiply dreams within which identities that are constructs of the profiler, the psychological tester, and the human resources manager, become crucial. All large organizations, equipped with the foresight of simulation, can screen out potential deviance from the organization as easily as the society at large.

It is the reality of how, increasingly, organizations use informatics' virtual worlds as they construct identities within which our lives will be lived. Our identity, more than ever, will be a social construction, but not necessarily one made under conditions of our own choosing. Organizations will increasingly adopt biosurveillance technologies, such as retina, fingerprint, and face scanning, and use this to monitor, restrict, and govern access. Such data, together with those identities that are coded from market-based information, credit records, credit cards, and other forms of transactions, will ensure that some elements of identity become less negotiable. Given the likely direction and speed of development of genetics, organizational capabilities will increasingly be prefigurative rather than retrospective; as Bogard (1996, p. 9) puts it, "genetic technology offers the fantastic possibilities of pre-identification, i.e., identities assigned in advance, profiles that we have seen can be used to target bodies for all kinds of future interventions and diversions." Potential pathologies for organizations—such as prediction of earlier than required executive demise due to genetic codes or lifestyle triggers—can be problems eliminated in advance. Normalization will no longer be remedial or therapeutic, no longer require the counseling interview as its major device, but will be anticipatory. Biopsychological screening is becoming ever more closely intertwined with genetic and security screening. Organizational elites will not only be able to reproduce themselves biologically but also to clone themselves socially, with ever more precise simulations.[8]

## CONCLUSIONS

The ideological signification of democracy in the organizational world is not only related to a kind of moral utterance. It is also the work of power, since democracy in economic institutions is antagonistic to oligarchic and bureaucratic practices and values. It is power not only in the mechanical sense of "force applied to a people by external government in the pursuit of its own objectives, but power regarded as arising from the people, transmitted by libertarian, egalitarian and rationalist ends so that it becomes, in effect, not power but only the exercise of the people's own will" (Nisbet, 1993, p. 40). The question arising from this quotation is not merely how far organizations can be truly democratic but concerns the peculiar interconnections between democracy, power, and morality. As Nisbet (1993) puts it, power without morality is despotism, while morality without power is sterile. Scholars must therefore think through the combination between democracy, power, and morality. So far, we have barely begun to do this in the contemporary practices of organizations. Can the political imagination usher in changes correlative with the new distributed forms of technology that are now available? The pen and the typewriter gave us bureaucracy; can virtuality give us democracy?

When a member of an organization faces a novel and morally charged situation he or she does more than merely apply a formulaic model or process, the organizational machinery, in order to decide on a course of action. In practice there will always be room for interpretation as various ethical models and calculations are *used* in relation to the activities of organizing and managing. Thus, organizational members have to make choices to apply, interpret, and make sense of various competing models of practice (including ethical ones) in specific situations. Such ethical work does not suggest a total "free play" but implies that moral choice proposes an oscillation between possibilities, where these possibilities are determined situationally rather than technologically or by rules. Ethics are *at stake* when norms, rules, or systems of ethics clash, and no third meta-rule can be applied to resolve the dilemma. We cannot avoid being moral beings that make choices "with the knowledge (or at least a suspicion in case efforts are made to suppress or deny that knowledge) that they are but choices. Society engraves the pattern of ethics upon the raw and pliable stuff of morality. Ethics is a social product because morality is not" (Bauman, in Bauman & Tester, 2001, p. 45). And if ethics cannot be articulated, it is invariably because power arbitrates on, overrules, and otherwise struggles to fix meanings.

Ethical codes, norms, and models, just as technologies, have important implications for organizational members. They are resources that skillful and knowledgeable members use freely in everyday management. As Foucault (1997, p. 284) suggests, "what is ethics, if not the practice of freedom, the conscious practice of freedom?" The moral agent, from a power perspective, is one who enacts agency rather than one whose actions are considered to be wholly determined structurally (see Lukes, 1974, 2005). One may agree or disagree with particular ethical dictates, but it is what one does in relation to them that determines the practice of ethics.

When formal systems of ethics such as codes of conduct are present, following Meyer and Rowan (1977), they can be expected to function as ceremonially adopted myths used to gain legitimacy, resources, stability, and to enhance survival prospects. The practice of the system far exceeds its explicit statements. Thus, to maintain ceremonial conformity, "organizations that reflect institutional rules tend to buffer their formal structures from the uncertainties of technical activities by becoming loosely coupled, building gaps between their formal structures and actual work activities" (Meyer & Rowan, 1977, p. 340). In their search for legitimacy, organizations use codes of conduct as standards to justify what they do (Brunsson & Jacobsson, 2000) as well as to fulfill a narcissistic obsession with looking "good" (Roberts, 2003). In this sense, codes of conduct become a "public relations exercise" (Munro, 1992, p. 98). Goffman (1961. p. 30) had their meaning nailed when he wrote about the partial reversal of transformation rules in encounters where "minor courtesies" are displayed to "women and children in our society" by men, honoring the youngest or weakest "as a ceremonial reversal of ordinary practice." The point he makes is that codes of conduct are not constructed out of a sense of esteeming and identifying with another who is like you but are instead an impersonal and productive convenience to secure selfish aims. Should we analyze organizations in terms of what they say they do in their formal documentation or should we study what they actually do? Clearly, we should do both, while acknowledging that rhetoric has its own practice and it is the relations between the practices, the situations in which they occur, and the audiences they invite, that is important (Corbett & Connors, 1999; Cheney, Christensen, Conrad, & Lair, 2004; Suddaby & Greenwood, 2005). Technologies change the rhetoric but they do so in ways that are not too dissimilar to the impressions managed through rules and other systems of subordination by individual principles.

## NOTES

1. Gerard Fairtlough, in thinking about alternatives to hierarchy, is not some ivory tower theorist, or hippie dreamer, we should add; in fact, he is one of the few current organization theorists to have run several multimillion-dollar enterprises (including Shell Chemicals UK and Celltech, the most successful European biotechnology company) and, as he explains elsewhere, many of his ideas were worked out in the practice of running these companies (Fairtlough, 1994). Sadly, Gerard died in Ryall, Dorset on December 15, 2007.

2. Other writers also recognize that hierarchy is by no means the only form through which power relations may be condensed and concentrated—nor is it necessarily the best. Manuel Castells (1996) argues that we are seeing the emergence and rise of the network society and Phillip Bobbitt (2002) sees the nation-state being replaced by the market state, wherein numerous diverse private organizations take over governmental function, thus reducing the role of hierarchical government.

3. By the end of the 20th century the Internet had enabled the vertically integrated multinational corporation, under unified ownership, to be replaced by networks of externalized relationships between associated but often autonomous firms. This wider separation of networks that link locations in East Asia with the U.S. and Europe is typified by the operations of electronics companies such as Texas Instruments, which distributes research and development between Austin Texas and Taipei. Smooth operation relies on a synchronized corporate database physically replicated on identical hardware at each end of the link using a high-capacity data link. The notion of "networked enterprise" promoted by Castells (1996) as a means of geographically and temporally constrained collaboration in order to enter and shape specific market has, however, already been superseded by more durable modes of operation. Companies such as ARM

Holdings (http://www.arm.com/) produce high-value intellectual property utilized by global corporations that rely, in turn, on third-party manufacturing facilities such as those provided by Flextronics (http://www.flextronics.com/). The actors located at each node of the network have a range of geographical locations available to them across which to distribute intellectual property and physical processes: the furthest development of ICT-dependent reconfiguration. Computerization within commercial and administrative organizations initially represented an extension of earlier office technologies designed to address internal efficiency. As the potential of computers to manage supply chain and customer relationships became apparent, organizational effectiveness became a primary objective. Finally, as the innovations in business models and interfirm relationships permitted by the synergies of networking became apparent, interorganizational management of the production and value chain became the focus of both local and global systems.

4. See http://www.mmm.merseyside.org/cd.htm and http://www.mmm.merseyside.org/project.htm

5. The second dispute is archived at http://mua.org.au/war/ and is discussed in Clegg (1999).

6. See http://mua.org.au/war/cloak.html; http://www.ilwu19.com/global/wharfie/update65.htm.

7. Despite the relative inadequacy of current WAP (wireless application protocol) mobile telephony, the combination of low earth orbit (LEO) satellites with global positioning systems (GPS) allows location-sensitive services to be delivered to individuals and groups on the move.

8. In the movie *Gattaca* (Niccol, 1997), the main character, Vincent, notes, ironically in the context of the corporate organization Gattaca, that "We now have discrimination down to a science." It is a science that attempts to ensure that one is what one is coded as being irrespective of what or who one might want to be recognized as being or becoming. The movie demonstrates that resistance is possible, insofar, as its tagline has it, "There is no Gene for the Human Spirit." In the film, human endeavor is exemplified by a self-disciplined subject who overcomes the fact of being someone with invalid genes, and aspires to and achieves what he desires, in a journey that is plotted quite consciously as one of redemption through resistance.

## REFERENCES

Apple, M. W. (2004). *Ideology and curriculum* (3rd ed.). New York: RoutledgeFalmer.

Bauman, Z. (1976). *Towards a critical sociology: An sssay on common-sense and emancipation.* London: Routledge & Kegan Paul.

Bauman, Z. (2004). *Wasted lives: Modernity and its outcasts.* Cambridge, UK: Polity Press.

Bauman, Z., & Tester, K. (2001). *Conversations with Zygmunt Bauman.* Cambridge, UK: Polity Press.

Bessis, S. (2001). *Western supremacy: The triumph of an idea.* London: Zed Books.

Bobbitt, P. (2002). *The shield of Achilles: War, peace, and the course of history.* New York: Knopf.

Bogard, W. (1996). *The simulation of surveillance: Hypercontrol in telematic societies.* Cambridge, UK: Cambridge University Press.

Brunsson, N., & Jacobsson, B. (2000). *A world of standards.* New York: Oxford University Press.

Carter, C., Clegg, S. R., Hogan, J., & Kornberger, M. (2003) The polyphonic spree: The case of the Liverpool dockers. *Industrial Relations, 34*(4), 290–304.

Cartwright, D., & Zander, A. (1953). *Group dynamics: Research and theory.* London: Tavistock.

Castells, M. (1996). *The rise of the network society.* Oxford, UK: Blackwell.

Cheney, G., Christensen, L. T., Conrad, C., & Lair, D. J. (2004). Corporate rhetoric in organizational discourse. In D. Grant, C. Oswick, C. Hardy, & L. L. Putnam (Eds.), *Sage handbook of organizational discourse* (pp. 79–103). London: Sage.

Chomsky, N. (1959). A review of B. F. Skinner's verbal behavior. *Language, 35*(1), 26–58.

Clarke, J. J. (1997). *Oriental enlightenment: The encounter between Asian and Western thought.* London: Routledge.

Clarke, T., & Clegg, S. R. (1998). *Changing paradigms: The transformation of management for the 21st century.* London: HarperCollins.

Clegg, S. R. (1999). Globalizing the intelligent organization: Learning organizations, smart workers, (not so) clever countries and the sociological imagination. *Management Learning, 30*(3), 259–280.

Clegg, S. R., Boreham, P., & Dow, G. (1983). *Class, politics and the economy.* London: Routledge & Kegan Paul.

Clegg, S. R., Pitsis, T., Rura-Polley, T., & Marosszeky, M. (2002). Governmentality matters: Designing an alliance culture of inter-organizational collaboration for managing projects. *Organization Studies, 23*(3), 317–337.

Corbett, E. P. J., & Connors, R. J. (1999). *Classical rhetoric for the modern student.* Oxford, UK: Oxford University Press.

Crozier, M. (1964). *The bureaucratic phenomenon.* Chicago: University of Chicago Press.

Derrida, J. (1988). Structure, sign and play in the discourse of the human sciences. In D. Lodge (Ed.), *Modern criticism and theory.* London: Longman.

Dunlop, C., & Kling, R. (Eds.). (1991). *Computerization and controversy: Value conflicts and social choices.* Boston: Academic Press.

Durkheim, E. (1983). *Pragmatism and sociology.* Cambridge, UK: University of Cambridge Press.

Elias, N. (1982). *The civilizing process: Vol. 2. Power and civility.* New York: Pantheon.

Fairtlough, G. (2005). *The three ways of getting things done: Hierarchy, heterarchy and responsible autonomy in organizations.* Greenways, Dorset, UK: Triarchy Press.

Foucault, M. (1977). *Discipline and punish: The birth of the prison* (A Sheridan, Ed.). London: Allen & Lane.

Foucault, M. (1997). *Ethics: Subjectivity and truth* (P. Rabinow, Ed.). New York: New Press.

Friedman, A. (1977). *Industry and labour.* London: Macmillan.

Friedmann, G. (1946). *Problèmes humaines du machinisme industriel.* Paris: Gallimard.

Giroux, H. A. (1997). Are Disney's films good for your kids? In S. R. Steinberg & J. L. Kincheloe (Eds.), *Kinderculture: The corporate construction of childhood.* Boulder, CO: Westview Press.

Goffman, E. (1961). *Asylums.* Harmondsworth, UK: Penguin.

Gordon, R. D. (2002). Conceptualizing leadership with respect to its historical-contextual antecedents to power. *The Leadership Quarterly, 13*(2), 151–167.

Hardy, C., & Clegg, S. R. (1996). Some dare call it power. In S. R. Clegg, C. Hardy, & W. R. Nord (Eds.), *The handbook of organization studies* (pp. 622–641). London: Sage.

Hickson, D. J. (1966). A convergence in organization theory. *Administrative Science Quarterly, 11,* 224–237.

Hogan, J., & Greene, A. M. (2002), E-collectivism: on-line action and on-line mobilisation. In L. Holmes, D. M. Hosking, & M. Grieco (Eds.),*Organising in the information age: Distributed technology, distributed leadership, distributed identity, distributed discourse.* Aldershot, UK: Ashgate.

Horkheimer, M., & Adorno, T. W. (1944/2002). *Dialectic of enlightenment: Philosophical fragments.* (E. Jephcott, Trans.) Stanford, CA: Stanford University Press.

Illich, I. (1970). *Deschooling society.* New York: Harper and Row.

Jacoby, R. (1987). *The last intellectuals: American culture in the age of academe.* New York: Basic Books.

Kalberg, S. (1980). Max Weber's types of rationality: Cornerstones for the analysis of rationalization processes in history. *American Journal of Sociology, 85,* 1145–1179.

Kalyvas, A. (2005). Popular sovereignty, democracy, and the constituent power. *Constellation, 12*(2), 155–291.

Kornberger, M., Carter, C., & Clegg, S.R. (2006). Rethinking the polyphonic organization: Managing as discursive practice. *Scandinavian Journal of Management, 22,* 3–30.

Langford, D. P. (1994, November). Langford quality and learning video conference. Mississippi State University, PBS Adult Learning, and Langford International.

Lasch, C. (1979). *The culture of narcissism: American life in an age of diminishing expectations.* New York: Warner Books.

Little S. E., & Clegg S. R. (2005). Recovering experience, confirming identity, voicing resistance: The Braceros, the Internet and counter-coordination. *Critical Perspectives on International Business* [Special issue], *1*(2/3), 123–136.

Lukes, S. (1974). *Power: A radical view.* London: Macmillan.

Lukes, S. (2005). *Power: A radical view* (2nd ed.). London.

Malone, T. (2004). *The future of work: How the new order of business will shape your organization, your management style, and your life.* Boston: Harvard Business School Press.

Meyer, J. W., & Rowan, B. (1977). Institutionalized organizations: Formal structure as myth and ceremony. *American Journal of Sociology, 83,* 340–363.

Munro, I. (1992). Codes of ethics: Some uses and abuses. In P. Davies (Ed.), *Current issues in business ethics* (pp. 97–106). London: Routledge.

Niccol, A. (Director). (1977). *Gattaca* [Film]. New York: Sony.

Nisbet, R. A. (1993). *The sociological tradition.* New Brunswick, NJ: Transaction.

Ogilvy, J. (1977). *Many dimensional man: Decentralizing self, society and the sacred.* Oxford, UK: Oxford University Press.

Perez, C. (1983, October). Structural change and assimilation of new technologies in the economic and social systems. *Futures,* pp. 357–375.

Pitsis, T., Clegg, S. R, Marosszeky, M., & Rura-Polley, T. (2003). Constructing the Olympic dream: Managing innovation through the future perfect. *Organization Science, 14*(5), 574–590.

Postman, N., & Weingartner, C. (1969). *Teaching as a subversive activity.* New York: Delacorte Press.

Prasad, D. (2005). *Education for living creatively and peacefully.* Hyderabad: Spark-India.

Roberts, J. (2003). The manufacture of corporate social responsibility: Constructing corporate sensibility. *Organization, 10*(2), 249–265.

Said, E. (1978). *Orientalism.* New York: Vintage Books.

Simmel, G. (1964). *Conflict and the web of group affiliations* (K. H. Wolff & R. Bendix, Trans.). New York: Free Press.

Sprague, R. H., & McNurlin, B. C. (1997). *Information systems management in practice* (4th ed.). London: Prentice-Hall.

Steinberg, S. R., & Kincheloe, J. L. (Eds.). (1997). *Kinderculture: The corporate construction of childhood.* Boulder, Colorado: WestviewPress.

Suddaby, R., & Greenwood, R. (2005). Rhetorical strategies of legitimacy. *Administrative Science Quarterly, 50,* 35–67.

van Krieken, R. (1990). The organisation of the soul: Elias and Foucault on discipline and the self. *Archives Europeénes de Sociologie, 31*(2), 353–371.

Weber, M. (1976). *The protestant ethic and the spirit of capitalism* (2nd ed.). London: Allen & Unwin.

Weber, M. (1978). *Economy and society: An outline of interpretive sociology.* Berkeley: University of California Press.

Zuboff, S. (1988) *In the age of the smart machine: The future of work and power.* New York: Basic Books.

# PART IV

CT ETHICS FOR SOCIAL ISSUES

CHAPTER 13

# MORALITY IN CONTEXT

## Reflections on Voice and Exclusion

**Gabrielle Durepos**
**Albert J. Mills**

This is a story; it's an ironic story about morality-in-use, which neglects its context. It is also a story about a monolith, that is, a monolithic knowledge-generating enterprise that legitimates and validates the lack of contextual analysis in the knowledge about morality-in-use. Sadly, it is a story about how the lack of reflection about the effects of this monolith and the lack of questioning of the instrumental authority of the knowledge-creating monolith have been thoroughly effective in systematically silencing diversity.

### INTRODUCTION

It would be a mistake to attribute the recent wealth of attention given to the business of ethics to the novelty of the field. Dressed up and given differing titles such as business environment, social issues in management, or business ethics (Paul, 1987), issues of social responsibility and the implications for organizations have been the subject of much waxing and waning since the mid-1950s (Paul, 1987). Indeed, sections on business ethics were regularly included in U.S. management textbooks (see, e.g., Jamison,

*Critical Theory Ethics for Business and Public Administration*, pages 283–297

1956).¹ Guided largely by concerns external to academia (Paul, 1987), the level of recent concern with ethical issues and the various implications for organizations has been attributed to the rise of unethical behavior in practice and the social awareness of these "business scandals" (Grey, 2003; Paul, 1987). Perception of a dramatic rise in unethical business practice (e.g., Enron, Worldcom, etc.) has been the subject of many scholarly articles and books within the last 15 years (Jackall, 1988), and has instilled a sense of expediency in the need for incorporating courses of business ethics in the business school curriculum (Bremer, Logan, & Wokutch, 1987). This has been further encouraged through the standards requirements of AASCB International—the Association to Advance Collegiate Schools of Business.²

Our sensitivity to the recent academic attention given to ethical issues is surprising due to the long-standing dedication of the study of ethics within the university. Specifically within programs dedicated to the study of business administration, the need to incorporate discussions around issues of social responsibility and ethical behavior began in the late 1950s (Bremer et al., 1987). The narrow prevailing focus on the internal functions of the workplace when training future managers was deemed inadequate. It was recognized that future managers would need a working knowledge of the environment in which their workplace was embedded. As a result, the social, political, and legal environment of business began receiving considerable attention (Paul, 1987). Through the maturity of the field of business ethics, two main orientations developed, one informed by philosophy and the other focused on technical management. Concerned largely with similar issues, the philosophy orientation takes a more abstract and theoretical focus, dealing with issues of morality and their application. The management-orientated scholars have tasked themselves with practical aspects of ethics and decision making within organizations while considering the effects on the implicated industry (Beauchamp & Bowie, 2004; Paul, 1987).

This chapter is concerned mostly with the management orientation of business ethics, but incorporates arguments from both orientations since the two cannot be understood as divorced or in isolation from one another. The chapter focuses on issues of "morality" as termed by philosophy-oriented scholars of ethics and the subsequent application of "morality" by management-oriented scholars as they theorize about practical aspects of ethics and decision making in practice. Therefore, business ethics is understood as moral theory in application, thus "morality-in-use." At its core, the chapter looks at the study of "morality-in-use" within the workplace. Primarily, it is concerned with the way in which studies of "morality-in-use" have neglected the context in which they are "in-use." Specifically, of interest is the way in which knowledge generated about "morality-in-use" has been effective in neglecting the workplace as a site of diversity, comprised of people of differing class, gender, race, and ethnicity (Mills, Simmons, &

Helms Mills, 2005). In neglecting the diversity of the workplace, studies of "morality-in-use" have also neglected the historical rooted nature of the organization, gender, class, race, and ethnicity (Calás & Smircich, 1997; Mills et al., 2005). As a result, the individuality of individuals, as they have been shaped by their specific context of socialization as well as their situated nature within the organization and society, has been neglected (Mills et al., 2005; Calás & Smircich, 1997).

An exploration of these various forms of neglect is the focus of this chapter. The chapter begins with an exploration of the current perspective in which knowledge about business ethics is generated and puts forth a detailed analysis of the field's current epistemological constraints. The oft-cited debate in ethics between Carol Gilligan and Lawrence Kohlberg is discussed as an example of the field's current epistemological limitation. Through this, it is proposed that the rules for validating and legitimizing knowledge in the study of "morality-in-use" have been effective in the systematic silencing of diversity. The chapter concludes with ways forward in generating knowledge about business ethics that offer potential in voicing previously marginalized voices. Above all, the chapter is concerned with drawing attention to a pressing problem, that is, current forms of generating knowledge about business ethics have systematically silenced diversity and epistemological issues are in extreme need of deliberation.

## FUNCTIONAL BUSINESS ETHICS AND MORAL THEORY

Perhaps due to the influence of modernist conceptions of thought (Prasad, 2005) and its stronghold on organizational scholars, studies of organizations have been dominated by analysis characterized by rigidity and concreteness (Chia, 1995). The study of organization within a modernist mode of thought has served to create fictitious categories within the organization, leading to the conceptualization of the various capacities of the organization as separate, isolated, and rigid entities (Chia, 1995). Included in these capacities are issues of gender, ethics, class, and ethnicity. Within a broad modernist discourse, issues of diversity have been treated as functions of the organizations and assumed a "thing-like" character. Attempts at rationally organizing the workplace have lead to a view of diversity and ethics as subsumed by the organization.

Knowledge generation on issues of ethics and diversity has been effective in legitimizing this modernist view of the organization and "morality-in-use." Through the analysis of hypothetical cases and "real-life situations abstracted from their intricate organizational contexts" (Jackall, 1988, p. 5), the much privileged objectivity and rationality within the study of business ethics has been maintained. Such abstractions are rooted in a functionalist view of the social sciences, which operate according to a positivist epistemology (Burrell & Morgan, 1979). Largely borrowing rules for generating knowledge from the natural sciences, positivist epistemologies support modernist streams of thought in that its suppositions for legitimizing and validating knowledge about the social world are based on assumptions of that social world as made of concrete social artifacts. Based on the assumption of the social world's independent existence of an individual's mental appreciation of it, extracting objective knowledge, that which represents or mirrors the social, has been the preoccupation of many attempts in understanding the diversity of the social world (Chia, 1995; Burrell & Morgan, 1979). As such, accurate knowledge of the social world has been gathered in a "progressive" quest, aimed at depicting "truths" in a neutral and impartial manner (Calás & Smircich, 1997; Alvesson & Willmott, 1996). The obsession with generating rational explanations of social affairs (Burrell & Morgan, 1979, p. 26; Calás & Smircich, 1997), through isolating phenomena, has contributed to the legitimacy of the vacuum-like conditions in which business ethics has been studied (Alvesson & Willmott, 1996). As a result, current theorization of business ethics are generated as divorced from context. From the business ethics researcher, isolating phenomena in hopes of understanding associations, to the business ethics student learning moral principles and then applying them to case studies (Calás and Smircich, 1997), the study of business ethics is plagued by the division of "morality-in-use" from its context of application. The field of business ethics in its current form is suffering from epistemological constraint and as such, the next section dissects these constraints (Walker, 1989).

## CURRENT EPISTEMOLOGICAL CONSTRAINTS IN "MORALITY-IN-USE"

Through acceptance of the authority of positivism, business ethics scholars have created a monolithic knowledge-generating enterprise, incapable of self-reflection or self-criticism. Knowledge generated has been a one-sided monologue (Calás & Smircich, 1997), lacking in contextual grounding (Jackall, 1988; Grey, 2003), ahistorical (Booth & Rowlinson, 2006), and promoting the fallacy of a concrete social order (Chia, 1995; Law, 1994) limiting the possibility of conceptualizing the "unthought, unseen and unheard" (Benhabib, 1987, p. 168). If the apparent immediacy for discussions of business ethics is not a passing fad, then ways of generating knowledge about business ethics are in need of examination (Booth & Rowlinson, 2006).

Theorizing about business ethics has been subsumed within a powerful modernist gaze. This gaze has been all pervasive in that it has created homogeneity of knowledge, lacking multiplicity and plurality (Calás & Smirich, 1997). Knowledge generation within this gaze has attempted to strip the complexity of the social through reductionist analyses, opting to explain the multifaceted nature of phenomenon through the isolated exploration of few incidents, and then generalizing its findings across populations. Inherent in the idea of a generalization is an impartial applicability to all involved, which falls short in accounting for possible differences, due to differing contextual socializations within a population. Generalizations limit the view of ethics as situated, rooted, and "parasitic on the circumstances" (Michaels, 1986, p. 178) of a specific place and time, informing its particularities (Mills et al., 2005; Michaels, 1986). As Walker (1989) notes, it is only with a move away from the privileging of the abstract and the objective that legitimizes generalizations, to the specific individualities of individuals, that an interpersonal view can be fostered. But, with the current modernist commitment to rationality and objectivity, legitimizing this interpersonal view is difficult to sustain. Part of the all-pervasiveness of modernity has been its normalization of the production of disinterested research written in a neutral language (Michaels, 1986), which has been instrumental in sustaining the authority of the rational (Alvesson & Willmott, 1996).

Positivist knowledge generation within the business school has tended to take a narrow focus of technical problem solving, concerned *centrally* with diagnosing problems and finding practical solutions (Burrell & Morgan, 1979; Calás & Smirich, 1997; Paul, 1987; Mills et al., 2005; Alvesson & Willmott, 1996). The study of business ethics too has taken a position of technical rationality and thus only issues deemed relevant to the orientation of technical problem solving have been considered important and worthy of analysis (Calás & Smirich, 1997). For the business ethics pedagogue, this technical problem-solving approach has meant that through the combination of lectures on universal ethics principles and analysis of a few abstract and decontextualized case studies, the student has been effectively educated in ethical decision making. But in essence, what this really points to is an effectively educated and socialized student, who can "see" the problem as it is narrowly defined by the business school. The trouble with this narrow approach is that it neglects the importance of understanding the *a priori* conditions of the problem, that is, the specific conditions that have enabled the problem's existence and those conditions that have lead the student in understanding the problem as "normal" and "natural" (Alvesson & Willmott, 1996).

The conditions that sustain and enable the prevalence of a mode of naturalness within the study of organizations, implying that the present status quo is pregiven in the order of things and that the world comes made in the categories that presently orders our existence (Martin & Knopoff, 1997), is often neglected or erased from sight. Left is a false illustration of the necessity in the current mode of organizing the social, or as Unger (2004) calls it a "false necessity." Naturalness is limited and dogmatic in that when it is assumed, all other forms of exploring and conceptualizing are erased from view. Flimsy arguments based solely on naturalness need exposing to delimit creative modes of knowledge generation. Writing in business ethics, due to its supposed quest for neutrality and objectivity appears to be universal and natural. But as Martin and Knopoff (1997) have shown, through a detailed deconstruction of text, it is often found to be masculine dominant.

Like organizational analysis from a positivist epistemology, business ethics or morality-in-use tends to be universal in approach in that it is assumed that the principles deemed appropriate for guiding moral behavior and ethical decision making are spatially and temporally constant (Benhabib, 1987; Calás & Smircich, 1997). Specifically, philosophical moral theorists understand ethics as the search for moral knowledge in the formulation of moral principles that are thoroughly applicable to a collective. It is assumed that in a situation of social exchange, moral principles put into use would ensure that all parties involved would have their needs met (Walker, 1989; Benhabib, 1987). But the very existence of a universal set of principles guiding behavior glosses over the notion of the organization as "located within a larger society possessing its own distinctive history, culture and social relations" (Mills et al., 2005, p. 206) as well as differing needs. Embedded in the very existence and notion of universal principles is an assumption that society is made of homogenized occupants devoid of individualized detail and intricacy. The doubt lies in whether a universalized set of principles will instill a sense of morality that will satisfy the diverse desires in the various social exchanges that connect these individuals (Walker, 1989). Universalism in moral theory creates a "generalized other" that is disembodied, disembedded, and stripped of complexity (Benhabib, 1987). To recognize the various differences that exist among individuals, to acknowledge their complexity and diversity and recognize "each and every rational being as an individual with a concrete history, identity and affective-emotional constitution" (Benhabib, 1987, p. 164), is to begin to accentuate their individual voice. Modernist conceptions have focused on commonalities that bring individuals together, but this has neglected their individualities. Instead, by focusing on differences, the intricacy of diversity can be thoroughly appreciated (Benhabib, 1987).

As has been previously noted, legitimized knowledge of business ethics has been "uni-vocal" (Calás & Smircich, 1997) in that it has privileged one voice at the exclusion of all others. This voice has been criticized as being patriarchal (Calás & Smircich, 1997; Ferguson, 1997; Martin & Knopoff, 1997). An example is evident through an exploration of moral philosophy's main focus, which has been to articulate qualities of character, or virtues of the morally good person. For some moral philosophers, reason, rationality, self-control, and strength of will are at the core of the morally informed person in that they guide their conduct. The privileging of reason, rationality, as well as self-control and strength of will in informing good moral behavior creates a binary in that all qualities associated with what is deemed moral are favored and celebrated while systematically excluding "other" qualities such as compassion, sympathy, kindness and emotional support (Blum, 1982). For the moral philosopher, emotions are impure since acting in an emotionally charged manner is deemed contradictory to acting disinterested and are therefore irrelevant to moral behavior (Michaels, 1986). The qualities privileged by the moral philosopher have often reflected commonly associated characteristics of the white, middle-class male living in a Western society (Blum, 1982). But to call qualities male and female does not mean characterizing gender solely through physiological differences. It means accepting that one's embodiment plays a large role in the process of socialization, while at the same time acknowledging that the social world is socially constructed and mediated (Calás & Smircich, 1997). For the most part, society's role in associating certain qualities with "what it means to be male" and "what it means to be female" is mostly predetermined by the community in which one is socialized. But it also means acknowledging the active process in which individuals are socialized into various gender identities (Blum, 1982). Studies in business ethics have appeared objective and impartial and have systematically ruled out the notion of the social world being socially negotiated. Instead, rationality, a traditionally male-dominated characteristic (Ferguson, 1984), has ruled the production of knowledge and methodology and through its dominance has imposed these rigidities on "others," ensuring conformity. The privileging of rationality through this white maleness has been so dominant and successful that the patriarchal biases are deeply embedded in the very fabric that makes up business ethics (Calás & Smircich, 1997; Ferguson, 1997; Martin & Knopoff, 1997). The Gilligan–Kohlberg debate is an excellent example of the patriarchy embedded in the very nature of business ethics and it is to this controversy that we shift our focus in the next section.

The preceding paragraphs have highlighted the current epistemological constraints of business ethics and have explored the effectiveness of a positivist epistemology in systematically silencing diversity. This problem is one that others have attempted to address. Voicing a previously silenced female voice in the study of "morality-in-use" has been attempted. The perceived success of this attempt in changing the monologue of ethics has largely been a matter of opinion, which need not concern our analysis. In an effort to treat knowledge symmetrically (Law, 1994), that is, treat truth claims as well as false claims, success and failures with the same level of sociological scrutiny, the following section analyzes the recent debate between Lawrence Kohlberg and Carol Gilligan.

## WHAT KIND OF "DIFFERENT" VOICE?

The purpose of this section is to provide an example of the all-pervasiveness of a positivist epistemology in silencing diversity. The well-known and oft-cited debate, featuring Carol Gilligan and Lawrence Kohlberg, is discussed to highlight the current epistemic constraints within "morality-in-use" as has been previously mentioned in the above paragraphs.

Kohlberg and Gilligan, scholars concerned with the study of ethics, have developed two differing and nonreconcilable perspectives on the subject. Kohlberg, firmly rooted in the tradition of moral justice, has described a view of ethics as operating on independent universal principles that guide the moral autonomous agent (Meyers & Kittay, 1987, Michaels, 1986). The principles of justice as discussed by Kohlberg are said to exist independently of any social or personal arrangements; they are abstract, general (Michaels, 1986; Meyers & Kittay, 1987), universal in that they "true for all persons, at all times, in all places" (Meyers & Kittay, 1987, p. 13) and are "strictly impartial" (Friedman, 1987, p. 200).

In an attempt to generate knowledge about moral justice and moral maturity, Kohlberg developed a scale of moral development consisting of six stages. The various stages were said to represent degrees in which an individual was able to adopt conventional morality. Kohlberg gathered data through the analysis of case studies and hypothetical dilemmas (Michaels, 1986). Implicit in his choice of method is an assumption that moral development is something that can be tested and evaluated rationally (Michaels, 1986). As Kohlberg notes, "justice asks for 'objective' or rational reasons and justifications for choice rather than being satisfied with subjective, 'decisionistic,' personal commitments to aims and to other persons" (Kohlberg, 1983, p. 93, as quoted in Friedman, 1987). As Michaels (1986, p. 179) notes, Kohlberg's use of "canned" moral dilemmas maintained his formal, abstract, and objective testing of moral development (Walker, 1989; Michaels, 1986).

When using his scale to test subjects, those showing "reasoned" appeals to principles of justice, which meant achieving within the higher levels of the scale, were said to have the highest level of moral development. Through this, it was determined that subjects showing high levels of moral development were more likely to have moral maturity (Meyers & Kittay, 1987; Michaels, 1986). It is important to caution that Kohlberg's notion of moral maturity is largely synonymous with the ideals of moral maturity as defined by the justice tradition; therefore, what is subsumed within his general notion of moral maturity is the fulfillment of that which is narrowly defined by the justice tradition (Meyers & Kittay, 1987). The subjects of Kohlberg's study were primarily male but when female subjects were tested using the scale, none were found to achieve the top stages of Kohlberg's moral development scale, leading him to conclude that women's moral reasoning is "defective" (Michaels, 1986, p. 179).

Largely reacting to and suspicious of a study that deemed female moral reasoning deficient, Gilligan became preoccupied with the distinct decision-making strategies of women and their specific course of moral development (Meyers & Kittay, 1987; Michaels, 1986). Gilligan began to develop what is now known as an "ethics of care" orientation to ethics. Her notion of a moral agent is one who is "enmeshed in a network of relations to others and whose moral deliberation aims to maintain these relations" (Meyers & Kittay, 1987, p. 10). Gilligan's notion of morality has differed from a tradition of moral justice characterized by universalism, in that it assumes that moral principles and responses are dependent on the specific situations in which agents are embedded (Meyers & Kittay, 1987). Gilligan attempted to measure and understand moral reasoning in women by looking at women immersed in actual dilemmas. Similar to Kohlberg, Gilligan assumed that moral development could be effectively understood by measuring women and their morality as they progress through various levels of moral development (Michaels, 1986). In constructing her study, Gilligan used narratives to provide the intricate detail of moral problems (Walker, 1989), and sought to elude abstract reasoning by understanding her subjects as embedded within a contextual frame (Friedman, 1987; Gilligan, 1982; Meyers & Kittay, 1987). Differing largely from Kohlberg's findings, Gilligan showed that progress from one stage of moral development to the next was guided by the individual's increasing awareness and understanding of the relationships in which they were surrounded. She found that progress in moral development was also fueled by the individual's attempt to assess specific situations before acting while maintaining care for one's self and being cautious not to neglect others as she acted (Meyers & Kittay, 1987). Conclusions to Gilligan's empirical study revealed a gender difference in morality, and led her to concede that there are two independent but equal systems in moral theory, which are irreconcilable (Meyers & Kittay, 1987). Women on one hand have an inclination to solve moral problems through an ethics of care perspective and men through an ethics of justice perspective (Gilligan, 1982).

The Gilligan–Kohlberg debate hints to an attempt to break the monologue of ethics by voicing a previously silenced female perspective. Kohlberg bases his study and findings on a tradition of morality that privileges reason, rationality, and impartiality and Gilligan is successful in showing that these hallmarks are male-dominant in that they do not accurately reflect the process by which female subjects become morally mature (Gilligan, 1982). Gilligan is successful in finding space and generating a receptive audience in the discussion of gender and moral theory. She is also successful in showing the deceptive nature of universalism in moral theory, but sadly she limits this to differences of gender and neglects the possibility of universalism being subject to other constraints such as culture, history, or economic class (Meyers & Kittay, 1987). In showing the defective nature of universalism, Gilligan recreates and thus reinforces the very same generalizations that initially discriminated women. In accepting Kohlberg's findings as legitimate when applicable to men, and deeming Kohlberg's scale of moral development inadequate to measure women's progress in moral development, she creates a scale along the same legitimizing criteria as used by Kohlberg to measure moral development in women (Michaels, 1986). She then generalizes her findings among all women. Implicit in Gilligan's generalization is the very universalism that was accountable in silencing women. Gilligan's newly created universalism is subject to criticisms in that it assumes women to be a homogeneous group, devoid of differences of class, race, ethnicity, and sexual orientation (Addelson, 1987). Gilligan's categorizing of women as a homogenous group casts light on another problem, which is her narrow construction of gender. Embedded in Gilligan's conception of gender is a neglect of differing social constructions of women's identities due to their individualized socializations, mediated by their class, race, ethnicity, or sexual orientation. The context as a site of socialization, where moral explanations are socially constructed, and negotiated through interactions within a collective is neglected (Addelson, 1987).

Fundamentally, these problems point to epistemological limitations (Benhabib, 1987). In Gilligan's attempt to voice a woman's perspective, she draws on ways of generating knowledge that are synonymous to that of Kohlberg's. For example, Gilligan's use of method (contextualized narratives) differs from that of Kohlberg's (abstract case analysis) to accentuate the different characteristics of women, but her construction of a scale to understand the moral development of women assumes that measuring and testing moral development is a valid method in generating legitimate knowledge. Gilligan's attempt in finding a "different voice" is caught within the modernist gaze of concreteness and subject to the limiting and patriarchal rules of a positivist epistemology. As a result, Gilligan creates homogeneous, universal, and generalized knowledge about women. She recreates the "univocal" (Calás & Smircich, 1997) nature of ethics, which ironically was previously criticized for silencing women.

The Gilligan–Kohlberg debate effectively illustrates the epistemological constraints of positivism in generating plural and diverse knowledge as well as warrantable knowledge about diversity. If ethics or "morality-in-use" is concerned with the identification of a "moral good" and through this the welfare of society then modes of generating knowledge that can account for the multiplicity of society are in need (Benhabib, 1987). Knowledge about business ethics has been generated within the modernist assumption that morality is a rigid and concrete "thing" that individuals *have*. A shift of focus is necessary. To comprehend the diversity within morality-in-use, business ethics must be understood in action, as a social activity that is negotiated among actors within a thought collective, who are embedded and situated within a particular context (Addelson, 1987). The modernist fixation with capturing what morality individuals have must be abandoned and replaced with a focus on the constant flexural process by which morality is constructed and negotiated in day-to-day operations (Jackall, 1988).

## TOWARD AN UNDERSTANDING OF BUSINESS ETHICS IN ACTION

Little work has been done in the detailed investigation of daily operations of work and its influence on the shaping of moral consciousness (Jackall, 1988). The idea of morality as an active process, where actors participate on a daily basis in negotiating what is "right" or "wrong," have received very little attention (Jackall, 1988). To be specific, the study of morality-in-use has been dominated by an assumption of morality as embrained (Blackler, 1995) by individuals, in which morality is understood as a set of capabilities that various actors within organizations should possess or already have. Business ethics as a social and organizational activity (Jackall, 1988; Alvesson & Willmott, 1996) shifts from this dominant cognitive focus to provide a relational view of morality as an active process. Instead of understanding morality as contained by the individual, business ethics as a social activity focuses on the various collectives in which moral consciousness is mediated (much like the respective thought collectives and communities of scientists of Fleck, 1979, and Kuhn, 1962).

A cultural and communal look permits the researcher to gather individuated knowledge, that which is situated and informed by the history of the actor, as opposed to knowledge about individuals (that which the individual has or possesses), to understand how actors are formed and shaped into their particularities. This processual focus not only demands that we acknowledge the socially constructed nature of actors but also the fluid process in which they renegotiate their "selves" (Calás & Smircich, 1997). Within a sociocultural lens, the previously deemed "naturalness" of social categories and practices, that is, the false necessity of social reality where actors are fooled by their status quo in that they unquestioningly accept it as the only enabler of their known mode of ordering (Unger, 2004) can be disturbed, offering opportunities for creative reflection (Ferguson, 1997). More specifically, through a sociocultural lens where contexts are understood as sites where notions of gender, ethnicity, and social class are shaped and shape activity, we can begin to produce previously neglected knowledge about business ethics and diversity (Calás & Smircich, 1997).

A sociocultural perspective creates knowledge that is contextual, improvised (Jackall, 1988), relational as well as situated while challenging the false necessity of social reality (Unger, 2004; Calás & Smircich, 1997). Knowledge creation from this perspective should focus on the various relationships that form the organization as a site where morality of managerial work is created, mediated, and recreated (Jackall, 1988). As such, business ethics should be understood as a process that is both relational and emergent, played out through the interactions of a diversity of individuals. Business ethics is thus an activity that both shapes actors as they engage in moral deliberations while simultaneously being shaped by actors as they renegotiate and define morality (Jackall, 1988).

A sociocultural view of business ethics seeks to construct knowledge that takes into account its situated nature. To produce situated knowledge about morality is to understand with intricate detail the specificities of a collective's frame of thought in negotiating morality, as located and influenced by a particular time and place (Jackall, 1988; Benhabib, 1987). This means locating discussions, that is, actors' negotiations, about morality within the broader context in which they are taking place to discern their meaning. It also means acknowledging that a collective's particular frame of thought (drawing on Fleck's, 1979, thought collective), is in a constant state of improvisation, in that it is continually revised, negotiated, and therefore emergent. Thus, the organization is understood as a situated effect of the collective's constant revision and negotiation (Chia, 1995).

Jackall (1988) provides an excellent example of the constant negotiation and improvisation of managers as they engage in "moral rules-in-use." Interestingly, he describes moral behavior as "often unarticulated" (p. 6) in various collectives. Jackall's version of business ethics discusses morality as emergent and processual, as an active process in which actors engage. Quite expectedly, "there is a dissonance with the ideological rhetoric of moral theory and the morality in use of Jackall's actors" (Alvesson & Willmott, 1996, p. 34). In describing the daily activities of various actors, Jackall never refers to an absolute or concrete system of morals that guide the autonomous moral agent. Instead, he describes social morality as situated within a particular time and place, and "parasitic" upon the circumstances of that particular time and place (Benhabib, 1987). He describes actors as effects of the organization in that their morality at work is shaped by the rules of their occupation that is the rules of bureaucracy. Actors are not only effects generated through the organization, they come to embody the very ethos of morality as it has been shaped by the unspoken rules and norms of bureaucracy (Jackall, 1988, p. 12). As Jackall notes, they are the principle carriers of this ethos and come to reflect it as it guides them in their engagement in daily activities.

This view of morality is largely at odds with that generated from a positivist epistemology. It paints business ethics as an active process, in continual flux, in which actors who have been socialized in differing manners engage in morality. It is a contextual view that focuses on the relational, processual, and situated nature of morality in which the modernist preoccupation with concreteness and motionlessness has no place.

## CONCLUSIONS

In the recent series of unethical behavior in practice, a certain expediency has been instilled in the need for discussions about business ethics. Through the transformation of business ethics into the busyness of ethics, the potential benefits or neglects in previously dominant ways of generating and validating knowledge have not been examined and have been unquestioningly reproduced. This chapter has sought to illustrate the current problems with understanding diversity and business ethics from a positivist epistemology. It has sought to illustrate that embedded in the nature of knowledge created from a positivist epistemology is a systematic silencing of diversity.

Specifically, a positivist epistemology has been deemed inappropriate in producing knowledge about ethicality due to its extreme focus on reductionist analysis, generalizations, and narrow technical problem-solving approach, universalisms, and patriarchy. These epistemological limitations have been illustrated through an exploration of the Gilligan–Kohlberg debate in ethics. Above all, the main point has been that voicing the previously silenced is not enough. The main task has been to illustrate that new ways of generating knowledge that take into account the historical and contextual rooted nature of the organization are in need. Generating knowledge in this manner can only be done by focusing on business ethics as an emergent activity that takes the context as a site where norms of ethics and diversity are constantly being crafted, negotiated, mediated, and sustained. We must break away from the all-pervasiveness of the modernist gaze to understand the organization as an effect generated through a diversity of situated actors engaging daily in morality.

## NOTES

1. In a section called "Code of ethical conduct" Jamison (1956, pp. 256–257) outlines in full the "ten ethical practices" of the Association of Consulting Management Engineers' "code of professional ethics."
2. In April 2003 the AACSB adopted revised standards of accreditation, which includes clause "E": "The institution or the business programs of the institu-

tion must establish expectations for ethical behavior by administrators, faculty, and students" (AACSB, 2006).

## REFERENCES

AACSB. (2006). *Eligibility procedures and accreditation standards for business accreditation.* Tampa, FL: Author.

Addelson, K. P. (1987). Moral passages. In E. F. Kittay & D. T. Meyers (Eds.), *Women and moral theory* (pp. 87–110). New York: Rowman & Littlefield.

Alvesson, M., & Willmott, H. (1996). *Making sense of management: A critical introduction.* London: Sage.

Beauchamp, T. L., & Bowie, N. E. (2004). *Ethical theory and business.* London: Pearson Prentice Hall.

Benhabib, S. (1987). The generalized and the concrete other. In E. F. Kittay & D. T. Meyers (Eds.), *Women and moral theory* (pp. 154–177). New York: Rowman & Littlefield.

Blackler, F. (1995). Knowledge, knowledge work and organizations: An overview and interpretation. *Organization Studies, 16*(6), 1021–1046.

Blum, L. A. (1982). Kant's and Hegel's moral rationalism: A feminist perspective. *Canadian Journal of Philosophy, 12*(2), 287–302.

Booth, C., & Rowlinson, M. (2006). Management and organizational history: Prospects. *Management and Organizational History, 1*(1), 5–30.

Bremer, O. A., Logan, J. E., & Wokutch, R. E. (1987). Ethics and values in management thought. In K. Paul (Ed.), *Business environment and business ethics* (pp. 61–86). Cambridge, UK: Ballinger.

Burrell, G., & Morgan, G. (1979). *Sociological paradigms and organizational analysis.* London: Heinemann.

Calás, M. B., & Smircich, L. (1997). Predicando la moral en calzoncillos?: Feminist inquiries into business ethics. In A. Larson & R.E. Freeman (Eds.), *Woman's studies and business ethics: Towards a new conversation* (pp. 50–191). New York: Oxford University Press.

Chia, R. (1995). From modern to postmodern organizational analysis. *Organization Studies, 16*(4), 579–604.

Ferguson, K. E. (1984). *The feminist case against bureaucracy.* Philadelphia: Temple University Press.

Ferguson, K.E. (1997). Postmodernism, feminism, and organizational ethics: Letting difference be. In A. Larson & R. E. Freeman (Eds.), *Woman's studies and business ethics: Towards a new conversation* (pp. 80–91). New York: Oxford University Press.

Fleck, L. (1979). *Genesis and development of a scientific fact.* Chicago: University of Chicago Press.

Friedman, M. (1987). Care and context in moral reasoning. In E. F. Kittay & D. T. Meyers (Eds.), *Women and moral theory* (pp. 190–204). New York: Rowman & Littlefield.

Gilligan, C. (1982). *In a different voice: Psychological theory and women's development.* Cambridge, MA: Harvard University Press.

Grey, C. (2003). The real world of Enron's auditors. *Organization, 10*(3), 572–576.

Jackall, R. (1988). *Moral mazes.* Oxford, UK: Oxford University Press.

Jamison, C. L. (1956). *Business policy.* Englewood Cliffs, NJ: Prentice Hall.

Kuhn, T. (1962). *The structure of scientific revolutions.* Chicago: University of Chicago Press.

Law, J. (1994). *Organizing modernity.* Oxford, UK: Blackwell.

Martin, J., & Knopoff, K. (1997). The gendered implications of apparently gender-neutral theory: Rereading Max Weber. In A. Larson & R. E. Freeman (Eds.), *Woman's studies and business ethics: Towards a new conversation* (pp. 30–49). New York: Oxford University Press.

Meyers, D. T., & Kittay, E. F. (1987). Introduction. In E. F. Kittay & D. T. Meyers (Eds.), *Women and moral theory* (pp. 3–16). New York: Rowman & Littlefield.

Michaels, M. W. (1986). Morality without distinction. *Philosophical Forum, 17*(3), 175–187.

Mills, A. J., Simmons, T., & Helms Mills, J. (2005). *Reading organization theory: A critical approach to the study of organizational behaviour and structure* (3rd ed.). Toronto: Garamond Press.

Paul, K. (1987). Business environment and business ethics in management thought. In K. Paul (Ed.), *Business environment and business ethics* (pp. 1–17). Cambridge, UK: Ballinger.

Prasad, P. (2005). *Crafting qualitative research.* Armonk, NY: M. E. Sharpe.

Unger, R. M. (2004). *False necessity: Anti-necessitarian social theory in the service of radical democracy: From Politics, a work in constructive social theory.* London: Verso.

Walker, M. A. (1989). Moral understandings: Alternative "epistemology" for a feminist ethics. *Hypatia, 4,* 15–28.

# CHAPTER 14

# ETHICS OF RECOGNITION

## *I / you (thou) / they*

**Hugo Letiche**

## INTRODUCTION

One of the Netherlands' major insurance companies has, now for more than a year, had an ethics committee composed of the CEO, the head of the Legal Department, a representative of the Works Council, the Director of Life Insurance, a senior staff member for corporate strategy and ethics, and one external academic member. Many issues brought to the committee really had little or nothing to do with ethics. For instance, inquires were made whether a corporate strategy of "transparency" meant that this or that ought to be done. These questions had not to do with the ethics of "transparency"—for instance, "Is any such principle really adequate to dealing with justice, or with one's obligations to the insured?"—but had only to do with how the corporate mission was to be understood. The committee sent these requests unanswered back to their originators.

At one point, the committee was asked to discuss a decision to withdraw an ethical investment product from the market. The problem was that the product had not achieved the hoped-for return on investment. SRI invest-

*Critical Theory Ethics for Business and Public Administration*, pages 299–317
**299**

ment choices tend to pay off better in the long run than in the short; and to require specialist financial management skills, none of which is specifically ethical. What the investment bankers meant (in practice) by "people, planet, profit" was "ethical." But, how does "people" manifest itself—as political parties, labor unions, new social movements? How does "planet" show itself—as Gaia, as an object of life science? And what exactly is "profit"—is it a social–economic concept, the "subject" of history, or what? If "people, planet, profit" are ontologically incommensurable terms—for instance, one is a *social actor,* one is an *object of scientific study,* and one is (maybe) the *first cause of economic* activity, what sort of triad do they form? Each has a different sort of agency and there is no common playing field. While radical critique of concepts like "people, planet, profit" or "sustainability" are much needed, such questioning doesn't solve much in a concrete SRI debate.[1] Goals need analysis if they are to be (more) successfully opperationalized. But such analysis goes much further than what the investment bankers were after.

Often, the ethics committee discovered that what was asked of it were rules of action. Issues arose regularly, such as: *If a client was convicted of a drug offense, should the insurance company cancel the client's health and auto insurance?* Here there is an ethical issue to be considered. On the one hand, the insurer had accepted a responsibility to not stimulate or be a party to illegal activities (i.e., running a marijuana plantation), but on the other hand, insurers must not try to play judge and/or jury (i.e., an offender's punishment is meted out by the courts and not by insurers). Furthermore, family or employees (of perfectly legal enterprises) should not be punished (i.e., lose their health insurance) because an employer or husband has been convicted of a criminal activity.

But how should an insurance company react when it knows that a significant percentage of employers in a sector, wherein it is the dominant insurer, are employing illegal labor? Does the insurer pay out to an illegal employee who has suffered a serious on-the-job accident? Illegal labor earns much less than legal labor and does not pay into the government health insurance system. Thus, the employer is cheating on social responsibilities, and those employers who do not cheat are stuck with higher costs. If the insurer pays out to the illegal worker, the insurance policies for all employers become more expensive. Again, the employer who cheats hurts the economic position of the employer who is honest. Here the ethical issue is one of how does one react with integrity to the accident victim, without penalizing the honest employer? Because reliable lists exist of those employers who respect employment laws, it is possible to offer them preferential rates, rewarding their integrity. Here the choice was made to try to stimulate integrity, rather than to "punish" improper behavior.

Often cases reached the committee that were really about reputation management, such as should the insurer insure prostitutes. In the Netherlands, prostitution is legal. But too much contact with the prostitution sector leads to bad publicity, but there is no question of illegal activity. Qua ethics, stimulating the use of condoms and the prevention of sexually transmitted illnesses, can be thought of as much more relevant than penalizing or punishing brothels. Ethically spoken, support for public health measures are to be valued, but qua reputation management one may not want to get too involved in the sector. The query that was addressed to the ethics committee assumed that reputation management was the same thing as ethics. The committee replied that, in fact, they contradict one another in this case. Prostitution is a legal economic activity, wherein as insurer one could support programs for the improvement of public health. Those brothels that are really committed to supporting public health measures are identifiable and one could offer them privileged insurance rates, as they are the better-managed and safer addresses. But would one want to get that involved?

Insurance is a matter of spreading risk, whereby the insured only pays a premium, instead of being exposed to the full risk. Insurers spread risk across large numbers of people, so the risk to each individual (in the form of the premium) can be borne without economic hardship. Thus, insurers are in principle agents of solidarity. The insurer's task is to spread risk, so that together, everyone is better off than the individual would be standing alone. But how do these principles match up to the actions of an insurer who has discovered that wealthy persons have fewer health problems than poor ones? The wealthy eat better, exercise more, and can afford better medical care for themselves. Furthermore, their work is physically less strenuous. Thus, one could launch a health insurance product for the rich, which costs less than the policies for the poor. Such a policy makes sense in terms of risk analysis and profitability. But it is a direct attack on the solidarity principle. There are no technical insurance reasons not to launch such a policy—it is purely an ethical issue. The ethics committee advised, successfully, that it would be irresponsible to develop such a product.

The most crucial issues an insurer must address include: (1) who does or does not get coverage; (2) how will the enormous financial resources of the insurer be invested; and (3) how does the insurer define solidarity. The ethics committee tries to define processes and principles for answering these conundrums. It does not see itself as a legislative body that enacts rules for the organization. It is primarily a consulting body that develops ethical thought in practice. It exists to show a way to the ethical consideration of key issues. Three underlying principles have been identified: (1) the root identity and *raison d'être* of the insurer is grounded in solidarity and the insurer must never betray its very right to exist; (2) as insurer, one needs to pursue active citizenship by facilitating the ethical success of constitutive sociability and the social self; and (3) as insurer one has "soul-making" responsibilities. The first principle has been axiomatically accepted. The second remains theoretically uncertain, but has been accepted in practice. The third is under intense debate.

The first principle is bound to a deontological statement of the insurer's identity. It defines what an insurer is and must continue to be if the insurer wishes to be trusted and seen to fulfill its social goals and purposes. It is assumed that organizations entail various processes of social interaction wherein successful maintenance of social interaction (see below) is crucial. If one assumes that the autonomous egoistic individual is the starting point for organization, then ethics does (or does not) have to impose some sort of social contract from the outside. If organizations exist for the utilitarian benefit of self-sufficient individuals, then the organization as social interact is well near irrelevant. Our assumptions are "communitarian" in the sense that we understand insurance as a process of social relationship wherein insurer and insured form a constitutive bond. Insurer and insured "speak to one another," defining common practices, norms, and values. In their interaction, there is considerable autonomy; the relationship is grounded in their differences in position, role, and purpose. Insurer and insured are part of a community of divergence and interaction. Difference, thus, forms a crucial dimension to their identity.

The second principle follows from the liberal democratic assumption that the insurer, as a significant social factor, must practice good citizenship. It carries on from the acknowledgment of difference, assumed in basic organizational identity. Only in relationship is there (the possibility of) autonomy. In autism, there is no autonomy. Human political freedom or social autonomy is a form of relatedness. It requires shared language, values, and understanding. When economic organizations destroy the social bonds of society, they create Hobbesian anarchy. Liberal democracy assumes that difference is manageable—that is, that one can regulate relationships of difference so that order and diversity both flourish. Liberal democracy is all about the tension between the same and the other, difference and repetition, established and changing. Liberal democracy ceases to exist if either "same" or "different," is imposed. The terror of "sameness" permits no discovery, experimentation, or individualization; the terror of "difference" imposes principles of separation, inequality, and hierarchy. It is a major challenge to deal with the complexity of contemporary social and economic difference without availing oneself of terror. This principle can best be voiced in terms of neoliberal political thought, such as that of Hanna Arendt, Micheal Polanyi, or Tzvetan Todorov (Arendt, 1998; Brohm, 2005; for Todorov, see below).

The third principle is based on the assumption that the insurer is a proactive liberal institution and should thus support ethical flourishing. It reflects, for instance, the ethics of Kwame Anthony Appiah. While the ethical commission has wrestled with the second principle, despite feeling a firm implicit consensus about it, the third principle has throughout remained thoroughly controversial. Does an insurer really have a pedagogical responsibility? The ethical committee (successfully) advised the insurer to not accept a commission for certain services because commission taking would destroy necessary impartiality in advice to the client. But some intermediaries are taking hidden commissions. Should the insurer make its position, action, and standpoint widely known; including its opposition to less scrupulous actors? The chairman of a celebrated football (soccer) team has repeatedly been caught in pedophile activity. He is a client of the insurer; should the insurer publicly refuse to do business with him? The insurer claims to not do business with parties who are ethically reprehensible. It claims to take responsibility for the quality and nature of the interaction with its clients; is this a client with whom that responsibility is no longer possible? Does he and others need to know that the insurer refuses "recognition" (see below) to those who impose themselves sexually on young boys? Is this a necessary, social, political, and educational statement?

## RECOGNITION

Discussion of "recognition" will take place in two steps. First, the assertion of recognition implies a fundamentally social concept of organization. Organizations are not utilitarian tools in the hands of purely self-interested individuals; but form the social and human context for existence. Organization is not merely instrumental; human identity is grounded in the language, knowledge and culture of interaction. Humans are able to become human via their participation in relationship, diversity, and interaction. Humanization is a process of shared event, activity, and action. Thus an ethics that assumes the atomistic individual as its absolute starting point is rejected. Autonomy is a historical, social, and political relationship—"autonomy" is a concept defined in terms of writers, events, philosophies, and desires. It, like any concept, is essentially social. No idea, language, or statement can ever be entirely individual without becoming un-understandable and incomprehensible. Thus "autonomy" is a social relationship—a complex of embedded relationships, textual references, and shared personal histories. In the first phase of the examination of "recognition," the focus will be on the social conceptual prestructure to ethics. Here (early) Hegelian intersubjectivity serves as the point of departure. In a second phase, I turn more to the practices of ethical intersubjectivity. Here Todorov's conceptualization of becoming ethical, or of the humanization of the social, is examined. Thus the first phase is philosophical/theoretical, and the second phase (social) psychological/practical.

**(1)**

Hobbes and Machiavelli, in effect, ask the opposite question to mine. They want to make relationships less important and to define more space for the individual. Their "individual" competes for power, wealth, and success. Ever-expanding trade and commerce had opened previously unseen possibilities of economic activity and the egocentric pursuit of self-benefit had triumphed. From classical Greece to Christian medieval Europe:

> ... human beings were conceived of fundamentally as entities capable of life in community, as zoon politikon, as beings who had to rely on the social framework of a political community for the realization of their inner nature. Only in the ethical community of the polis or civitas—whose intersubjectively shared values sharply distinguish them from merely functional nexus formed by economic activities—could the social character of human nature genuinely develop. Starting from this teleological conception of human beings, the traditional doctrine of politics set itself the theoretical task of defining the ethical order of virtuous conduct within which individuals' . . . development could take the most appropriate course. (Honneth, 1995, p. 7)

But from Machiavelli to Hobbes, and onto Kant, individual economic and political self-interest surfaced stronger and stronger as the background to social thought. The collectivist or communitarian assumptions of the "polis" were swamped by the possibilities for economic and political expansion. The individualistic assumptions of Kant's thought rejected the prioritization of the intersubjective; the single rational being was to be taken as the unit of analysis, the social was (or was not) just added on. The basic assumption of subjects, isolated from one another, fits the expanding conditions of market production, distribution, and consumption, but leads at best to a "unified many" rather than to a "community."

Hegel's reaction to this lack of "community" was to try and define an "organization of society whose ethical cohesion would lie in a form of solidarity based on the recognition of the individual freedom of its citizens" (Honneth, 1995, p. 14). Thus, the growth of individuality and particular economic and political power was acknowledged, but nonetheless the attempt was made to preserve the intersubjectivity and mutuality of relationship in community. Hegel made this effort early in the 19th century in Jena and abandoned it fairly quickly thereafter. In this thought, the self-sufficient individual is not taken as the point of departure. Put in liberal phraseology, the "autonomy" of the subject is not the bedrock of the analysis. Persons are understood as formed, cared-for, and brought forth in relationship to others. The human child requires physical and emotional nurturing to ever become an adult. Not autonomous subjects, but dependent, incomplete, and relational babies are born. The bonds of nurturing, and the social context(s) of language, knowledge, and culture, make human individual existence possible. Isolated subjects are abstractions, reflective constructs drawn out of concrete relationships, interactions, and events. One must not prioritize the abstractions above the phenomenological processes.

Thus, the social ethical problem is not one of overcoming basic human egoism; for instance, via a social contract. Human existence is dependent, interrelated, and socially constituted from the start. But understanding identity formation is a crucial problem. How do humans come to self-conceptualize themselves, for instance, as autonomous or free individuals? Hegel saw the concept of recognition as the key to this process (O'Neill, 1996). He conceptualized recognition as a double movement of externalization and return (Honneth, 1995). In organizational studies, Karl Weick has basically repeated the same ideas but without referencing Hegel. Weick's *Social Psychology of Organizing* (1979) repeats Hegel's logic of recognition as the "double interact." The basic constitutive unit of human interaction is posited to be one person communicating with another, aware that communication is taking place. Thus A speaks to B, aware of B's acknowledgment of being spoken to. There is speech and "communication"—that is, speech with recognition. Mere monologue—speech without evident or expressed recognition — may or may not be communicative. The monologue may or may not be heard; and if not heard, it cannot contribute to organizational coherence. Organization depends on speech with recognition. And this, exactly, was Hegel's point. But Hegel realized, while Weick avoided or ran away from, that recognition is essentially conflictual.

In a logic of recognition, who recognizes whom? Who has control over the process? Hegel explored this concept, as the "master/slave" relationship. The assumption of difference is crucial. The one is different from the other; the one voice varies from the next one that follows it. Difference makes recognition possible. If we were all the same, there would be no motor to recognition—recognition has to do with the acknowledgment of dissimilarity or divergence. But in diversity, there is "not-sameness" or inequality. Kant's individualism actually leads to a pretense of "sameness"— all humans supposedly possess the same rational abilities, the same "truths" are (potentially) valid for all. But in a regime of difference, what the one understands, knows, or possesses is always different from the other. And difference makes for tensions, jealousy, and competition. In Weick's "double interact" he does not problematize who initiates and controls the conversation and who not. From conversation analysis, we know full well that turn-taking will impose its procedures on the conversation. The manager will control who speaks, when, and how; the "subaltern" will have the role of acknowledging what the boss says (Spivak, 1996). The latter acknowledges and recognizes; the former alone has voice and speaks. In the relationship between the speaker and the spoken to, only the speaker can be "recognized." What "recognition" adds to the analysis of communication is awareness of how one-sided the subject position really is. The speaker is subject only just as long as the listener is not subject. The social psychology of organization depends on double interacts wherein speakers are recognized, which means in effect that the listeners continually affirm their secondariness. The double interact is a logic of managerial firstness, and employee secondness.

The problem is that managerial "firstness" will eventually run out of energy. The managerial role of speaking and being acknowledged demands that one goes on and on speaking. If one stops and another takes over the role, one loses one's "firstness." Identity depends on the acknowledgment of one's presence; if one's being goes unacknowledged, it socially collapses. Thus "firstness" is inherently dependent on "secondness." Identity, or the speaker's role, only exists insofar as there is a listener—and the listener acknowledges somehow (for instance in organization, through actions) that listening has taken place. If the employees stop following orders, if colleagues ignore what one says, if one's proposals all come to naught, then one loses one's identity. To use Hegel's terminology, the "master" is only so strong as the "slave" permits.

The key role that difference plays in this analysis is almost contemporary. Recognition depends on the acknowledgment of difference—it trades in difference. But difference has to be maintained. A possible solution to the conflict implicit in the double interact is a mutuality of acknowledgment. The One acknowledges the speech of the Other, and the Other acknowledges the speech of the One. Herein, firstness and secondness are rotated and exchanged. Each party opens up to the other—identity is mutually developed, exchanged, and rotated. This makes awareness, learning, and appreciation possible. But it reduces or even aborts difference. The one and the other merge into their mutual discourse, awareness, or practice(s). The solution to the conflict is a mutuality of identity. But then, recognition collapses and new difference has to be sought and/or created for the process of recognition to continue. Identity or the psychological ability to feel one's own quality of aliveness or existence depends on interacts of difference. Relationship has socially, intellectually, affectively, and sexually to do with differences and their dynamics. Without difference, there is no awareness, dynamism, or life. Mutuality offers a solution to the conflict of recognition, but the generation of difference is necessary to retain one's perception of existing. In this logic, Hegel comes close to being a precursor of existentialism—wherein identity is created via difference (Kojève, 1969).

Humanity is a whole that constructs itself out of difference. Not individual human nature, but complex social processes of interaction and difference are crucial to human interaction. And turning to organizational (or business) ethics, what we have to attend to are the qualities and complexities of interacts and not the a priori preservation of individual autonomy. Business ethics tends to be Kantian—that is, to assume that the preservation of principles or absolute points of departure will ensure virtue. But organizational ethics needs to be post-Hegelian and to attend to the logic and processes of difference and recognition. Organization is attempted coherence, constructed out of difference—that is, a process of emergence, negotiation, and activity; wherein the One and the Other find (temporary) balance and dynamic grounds for interaction. The ethic of such a process has to ensure that the mutuality, negotiation, and creative interaction remains ongoing. Stasis or death has to be avoided; activity or generativity has to be supported.

Organizations do not need rules so much as they need life. Doing justice to one another, to circumstances and to others, is life-giving. That is, "doing justice" to the other is the same as recognizing the dialogue of differences. Ethics in organization, in this perspective, is about creating and preserving life or existing, and not about defining rules. Rules are reifications of past moments of recognition—they can be handy, but they always prioritize past instances of recognition more than they value living interaction. An organization can only take so much rule-making. Rules circumscribe and limit difference—within the rules there is no room for living difference and experienced recognition. Rules are the dead repetition of circumstances of recognition that have taken place. If past recognition dominates present recognition, if rules are prioritized above interaction, the organization ceases to live.

In Hegel, the position of the One and the Other is unstable. The slave can overtake the master. The One (the master) has great difficulty experiencing difference. As recognized, the subject feels and experiences Self—but self without other is not able to change, develop, and transcend itself. The Other is constantly challenged to learn and to change. The Other can develop and self-transcend whereby it overtakes the One. In actual social relationships, there are all sorts of status, educational, and social impediments blocking the Other from overtaking the One. But the conflict of recognition—played out between groups, generations, organizations, nations, etc.; is all too evident.

## (2)

Recognition, in practice, is a social psychological principle and the social psychology of recognition leads to democratic practice. These complementary claims form the crux to Tzvetan Todorov's exploration of humanism. According to Todorov, in *Jardin imparfait* (Imperfect Garden), humanism entails: "The autonomy of the *I*, the finality of the *you (thou)*, and the universality of the *they*" (Todorov, 2002). Summarized briefly, the *I* is a conscious subject that is not only a product of nature formed by material laws or so-cially determined. The *I* exists situationally, but is capable of individual-izing how it experiences and deals with circumstances. The *I* is never only other, culture, or society. But the *I* can identify itself with taking initiative—it can lose itself in activity. Most important, the *I* can experience love. Only a specific other person, or *you*, can be loved. Love is specific—that is, a particular, concrete, explicit other is loved. One does not love an idea or a generalization of the other; one loves a concrete, individual other human. The gaze of recognition, and therein the acknowledgment of mutual hu-manity, makes love so important. In love, shared humanity is taken to be the highest possible measure of value. Love is about living persons and actual relationships—it is not about scientific truth or theology. Love is specifically human, because it is a relationship that occurs in time—it refers to inter-action in a dynamic, temporal universe, inclusive of death. Love refers to affective and existential recognition, occurring in a changing and unstable universe. The *I* / *you* (thou) relationship of love is exclusive, but there is also the *they*—that is, society, history, and politics. In love, the *I* learns about the other (or the *you*), and thereby about difference and diversity. These lessons hold a mirror up to the *I*, whereby the *I* experiences itself as a *you*. The *I* learns about self and other, about I and thou, about love and differ-ence. And the *I* attempts to recast what it has learned in terms of thoughts, principles, and processes. Hereby the *I* co-creates the *they*. The *they* is an ab-stracted record of the one and the other, or of the self and the loved one, or of the I and the thou. But in the abstraction, there is no living relationship, no actual recognition of an Other. The unicity of the *I* / *you* (thou) interac-tion is lost in the abstracted universe of the *they*. The existential grounding of recognition can never be replaced by mere abstraction (*they*), humanism has to include living relationships, or it is dead.

When in interaction, there is recognition, when there is a dialogue of friendship and/or love, then there is the possibility of humanly worthy ac-tion. But when abstractions or ideas overpower interaction and lived rela-tionship, then the human ground to existential authenticity is abrogated. Recognition as a humanist principle acts as an existential basis for humanly respectful and worthy interaction. Organization grounded in recognition is embedded in respect for the other, and in the dynamic process of the one and the other in genuine relationship to one another. Such a process of re-spect, mutual interaction, and relationship underpins human flourishing. The institutions that match such processes are democratic. They respect au-tonomy in relationship, and individuality in association. Their social bond is characterized by radical respect for the other. Experiential governance explores the self and the other, the *I* and the *you*, in relationship. Democ-racy is grounded in respect for the *you* (thou) and the ability to see the *I* as a *you* (thou). The gaze of recognition is crucial to respectful interaction and thereby to self-recognition. The *I* that experiences recognition and its own ability at recognition is dialogical; "democracy" is a name for such dialogical organization. Institutions can be dead—so-called "democracies" can be lacking in the dialogical process. But without a living *you* (thou), there are no living humanist institutions. Abstract *they* humanism can exist; but such theoretical positions have no flesh and bones, no living recognition, no shared gaze. *I* and *thou* can only exist in relationship to one another and not apart. They are a form of a living relationship, which is identity creating and supporting, as well as a prerequisite for democracy. The (social) psychological processes of humanist relationship lead on an individual aggregation level to identity formation; and on a collective aggregation level, to democracy. Todorov's goal in his writing has been to clarify this psychological genealogy of self and democracy.

The book wherein I believe Todorov most convincingly explores the interrelationship(s) of self-formation and politics is *The Conquest of America*[2] (1984). In this book, Todorov explores the Spanish conquest of the Americas from Columbus to Cortez, to the missionaries. Five differing positions of (non-) (partial-) (encompassing-) recognition are defined and explored in both their psychological and political significance. This is Todorov's most "Hegelian" book, in the sense that the analysis clearly centers on patterns of recognition. And unlike his studies of 20th-century history, he never becomes a combatant, but maintains a respectful distance. In his examination of the psychology and politics of the 20th century, Todorov is all too clearly a Bulgarian anticommunist refugee who has his own axe to grind (Todorov, 2003). Sixteenth-century Mexico is a human drama of even greater proportions than 20th-century Europe. The native Mexican population was decimated, dropping from 25 million to 1 million in a century. The story told is of genocide on an even greater scale than Nazi-ism or Soviet communism.

Todorov's account of relationships in 17th-century Mexico can be schematicized as follows:

|  | I | You (thou) | They |
|---|---|---|---|
| Columbus |  |  | ✔ |
| Cortés | ✔ |  | ✔ |
| Montezuma |  | ✔ | ✔ |
| Las Casas |  | ✔ |  |
| Durán/Sahagún | ✔ | ✔ | ✔ |

Columbus comes into contact with Caribbean populations, but only sees what he is pre-prepared to see. He literally "collects" natives to take back with him to Spain, but they are "specimens" to be displayed. The native other is an "object" for him; there is no recognition on Columbus' part of separate being. In the beginning, he saw the natives as implicitly identical and tried to understand them as if they existed in the same culture as himself; but when that failed, he came to see them as potential servants or slaves. He never entertained the idea that they could be "other." For Columbus, there is only one episteme or language, his. He names everyplace he visits (a few times, by mistake, twice), assuming a natural ontology to naming—that is, by naming an island with a Spanish name, it becomes a Spanish possession. Things are their names. He cannot imagine human difference or diversity. For instance, he assumes that the Indians must have "judges," "nobles," "governors," etc., because the Europeans do. For him, there is only one reality and it has been named. He does not seek new truths but only to confirm already existing political and religious truth. He lives in the logic of *they*. The world is already known and understood, interpreted and named. He does not make discoveries, but finds things where and how he "knew" they would be. His "knowing" is grounded in prescience and authority, and has little or nothing modern about it. Human individuality and particularity has no place in Columbus' hermeneutics.

Cortés is much more self-conscious than Columbus. He is continually aware of what impression he makes on the Mexicans. His achievement was with a few hundred men to seize the Kingdom of Montezuma with its nearly unlimited (several hundred thousand troops) resources. If he had understood the Mexicans as equal others, his (self-appointed) task would have seemed an impossible folly. How could such a little force conquer a large, well-organized empire? Cortés went about it by making the Mexicans into his *they*. The Mexicans were for him an object of study to be analyzed and manipulated. He quickly managed to find interpreters who could tell him what the Mexicans said, thought, and did. Knowledge accumulation was one way Cortés empirically studied the Mexicans, he acted as a proto-anthropologist. The Mexicans (see below) remained (much like Columbus) imprisoned in their preexisting assumptions and unable to understand Cortés as "other." Cortés understood that the Mexicans were "other," but rejected any claim from them for recognition. By denying the thou (*you*), the Mexicans were kept off balance and unsure of themselves. Cortés constantly produced equivocal and self-contradictory images of who he was and what his intentions were. He played at being friend and enemy, cruel and just, God and politician. In part, his success was political—he organized minority popular discontentment around high taxes; destabilizing the central power's position. Cortés was politically self-conscious—to put it all too contemporarily, he was his own "spin doctor." But to succeed, he had to know and understand the Mexican political and taxation situation. Cortés believed that he was the cause of events—he was, in fact, the only one to act; the Mexicans tried to preserve what already was and only reacted. Cortés assumed linear time—change and event occur as processes. For him, the political reality is emergent; a process open to influence and that one can try to control. Cortés had a rather modern sense of the subject as autonomous actor. He understood that meaning was not pre-determined but was something that he could make. Thus, he "arrested" the central government's tax collectors and gained allies. He never assumed that things were what they were, but constantly redefined the situation to his own benefit. Meaning was social and political for Cortés, but the audience was never considered to be equal. He manipulated what the Mexicans saw. There was no mutuality or dialogue in his relationship to the other.

Montezuma was the Aztec emperor who Cortés defeated. Montezuma's hermeneutic was grounded in rules, not processes. In Aztec belief, time was circular. Change did not exist. Occurrence was always repetition. Existence was circular—characterized by patterns or cycles of life and death, growth and decline, expansion and withdrawal. Thus when Cortés showed up, Montezuma's problem was how to understand him. Montezuma was caught; if he understood Cortés as a unique new event, he would destabilize his own mindset and legitimacy. The emperor ruled in inevitability. Reality was, as it had to be—as ontology determined. Fundamental order was God given— absolute and ahistorical. If one admitted the unicity of events, then the logic of the whole culture and empire came in for examination. Thus Montezuma had the arms to defend his empire, but if he used them in a modern European manner, he would have destroyed the cultural glue of his world. Thus he sat in his palace and did nothing—allowing events to unfold as they would. He remained reactive because in his fundamental beliefs, he understood humanity to be reactive. In effect, he was conquered by a hermeneutic. For Montezuma there was only *you* and *they*—there was no autonomous actor or self. Montezuma's information collecting was accurate and fast; he knew long before Cortés entered (what is now) Mexico City where Cortés was and that he was proceeding toward the capital. Thus Montezuma knew that the *you* existed, but he could not deal with it. For him any *you* should form part of the known *they*, and when Cortés formed an exception Montezuma lacked an *I* capable of interpreting and (re-)acting. In Aztec culture the *you* and *they*—that is, the social processes and the social rules—so closely matched one another, that no differences could appear. For Aztecs, the immediate and the heavenly, the historical and the religious, the particular and the absolute, were seamlessly connected. There was no place in their logic for innovation, unique events, or improvisation—that is, for Cortés.

Las Casas was a Spanish missionary who "loved" the Indians, but his "love" was an act of Christian belief. On the one hand, he was genuinely concerned with the Indian's plight; but on the other, he could not "know" them in any significant way. His Indians were a Christian *you*—nothing more or less. There is only one possible you for Las Casas, that of Christian belief. Las Casas does not consider his belief to be personal—it is not *his* belief that counts—but the one true universal truth that is important. Thus for Las Casas, there is no *I* involved. He is "full of kindness and humanity" in regard to the Indians, but there is not much that he can do against the cruelty of Spanish rule; in his own words:

> And just as the young man came down, a Spaniard who was there drew a cutlass or half sword and gives him a cut through the loins, so that his intestines fall out . . . The Indian, moaning, takes his intestines in his hands and comes fleeing out of the house. He encounters the cleric [Las Casas] . . . and the cleric tells him some things about the faith, as much as time and anguish permitted, explaining to him that if he wished to be baptized he would go to heaven to live with God. The poor creature, weeping and showing pain as if we were burning in flames, said yes, and with this the cleric baptized him. He then fell dead on the ground. (quoted in Todorov, 1984, p. 169)

Las Casas' is not politically progressive; his dream was of a medieval theocratic Christian state. But he did not want to enslave or imprison the Indians. His motives were complex; he was convinced that the King of Spain had more economically to gain via assimilated than enslaved Indians. His description of Spanish crimes and violence against the Indians was certainly a powerful attack on "white supremacy," but he acted in the name of a more humane and thereby more effective colonialism. As religious, not only was his own *I* irrelevant in his analysis, the Mexican's *I* was also irrelevant. He spoke always in terms of the *thou*, a *thou* that he would have wished to be a *they*, but which was not one. The *they* of Spanish America remained dominated by violent profiteering and inhuman exploitation. One of the principle causes of Indian deaths was the overexploitation of their labor, for instance in the mines. The Spanish literally worked the Indians to death. The Indians were expendable—objects to be used and thrown away. To illustrate: Indian flesh was used to feed remaining Indians or dogs. Indians were killed to boil down into grease to be used by Spanish on skin wounds. We know about these cruelties because Las Casas reported on them. Las Casas in his writing parallels in some ways Cortés—knowledge of the Indians was supposed to lead to more effective (i.e., in the economic and political interests of the Spanish) rule. But unlike Cortés, Las Casas looked for a win/win relationship wherein the Indians would also profit from change. Aztec cannibalism and human sacrifice were certainly to be improved upon. And Aztec culture with its circular concept of time and history did not permit much opportunity for development. Furthermore, the Aztec civilization was an oral culture, wherein enormous human resources had to be invested in memorizing the body of knowledge; written culture communicates much more efficiently. Thus, the Spanish may have brought cruelty, violent exploitation, and small pox, but they did bring literacy and the principle of human change. Las Casas, at the end of his life, adopted *perspectivism*. He came to accept the Aztecs as reverent believers who really had been and were religious; the forms of religious expression really were less important than their substance. For Las Casas, there is one God, and His forms of worship transcend human understanding or judgment. Herein the universality of Christian egalitarianism comes into its own. Christianity is equated with the principle of love. But alterity is denied—there is one principle of love, Christianity's. All humanism—all respect of the *you*—is an outing of the Christian God. A sort of *thou* prevails, but at the cost of denying diversity and difference.

Finally, there are the witnesses of hybridization of cultures, positions, and persons. Polyglot identity is neither Mexican nor Spanish, Pagan nor Christian. It neither colonizes nor is it colonized. Durán came to Mexico as a child and grew up knowing both worlds. Sahagún lived 60 years in Mexico. Durán interpreted Indian beliefs and ideas to the Spanish audience. He described and explained; he clarified what the Indian customs "meant". Thus he was the inside outsider—someone who knew Mexican Indian culture so well that he could explain its rites, beliefs, and society. But such explanations externalize the culture—remaking it into an object of European knowledge and into text. Sahagún wrote his descriptions, first in Nahuatl (the Mexican Indian language), and thereafter he decided to produce a second Spanish version of his text. He described Mexico at "degree zero"—that is, without interpretations, judgments, or evaluation. With Durán and Sahagún we have, in some sense, near modern writers. They wanted to know, understand, and describe. Their work was an interaction of several voices drawn from their native sources and their European perspectives, and included their righteous outrage at the Spanish genocide as well as their awareness of Spanish political and economic interests. They wrote in complexity, where no one point of view triumphs. Truth is interactional, partial, and ongoing. Sahagún wrote from the exterior position, without judgments or interpretations. Durán wrote from the polyglot position of alternatively identifying with the Indian and then the Spanish perspective. In the work of both, two voices, two cultures, and two perspectives can be identified. Durán tries to understand and runs the risk of reducing everything to himself; Sahagún tries to honor and respect otherness, running the risk of not understanding or of not sufficiently working through the differences. Thus, their dilemmas in handling self and other, difference and comprehension, were nearly modern. They knew that the author or *I* understands via empathy—by engaging with the other as *thou*. But all knowledge requires text that can be read and understood—that is, operates within an accessible hermeneutic or *they*.

## (iii) The Ethics of Understanding

Todorov's examination of the conquest of America is not just intended to be an interesting history—though it is also that. It is meant to pose fundamental questions about knowing and judging—about both the organization of ethics and the ethics of organization. It is his judgment that neither the ego-centric *I* nor the empty *I* can be ethical. The *I* that only sees its own categories, prejudices, and assumptions whereever it looks cannot see the other at all (Columbus). It can never respect, care for, or react to the other. It cannot live in the sense of change, participate, and innovate. It is doomed to repetition and stagnation (as were the Mexicans). The opportunist *I* is all too aware of its surroundings (the *they*) and able to exploit them (i.e., Cortés). This is knowledge as power, grounded in *I* / world relationships determined by use value. Understanding can lead to control, misuse and manipulation. Todorov implies that knowledge without the *I* / *you* relationship leads to genocide. If there is no *I* / *you* (thou) relationship, there is nothing to stop totalitarianism; or the powerful, taking advantage of the weak; or the one, refusing to recognize the humanity of the other. Ethics depends on recognition or "the discover of the other in oneself" (Todorov, 1984, p. 249). But how can we really discover the other without sacrificing our own perspective? This is the problem posed by Durán and Sahagún. A strong *I* / *you* (thou) relationship leads to a weak *they*. A society, fairly obviously, cannot be constructed of monads—the autonomous and atomistic *I* has no language, knowledge, psychological security, ability to cooperate, or chance of surviving infancy. But a society cannot be constructed only of dyads—*I* / *you* (thou) pairs, alone, become symbiotic. Excessive recognition leads to the psychic fusion of the one with the other, which permits no autonomy, development, or change. One needs exteriority as much as one needs the *I* / *you* (*thou*)—that is, the ability to see the other as genuinely other, as separate, distinct, and knowable. Recognition as a subject is crucial to humanization; but the ability to maintain some distance and thereby think critically is also crucial. Thus, what is ethics? My answer is based on the reading of Todorov: *Ethics is the examination of problems and issues within relationships in the perspective of the recognition of the complexity of I / you / they interaction(s).*

## "SOUL MAKING"

Todorov provides a rich conceptual vocabulary for understanding ethics as a social process. Ethics, obviously, is not identified here with (natural) rights or universal truths. A question is ethical if it involves the structures and relationships of human identity. The key question is: Does this problem involve principles of relationship, identity, and social well-being? If human flourishing and its interrelational foundations are involved, then the question is ethical. If recognition, gaze, and the processes that allow us to be(-come) human are involved, then the issue involves ethics.

A separate, additional question is that of what Appiah has called "soul making":

> By "soul making" I mean the project of intervening in the process of interpretation through which each citizen develops an identity—and doing so with the aim of increasing her chances of living an ethically successful life. (Appiah, 2005, p. 164)

Should the insurer want to proactively influence how contemporary citizens or their clients understand autonomy, flourishing, and their relational structures? Appiah identifies ethical well-being with self-authorship. Only the life that is chosen is considered to be worth living. Appiah's political liberalism is far more restrictive than Todorov's social liberalism. Todorov in his writings on Jean-Jacques Rousseau and Benjamin Constant makes it clear that he is a social liberal (Todorov, 1999, 2001). His thought centers on how the self lives relationship(s) and how it is thereby juxtaposed to others and in the process understands itself. Appiah tries to address ethics via rational choice—that is, what project does one choose from one's possibilities and circumstances for one's life. Todorov studies inter-relationship, recognition, and the hybridity of interaction. It is amply clear that I—and to my enormous satisfaction the insurer's ethics committee with me—have chosen for Todorov's approach. The so-called rationality of free choice is not what in real societies and relationships is at stake. Nor do we need rules to fill in ahead of time how others should choose. Liberal ethics tends with one hand to offer individual choice, and with the other to try via rules to predetermine the possible results of choices. Our approach does not entail such entanglements. But we must constantly query the nature, result, and significance of interrelationship as a vehicle, (not) of recognition.

We have been called upon to undertake "soul making"—that is, to act pedagogically. Some voices claim that we need to publicly display our process ethics—that is, to make it more visible what we do and do not find relationally acceptable. Up to now, the ethics committee has found it demanding enough to try and apply our relational logic to current issues, without seeking out cases of nonrecognition to allow us to "make a statement." Interestingly, Todorov is mute on this question. He writes about the holocaust, concentration camps, totalitarianism, and colonialism, but he is in each of these looking back to what happened, and not intervening in current debates. His pamphlet on the new world disorder attempts intervention into current events (Todorov, 2005). But while this polemically reveals contradictions and hypocrisies, it fails as an ethics of recognition. What Todorov seems to have understood so powerfully in his historical texts—that ethics is all about persons in interrelations—he forgets when he addresses the here and now. In his book on Rousseau, Todorov explores the tensions between

Rousseau's theoretical grasp of sociability and his own hunkering for solitude. And in the book on Constant, Todorov analyzes how care for the other, as a first principle of relationship, leads to democratic politics but also to a personal inability to choose. Both times personal structures and social issues are shown in their interrelationship(s). Ethics is about ways of being to and with others. Texts on ethics put the *I / thou* into the *they*—ethics as knowledge is an abstraction of forms of recognition. But when Todorov addresses the contemporary, he forgets all about the radically human grounds to ethics and makes a series of political statements. From this, I conclude that even Todorov has enormous difficulty converting his concept of ethics into proactive practice. Thus I think that for the time being, the ethics committee is well advised to attempt a more reactive stance, wherein problems that are brought to us are examined, analyzed, and judged. "Soul making" remains, certainly for the time being, a bridge too far.

## CONCLUSION

Based on Todorov's humanist ethics of I / you (thou) / they, I have described an ethics of recognition and interrelationship. It is a process ethics, which has been put into practice in the ethics committee of a major Dutch insurer. Instead of increasing bureaucratic rule making, such an ethics strengthens the awareness of the justness or injustice of relationship(s). The organization is, we believe, qualitatively strengthened in the process. This practice of ethics facilitates relationships between the I and the other, and between the organization and its (human) environment. It is an organizational ethics of recognition, rather than of constraints. Ethical practice, hereby, is brought into development.

## NOTES

1. If "sustainability" literally means leaving the earth as one found it, it is an amazingly conservative goal, making all human-driven change impossible.
2. The analysis that follows examines an earlier book of Todorov's (1984) in terms of concepts developed in a later one (2002). Thus I (as much as Todorov) must be held responsible for this particular theoretical "move" or construct.

## REFERENCES

Appiah, K. A. (2005). *The ethics of identity.* Princeton, NJ: Princeton University Press.
Arendt, H. (1998). *The human condition* Chicago: University of Chicago Press.
Brohm, R. (2005). *Polycentric order in organizations.* Rotterdam: ERIM.

Honneth, A. (1995). *The struggle for recognition* London: Polity Press.

Kojève, A. (1969). *Introduction to the reading of Hegel.* New York: Basic Books.

O'Neill, J. (1996). *Hegel's dialectic of desire and recognition: Texts and commentary.* Albany: State University of New York Press.

Spivak, G. C. (1996). *The Spivak reader* (D. Landry & G. MacLean, Eds.). London: Routledge.

Todorov, T. (1984). *The conquest of America.* New York: HarperPerrennial.

Todorov, T. (1999). *A passion for democracy.* New York: Algora.

Todorov, T. (2001). *Frail happiness.* University Park: Pennsylvania State University Press.

Todorov, T. (2002). *Imperfect garden.* Princeton, NJ: Princeton University Press.

Todorov, T. (2003). *Hope and memory.* Princeton, NJ: Princeton University Press.

Todorov, T. (2005). *The new world disorder.* London: Polity Press.

Weick, K. (1979). *The social psychology of organizing.* New York: McGraw-Hill.

CHAPTER 15

# GOOD ORDER

## Ethics and Disposition

Heather Höpfl

## EASTERN ACADEMY OF MANAGEMENT, SAN JOSE, COSTA RICA 2001

There were several practitioner speakers but the most impressive was the young man from a large well-known multinational. He was very good. He looked good. His talk was persuasive and his overhead transparencies color coordinated with his tie. He was well groomed with a Kurt Russell haircut and an all-American smile. He demonstrated by reference to slide after slide that his company was doing well in Costa Rica. He showed us targets and how the company had exceeded them. He told us his corporation was good for Costa Rica and then showed us slide after slide to demonstrate how and why. His company was making things better for the local people. He was an emissary for good. He brought a commitment to corporate values and to corporate America. He was disposed to do good where good was synonymous with these values.

His presentation was polished. He exuded charm, enthusiasm, and professionalism. He was so clean, he shone. He was a real star. He wasn't only

*Critical Theory Ethics for Business and Public Administration*, pages 319–331
Copyright © 2008 by Information Age Publishing
**319**

good, he was exemplary and outshone his fellow speakers. It was all so good, so wholesome, so well coordinated. He was young and a believer with all the fanaticism of the zealot. He desperately wanted us to believe his story. This was corporate evangelism at its best. His company was fighting for social justice, to end poverty, to bring not just material gains but dignity and self worth. Although he did not say it in so many words, his company sought to bring light into dark places, to lead the Costa Ricans into the saving grace of the market, to salvation. This spectacular performance was received in different ways by the audience but mainly it was received as meaning exactly what was said. In the main, he was preaching to the converted. The majority of the audience of business school academics and consultants believed him to be entirely right. His view of the world was wholly compatible with their own. He was most likely a product of their making and a successful one at that. He wore the same stamp of manufacture as the audience. He was a *paragon of virtue*: a shining example of manufactured good.

## EASTERN ACADEMY OF MANAGEMENT, SAN JOSE, COSTA RICA, 2001

The man moves toward the lectern: slowly and with dignity. He is sure of himself and yet not proud. He is a man who knows power and is comfortable with it. He has the attention of the audience and he is aware of it. Yet he has a natural humility. This is a man who has seen suffering and he has the kind of deep, melancholic smile that comes from maturity and wisdom: a rather shy, self-effacing smile. He is a man of contrasts: profoundly human. His mere presence touches the audience. He is Oscar Arias Sanchez, President of Costa Rica (1986–90).[1] He talks about the revolutionary pronouncement of Jose Figueres in December 1948, which abolished the national army and gave economic priority to schools and hospitals, a principle that has continued for over 50 years. He spoke about how this decision had kept Costa Rica out of the mounting poverty, military repression, brutal regimes, guerrilla movements, and foreign intervention that had affected its neighbors in Central America. He brings the message of demilitarization and the importance of ending rule by "men with guns." He talks about the importance of housing, education, and health. He has tremendous gravitas and clarity of vision. His presidential election campaign slogan in 1986 was "Roofs, jobs, and peace." He won the Nobel Peace Prize for his peace-keeping work in Central America in 1987. In an interview in 1995 at Amherst he had said,

> I think the most important thing for the future generations is to understand that it is necessary to have ideals, to dream, to live a life of principles. It is necessary to understand that the brotherhood is more important than the self.

It is necessary to comprehend that the problems of a neighbor in some way affect us too. It is necessary to live in a transparent, crystal-like world where everyone practices what they preach, to end hypocrisy and to have the courage to fight for what you believe in. I would say don't give in to the naysayers, not to give up one's dreams of bettering the world. Understand that by fighting for the impossible, one begins to make it possible. In that way, no matter how difficult the task is, one will never give up. And it doesn't matter if they call us dreamers, idealists. I always said I would rather be Don Quixote than to be Pancho. Understand that the idealists of today will be the leaders of tomorrow. And we can't stop dreaming.[2]

Arias Sanchez is passionate and charismatic. He is driven by his convictions. He sets a high humanitarian tone for the conference. "The world needs more love. We all know that," he says. "We need new leaders: a new ethics."

## POSITION AND DISPOSITION

In fact, despite the order in which these two accounts have been presented above, it was Arias Sanchez who spoke first. His address opened the conference and was followed by a session on international business in Costa Rica. The order in which they are presented in this chapter fulfills a rhetorical function in the unfolding of the text. It presents contrasts. Two men: one young and one old; both committed to a set of values; both with a vision of what they can do from their own standpoints. Clearly, they are not simple opposites. What they represent in the argument presented is disposition and character. The Greek word ethikos (from ethos) means precisely this: personal character and disposition. How one is disposed toward the world is one's ethical position. This chapter seeks to examine the concept of "good" in relation to disposition.

## A GOOD SET OF RESULTS

In organizational terms, the strategic direction of the organization involves the construction of the organization as a purposive entity with a trajectory toward a desired future. Consequently, organizational strategy as an indicator of movement toward this future is about the way in which such a desired state can be reached, targets set, achievements measured. In such movement toward better and better performance, it is inevitable that the purposive nature of the action takes precedence over the individual in the service of (Latin, ad-ministrare, to serve) desired results. The organization constructs itself in textual and representational terms in relation to such desires. These representations range from the explicit use of rhetoric in marketing its products and images to the more subtle construction of the organization as a fictive entity in the construction of statements, strategies and structures, and function to regulate the organization through definition (Latin, de-finire, to finish, to finalize). The fundamental characteristic of the organization as a purposive entity is its directedness and, clearly, there is a relationship between the direction (as orientation) and direction (as command) of the organization and the rhetorical trajectory. In a specific sense, the organization as a rhetorical entity wants something of the employee, of the customer, the competitor, the supplier, the general public and, therefore, what is not the organization is always defined as deficient in relation to it: not as good as that from which it complements. Therefore, representations of the organization—images and texts—need to be received as convincing by its various audiences. For example, recent years have seen the elaboration of the rhetoric directed toward employees in the pursuit of greater commitment and improved performance, in terms of invocations to quality and in the construction of ornate narratives of organizational performances; in exhortations toward greater goodness. However, in such representations, the organization is an abstract entity removed from the activities of the physical bodies of which it is made up. Without a body, the pain of labor itself becomes an abstraction so that embodied pain is exiled from the organization as a site of production. Such an elaborate vision of goodness, truth, and beauty cannot admit the possibility of what counterdefinition must construe as ugliness and dissent. Consequently, it is the abstract "good" that is venerated and administered and not the laboring bodies, which are in need of ministry.

## ADMINISTRATION AND MINISTRATION

The notion of a discourse of maternity subverts the dominant social discourse to challenge order, rationality, and patriarchal regulation. What this contributes to organizational theory is the capacity to make transparent the effects of the production of meaning, to render explicit the patriarchal quest of the organization, to make problematic the notion of trajectory, strategy, and purpose, to question "ordinary" notions of the good. Therefore, by presenting the organization as maternal, this chapter seeks to offend conventional definitions of the goods of organization in order to allow the mother/ motherhood/ maternal body to enter. Thus, whereas the text of the organization is about regulation and representation, of rational argument, perfect and perfectible relationships and rhetorical trajectory, the embodied subject speaks of division, separation, rupture, tearing, blood, and the pain of labor. So good becomes defined in terms of a recursive seduction to the notion of order and what is not good, the physical, becomes the province of hysteria. Consequently, despite management desires to demonstrate success and achievement by recourse to metrics, comparatives, benchmarks, and results, organizations are more of metaphysics than of matter.

One might provocatively characterize this relationship in terms of the ways in which organizations as purposive and rhetorical entities define themselves in counterdistinction to notions of the feminine and madness. Lacoue-Labarthe (1989, p. 129) speaks of the major threats to representation as being women and madness and, in part, this is because in the hystera (Gk. *womb*) and the psycho*logical* condition of hysteria (as a disturbance of the nervous system thought to be brought about by uterine dysfunction) there is a common concern with the function of reproduction: a contest between representation and definitions of reproduction, between reason and body. In the organizational world, disorder cannot be badness or madness because the logic of organization assumes that these conditions can be corrected by reason. In this sense, redemption and cure requires submission to *psychology* (regulation of the psyche by the logos). If that which is defined as deficient, the employee, the organizational member, will only submit to superior logic he or she will *realize* the extent of his or her disorder. He or she can be turned around (*converted*) and induced to "make a clean break between fantasies and reality" (Irigaray, 1985, p. 273). He or she can be converted by and conformed to psychology: "the wisdom of the master. And of mastery" (Irigaray, 1985, p. 274). When organizations exhort their employees to specific standards of performance, behavior, conformity, and so forth, they hold up a mirror to the deficient condition of their members and confronts them with "reality." However, this is a reality that kills. The physical is destroyed by the reflection and as mere reflection, is rendered inanimate. All that is now permitted to be reflected back is the organization's own construction, a sublime illusion, and so what the organization member can reflect back to him/herself is mortification of the body. If the organization can convert its members to the power of the logos, it is able to demonstrate control over hysteria and disorder and by implication over the physical and embodied reproduction. So defined, organizational members are infinitely reproducible and reproduced assured that goodness and an absence of madness are synonymous with order and sanity. However, *in order* to sustain this logic, the focus must remain on the organizational speculum so that a consistent reflection is maintained. The organizational member must be conformed to the rule of the logos and possessed by it, must become the property of that logos in the sense that as *property*, the member maintains what is *proper* to that construction. So organizations seek to *cure* their members of their disordered otherness and to offer alternative and convincing definitions of reality. All this in the service of good order.

## THE PSYCHOLOGY OF GOODNESS

In other words, the (hysterical) disordered state must be subjected to regulation by psycho-logy: regulation by (logical) discourse. Organizations thus construct themselves as means of salvation, as bulwarks against destruction and danger. So strong is the conviction that the right path of the organization leads to good that the organization believes it can serve to restore a proper way of seeing things. However, if this cannot be achieved there is no option, the organizational member must conform to propriety or be exiled from it. Mortified in the flesh and now annihilated even as mere reflection, a lack of propriety cannot be admitted. If the organizational member cannot be cured or refuses to be conformed, this is a considerable challenge to the trajectory of the organization and so the masculine identity of the organization hangs in the balance. The improper must be eradicated to sustain the illusion of purpose, to preserve good order and for the good of the organization.

So it seems, organizations have a purposive commitment to the pursuit of some notion of good, circumscribed and defined, logical and metrical. Jung has argued that the pursuit of "sterile perfection" (Dourley, 1990, p. 51) is one of the defining characteristics of patriarchal consciousness. Order and rationality function to exclude the physical. Whitmont puts forward the view that the *control* of passions and physical needs traditionally have been valorized because they idealize maleness and gives emphasis to the "*merely* rational" (1991, p. 243, emphasis added). Organizations then, as expressions of collective expectations, render physicality "dirty," corrupting, and, by implication, not good. Indeed, the corollary of this emphasis on rationality is a distrust of natural affections and the loss of compassion (Whitmont, 1991, p. 245). Without compassion, the organization cannot *admit* the suffering that is caused by the pursuit of rationality. Goodness it seems is self-referential and abstract.

## COMPASSION

Without compassion, the paternal discourse of organization, dominated by the rationality and the rejection of dependency, reduces the notion of the maternal to nurturing, domestic, and servicing functions. For an organization the loss of the maternal leaves the questing behavior of organizations as unrelieved rationality and power motivation. Whitmont puts forward the view that historically it has been fear of the feminine, [as disorder or hysteria], which has led to the degradation of women but he also goes on to say that there is a contemporary problem of masculinization. This he argues has resulted in abstract dogmatic mental attitudes and a sterile and over-rationalistic social world (1991, p. 200). It is precisely in this excessive rationality and the preoccupation with measurement that embraces goodness in order to exclude it. Consequently, organizations are given to producing totalizing discourses that seek to capture all aspects of organizational life. These are totalizing if only to provide comfort from the physicality that they lack. They can never offer completion but they need to be totalizing precisely to preclude the possibility of otherness. Therefore, they seek to exclude and, more particularly, they seek to exclude the possibility of the maternal. This is because the maternal threatens to disrupt the discipline and sterility of the paternal logos. The maternal poses a threat to the logic of the self-serving and totalizing narratives of the organization.

At a simplistic level, this is one reason why organizations, as collective expressions of one-dimensional patriarchy, have been keen to turn women into homologues of men: a task greatly assisted by the equity feminists. However, they have also sought to turn men into ciphers of masculinity through the relentless pursuit of perfectionism and rationality. By containing the feminine within the purposive logic of futurity, organizations as directive entities have sought to defend themselves against the threat posed by their very presence, ambivalence, and physicality. Yet, the result of all this purposive striving and collective questing is, nonetheless, an inevitable sterility. This is because the patriarchal logos substitutes words and exhortations and their reproduction as text for bodies, physicality, and embodied reproduction. In privileging constructions over physicality, the organization comes to reproduce itself as text and understand itself in metaphysical terms as the product of its own reproduction. Within this logic, the organization seeks to reassure itself of its own beneficence: the good is whatever the organization says it is.

## REPRODUCING GOOD

As part of the obsession with definition, organizations have been fanatical about metrics and monitoring. Elsewhere, I have examined the etymology and significance of the matrix as an organ and instrument of reproduction (Höpfl, 2000a, 2000b, 2002) and argued that embodied reproduction is replaced by the reproduction of text. The matrix is regulated so that its cells show location and defining characteristics on the basis of power relations. This power derives from the ability to define, to authorize, and to regulate the site of production. Understood in this way, the matrix defines what the organization regards as good and what is worthy of reproduction. In the substitution of words for the natural products of the embodied matrix, reproduction of homologues is guaranteed. Men and women in the service of the organization reproduce themselves in relation to what is defined as good and, therefore, produce only sons.

The appropriated matrix deals on the level of the abstract alone. Despite the totalizing rhetoric that it produces, it is not sustainable and therefore seeks to construct for itself icons of what it lacks. For the paternal matrix, perfection comes from striving. Consequently, the matrix gives birth into a world of obsessive reproduction and insatiable desire. Paternal reproduction arises from the sense of lack that only the acknowledgment of the maternal matrix could satisfy. However, so configured, the paternal matrix can only construct for itself representations of the things it lacks. Consequently, care, creativity, quality, ethics, emotions, and so forth become the abstract products of the sterile matrix: acknowledged to be good but divorced from goodness.

## NO GOOD AT ALL

In this context, it is not surprising that organizations function at variance to the bodies who work in and for them. Consequently, people in organizations are always struggling with issues that arise from the substitution of textual matrices for physical ones. They are rendered abstract by loss of contact with their physicality as organizations reduce them to categories and metrics. But, from the point of view of the maternal, the position is more serious. In the relentless pursuit of future states, organizations as purposive entities seek to construct for themselves the empty emblems of the object of the quest: high quality standards, improved performance, an ethical position, dignity at work, care for staff, and so forth. In part, this is because the purposiveness of organizations is without end—indeed can never end—and, therefore, the notion of any real completion is antithetical to the idea of trajectory. Strategy gives birth to more strategy, rhetoric to more rhetoric, text to more text, and so on. The good is never attained. The construction of goodness as abstract organizational categories is intended to console in the absence of the hope of restoration. Moreover, the vicarious and representational has more seductive power than the physical and disordered other. These emblems function as an anamnesis to register the loss as representation. For this reason alone, the emblem of loss is melancholic and pervades the organization with melancholy. It cannot offer consolation because ironically it can only recall that there is a loss. So, the emblem of the lost object provides a false reassurance that completion itself can arise from a construction. So, when an organization lays claim to goodness, it constructs a notion of goodness that serves its strategic ends.

The argument presented here makes the case for a greater understanding of the way in which there is an organizational angst about the feminine as dissident, disorderly, and disjunctive. That the feminine is not so easily seduced into the illusions of future satisfactions and abstract relations causes a number of tensions and oscillations. These occur between the purposive nature of organizational trajectory and progress into the future and the ambivalence of compassionate members of organizations as dissident. The paradox at the root of this argument is one of power. Those who are not easily seduced by corporate promises, by subjugation to futurity, and by notions of perfectibility are dangerous and disordered. Such positions are equated with the feminine as hysterical and needing to be cured by submission to logic and good order. Where organizational members do not accept these definitions or merely pay lip service to them, the extent of their participation is controlled and regulated. These positions cannot easily be reconciled because they pose the physical against the metaphysical and in doing so implicitly challenge the organization's construction of good. Yet ambivalence and dissidence have important political significance for changing the nature of work.

In seeking to construct themselves both as sublime manifestations of male desire and as unattainable ideals, organizations lay themselves open to inevitable failure. The therapeutic project of *saving* the organization via the rule of logic, via insistent authority, and via psychology is a process of mortification. Moreover, it is founded on a masculine sublime fabricated to reflect the male ego, narcissistic and inevitably melancholic. The feminine has no place, no reflection, no role in this construction other than to the extent that, in an entirely selective way, it serves as an object within the construction. In this construction, the feminine is hysterical and has to be kept out because, by posing a threat to its mere representational form [to mimesis], it threatens good order. Only if the feminine is prepared to submit itself to the symbol of the masculine construction (the erection) can it even enter into reflection. However, even then it must show a *proper* reflection *appropriate* to its status as a *property* of that construction. Where the feminine lacks *propriety* it is reduced to nothing. The goodness of the organization is textual and representational. It has nothing to do with compassion and virtue. These are the defenses that protect psychology as regulation by the logos from failure and subversion. It is a phallocentric psychology that credits itself with initiative, achievement, and purpose and that defends its position by either relegation and cancellation. Clearly, part of this defense rests on power over the control of reflection, theorization, and discourse, and on the control of categories and their meanings.

## THE HEROIC GOOD

Organizations want to create a heroic notion of the good, a confidant and bold representation of the future—and this is inevitably a masculine construction.

The feminine is required to remain silent or to present itself according to its representation as viewed through the male gaze: to produce itself in a way that ensures its own annihilation. What then does the idea of the maternal contribute to an understanding of goodness and organizations? In part, it is to do with borders and their demarcation, exile and homelessness, strangeness, estrangement, the boundary of the body, and sociality and love; it concerns ethics and motherhood. These are complex issues that deserve further elaboration. Certainly, the writings of Julia Kristeva are a good place to start (Höpfl, 2000b). Maternity, motherhood, and the maternal body play a significant part in the dynamics of her psychoanalytical writing.

Kristeva sees the client–patient relationship as rooted in love and characterized by what she terms, "herethics of love" (1987, p. 263) an implicit ethical practice. These are writings from exile and according to Docherty (1996) there is considerable potential in this position. He argues that "the postmodern narrative of characterization . . . eradicates the distinction between the ethical and the political" (p. 66) because it draws the reader into "disposition" [sic], in other words, it puts the reader into a suitable place, it inclines the reader, or to use the Greek word for this disposition, *ethos*, it establishes the place of the ethical by involving the reader in the search for *"the good"* so, Docherty argues, reestablishing the place of the political. Thus, for Docherty, "to read postmodern characterization is to reintroduce the possibility of politics, and importantly of a genuinely historical political change, into the act of reading" (pp. 66, 67).

## WRITING FROM EXILE

Postmodern characterization then involves "first, the confusion of the ontological status of the character with that of the reader; secondly, the decentring of the reader's consciousness, such that she or he is, like the character, endlessly displaced and 'differing'; and, thirdly, the political and ethical implications of this 'seeming otherwise,' shifting from appearance to different appearance in the disappearance of a totalized selfhood" (Docherty, 1996, p. 67). This has political consequence, that is, that there is "a marginalization of the reader from a centralized or totalized narrative of selfhood," which renders "the reading subject-in-process as the figure of the dissident" (p. 67). To support this view, Docherty refers to Kristeva's identification of the experimental writer and, as Docherty says, "crucially, women" as types of dissident. So, the argument runs, what these two "share is the impetus towards marginalization and indefinition; they are in a condition of 'exile' from a centred identity of meaning and its claims to a totalized Law or Truth" and, further, he adds that exile itself is a form of dissidence "since it involves the marginalization or decentring of the self from all positions of totalized or systematic Law (such as imperialist nation, patriarchal family, monotheistic language)." Hence, Docherty puts forward the proposition that postmodern characterization, "construed as writing in and from exile, serves to construct the possibility, for perhaps the first time, of elaborating the paradigmatic reader of these new novels as feminized" (p. 68) "always dispositioned towards otherness, alterity." Hence, postmodern characterization permits the ethics of alterity and the opportunity to explore what it means "to speak from the political disposition of the Other." Docherty's view of postmodern writing raises some important issues not least the problem of authorship and authority (Höpfl, 2003), but it does make an important contribution to an appreciation of the role of exile and estrangement. Here is the possibility of the political and a challenge to grand notions of goodness. Here is the possibility of the ethics of the interpersonal, the encounter with otherness, the reconciliation of logos and physis. The idea of men accepting and valuing their feminine qualities would not be considered strange within a community of nurturing, which had a genuine concern for the other, which adopted an embodied notion of the good. However, there are broader issues here, which require careful analysis.

Eagleton argues that against the "ideal of compassionate community, of altruism and natural affection...(there is) a threat to rationalism" and says that "the political consequences of this are ambivalent" (1990, p. 60). On the other hand, for the feminine, this site of ambivalence might be the very starting point of a political praxis within the discourse of maternity. And whereas Eagleton warns against "a fantasy of mother and father in one, of love and law commingled" (p. 263), it is perhaps this very conciliation that might bring the pursuit of ends and goodness together (see also Whitmont, 1983). In other words, to redefine the good. However, a serious caution must remain and that is one put forward by Baudrillard in his critique of rationality in which he argues that the reduction of male and female to categories has produced an artificial distinction that objectifies the feminine. By this line of argument, the feminine is now constructed as a category of the masculine and, by implication, the power of the feminine to manifest itself in ambivalence is lost. In other words, Baudrillard (1990) sees femin-*ism*, per se, as ensnared within the construction of a phallic order. This is a position with which Kristeva (1984) is familiar. As her biographer Toril Moi puts it, "The problem is that as soon as the insurgent 'substance' speaks, it is necessarily caught up in the kind of discourse *allowed by* and *submitted to* by the Law" (p. 10, emphasis added). The desire to confront this problem of inevitable capture is fundamental to Kristeva's work and yet she acknowledges that to attempt to use language against itself is to create an untenable position: a position that is all too familiar to women writers when they attempt to deviate from the notion of mastery and this piece of writing is itself not excluded from this judgment. Writing is inevitably about coming up with the goods and in academic life this is about producing good textual sons.

So after all, this chapter is about *good* practice, about behavior, gesture, ways of interacting, about the micropolitics of organizing. It is not about abstract goodness and unattainable futures. These belong to the province of insatiable organization. This is a chapter about the primacy of the personal, the significance of character, about disposition, about ethics. Here is simply the hope of a compassionate community and an invocation to the practice of goodness. As President Oscar Arias Sanchez says, "to have ideals, to dream, to live a life of principles." Politics begins with the individual.

## ACKNOWLEDGMENT

An earlier version of this paper was published in *Tamara*, 2(3), pp. 28–35.

## NOTES

1. Reelected to the Presidency in 2005.
2. http://www.galegroup.com/free_resources/chh/bio/arias_o.htm (accessed February 8, 2006)

## REFERENCES

Baudrillard, J. (1990). *Seduction*. London: Macmillan.

Docherty, T. (1996). *Alterities*. Oxford, UK: Clarendon Press.

Dourley, J. P. (1990). *The goddess, mother of the trinity*. Lewiston, ME: Edwin Mellen Press.

Eagleton, T. (1990) *The ideology of the aesthetic*. Oxford, UK: Blackwell.

Hoad, T. F. (1986). *The concise Oxford dictionary of English etymology*. Oxford, UK: Oxford University Press.

Höpfl, H. (2000b). The suffering mother and the miserable son: Organising women and organising women and organising women's writing. *Gender Work and Organization, 7*(2), 98–106.

Höpfl, H. (2000a). On being moved. *Studies in Cultures, Organisations and Societies, 6*(1), 15–25.

Höpfl, H. (2002, January). Corporate strategy and the quest for the primal mother. *Human Resource Development International*, pp. 11–22.

Höpfl, H. (2003). The body of the text and the ordinary narratives of organisation. In B. Czarniawska & P. Gagliardi (Eds.), *Narratives we organise by*. London: Routledge.

Irigaray, L. (1985). *Speculum of the other woman* (G. Gill, Ed.). Ithaca, NY: Cornell University Press.

Jung, E., & von Franz, M. L. (1998). *The Grail legend.* Princeton, NJ: Princeton University Press.

Kristeva, J. (1984). *Desire in language: A semiotic approach to literature and Art* (T. S. Gora, A. Jardine, & L. Roudiez, Trans.). Oxford, UK: Basil Blackwell.

Kristeva, J. (1987). *Tales of love* (L. Roudiez, Trans.). New York: Columbia University Press.

Lacoue-Labarthe. (1989). *Typography.* Stanford, CA: Stanford University Press.

Moi, T. (Ed.). (1986). *The Kristeva reader.* Oxford, UK: Blackwell.

Whitmont, E. C. (1983). *Return of the goddess,* London: Routledge & Kegan Paul.

Whitmont, E. C. (1991). *The symbolic quest: Basic concepts of analytical psychology.* Princeton, NJ: Princeton University Press.

CHAPTER 16

# CRITICAL SPIRITUALITY, MORAL PHILOSOPHY, AND BUSINESS ETHICS

**Michael Whitty**
**Jerry Biberman**

## INTRODUCTION

*There is no right behavior within the wrong world.*

—Adorno (1963/2000, p. 174)

In the spirit of For Ethics (Jones, Parker, & ten Bos, 2005), we invite the reader to reflect on unfinished ethics and political philosophy. Much as critical theory and critical management studies seek to bring balance and forward movement to the study of business ethics, so too can the insights of moral philosophy bring balance to an otherwise predatory capitalism. A critical postmodern ethics may be needed to deconstruct the dominant managerialist paradigm. It is our purpose in this chapter to take the discussion of spirituality in business ethics, as well as the impact of religion on business ethics, beyond the assumptions of common-sense business ethics. We suggest that scholars with commitments to their versions of spirituality

*Critical Theory Ethics for Business and Public Administration*, pages 333–346
Copyright © 2008 by Information Age Publishing
All rights of reproduction in any form reserved.

or religion guard against allowing the philosophy of ethics and their belief systems to simply become utilitarian and political instruments of contemporary ideology or currently popular cosmology. Great thinkers and great thoughts in every era risk co-option into the dominant power structure of the day.

Philosophy and religion too often serve the king, human progress and possibility often take a back seat. This chapter urges scholars of management, spirituality, and religion to offer more depth, context, and vision to the all too narrow scholarship of business ethics. Critical theory can offer a new paradigm for ethics as well as criticism of the current norms of ethics.

## CRITICAL THEORY AND POSTMODERN ANALYSIS HELP KEEP DIALOGUE DEEP AND WIDE

While the field of spirituality in the workplace is dominated by the modernist paradigm, a modest alternative paradigm of what Boje (2000) calls "spiritual capitalism" has reappeared in the literature (Karliner & Karliner, 1997); Mokhiber & Weissman, 1999; Steingard & Fitzgibbons, 1995; and Biberman & Whitty, 2000). From the perspective of critical theory, both spirituality addressing economics, as well as business ethics in its traditional, narrow construct, have been largely co-opted by larger meta-systems of conformance and control. Thus, neither field can fully assume its full potential as part of the human intellectual journey toward higher consciousness. The best that moral philosophy, spirituality and critical theorists can do is keep the fundamental questions of human potential open and debated in modern organizational settings. Otherwise, virtually every spirituality and ethical system is put to work for whatever dominant dialectic is in fashion in any particular era or eon.

Critical theorists have applied their critiques to all academic disciplines from philosophy to economics. Leading thinkers such as Boje have observed that the integral spirit utopians have not incorporated the Darwinian character of economics and materialism, while, at the same time, the Darwinians have not fully considered a post-capitalist necessity to a healthy ecohumanity. Boje (2007) proposes injecting a Hegelian dialectic into the scholarship of business ethics and the new field of spirituality in economics.

Within the paradigm of reform-oriented spiritual capitalism, Boje (2000) has identified six schools of thought. He suggests that each worldview affects scholarship, resulting in very different conclusions and remedies, from the affirmative postmodernists, as contrasted with the skeptical postmodernists. Some of the critics of the mainstream or dominant modernist paradigm of business ethics are found within postmodernism and critical theory. The six schools of thought that Boje identifies are as follows:

1. **Affirmative postmodernism**—assuming continuing, favorable paradigm shift toward newer forms of progress.
2. **Skeptical postmodernism**—the matrix and the shadow side of humanity; a continuance of power over and dominance and scarcity et al.
3. **Fundamentalist–traditionalist** assumptions about work and ethics. Both Islamist and Christian conservatives are on the march and control much capital and business thought. They have a voice in popular media and popular culture worldwide both in the west and in the east. Ultimately the universe will adopt a new live-and-let-live thesis reconciling unity in diversity thus resolving the current clash of civilizations. Higher consciousness will absorb the various currents of belief into a oneness state, a form of human unity seen only in higher states of consciousness, the oneness state that is our common destiny.
4. **Ecological bioneers** believe nature is taking us somewhere wise and we will see it in time to save humanity and the planet. Liberal religion with the stewardship principle and much of spirituality movement has aligned with the new bioethics. They believe a green business ethics will help save the day.
5. **Managerialist** assumptions about business ethics are reflected in law and business higher education. A strong critique is badly needed. Where are B schools holding things back?
6. **Humanist**—this camp can include several subgroups such as religious humanists, secular humanists—some in the case of status quo ethics and others seeking to enlarge or break the existing paradigm. Critical theorists and radical humanists often are aligned with movements for social justice and believe a better world is possible.

Many new ecospiritual and humanistic paradigms have arisen offering a more dialectic approach to future evolution. This new set of stories accepts a dialectical and evolutionary process of give and take in all fields (i.e., a dialectical democracy). Thus, a humanistic and progressive spirituality can provide a much-needed ally to the forces associated with critical theory and true democracy.

Some new thinkers are very affirmative in their vision (Wilber, 2000; Hawkins, 2002), while others remain unconvinced of the so-called progress myth (Boje, 2000). The ecologist perspective and the sustainability movement are also current versions of affirmative paradigms lodged in both modernist and postmodernist scholarship.

## CRITICAL REVIEWS OF SPIRITUALITY IN ORGANIZATION AND SOCIETY

Critical reviewers have pointed out a number of ways in which spirituality can be misused or be used as an addiction in an organization. Some of these are as follows: (1) in an addictive organization, or in an organization where the top leaders are addicts, spirituality can itself be used as an addiction, and as a way to avoid or deny dealing with real organizational problems; (2) an organization or leader may impose spiritual or religious beliefs on its members; and (3) organizations can use spirituality or religion as a management tool.

While the literature on spirituality in the workplace has largely considered spirituality to be an individual phenomenon (e.g., Ashforth & Pratt, 2003), workplace spirituality has also been advocated as a means for improving organizational performance (Mitroff & Denton, 1999; Neck & Milliman, 1994). Spirituality has also been described as a way to increase employee motivation (Tischler, 1999) cohesion (Dehler & Welsh, 1994), and better performance (Guillory, 2000; Mitroff & Denton, 1999). Spirituality has thus been depicted as a means of supporting "longer term enterprise stability, growth and profitability" (Burack, 1999, p. 280) and "real bottom-line improvements" (Leigh, 1997, p. 26).

Critics of organizational spirituality (e.g., Bell & Taylor, 2003) have argued that the spirituality discourse is totalizing because it seems to advocate, implicitly or explicitly, the idea that individuals have to accept the social structures in which they work, and more importantly, come to see these structures as meaningful and good. They further argue that the spirituality discourse is totalizing because it provides mechanisms through which individuals are better able to cope with all, including exploitative and dysfunctional, aspects of capitalist systems but no mechanisms by which to recognize or critique them as exploitative and dysfunctional (Bell & Taylor, 2003). This legitimizing of current organizational structures and getting individuals to believe in them as the manifestation of "a sacred power" (Bell & Taylor, 2003, p. 340) leads to the individual being placed in a position of potentially increased conformity (Ashforth & Pratt, 2003), a position from which the individual may lack critical distance and the impetus to resist or change dysfunctional organizational structures (Nadesan, 1999).

Bell and Taylor (2003) further suggest that spirituality in organizations goes further and seems more totalizing than the Protestant work ethic in positioning work as one or perhaps the only path for self-fulfillment and spiritual transformation. Critics have raised further concerns that spirituality may be misappropriated as a tool for "material gain" (Benefiel, 2003) or of increased managerial control (Brown, 2003; Elmes & Smith, 2001).

Some critical theorists have seen a more positive role for workplace spirituality in organizational transformation. Boyle and Healy (2003), for example, suggest that organizational spirituality may be a tool for increased managerial control, but that it may also be illusionary to believe that employee spirituality can ever be totally controlled and that it may not also lead to employee resistance. That is, by creating a space for individual spirituality, the organization may also create a space for individual resistance. Furthermore, Boje (2000) has suggested that organizational spirituality should lead to the rejection of existing paradigms and the adoption of a new business paradigm characterized by nonviolent business practices, sustainable growth, ecological awareness, and the cultivation of personal development. He therefore agrees with Horkheimer and Adorno (1997) that "the maxim that would be made universal, be done at the level of people organizing with others to change the social system that is producing the unethical behaviors" (Boje, 2007).

Postmodern critics argue that most spirituality writings are pro-management, overly optimistic, and don't pay attention to the social and environmental consequences and other injustices brought about by business practices—even spiritually oriented practices. Against their assertion, we argue that criticism alone of the existing system will not, in and of itself, bring about change in the system—but will, instead, simply result in current practitioners of the system digging in their heels and defending the status quo. Rather than criticize the status quo, we suggest that individuals engage in personal growth and other spiritual practices that will bring about their own personal transformation and change. Our hypothesis is that as a person grows into progressively higher levels of consciousness, the person's commitment to ethics and social and environmental issues naturally deepens—resulting ultimately in practices and policies that create organizational and political system change. Such change may ultimately usher in a new spiritual organizational paradigm.

## SPIRITUAL PARADIGMS INTEGRATING INTO BUSINESS VALUES

Organizations and their executives both in Japan and in the United States are beginning to show an interest in spirituality and spiritual values (e.g., Brandt, 1996; Labbs, 1995; Vicek, 1992). A number of organizational writers are urging organizations and their members to pay more attention to spiritual values and spirituality (e.g., Bolman & Deal, 1995; Gunn, 1992; Russell, 1989; Schechter, 1995; Scherer & Shook, 1993; Walker, 1989).

Some authors have related spirituality to organizational learning processes. Mingin (1985), for example, describes how information-based technology will lead to "spirituality oriented fundamental abstractions." Vail (1985) proposes a "process wisdom" explanation of organizational transformation that involves four elements: grounding in existence, appreciation of the openness of the human spirit, understanding of human consciousness, and an appreciation of the spirituality of humankind. Hawkins (1991) relates the spiritual dimension in learning organizations to Gregory Bateson's concept of double-loop Level III learning.

Interest in organizational learning and creative thinking has also led to the increased use of certain spiritual practices—particularly meditation—among organization members, and an increased interest in intuition and whole brain thinking in organization decision processes (e.g., Agor 1989). Increasing numbers of executives and managers are turning to various types of meditation and spiritual disciplines as a way of coping with stress and for finding meaning in their turbulent work environments (Dehler & Welsh, 1994) and in dealing with recovery from job loss (Byron, 1995).

At the same time that organizations and managers are paying more attention to spirituality and to whole-brain thinking and learning, global competition and other conditions are bringing about increased attention to team development and employee empowerment. When one examines the various descriptions of organizations using work teams (e.g., Levine, 1994) one is struck by the similarity of values, behaviors, and processes that emerge from these teams to those described in relation to spirituality, creativity, and organization learning. Indeed, Poe (1991) points out that the Japanese, with their knowledge of Zen Buddhism, understood Deming's Plan–Do–Study–Act (PDSA) cycle as a spiritual discipline. As employees master this PDSA discipline, they continually trade information with each other until individual wisdom fuses into powerful group intelligence. Poe says that excessive reliance on logic and reason led many Westerners to misunderstand this aspect of Deming's theories. Similarly, Fort (1995, p. 16) describes how total quality management's emphasis on fulfilling the needs of customers and stakeholders is a contemporary managerial articulation of what Pope John Paul calls solidarity, or the goodness of understanding the self in terms of the self's dialectical relationships with others. Fort asserts that "this expresses an overlapping wisdom that grounds a spirituality of connectedness in all aspects of life, including business."

What do these emerging trends have in common? It is our contention that they represent a postmodern management paradigm that is emerging—one that emphasizes spiritual principles and practices, as opposed to the current prevailing modern management paradigm. Moral philosophy is a practical and theoretical starting point for critical postmodern theory to explore in its search for new scholarship in the field of organizational ethics.

Rose (1990) describes a new paradigm that is beginning to develop among managers and executives that incorporates ideas from quantum physics, cybernetics, chaos theory, cognitive science, and Eastern and Western spiritual traditions. It contains two main components: everything is seen as being interconnected, and there is a focus on empowering people. Rose attributes the vogue for Japanese management techniques, the spread of technology, and the spread of idealism as fueling the trend. Fox (1994) describes many of these same characteristics as depicting what he calls the green (sheen) era of Creation as Sacrament paradigm. James Redfield (1993, 1996) has summarized many of the components into the 10 insights described in the *Celestine Prophecy and the Tenth Insight,* and Deepak Chopra (1994) has distilled the spiritual laws involved in this paradigm (from the Indian Vedic tradition perspective) into the *Seven Spiritual Laws of Success.*

It is our contention that this paradigm is continuing to emerge, and will become more widespread in future years, and that the existing stress that managers and organizations are experiencing may actually produce the catalyst for organization spiritual transformation, in ways similar to that in which personal crises have led to personal spiritual growth and transformation (Grof & Grof, 1989).

Persons operating from a spiritual paradigm perspective would be open to change, have a sense of purpose and meaning in their life, appreciate how they are connected with a greater whole, and have individual understanding and expression of their own spirituality. In contrast to a scarcity belief, they possess what has been referred to as an "abundance" mentality—a belief that there are abundant resources available to all, so that there is no need to compete for them. They would also be more likely to trust others, share information and work in concert with teams and coworkers to accomplish mutual objectives, and to empower their coworkers and people below them in the organization hierarchy. They would be more likely to use intuition and emotions in reaching decisions. They would also be more likely to use win–win collaborative strategies in conflict situations.

Organizations that operate from the modern paradigm possess rigid, bureaucratic structures and hierarchical chains of command. They are more likely to use formal communication channels and have very formal policy manuals and procedures for every activity and job title in the organization. They are more concerned with following policies and procedures than in pleasing either internal or external customers. The belief in scarcity of resources leads to competition between organization units for budget, personnel, and other resources, and leads to politics and power struggles between units.

In contrast, organizations that operate from the spiritual paradigm would be expected to have flatter organization structures and a greater openness to change. Their belief in abundant resources would lead to greater interconnectedness and cooperation between organization units, and empowerment of workers at all levels of the organization. Rather than believing in the preservation of the self at all costs, these organizations would be more concerned with existing in harmony with their environment, and would thus be more supportive of the ecology and environment, and more concerned with meeting the needs of internal and external customers. These organizations would be more likely to encourage creative thinking and the working together of organization units to establish and accomplish mutually agreed-on mission statements and objectives for the organization.

It is our contention that the human relations movement, organization development, and its attendant concepts developed as a reaction to the prevailing modernist paradigm, and existed within it, rather than trying to create a new paradigm. Thus, the proponents of the human relations movement and organization development accepted most of the underlying tenants of the modernist paradigm—such as the belief in the scientific method—as true and as fact, and then attempted to use the methods of that paradigm to call for what were largely cosmetic changes in the way organizations were managed.

We predict that more and more organizations and their workers can be expected to shift to this new spiritual paradigm in the coming years. This shift is not only likely to occur for the reasons Boje and others cite as pushing organizations into postmodern practices, but also because of the shift in the consciousness of workers and managers at all levels of organizations that is already beginning to occur as workers and managers seek to find more meaning in their work.

Organizational soul and the spirit of the workforce have been too often ignored or neglected. Nonetheless, the history of economic reform movements and the thread of social justice in philosophy and religion have long called for a basic change of heart in human behavior. This has always implied a more communal approach to organizational theory and practice as well as a more humanistic psychology for individual behavior. These democratizing concepts were often introduced by social democrats in alliance with unions. Liberal religion supported these community-building reforms.

Religious faith has also played a role in the thinking of critical theorists. For example, the writings of Horkheimer and Adorno are influenced by their Jewish faith, especially the case when they talk about Jews and Fascist Germany anti-Semitism (Horkheimer & Adorno, 1997), and Boje's writings have been influenced by the Jainism (Boje, 2000). We suggest that as critical theorists continue to pursue their own spiritual practices, and as they grow into progressively higher levels of consciousness, their commitment to ethics and social and environmental issues will naturally deepen—

resulting ultimately in a reconciliation of their spirituality and their critical ideology.

Spirit-based organizational theorists might profit from further interdisciplinary research into aspects of all major work reform movements of the last 200 years. With the rise of modernism came a heightened materialism that marginalized sharing and caring. Industrialism weakened community and sidelined religion. Employees were often excluded stakeholders. Now a post-industrial age yearns for community and spiritual nourishment in both personal and organizational terms. Selfishness seems dysfunctional to many global thinkers. Only by reinventing work from the inside out will individuals acquire a sense of deeper purpose in work.

In the postmodern future, humankind's eternal search for meaning may require not only reinventing work and the workplace but also a renewed reflection on the deepest intentions behind human activity. Spirit-based organizations might also profit from such an arrangement. Cooperation may be good for the future of organizational culture and for people's sense of shared destiny.

## A CRITICAL ETHICS MAY REQUIRE NEW PARADIGM THINKING FOR MORAL PHILOSOPHY

A critical postmodern moral philosophy of work can be the common ground for the new work community. The philosophy of participation adopted from the team concept model could be expanded in the 21st century to involve human unity and higher consciousness as well as continuous improvement. This may require a fuller understanding that management makes decisions that have far-reaching impacts on the spiritual lives of employees. Work life reaches into the very soul of all working people. Employees in touch with their spirituality seek to have more input into those decisions. Rekindling the spirit in work will deepen these efforts. The final step would be a corporate attitude of servant leadership toward all stakeholders. Visionary groups such as the Greenleaf Center for Servant Leadership and the Noetic Sciences Institute have path-breaking conferences and workshops designed to encourage new paradigms in business. These groups believe that shared power will ensure that the future "borderless world" values diversity, embraces pluralism, and provides global servant leadership. Workplace unity and high purpose can create a service-learning atmosphere which will result in high standards, adequate competitiveness, and an agile business system for the century to come. A deepened form of organizational stewardship could evolve from reforms in organizational decision making. A new work community based on spirit at work will result in economics as if people mattered, thus reinventing the purpose of business ethics.

Working people and human evolution itself are constantly seeking meaning, purpose, and a sense of contribution to work life. These needs are served and deepened when a spiritual paradigm frames the intentions of all stakeholders. Real human nourishment is provided by the soulful organization.

The postmodern work organization can transform the purpose and meaning of work without excluding employee stakeholders. During the rest of our professional lives we can teach the wisdom and skills of organizational harmony and evolution. Reframing the meaning of work has support of the servant leaders worldwide who see that a life of service best fits the basic human need for relevance, recognition, meaning, and self-transcendence. Critical theory has been a major thought leader in the postmodern deconstruction of ethics, human organization and political philosophy.

If critical postmodern theory and critical management studies could expand to embrace consciousness studies as well as an updated Marxist humanism, the basis for an empowered ethics could arise. This chapter is one step in that direction: a new interdisciplinary paradigm not only for business ethics but the meaning of life and the possible future.

## CONCLUSION: UNFINISHED ETHICS: HOPEFUL IDEAS FOR CRITICAL POSTMODERN THEORY

Our conclusion is eclectic and dialectic. Critical theory could profit from expanding its own ideological and philosophical framework to include the new science, transpersonal psychology, post-postmodern visionary moral philosophy, and postcapitalist economics. We suggest a gradual process of convergence of several hopeful themes and trends will result in continued upswings of higher levels of consciousness by ever larger numbers of thought leaders. The diverse contributions in this reader are a prophetic sign that significant intellectual scholarly trend is underway to enlarge the philosophical scope and authority of business ethics and societal politics in general. All of this results from a combination of several of the visionary political reform movements with the evolutionary shift to a post-postmodern theory used to inspire a new radical moral ethic for business, commerce, and economics. This new business ethics may transform economics, work, and the politics of meaning for the human race.

We appreciate the usefulness of the dialectical method and the various schools of critical theory as applied to the field of business ethics and see much value in its methods. This has implications for the application of critical theory not only in the teaching of business ethics but also the entire fabric of the oncoming knowledge society. Philosophy, economics, business, technology, science, and education as well as the field of ethics are now offered a new cosmology with a hopeful view of the future. Philosophy can profit from a healthy dose of science and futurism, while economics can benefit from more ethics, compassion, love, and generosity.

Ethics, business, science, and technology may need a postmodern re-definition of their ultimate purposes and intentions. We may rethink the human uses of materialism from the perspective of evolution and higher consciousness. Ethics along with critical theory might look forward to the possibility of achieving the preferred future.

Education is catching up with the hopeful megatrends of the future. Education for higher consciousness could facilitate a new leadership class holding global ethics requiring not only sustainable economics but a sustainable human ecology. Our vision of the future is post-Hegelian, a step beyond criticism to a new level of seeing premised on a post-philosophic evolution to higher consciousness, which may already be underway (Wilber, 2004).

We propose that spirituality's contribution to business ethics, as seen through the lens of critical theory and postmodernism, is to offer new ways of seeing the future. A future with an ongoing, organic evolution of human ethics and human behavior is already documented by mainline forecasting groups such as the World Future Society. This way of seeing is the way of the great inventors, scientists, and visionary philosophers, and—dare we say—the way of the mystics.

Business ethics infused with a critical post-modern theory, consciousness, and moral philosophy can be both a critical social science and a progressive social practice. Within the framework of an inclusive, open-ended critical theory, combined with an appreciation of the evolutionary shift to higher consciousness, the field of business ethics could empower people to reject false consciousness in its theory and practice. Critical theory is vital for this process to affect economics, accounting, strategy, or deep cultural norms such as the "creed of greed." Consciousness theory or spirituality is a new mega-theory that can offer a hopeful scenario to the field of postmodern ethics and critical theory.

Just as business ethics has no business simply acting as an ideological prop for dominance and power holding, so too must spirituality guard against being used as thought control. The progress myth is just that—a question-able assumption that our species is guaranteed to prosper and prevail. A little intellectual and spiritual humility is in order in an age of utilitarianism and rationales for social Darwinism. Wrong economic ethics undercuts the personal codes of business ethics in every greed centered economic system. Life cannot be lived rightly in a system based on false consciousness, fear, greed, and power seeking.

Scholars of business ethics can question the "progress myth" (Boje, 2000) while still drawing some inspiration from those with an affirmative vision—whether modernists or postmodernists. The current evolution (or devolution) of capitalism has even given pause to optimists such as Wilber and many of the mainstream scholars of business social responsibility.

With that having been said, we still hold out the torch of human possibility, the possible human, and the possible future as a human potentiality. We offer the hopeful, visionary possibility of evolution to higher consciousness and with it the liberation of the corporate soul. We offer the postcapitalist premise of business ethics being implemented as if people really mattered and money was only a means to a much more sacred end.

# REFERENCES

Adorno, T W. (1963/2000). *Problems of moral philosophy.* Stanford, CA: Stanford University Press.

Agor, W. H. (1989). *Intuition in organizations.* Newbury Park, CA: Sage,

Ashforth, B. E., & Pratt, M. G. (2003). Institutionalized spirituality: An oxymoron? In R. A. Giacalone & C.L. Jurkiewicz (Eds.), *Handbook of workplace spirituality and organizational performance* (pp. 93–107). Armonk, NY: M.E. Sharpe.

Bell, E., & Taylor, S. (2003). The elevation of work: Pastoral power and the New Age work ethic. *Organization, 10*(2), 329–349.

Benefiel, M. (2003). Mapping the terrain of spirituality in organizations research. *Journal of Organizational Change Management, 16*(4), 367–377.

Biberman, J, & Whitty, M. D. (Eds.). (2000). *Work and spirit: A reader of new spiritual paradigms for organizations.* Scranton, PA: University of Scranton Press.

Boje, D. M. (2000). Another view: Approaches to the study of spiritual capitalism. In J. Biberman & M. D. Whitty (Eds.), *Work and spirit: A reader of new spiritual paradigms for organizations* (pp. xxv–xxxii). Scranton, PA: University of Scranton Press.

Boje, D. M. (2007). *Critical theory ethics for business and public administration.* Greenwich, CT: Information Age.

Boje, D. M., & Dennehy, R. F. (1994). *Managing in the postmodern world: America's revolution against exploitation* (2nd ed.). Dubuque, IA: Kendall Hunt.

Bolman, L. G., & Deal, T. E. (1995). *Leading with soul: An uncommon journey of spirit.* San Francisco: Jossey-Bass.

Boyle, M. V., & Healy, J. (2003). Balancing mysterium and onus: Doing spiritual work within an emotion-laden organizational context. *Organization, 10*(2), 351–373.

Brandt, E. (1996). Corporate pioneers explore spirituality, peace. *HRMagazine, 41*(4), 82–87.

Brown, R. B. (2003). Organizational spirituality: The skeptic's version. *Organization, 10*(2), 393–400.

Burack, E. H. (1999). Spirituality in the workplace. *Journal of Organizational Change Management, 12*(4), 280–290.

Byron, W. J. (1995). Spirituality on the road to re-employment. *America, 172*(18), 15–16.

Chopra, D. (1994). *The seven spiritual laws of success: A practical guide to the fulfillment of your dreams.* San Rafael, CA: Amber-Allen.

Dehler, G. E., & Welsh, M. A. (1994). Spirituality and organizational transformation. *Journal of Managerial Psychology, 9*(6), 17–26.

Elmes, M., & Smith, C. (2001). Moved by the spirit: Contextualizing workplace empowerment in American spiritual ideals. *Journal of Applied Behavioral Science, 37*(1), 33–50.

Fort, T. L. (1995). The spirituality of solidarity and total quality management. *Business and Professional Ethics Journal, 14*(2), 3–21.

Fox, M. (1994). *The reinvention of work: A new vision of livelihood for our time.* San Francisco: Harper San Francisco.

Grof, S., & Grof, C. (Eds.). (1989). *Spiritual emergency: When personal transformation becomes a crisis.* Los Angeles: Tarcher.

Guillory, W. A. (2000). *The living organization: Spirituality in the workplace.* Salt Lake City: UT: Innovations International.

Gunn, B. (1992). Competruism: Ideology with a sustainable future. *Futures, 24*(6), 559–579.

Hawkins, D. R. (2002). *Power vs. force.* Carlsbad, CA: Hay House.

Hawkins, P. (1991). The spiritual dimension of the learning organization. *Management Education and Development, 22*(3), 172–187.

Horkheimer, M. (1933/1993). Materialism and morality. In *Between philosophy and social science: Selected early writings, Max Horkheimer* (pp. 15–49). Cambridge, MA: MIT Press.

Horkheimer, M., & Adorno, T. (1997). *Dialectics of enlightenment.* London: Verso

Karliner, J., & Karliner, J. (1997). *The corporate planet: Ecology and politics in the age of globalization.* San Francisco: Sierra Club Books.

Jones, C., Parker, M., & ten Bos, R. (2005). *For business ethics.* London: Routhledge.

Labbs, J. J. (1995). Balancing spirituality and work. *Personnel Journal, 74*(9), 60–76.

Leigh, P. (1997). The new spirit at work. *Training and Development, 51*(3), 26–34.

Levine, L. (1994). Listening with spirit and the art of team dialogue. *Journal of Organizational Change Management, 7*(1), 61–73.

Mingin, W. (1985). The trend toward being: what's after the information age? *ReVISION, 7*(2), 64–67.

Mitroff, I. I., & Denton, E. A. (1999). *A spiritual audit of corporate America.* San Francisco: Jossey-Bass.

Mokhiber, R., & Weissman, R. (1999). *Corporate predators: The hunt for mega-profits and the attack on democracy.* Monroe, ME: Common Courage Press.

Nadesan, M. H. (1999). The discourses of corporate spiritualism and Evangelical capitalism. *Management Communication Quarterly, 13*(1), 3–42.

Neck, C. P., & Milliman, J. F. (1994). Thought self-leadership: Finding spiritual fulfillment in organizational life. *Journal of Managerial Psychology, 9*(6), 9–16.

Poe, R. (1991). The new discipline. *Success, 38*(6), 80.

Redfield, J. (1993). *The Celestine prophecy: An adventure.* New York: Warner.

Redfield, J. (1996). *The tenth insight: Holding the vision.* New York: Warner.

Rose, F. (1990). A new age for business? *Fortune, 122*(9), 156–164.

Russell, P. (1989). The redemption of the executive. *Leadership and Organization Development Journal, 10*(3), i–iv.

Schechter, H. (1995). *Rekindling the spirit at work*. Barrytown, NY: Barrytown.

Scherer, J., & Shook, L. (1993). *Work and the human spirit*. Spokane, WA: John Scherer & Associates.

Steingard, D. S., & Fitzgibbons, D. E. (1995). Challenging the juggernaut of globalization: A manifesto for academic praxis. *Journal of Organizational Change Management, 8*(4), 30–54.

Tischler, L. (1999). The growing interest in spirituality in business: A long-term socio-economic explanation. *Journal of Organizational Change Management, 12*(4), 273–280.

Vail, P. B. (1985). Process wisdom for a new age. *ReVISION, 7*(2), 39–49.

Vicek, D. J. (1992). The domino effect. *Small Business Reports, 17*(9), 21–25.

Walker, R. G. (1989). The imperative of leaders to create leaders. *Directors and Boards, 13*(2), 21–25.

Wilber, K. (2000). *A brief history of everything*. Boston: Shambala.

Wilber, K. (2001). *Sex, ecology, spirituality: The spirit of evolution* (2nd rev ed.). Boston: Shambala.

CHAPTER 17

# CRITICAL PEDAGOGY AND ETHICS

## An Epic Four-Quadrant Model

**Grace Ann Rosile, Mark Horowitz, Stephen DeGiulio, and Janet Marta**

This chapter combines a narrative analysis with a critical perspective to offer a critical narrative analysis of ethical issues in business management pedagogy. Starting with a story of cheating in a business classroom, a critical deconstruction of the dominant or status-quo story explodes the neatly focused tragic story of crime and punishment. Eight deconstruction steps (Boje, 2001) shatter the unitary tragic story into the polyphonic epic narrative of multiple characters, settings, and plots.

Yes, some students cheated in a class. But what about the pressures to teach larger classes, which require objective multiple-choice testing rather than essays? What about those honest students who observed the cheating and did nothing? What about teachers who take graduate students' work and publish it as their own? What about the obsessions with objective testing for "outcomes assessment" and funding decisions? Is it fair to fail a student for proven plagiarism or cheating when we know so many go un-

*Critical Theory Ethics for Business and Public Administration*, pages 347–372
Copyright © 2008 by Information Age Publishing
**347**

punished? What about the growing gap between the rich and the poor? All these issues and more are relevant to developing a pedagogy for addressing ethics from a critical perspective in business schools.

How do we approach the plethora of issues (stories) relevant to this epic version of ethics pedagogy in business? Ironically, one of those linear reductionist $2 \times 2$ models can help to sort these multiple stories into a framework. First, the stories are sorted into the perspectives of either insiders in the world of business education or outsiders, yielding emic and etic viewpoints. Next, the epic narratives are split according to their micro focus on individual students versus a more macro focus on classroom culture and even broad social systems.

Rosile (2004) has developed the Epic Four-Quadrant model. In order to better reflect the multiple voices of a critical perspective, Rosile includes three other authors in presenting perspectives of three of the four quadrants, as summarized next.

## SYSTEMIC ROOT CAUSES OF CHEATING:
## THE FOUR-QUADRANT MODEL[1]

In a complex situation like cheating in the classroom, expanding the view of the problem, through deconstruction or other means, is essential to understanding the root causes of the problem, and to resituating the epic story and counterstory. This broader view developed above allows us to trace the systemic root causes of academic dishonesty by clustering the various storylines.

One way to cluster story lines is by author. A contribution of the narrative approach is to recognize the voice of the author in her/his particular context, rather than to assume the author is an impersonal omniscient rational voice. In the context of academic dishonesty, it is apparent that the story of dishonesty (the diagnosis of the problem) varies according to whether the author is an insider in academia or an outsider.

Insider stories are the author's stories about themselves, and outsider stories are external persons viewing and interpreting situations in someone else's milieu. According to attribution theory, we know that when people seek the reasons for their own failures, they attribute these failures to elements of the task or the situation, generally termed *external* causes because they are external to the person. When I seek the reasons for someone else's failure, I look at their internal qualities of ability and effort.

A simple example demonstrates the internal–external perspective. You are a student who has just failed an exam. Why do you think you failed? Usually you will cite friends who distracted you from studies, work or family demands, the difficulty or irrelevance of the subject matter, and the lack of ability of the instructor. Some will claim "tricky" test questions or an instructor who does not like them. In other words, it was not your fault, there were external circumstances that caused your failure.

Next, assume you are a student whose roommate just failed an exam. Why do you think they failed? You will likely think your suspicions have been confirmed, that the roommate is not as smart and motivated as you thought. You were there the evenings they partied instead of studied. They are a bit less intelligent and less hard-working than you are (i.e., a bit stupid and lazy), although a great friend. In other words, you blame the roommate's lack of personal qualities for their failure.

Now assume that the semester after your roommate failed the exam (the above example), that you are taking the same course. You fail the same exam, despite reasonable efforts to study for it. Suddenly, you will see your roommate's previous "excuses" in a different light. You are likely to have a greater appreciation for the difficulties inherent in the situation.

The same attributional biases will likely apply to our perception of causes in a cheating situation. The stories of academic dishonesty are quite different when seen from the attributionally different vantage points of actor or observer. To the extent that cheating is seen as a failure, we can expect that if I am the actor and am referring to my own case of cheating, I will be more likely to blame external circumstances for "causing" my cheating. If I am observing you cheat, I will blame your lack of personal qualities (poor moral character or laziness) more than the external circumstances as the cause for your cheating. Thus the narratives about why cheating occurs are likely to vary according to whether the person is referring to themselves or to others who have cheated.

The Epic Four-Quadrant Model sorts the stories (problem statements) about cheating into whether these stories are told from the perspective of the actor (the person/group who has done the action) or the observer (a person/group observing others' actions). Borrowing terms from ethnographic research, the first dimension of the model is Insider/Emic and Outsider/Etic. Emic refers to concepts that arise from within a culture; etic refers to concepts imposed on a culture from the outside.

The second dimension of the Epic Four-Quadrant Model refers to the micro or macro nature of the story. Micro stories will tend to be more narrowly focused tragic stories. Macro stories will include more epic stories with a broader systemic perspective.

The analysis is narrative because we are looking at variations in the stories based on who is narrating and what is their context, how they are embedded in the situation. In contrast, if we were looking at some "objective" empirical research based on statistics, say about the effects of the death penalty on crime rates, theoretically we would consider only the rigor, validity, and reliability of the research methods and statistical analysis. Theoretically, we should not be interested, nor should we take into consideration, the fact that the author of this research is a death-row inmate. Nor would it be relevant if the author were instead the parent of a murder victim. But in narrative analysis, the identity and context of the narrator who is telling the story is a crucial piece of data. We understand the narrator's story differently when we see the narrator in different contexts.

## THE EPIC FOUR QUADRANT MODEL: FOUR ROOT CAUSES

The Four-Quadrant Model shown in Table 17.1 sorts the root cause narratives of cheating into micro and macro narratives, and narratives told from an insider versus outsider perspective. Each quadrant has some of the narratives derived from the eight steps to deconstruction offered in Rosile's Quadrant III.

## QUADRANT I CRIME AND PUNISHMENT: MICRO INSIDER APPROACHES TO ETHICS

The first quadrant represents micro (individual-level) attributions from the actor's perspective. In other words, the narrator is talking about themselves personally or their social group. The story here is one of "Crime and Punishment." Since the self-serving attributional bias operates to protect the self, most individuals will attribute their own failure to external causes.

**TABLE 17.1   Root Causes of Cheating**

|  | Insider/Emic | Outsider/Etic |
|---|---|---|
| Micro | **I. Crime and Punishment**<br>*"A few bad apples"*<br>1 Bad students cheat not good ones<br>1 Athletes and males cheat more<br>1 Honest students are not seen as part<br>  of the problem | **II. Collusion and Complicity**<br>*"Beating the System"*<br>4 Cheaters are heroes opposing a<br>  corrupt system<br>5 Teachers helping students to cheat<br>5 Teachers who steal students' work |
| Macro | **III. Classroom Culture**<br>*"McDonalization of Education"*<br>1 Honest students are not seen as part<br>  of the solution<br>2 Teachers who don't care<br>5 Teachers who cheat<br>6 Untold stories of honest students | **IV. Complete Corruption**<br>*"Systemic Abuse of Power"*<br>3 Corporate crime<br>5 Cheating is only way to success<br>7 Irrelevant curriculum/not real world<br>  (standardized testing/performativity) |

*Note:* The numbers correlate with the deconstructions of the cheating story listed above.

Thus in this quadrant, the blame may be on "us" but it usually is not taken on the self. Rather, it is "a few bad apples" among "us."

Horowitz offers one strategy to avoid the self-protection self-serving bias. He explains that to ethically pose ethical questions from a critical perspective requires that we professors abandon the illusion of objectivity and reveal our personal relationship to the material being presented. He prefaces his classroom analogy critiquing global business practices with a discussion of his experiences with maquiladoras (foreign-owned manufacturing plants in Mexico).

## QUADRANT II COLLUSION AND COMPLICITY: MICRO OUTSIDER APPROACHES TO ETHICS

Quadrant II includes the stories of external narrators who are talking about those "others" who cheat. Told by an outsider, this story typically exaggerates the weak moral character or personal flaws of the "others" who are the guilty insiders. It is the story of "Collusion and Complicity," of corrupt teachers who help students to cheat, and all those "others" who are out to "beat the system."

There might be good reasons why business faculty report they see less cheating, and why fewer still report what they do see (McCabe & Trevino, 1995, p. 216). Maybe penalties are perceived as too harsh, maybe the administration does not support faculty efforts to enforce penalties for cheating. Nevertheless, from the outside, this behavior looks like complicity. Deconstructions 4 and 5 fall into this quadrant.

In Quadrant II, author Marta is the "outsider" as a faculty member viewing the reward and punishment systems supporting classroom integrity. Marta takes a "folly of rewarding A while hoping for B" approach. A newcomer (therefore outsider) in her educational system, Marta stands outside the system to critically reflect on whose interests are being served. At first, Professor Marta could not find anyone else among her colleagues who had failed a student for plagiarism. Eventually she discovered that there had been a few cases, but they were rare and enforcement did not appear to be systematic.

Marta asks what behavior is being rewarded in this system.

## QUADRANT III CLASSROOM CULTURE: MACRO INSIDER APPROACHES TO ETHICS

Quadrant III reflects the external attributions made by insiders to excuse their guilt. It is the story of the "Classroom Culture." The fault here is attributed to what might be generally termed the McDonaldization (Ritzer, 2000) of education, where the pressures for calculability (see McNeil, 2000, for a discussion of standardized testing), predictability, and control displace education as the goal. Also important here is the role of the "innocent by-stander" or honest student. Deconstructed narratives 2, 5, and 6 may fall into this quadrant.

Rosile questions the role of the "innocent bystander" student who has not cheated. Most narratives of the cheating story put the honest students on the sidelines as (thankfully) "not part of the problem" or simply irrelevant. This author expands the cheating story from tragic crime-and-punishment to an epic tale involving everyone in the class.

## QUADRANT IV COMPLETE SYSTEMIC CORRUPTION: MACRO OUTSIDER APPROACHES TO ETHICS

Finally, Quadrant IV is the story most visible to outsiders who readily see the implicit (and faulty) assumptions in the larger system belonging to the "others." DeGiulio's critical pedagogy perspective looks at deeper ethical questions buried in the fabric of educational systems. From this perspective, systemic abuse of power arises not from individual characteristics but from the nature of the system itself (Freire, 1970). The educational system may seek to maintain itself at the expense of educational goals. Deconstructions 3, 5, and 7 may fit into Quadrant IV.

Included in Quadrant IV is relevance of the curriculum. Relevance (or lack of it) is an excuse used by some who admit to cheating in the classroom (McCabe, 2005). Scholars within the management field itself question the usefulness of management and organizational behavior curriculums (Miner, 2003; Pfeffer & Fong, 2002), noting "the relatively small impact of business school research" on management practice (Pfeffer & Fong, 2002, p. 88). Even more shockingly, no one seems very surprised. If an educational program is viewed by students as a union card rather than preparation vital to their performance in the field, such lack of relevance may contribute to cheating (McCabe, 2005).

In the next section, each author offers a response to academic dishonesty by focusing on one of the quadrants described above.

## QUADRANT I CRIME AND PUNISHMENT: MICRO INSIDER APPROACHES TO ETHICS AND RECOMMENDATION OF "APPLIED ETHICS"

### by Mark Horowitz

What do the lessons of critical theory tell us about fostering an ethical environment in the classroom? In this section I show how we, as critically minded educators, might avoid dogmatism in the classroom and protect against self-serving biases. To do so I suggest that we acknowledge both the inherently ideological nature of knowledge production and the implication of our own identities in the classroom. Knowledge is ideological because there is no clean distinction between facts and values. Our identities are implicated in our teaching because our standpoints vis-à-vis the knowledge we produce are necessarily communicated to students in the narratives we project and the very language we use to define phenomena of interest.

To illustrate these ideas I discuss below the evolution in my approach to teaching students about "sweatshops" in the global economy.

### Teaching About Export Factories—or "Sweatshops"?

The proliferation of global export factories, or "sweatshops," has spurred significant controversy in recent years. According to the International Labor Organization (2003), the number of countries making use of export processing zones has increased from 25 in 1975 to a staggering 116 in 2002. Such dramatic growth in export production raises the key politicoethical question of appropriate corporate behavior around the globe.

Notice above my placement of quotes around the term "sweatshops." I do so, of course, to note the controversy regarding that designation. I do not add quotes to the phrase "export factories," as it appears to be simply a neutral description of the phenomenon. However, how do we define sweatshops? The Department of Labor identifies a workplace as a sweatshop if it violates two or more basic labor laws, such as overtime pay, minimum wage, child labor, and the like. Following this definition, are export factories around the world sweatshops? And if so, would it not then be more appropriate to use the term "sweatshop" in the classroom?

The prevalence of labor violations in export factories globally is unknown. It is an empirical question that warrants investigation. Yet if we examine debate on the issue we find wildly divergent claims by interested parties. Business groups contend that labor abuses are the exception to otherwise lawful workplace practices around the world (see Mathiasen, 1998, chap. 3). Activist groups claim that abuses are rampant, more likely the rule than the exception (see, e.g., Kamel & Hoffman, 1999). My aim here is not to resolve the debate but to use it as an opportunity to highlight the dilemmas of language, power, and identity in the classroom. In my teaching career, my use of the terms "export factory" and "sweatshop" followed a certain trajectory. As a labor organizer in ABD status, I used the term "sweatshop" consistently in my first Social Problems course. Shortly thereafter, however, I switched to the term "export factory" to discuss the issue more "objectively" with students. Later yet, I decided upon the phrase "critics use the term 'sweatshops'" to present the debate. Presently, I maintain the latter practice, though I make it clear to students that I personally identify as a critic, engaged in the process of trying to transform the conditions of export factories along the Mexico–U.S. border and elsewhere.

### *Is my revelation of my activist identity appropriate in the classroom?*

I would argue that it is both appropriate and ethically requisite. Indeed, it would be irresponsible to conceal my commitments, given that my identity as an activist shapes—even if unconsciously—my selection of texts, presentation of material, intonation, and so on. Although this is not the space to contend fully with the hoary debate over politics in the classroom, we might ask: Would it be any less "political" to present the issue as a disengaged scholar? Does not our nonchalance (or, to the contrary, our passion) in presenting material of social and political import convey to students the nonchalance or gravity with which they should judge its significance?

Obviously, there are no easy answers to these knotty problems. My point here is simply that our personal identities cannot be liquidated when we enter the classroom. This is especially the case in carrying out critical social science, where we examine issues with an eye to their transformative societal possibilities. In the spirit of critical theory, how might we teach about sweatshops with an eye to progressive social change?

My globalization course begins, perhaps, conventionally. We discuss the historical and political-economic context of the proliferation of global export factories. Then we examine theoretical debate about the implications of the factories as a manifestation of wider neoliberal change, including consideration of the pros and cons of the factories in both the academic and popular press. Finally, we appraise possible solutions to the "problem" (semesters differ in the mix of students who view the factories, on the whole, as a problem).

My goals in the discussion are to spur critical thinking regarding key sociological theories, as well as to *grapple with students* about the sweatshop problem. To present the sweatshop issue as a problem, of which I have substantial but certainly limited knowledge, shifts the process of learning, at least in part, to one of collaboration and shared engagement. Typically, I will gauge the outlook of the class and then inform students that I will play devil's advocate for the less popular position. In any event, I use a variety of teaching strategies (papers, popular media, videos, class debate) to expound as convincingly as possible the views of all sides, including my own.

Advocates of export factories make a number of consistent arguments.[2] First, labor and other factory abuses are the exception, not the rule. Next, low wages and often harsh conditions are not unexpected given the trajectory of countries' development. Consonant with the Industrial Revolution in the West, export factories are but a "step on the road to prosperity" for poor nations. Third, export jobs typically pay wages as high if not higher than local averages, and thus are certainly "better than the alternatives" available to the local population, who may otherwise have to turn to dangerous work in the informal economy. Finally, companies do not force people to migrate, often en masse, from rural zones to take export jobs. Indeed, companies offer desperate workers opportunities that otherwise would not be available.

Critics, on the other hand, typically argue that labor and other abuses are widespread. Regarding wages, they contend that since companies *could* pay more, they *should* pay more. Next, they argue that although migrants choose to work in the factories, their choice is free, but not *fair*, due to the severely uneven bargaining power between employer and employee. Finally, critics contend that we need not repeat the mistakes of the industrial past. This is especially so given that the developmental paths of poor countries today differ decisively from those of the past, as they must develop in the context of a global economy already hemmed in by wealthy nations.

### Which position is correct?

As with other ethically relevant issues, there can be no "scientific" resolution. Science can bring us theories, facts, clarity, and an appreciation of causal factors, but it cannot ultimately adjudicate between moral alternatives. At the end of the day I can only share with students my own standpoint, open to revision, of what is desirable. Hence I express my view that labor and environmental standards between rich and poor nations should be harmonized upward; that the only way to attain such standards is through internationally enforceable rules, via a democratically accountable World Trade Organization or UN mechanism, which has the power to sanction countries that do not respect basic labor rights (child labor, collective bargaining, discrimination, etc.). As such a mechanism could only be created through adequate political pressure by civil society on governments world-wide, I make it clear to students why I have been involved for years in cross-border solidarity and political efforts aimed at fostering that political will. I then introduce students to a host of organizations grappling with this issue in varying ways. We go on to discuss the potential dangers in working toward international mechanisms (i.e., the specter of world government), and I share my view that world governmental structures are a necessary evil to change a world where young Asian girls live year round in factories making childrens' toys with which they will never play.

Space does not permit discussion of the many counterpoints to my strategic views. I do not present them to students because I believe they are unassailable. On the contrary, I present them to invite challenge and debate in a process of ongoing adjustment of my views to find the most viable possibilities for progressive social change. That is, I aim to work with students to both understand the sweatshop problem and defeat it. Today's students will be tomorrow's managers, administrators, and public officials. As educators we are inevitably bound up with the kind of citizens our students will become.

## The Quicksand Analogy

I close my personal narrative with brief reference to the final weapon in my anti-sweatshop arsenal—the quicksand analogy. I developed the quicksand analogy as a way to most effectively confront the arguments of advocates of export factories. It also shows my use of ethical narratives as a tool in the classroom.

First, I suggest to students that they imagine they are visiting their local neighborhood swamp with a hefty stick in hand. Suddenly, they witness a man in the swamp, holding on to dear life, up to his neck in quicksand. I then ask students if it would be justified to offer to save the man on the condition that he sign a contract promising to pay you $10,000. The answer is always unanimously negative. And then I ask students a series of questions: Did you put the man in the quicksand? Isn't the man better off with you there than without you there? Are you forcing the man to accept your offer? After the students respond I ask whether the facts justify the business arrangement. By then, if a student in class does not make the point for me, I reveal with characteristic candor my own position: The arguments made by transnational corporate advocates in support of the wages in export factories cannot change a basic moral fact—that the companies are profiting from the exploitation of third-world people's desperation.

## QUADRANT II COLLUSION AND COMPLICITY: MICRO OUTSIDER APPROACHES TO ETHICS AND RECOMMENDATION OF REWARD SYSTEM REFORM: WHY COLLEGE STUDENTS CHEAT

### by Janet Marta

On my office door, at the university where I teach, is a collection of quotes, with one set prominently in the center: "The system always wins."[3] This means, to me, that when you see behavior patterns emerging, a system is usually driving them, rather than individuals. This is what we teach in management courses as the "fundamental attribution error." If something is going on that you don't like, look to the system first, rather than to the individuals exhibiting the behavior.

Students are cheating their way through college. This is not news, though some may be unaware of the scale on which it happens. The news is this: schools are enabling and encouraging this behavior.

"Not at my school," you respond. "There's an entire section in the catalog that describes different kinds of academic dishonesty and prescribes corresponding sanctions. A student fails a course at the first instance of plagiarism, for instance, and is dismissed from the university if it happens again. We take it seriously. We're not enabling and encouraging cheating at this university."

But have you ever flunked a student for plagiarism? Do you regularly check for it? Almost all our universities have policies about academic dishonesty, to which we can point virtuously. The problem is that they are not enforced. It becomes hard to tell where the enabling shades into encouraging.

### Ever Heard of Unintentional Plagiarism?

You haven't? Well, that's what *all* of it is. The assumption is that the student didn't intend to plagiarize, which is a reasonable assumption given the sanctions on the books. Why would a rational person plagiarize, knowing they would get an "F" for the course? The answer is that they know they *won't* fail the course; thus, the system creates and perpetuates the behavior. There is no such thing as intentional plagiarism. "But officer, I didn't intend to exceed the speed limit."

### A Cautionary Tale, in an Unknown Number of Acts

At the end of my first semester as an assistant professor (in 1999), I received two papers that contained instances of plagiarism. I had limited the students' potential sources and was familiar with the style and content of most of them. One instance was the kind that some call "intentional": the student had placed a citation at the end of the paragraph, but indicated no direct quotes. The paragraph was, in fact, quoted directly from another source. But the other example was "unintentional": the student had put the citation in parentheses after the quote, but there were no quotation marks. My chair observed that it didn't look like the student was trying to cheat. I responded that I couldn't divine the student's intent, but I could recognize plagiarism. He was supportive, and the students failed the course.

The next semester, it happened again—another two students. One told me he'd been writing like that his entire academic career. I believed him, as I had checked with my middle- and high-school-age sons, who observed that in their experience it goes on all the time and teachers never punish students for it. "They tell us we can use whole sentences or paragraphs, Mom, if we just change a word here or there." The result for the student who had been trained this way and then ran into me his senior year was an "F." His fault, or the system's?

The other student's case, however, was quite different. She was a non-traditional student who had been out of school for 10 years. She became concerned when I warned in class about plagiarism, unsure that she remembered how to cite things properly. I recommended that she take her paper to the campus writing center and have them check it, before she turned it in. When she did, I found several plagiarized sentences in her paper, and, puzzled, called the writing center. Yes, the student had been in, and yes, they had checked her citations. Where the wires were crossed is that they had checked the citation *style*, which was indeed correct, but the student was assuming they had checked that she had handled attribution properly. In the end, I recommended that she appeal my decision to the appropriate university committee and I supported the appeal, which was ultimately successful.[4]

Well, this whole end-of-semester mess was beginning to look like an ulcer in the making. My first thought was to drop the research component of my classes, as many business professors have done. The chair encouraged me to rethink that idea: "someone has to teach writing." One of the main complaints from business about business schools is that graduates don't write well. I had been an undergraduate English major and had worked as an editor; therefore, I am capable of evaluating writing and our students deserve to be required to write decently.

The next step was to check with colleagues. The English department professors all said that they teach about how to avoid plagiarism in all freshman comp classes. The students know, they claimed. Had they ever flunked a student for plagiarism, or any form of academic dishonesty? No. The chair of our department and several others began to be curious and we asked around, in informal settings. *No one ever flunked students for academic dishonesty.* The general practice seems to be warn against academic dishonesty, but don't check for it. If it jumps out at you, either give the student the opportunity to fix it (coupled with a stern warning) or give them an "F" on the paper.

The following semester it was a graduating senior committing "unintentional" plagiarism. One of my department colleagues, the student's advisor, told me they were going to fight this, because it would slow down the student's graduation. A committee was formed, which recommended that the student only get an "F" for the paper, given the fact that nobody on the committee would have acted as I did. The student graduated; we found out later, from some of his friends, that he had cheated his way through school.

Okay, I was not going to knuckle under, but I had to find a way to lower the emotional price I was paying each semester. I designed a sheet that defined plagiarism, described how to handle citations properly and delineated the penalty. Students were to sign and date the paper, and hand it in with their research. I showed the paper to the head of the "appeals" committee, who thought it a good idea. "Do you teach about plagiarism in class?" she inquired. No, I teach marketing and international business, not composition or any portion of a knowledge base that I assume I can build on. "Well, this is good. You really should establish a paper trail." And why is that? I understood my part to be identifying the academic dishonesty and reporting it, then letting the committee handle it. "This will make it easier for your department to support you." The implications of this comment are disturbing: who's the bad guy here?

## What, Actually, Are We Doing Here?

So the system at first enables plagiarism and over time encourages it. In fact, the system teaches students far more powerfully than I do, because it molds them every day, in every class. These are some of the lessons it teaches:

- The ends (grades, GPA, diploma, etc.) justify the means
- You don't get caught
- "Nobody ever told me" is a convincing justification
- Honesty is a concept unrelated to your actions

It is *not* teaching them to think for themselves, to weigh arguments, to construct a satisfying synthesis. They'll never write as well as those people whose words they steal, because they haven't practiced. The system doesn't teach them knowledge, let alone wisdom. And knowledge is only part of wisdom. So is honesty.

## Crime and Punishment

One of the most important days of my life was the one on which I got caught cheating on a geometry quiz in junior high school. I resolved that I would never do it again; it was too muddling and painful for my spirit. The teacher who held me accountable accomplished something fundamental in my life. If the system, in its current state, wins, my students will not benefit from that same service.

## QUADRANT III CLASSROOM CULTURE: MACRO INSIDER APPROACHES TO ETHICS AND RECOMMENDATION FOR CULTURE CHANGE VIA STORY

### by Grace Ann Rosile

This is my epic story of cheating. I want to begin my epic story with the untold story of honest students. My ultimate goal is to shift our classrooms and our culture from the dominant oversimplified tragic story of cheating to a new epic story that leads to an academic culture of integrity. Center-stage is the majority of silent "honest" students whose "innocent bystander" attitude permits cheating to flourish. Co-starring are the faculty who do not seem to be aware of cheating—or are they?

### Key Case Example

Here is the key case example: When I discovered widespread (9 out of 44 seniors) cheating in my class 2 years ago, I realized that from the students' perspective I was likely to be cast as the villain of this story. An even worse prospect was that my students would be cast as the villains. Neither option was appealing to me. I wanted to be a hero to my students, and I wanted them to be winners, not losers. So after I got over the initial "why me?" stage, I asked myself, "How can I change this story? Can I make a new story where everyone can be a hero?" I recognized the old storyline: students are constantly trying to cheat and faculty are constantly trying to catch them. But what else was going on? What were the untold stories, the marginalized voices? If nine students out of 44 were cheating, at least nine more had to know something about what was going on. What was the story of these "innocent bystanders"?

In my research on narrative approaches to organizational studies, I had adapted an approach to personal and organizational change called "restorying." Could I restory my situation? I decided to try.

## Out of the Closet

My process involved people telling their stories, both the students in that fateful class and my faculty colleagues. I discovered that cheating seemed to be a taboo topic. Since beginning my teaching career over 25 years ago, no students had ever initiated a discussion with me about cheating, and neither had any colleagues. But during and after my infamous situation 2 years ago, I discovered that when I mentioned cheating in a conversation, virtually every colleague had at least one cheating story they were eager to tell. It was like opening floodgates of pent-up outrage, helplessness, and pain. These reactions convinced me there was much beneath the surface and a researchable topic here.

## Expand the Cast of Characters

My first step was to move beyond the tragic two-character story of the professor who fails the bad student for cheating. I expanded the story to include everyone in the class. Some must have known what was going on. Some may have purposely looked the other way. I gathered the stories of everyone in the class.

Moving from the tragic crime-and-punishment story to the epic complicity story of cheating, we broaden the focus to multiple plots and a broader cast of characters. This shift brings out the hidden, forgotten, overlooked, and untold stories.

By publishing student comments in class and anonymously, I recognize students' views and bring them into the open in the class. This honors their perspective and also serves to offset the power of those cheaters who claim that everyone cheats and that it is accepted. Looking at student's actual anonymous comments removes credibility from claims like "everyone does it" and "no one cares" and reveals untold stories.

## Deconstructing the Cheating Story

Deconstructing a story (Boje & Dennehy, 1993; Boje, 2001) means to take it apart to reveal its construction. The construction of any story involves us choosing some aspects of experience to include in the "dominant" story and some to exclude. We ask questions to discover what has been left out in the construction of a particular dominant story. We can question the parts as well as the whole.

Stories are not static. They are constantly shifting, falling apart, incorporating new pieces while excluding others: they are constantly deconstructing and being constructed. Re-storying works with these ongoing processes to shape a new story. White and Epston (1990), the founders of narrative therapy discussed in Chapter 5, believe that understanding deconstruction and deconstructing the dominant story is necessary for more effectively changing that dominant story. But before we get to changing (restorying) the problem, this taking-apart (deconstruction) process helps us to better understand the problem-story. Boje and Dennehy (1993, p. 340; Boje, 2001) suggest seven methods of deconstruction, plus an eighth step that is a culmination of the previous seven:

1. Duality search
2. Reinterpret
3. Rebel voices
4. Other side of the story
5. Deny the plot
6. Find the exception
7. State what is between the lines
8. Resituate

Applying these methods of deconstruction to some pieces of the cheating story might yield the following:

1. **Duality search.** There are several "dualisms" within the cheating story. Dualisms are black–white type polar opposites, with the opposites either stated explicitly or implied. Furthermore, one of the opposites usually is preferred over the other. Most often the preferred member of the pair is the first one that is mentioned, as in "male–female" connoting a preference for males, whereas if we commonly said "female–male" this would indicate preferred status for females. In the cheating story, cheating vsersus honesty is the first obvious dualism. Also, dualisms implied in this story are the teacher–student dualism, fair–unfair, knowledge–ignorance, right–wrong, honest–dishonest, and many more.

   Another very powerful dualism in the cheating story is success–failure. According to David Callahan (2004), the gap between rich and poor is widening, and the resulting winner-take-all approach fuels the trend to increased cheating in all aspects of society.

Finally, a very important dualism in this context is cheaters and non-cheaters. The dominant story says the cheating problem is about students who cheat, not about students who are honest. However, the willful blindness or implicit condoning of honest students who could or should be aware of cheating makes the honest student complicit in the problem. Without the silence of the "innocent bystander," much cheating would not be possible.

2. **Reinterpret.** The dominant story implies that faculty valiantly oppose the overwhelming trend of students cheating. The "reinterpret" strategy might yield a story about cynical burned-out faculty who really do not want to be bothered to exert more effort to police cheating. It is not their job, they are overworked as it is, and students hate them for any efforts in that direction. Another reinterpretation is that in this age of litigation, faculty may feel so harassed by the prospect of students with attorneys that prosecuting cheating becomes self-destructive. (This is not so far-fetched, as I lost an appeal to a student who had an attorney. This episode is described in another chapter.)

3. **Rebel Voices.** One of my students wrote: "Corporations cheat and steal from people all the time." So "rebel voices" challenge the dominant story that it is only students who cheat. Corporate crime was not even considered crime until fairly recently (early 1900s, *Wall Street Journal*) when the term "white-collar crime" was coined to refer to the kind of cheating occurring in corporations. Previously it seems corporations did whatever they could get away with doing: lying to customers, making false promises, etc.

4. **Other Side of the Story.** The dominant story says we cheer for the teachers in white hats; they are heroes and the cheating students are the villains. (Note that hero–villain is also a dualism.) The strategy of viewing "the other side of the story" might suggest we cheer for the cheaters. This side of the story might depict the cheaters as the down-trodden of society who have little chance of ever improving their socioeconomic status except through cheating—at least it appears that way to them. Many years ago, a government decided that Nelson Mandela was a criminal and put him in prison. In the "other side of the story" we would say Nelson Mandela was not a criminal but a hero fighting injustice. The latter has become the dominant story worldwide for many years now.

5. **Deny the Plot.** The dominant story says, "No one made them cheat; no one held a gun to their heads." Denying the plot says maybe they were forced to cheat. Maybe some people feel so disenfranchised, with no money and no education, they may feel cheating is the only way to get ahead.

The dominant story says teachers are honest, it is the students who are cheaters. Therefore, "It is OK to plant false answers (create a "sting") to catch cheaters." This argument suggests it is OK to deceive in order to catch deceivers. Denying this plot might question the "sting" as an end-justifies-the means argument. Is deception different when practiced by teacher rather than student? Or is the sting a "white lie" that does not hurt the innocent, only those who are dishonest themselves?

The dominant story says students cheat and teachers catch them. Reversing the plot says teachers cheat and students know about this too. It does appear that unethical practices by faculty have an impact on the moral views of students. Certainly the most clear example of this is with graduate faculty who might steal graduate students' ideas or writings. Students who see this surely must be affected.

6. **Find the Exception.**    The exception to the dominant story line may be an untold story, like the majority of students who conduct their daily work with integrity. Even one exception, like the student who asked me to take his name off of the ethics term paper because he had not worked on it, offers an alternative storyline. It is evidence that a more desirable outcome is possible.

7. **State What is Between the Lines.**    The dominant story says the classroom is not the "real world," that the two contexts are different. However, "between the lines" we see that students' academic preparation (or lack of it) will have "real-world" impacts with subsequent role performance of the graduate. Is cheating in the classroom predictive of cheating in the boardroom?

The nature of the connection between classroom and "real-world" misconduct is especially interesting after Enron and other spectacular corporate scandals. The *Wall Street Journal* created a special column called "Executives on Trial." Most of the infamous executives are graduates of some of the best business schools in the nation. Is their scandalous behavior attributable to their B-school educations? As I wrote in 2004:

> This has been hotly debated in the Academy of Management. Fiery email exchanges and heated discussions have occurred since the summer of 2002, continuing in meetings and in print (see Chronicle of Higher Education, Fall 2002; and Management Communication Quarterly special issue on "Corporate Meltdown" 17(1), 2003). Are we Dr. Frankensteins, or are we merely impotent, or even worse, irrelevant? (Rosile, 2004)

8. **Resituate.**    The culmination of the previous steps is a story that can be resituated from a tragic story with few voices and characters and

only one beginning–middle–end-type plot to an epic constellation of stories and counterstories.

In summary, the dominant story about this issue of academic dishonesty will tend to be a narrowly focused "tragic" story of individual students cheating in classrooms and sometimes being caught and punished. Deconstructing that story reveals many hidden counterstories and a more "epic" or broader systemic type story of cheating. This epic story includes the complicity of silent bystanders, the pressure from funding sources, and even the nature of our job market and economic system. This broader epic story is reflected in the four-quadrant model of cheating (see Table 17.1).

## QUADRANT IV COMPLETE SYSTEMIC CORRUPTION: MACRO OUTSIDER APPROACHES TO ETHICS AND RECOMMENDATION OF LIBERATORY PEDAGOGY CHEATING FACULTY: AN ETHICAL RESPONSE TO SYSTEMIC DECEIT

### by Stephen DeGiulio

The global, corporate academy claims the noble pursuit of "Truth," but functions to impose a distorted master narrative favorable to the interests of small elites who wield actual power and ownership. From this critical point of view, ethical conduct, whether of students, faculty, administrators, or funders (corporate, governmental and "personal") must be judged by how well it enables the autonomous pursuit of truth, by individuals, within this oppressive professional and cultural environment. This lowercase, but higher and pluralistic truth must necessarily be counterhegemonic and liberatory, and to approach it we need to question the concepts that sustain hegemony and consult models from both inside and outside the globalized Western tradition.

Works of scholarship and art and the work of instruction are marketed and assigned monetary and system dependent status value—that is why they are signed by their authors. But can scholars, teachers, and artists (henceforth "scholars") be directly judged and rewarded by the value others derive from their work, unmediated by oppressive institutions and financial markets geared toward other ends? The pressure to fake the work and make it fit market demand is obvious; the demand of the system for fake work, less so; and the hostility of institutionalized instruction toward learners and scholars well occulted. The monetary and status rewards offered do not begin to compensate for the loss of self that accompanies false work, and the impoverished, stressed, and depressed lives that result.

Difficult as it may be, when scholar or teacher steps out of the hegemonic culture industry (Horkheimer & Adorno, 1944, 2002) to behave ethically
and responsibly, she will elicit respect and inspire learners to also behave
ethically and responsibly—as corporate managers and leaders, if that is
what they are learning to become. Of course, one must also become skillful
at maintaining a low profile and avoid becoming a target for those invested
in maintaining a corrupt system.

Marx and later critical theorists have accounted for most of the facts of
modern corporate hegemony, from control of the physical means of production to the psychological and spiritual terror that prevents individuals
from believing their own senses, and cows them into accepting a reality substitute that scholars labor to elaborate and polish, along with entertainers,
athletes, journalists, businesspeople, and politicians. Outside the global hegemony, however, people have developed many technologies for establishing autonomous habits of reality-based consciousness—always in the face of
the "culture industry" of particular times and places.

The Frankfurt School thinkers lived the horror of the violent implo-
sion of western colonial expansion when it literally ran out of new places
to feed upon and lay waste. It seemed at that historical moment as if the
colonial powers might destroy one another. However new the scale was,
though—and the nuclear weapons that were so eagerly deployed in the
final orgy of killing were truly to planetary scale, as was the Holocaust—the
phenomena of hegemony is ancient. Unfortunately, what arose out of the
firestorms, the mushroom clouds, and the gas chambers was a systemicity
tighter than before, an armored culture industry that conditions whole
populations from birth through a wide variety of means, including adulter-
ated food and invasive pharmacology; police bullets and judicial sentences;
dehumanizing work and schooling; and deep-seated gender, class, racial,
ethnic, and lifestyle biases—ensuring that little opposition emerges. The
relatively privileged become workers and service providers—the "slaves" of
classical Marxism—obedient and subservient voters, soldiers, and citizens.
The millions who cannot, or will not, be well exploited are simply discard-
ed in the barrios and ghettos; the secret Gulags and acknowledged prisons;
and the refugee camps that are not marked on any maps (Bauman, 2004).
Today, with literally no place to escape to, ethics that allow one to develop
the extraordinary inner resources needed to counter hegemony are not
a luxury, they are necessary on a scale that gives existing educational institutions a life and death importance based, precisely, on the degree of
genuine academic honesty that can be created and sustained. Institutions,
of course, are not necessarily the best places for learning, as Illich (1970,
1999) suggests in "Deschooling Society."

## Scholarship as a Medium of Growth

Discourses on deconstruction, multitextuality, and postmodernism in general are gestures of a civilization in crisis that suggest authorship as intellectual private property may not be a tenable concept, while physical evidence suggests that private real property and economic growth may not be tenable concepts either. The global west's suppression of creative activity of all kinds, and its hermetic denial of value outside itself, effectively stifle the emergence of viable alternative ideas from inside, or their adoption from outside—ideas like shared authorship and property, sustainable industry and agriculture. Facilitating the emergence of fruitful points of view, useful analyses and deep insight is the ethical work of scholars, and refusing to train (and be trained) for obedience and conformity is an ethical subversion of the unjust corporate university (Postman & Weingartner, 1969; Jacoby, 1987).

Edward Said's (1978) foundational analysis of the cooption of the nonwest has not barred orientalist bias from its role of blinding corporate scholarship from seeing beyond its own reflection any more than Mohandas Karamchand Gandhi, Martin Luther King, and Nelson Mandela's campaigns for social justice have put a dent in white supremacy (Bessis, 2001); or Noam Chomsky's (1959) intellectual demolishment of behaviorism has shamed managers from using behaviorist techniques for exploiting both workers and markets—they just call it something else. The erasure from western history of the long story of the west's adoption of ideas and technology from outside is indirect proof of the poverty of what is genuinely western in western culture (Clarke, 1997); and this accompanies the erasure of the incalculable atrocities and multiple genocides of colonial violence. This profoundly false self-representation helps kill the natural urge for reflection—the root of respect for the otherness of the other—and replaces it with widespread obsession with horror, violence, and perversion. The inner life cannot be outlawed, but it can be quite effectively suppressed through psychological mechanisms like self-hatred, formed in narcissistic family and social structures (Lasch, 1979) and aggressive mental colonization by invasive media. And when, in addition, the body is poorly rested and nourished, but overfed, overmedicated, and unfit, it's no wonder that so few adults successfully resist hegemony.

Let us take the development of a rich, reality-based inner life to be the ethical purpose of research, and fomenting this development to be the ethical purpose of teaching. Beyond predatory corporatism lie ethics we can use to become fully responsible cultural workers. We remain scholars because, once or twice, we have been in a lecture hall or seminar room where the magic was transformative—and we need to pass that on like we need to breathe. This is the ethics that will heal the corporate academy, and the corporate culture. Rather than create fearful, petty, private selves—trademarked, registered, licensed, and necessarily dishonest—we want to be answerable *as* the world, fearless, free, and rich in spirit.

So what can be ethically wrong with signing an academic book or a work of art? Of course we are not saying this *is* wrong—the utility of sharing one's work while taking responsibility for it is clear—we are trying to imagine alternate cultural spaces from which profitably to view our predicament. I will briefly sketch an experience with scholarly/artistic documents whose authors did not feel the need to attach themselves to their work:

> Going through a sculpture exhibit of less than life-size Buddha heads in New Delhi's National Gallery of Art, my mind gradually stopped generating thoughts as I looked at dozens of faces, one after another. Time withered away along with my thoughts. I became aware of form, independent of the various materials, though what met my eyes was an infinite variety of arbitrary surface patterns in dull grays, browns, and greens, patinated through centuries of weather, the breaths of other viewers—in settings I could hardly imagine. As I sank into the subtle expressions, the variously set jaws, held lips, directed eyes, I felt the inner space I inhabited growing, as though the world to which the Buddha pointed was directly accessible simply by looking, simply by existing.
>
> I left nothing behind in those rooms, and carried nothing forward; I was empty in a comfortable, wonderful way, without expectation or desire to see anything else, without thought or desire to think. A few steps then brought me to the entrance of another gallery, and, as I turned to enter, I found my-self face to face with a large Tibetan Tanka (splendid curatorial move!). The effect was like a silent explosion. I was again "with" exactly what I had been with in the previous gallery, but the form was completely different—here the colors were brilliant, the lines sharp, and the simple familiarity of the human face was replaced by an incredible intricacy of images and symbols. It was almost too much; I staggered out of the museum, hardly looking at anything else, and slowly rejoined my life.

These works of scholarship and art were not signed, and, in a western sense, they were not originally marketed or owned either. The objects themselves are encoded knowledge used in a coherent cultural community for the education of individuals, just like scholarly writings, and the master scholars/artists enjoyed a respected status and a good living from their work, which included passing their specialized maker's knowledge on to the next generation of makers in a personal process beyond the content of the scholarly works that they produced. The parallel is strong. The fact that these artifacts survived the living community that produced them, and continue to be powerful, readable documents across huge cultural, geophysical, and temporal distances tells us that our quest to reach some peaceful, cooperative understanding of the otherness of others is feasible.

The fact that the content of these particular works is precisely the development of the inner life that, as scholars, we seek to foster suggests that ethical conduct in our profession, however difficult, may be possible under any circumstances.

It is the one-to-one relationship between teacher and learner that is most prominent in nonwestern educational practice generally, and this has been all but eliminated in today's academy. Instead of the intimacy and efficiency of one-to-one teaching/learning relationships, we socialize and train in large cohorts. Pressure on teaching faculty to promote themselves is constant and only one aspect of a professional socialization process that privileges the superficial over the meaningful, training faculty to pass minimally trained students into the "world of work" after filtering out the non-compliant. Another aspect of this professional socialization process is the pressure to teach a corporate-friendly curriculum, if not always in terms of content, then in terms of an unspoken curriculum of power relations (Apple, 2004). The first ethical requirement of a teacher, we think, is to respect the learners by presenting them a picture of the whole subject in context— including the institutional and historical matrix in which they find themselves. This implies teaching history, economics, science, etc., that has been erased from the textbooks. Thus the first principle of valid academic ethics is conscientization of self and one's learners and readers–so they, in Freire's celebrated phrase, (1970, 1995) "learn to read the world." The second is to survive while doing the first.

Without the corporate imperative for scholars to compete and commodify for the monopolistic academic market, there would be no need to excessively publish or even to attach one's name to scholarly work. Better to launch it, observe how well it floats on its own merits, and accept as obvious that most of what we create is only rearranged and passed on from our sources and our teachers. Just imagine the human energy that would be released if scholars were free to concentrate on their work, releasing only what is likely to be useful to others, instead of dressing up their false starts and failed projects in peer-juried drag and announcing them as serious contenders!

Out of what has gone before them, scholars create transitional knowledge, and, once grounded themselves, secure the profession by initiating a new generation of practitioners. They sleep well because they play a modest role in the healthy evolution of a community that can extend widely in space and time. This ideal attracts many to the academy. The reality they meet is otherwise. They teach in programs that limit their contact with learners to a span too short for habits of thinking and feeling to begin to shift, let alone for new voices to emerge. During this time teaching faculty are kept so busy they cannot even meet most of these "learners," who are left to their own devices, which means their class, gender, and ethnic status can assume the weight of life sentences. Drained by compulsory participation in ritualized committee meetings and conferences, and weighted down by corporate curriculum, faculty soon lose whatever vision they may have had of a community of learning and settle into the role of clerks, perhaps with pharmaceutical help to dull the conscience, and the distractions of the classy films, books, and hobbies they can afford.

This is accepted due to fears and self-hatred that are deeply seated by the time a typical contemporary child reaches adolescence. Corporate hostility to children and their caretakers takes the form of undercutting any form of security that might give children a chance to reflect peacefully on the world and express themselves creatively (Prasad, 2005). Children are largely confined to indoor environments and limited to contact with their age-group peers, their unstable assortment of parents are themselves ragged and stressed, and the schools are deadly boring and unsafe.

Corporate marketing to children is key to understanding the death grip the culture industry has on global professional and working classes (Steinberg & Kincheloe, 1997). With schools little more than holding pens, the family in subnuclear confusion, and organized religion largely marginalized, monopoly marketing of commodified substitutes for what children need has free reign: intimacy with real people is not available, so cartoons, tv, and films (Giroux, 1997) fill in; fun is not available cooped up inside, so we have theme parks and virtual adventures; affection is absent so the products are all cute, bright, soft, furry, smooth, flexible . . .; physical activity is restricted, except for competitive team sports; diet lacks nutrition and drugs are used to control newly medicalized behaviors. Then in preadolescence alcohol and illegal drug use begins, and the sexist norms of the criminal justice system leave millions of young girls abandoned with infants. The details change with social class, but not the essentials. The immediate purpose of this marketing may well be profit, but the long-range result is that children have little direct experience with unmediated, ordinary experience of the world upon which to build ideas about reality, and thus make ideal corporate subjects, easy to warehouse and sort into available job slots, including that of scholar.

It is not surprising that university students often cut corners and turn in substitutes for original work—that is what they have been taught to value, under conditions that are abusive. What *is* surprising is that so many youth are aware of, if not articulate about, how they have been cheated. Cynically, many do not even bother cheating because they know that grades count for little, and that graded tests and projects are of little use in learning anyway, in a pedagogical situation where they are denied live interaction with a teacher and given a commodified substitute—the teaching academic. The astonishing thing about the next generation—battered and dazed, they still retain the spirit to win autonomy in spite of their "education"—but few will succeed without help.

We remain scholars because, once or twice, we have been in a lecture hall or seminar room where the magic was transformative—and we need to pass that on like we need to breathe. This is the ethics that will heal the corporate academy, and the corporate culture. Rather than create fearful, petty, private selves—trademarked, registered, licenced, and necessarily dishonest—we want to be answerable *as* the world, fearless, free, and rich in spirit.

\* \* \* \* \*

In conclusion, we have moved from the narrowly focused tragic story of the cheating student caught by the honest faculty member, to the epic story of cheating.

From the above analysis, it is clear that the causes of cheating go far beyond personal flaws. Each of these four root cause narratives suggests the direction of potential responses to the cheating problem. Each of the four coauthors addresses a response associated with one quadrant. Problems rooted in all four narrative viewpoints must be addressed before we can create a happier ending to this story of cheating.

**TABLE 17.2  Recommendations**

|  | Insider/Emic | Outsider/Etic |
| --- | --- | --- |
| Micro | I. Crime and Punishment *"Applied Ethics"* | II. Collusion and Complicity *"Reward System Reform"* |
| Macro | III. Classroom Culture *"Culture Change Via Story"* | IV. Complete Corruption *"Liberatory Pedagogy"* |

*Source:* From Rosile (2004).

## NOTES

1. Parts of this discussion are taken from Rosile (2004).
2. This section draws in part from Mathiasen et al. (1998), chaps. 1–3.
3. Langford, David P., Langford Quality and Learning videoconference, November 3 & 10, 1994. Mississippi State University, PBS Adult Learning, and Langford International.
4. Why go through that whole process if I was going to support the appeal? Because that's the procedure we have in place and there are at least three reasons to follow procedure: to ensure consistency, to protect myself, and to expose faulty procedures. If nobody follows a procedure, nobody knows if it's a good or bad one.

# REFERENCES

Anderson, J. A. (2003). Ethics in business and teaching. *Management Communication Quarterly, 17*(1), 155–164.

Boje, D. M., & Rosile, G. A. (2003). Life imitates art: Enron's epic and tragic narration. *Management Communication Quarterly, 17*(1), 85–125.

Boje, D. M. (2001). *Narrative methods for organizational and communication research.* London: Sage.

Boje, D. M., & Dennehy, R. F. (1993). *Managing in the postmodern world: America's revolution against exploitation.* Dubuque, IA: Kendall-Hunt.

Callahan, D. (2004). *The cheating culture: Why more Americans are doing wrong to get ahead.* Orlando, Fl: Harcourt.

Freire, P. (1970). *Pedagogy of the oppressed* (M. B. Ramos, Trans.). New York: Seabury.

Freire, P. (1995). *Pedagogy of hope.* New York: Continuum.

International Labor Organization. (2003, March). *Employment and social policy in respect of export processing zones (EPZs).* International Labor Office, Committee on Employment and Social Policy.

Kamel, R., & Hoffman, A. (1999). *The Maquiladora reader.* American Friends Service Committee.

Mathiasen, C. (Ed.). (1998). *The sweatshop quandary.* Washington, DC: Investor Responsibility.

McCabe, D. L. (2005). Presentation at the Center for Academic Integrity's annual conference, Oct 20–22, 2005, at Virginia Tech, Blacksburg, VA.

McCabe, D. L., & Trevino, L. K. (1995). Cheating among business students: A challenge for business leaders and educators. *Journal of Management Education, 19*(2),205–218.

McNeil, L. (2000). *Contradictions of school reform: Educational costs of standardized testing.* New York: Routledge.

Miner, J. B. (2003). The rated importance, scientific validity, and practical usefulness of organizational behavior theories: A quantitative review. *Academy of Management Learning and Education, 2*(3), 250–269.

Pfeffer, J., & Fong, C. T. (2002). The end of business schools?: Less success than meets the eye. *Academy of Management Learning and Education, 1*(1), 78–95.

Ritzer, G. (2000). *McDonaldization of society: New century edition.* Thousand Oaks, CA: Pine Forge Press/Sage.

Rosile, G. A., & Boje, D. M. (2000, November). Enron whodunit?: Storytelling and plots. *Ephemera.*

Rosile, G. A. (2004). McCheating: Narrative analysis of root causes. In C. Gardner & A. Alkhafaji (Eds.), *Business Research Yearbook, XI.*

Restorying and the Case of the Sci Fi Organization. (1998, August). In "Organizational Storytelling II: Narrativity and the Case of a High Tech Organizational Consultation" sponsored by ODC, MED, and RM divisions at the Academy of Management, San Diego, CA.

Stablein, R. (2003). Teaching business ethics or teaching business ethically? *Management Communication Quarterly, 17*(1), 151–154.

Yballe, L., & O'Connor, D. (2000). Appreciative pedagogy: Constructing positive models for learning. *JME, 24*(4), 474–483.

White, M., & Epston, D. (1990). *Narrative means to therapeutic ends.* New York: W.W. Norton.

CHAPTER 18

# ENVIRONMENTAL ETHICS AND BUSINESS

## Toward a Habermasian Perspective

**Robert P. Gephart, Jr.**
**Michael Kulicki**

How should we live, work, and manage organizations in an age where decades of wealth accumulation have resulted in environmental risks and disasters (Beck, 1992)? It has long been widely accepted that "the crisis of environmental sustainability is no longer a matter of speculation" (Purser, 1994, p. 4) and that organizations are a key factor in the creation of environmental risks and disasters (Gephart, 1984). Thus it is imperative for managers and citizens to develop a normative framework for business management that addresses environmental issues and that limits the impacts that organizations have on the environment.

In this chapter, we have two broad purposes. First, we introduce the reader to theoretical debates within the field of environmental ethics and explore how these debates have influenced scholars of business management. Second, we explore the relationship between Habermasian critical theory and environmental ethics, and consider whether Habermas's critical

*Critical Theory Ethics for Business and Public Administration,* pages 373–393
Copyright © 2008 by Information Age Publishing
All rights of reproduction in any form reserved.

theory (in particular, his theory of communicative action) could provide a viable normative approach for thinking about and advocating environmental concerns. Our overall goal in this chapter, then, is to make manifest the enormous complexity of the issues surrounding debates over environmental policy and explore how Habermas may be useful for articulating and defending environmental values. But while we find Habermas's critical theory attractive in many respects, we cannot hope to provide in this space a sufficient defense of it. Rather, in opening up the issues involved, we hope to inspire further thinking on these matters with the aim of working toward their future clarification.

It requires several steps or stages to achieve our purposes in this chapter. First, we briefly review philosophical literature on environmental ethics, as well as the business literature on environmental ethics, to uncover the main approaches to environmental ethics that have been formulated, and to highlight why Habermas's critical theory may be worth considering when it comes to these issues. Briefly put, we find that Habermas's critical theory may provide a way of avoiding the epistemological and ontological impasses that (as we describe below) tend to arise within many theories of environmental ethics, and that tend to make them problematic for advocating environmental concerns. Moreover, while Habermas's critical theory has points in common with a lot of environmental philosophy (especially on issues related to the need for more participative and democratic decision making, and a need for structural/political change in order for environmental concerns to get a fair hearing), it attempts to articulate these concerns from a "post-metaphysical" basis, while accepting the wide plurality of views on ethical matters that are at the heart of liberal democracy. For these reasons, then, we find Habermas's theory attractive.

However, Habermas's theory has opened up considerable debate among environmental philosophers over the issue of whether it could be compatible with environmental concerns. Thus, we want to explore this debate and suggest that it is not evident that there is any fatal problem within Habermas's theory when it comes to defending the value of the natural world around us. While there may be other theoretical weaknesses with Habermas's theory (see, e.g., Benhabib & Dallmayr, 1990), the articulation of environmental concerns from within the theory is not one of these. Rather, given the diversity and the importance of the values at stake (i.e., not only including the value of the natural world, but also, e.g., the need for human beings to transform the natural world to some degree in order to live), we suggest that Habermas's theory is helpful in thinking about the hard questions about the environment that citizens, stakeholders, and business managers must grapple with everyday. Thus, as we face dwindling natural resources and difficult environment challenges ahead, we believe Habermas's critical theory could be especially relevant to business and for thinking about environmental limits to the business environment.

## ENVIRONMENTAL ETHICS: THE VIEW FROM PHILOSOPHY

Environmental ethics has developed as a response to what is regarded by environmental philosophers as a serious deficiency to be found within traditional ethical theory. Traditional ethical theories—such as virtue ethics, utilitarianism, and deontological (rights-based) theories—have been viewed as being anthropocentric; that is, these theories at bottom adopt a stance "that limits moral standing to human beings, confines the scope of morality and moral concerns to human interests, and regards nothing but human well-being as valuable intrinsically" (Attfield, 2003, p. 188). For example, virtue ethics has traditionally been concerned with delineating those virtues of character that could be seen to be the mark of a good or 'virtuous' human being, while having little to say about the proper relationship between human beings and the rest of nature, or taking for granted the right of human beings to enjoy dominion over the rest of nature. Furthermore, this neglect of the rest of nature can also be found within traditional deontological theories of ethics (which have focused on describing the rights and duties human beings owe to one another) as well as traditional versions of utilitarianism (which have mainly focused on attempting to determine whether the consequences of any policy are beneficial or detrimental as far as they impact other human beings).

Moreover, it is precisely this anthropocentric outlook within traditional ethical theory that is regarded as problematic by many environmental philosophers because it is viewed as legitimating environmental exploitation and contributing to the present environmental crisis. After all, if human well-being is the only thing in the world with any intrinsic value, why should we be concerned about the welfare of other species or the natural environment, except perhaps for instrumental reasons of our own (e.g., aesthetic reasons, mental health reasons, etc.)? Why should we be concerned about environmental limits to economic growth except for those minimally necessary for preserving and/or enhancing human well-being? Why should we not view the rest of nature as a mere "resource" to be used in whatever way we deem fit, regardless of the effects on other species?

Broadly speaking, environmental philosophers have adopted one of two general approaches to integrating environmental concerns within an ethical framework. First, many philosophers have attempted to amend traditional ethical theory in such a way as to better account for environmental values. For example, Peter Singer (2002) is well known within philosophy for his variety of utilitarianism which seeks to expand the zone of moral concern to include nonhuman but sentient beings. On the other hand, Tom Regan (2004) is an example of a philosopher who attempts to defend the interests of sentient animals on the basis of a deontological (rights-based) theory. Meanwhile, Thomas Hill (1983) attempts to show that, when the virtue of a human being is rightly understood, it would be the mark of a virtuous human being to integrate concern for environmental welfare into one's life.

While these philosophers do indeed have radical differences among themselves (corresponding to the radical differences in approach found in utilitarianism, deontology, and virtue ethics), they nonetheless share an important commonality: They believe that traditional ethical theory as such is not "fatally flawed" and that it is possible to amend it in order to take into account environmental values. However, another very broad group of philosophers rejects this view. They argue that anthropocentrism runs too deep within traditional ethical theory and that it thus must be rejected in order to address environmental concerns. This broad group of philosophers has attempted to establish the grounds for a radically new ecocentric ethical theory, one that would not categorically privilege human desires and interests over the well-being of the natural environment, but that would attempt instead to establish appropriate limits to human interests when they conflict with the well-being of other aspects of the environment.

Of course, there are a number of widely differing views to be found among this diverse group of ecocentric philosophers, and we can do no more here than describe them in passing. Curry (2006) notes several popular perspectives on the environment that embrace ecocentric principles, including the land ethic of Aldo Leopold, Gaia theory (which assumes the earth is like a living organism), deep ecology, deep green theory, left biocentrism, the Earth Manifesto, and ecofeminism. We will touch upon two of these below—deep ecology and left biocentrism—both in order to provide a sense of the themes animating these theorists, and because we will return to some of these themes later on in our discussion of Habermas.

Deep ecology is based on eight principles that emphasize the intrinsic value of nonhuman species. According to this view, there is thought to be a need to preserve species richness and diversity; to limit interference with the nonhuman world; to decrease the population; to change social policies and ideologies so as to encourage quality of life; and to urge people with ecocentric views to express these views and change society. Somewhat relatedly, left biocentrism attempts to work within deep ecology, and it focuses on issues related to social justice and political radicalism. It thus combines deep ecology with a left-of-center political view that is anti-industrial and anti-capitalist, opposing both economic growth and consumerism. It assumes that nature, not labor, is the source of all wealth. And it assumes that both capitalism and traditional theories of socialism are anthropocentric, although it views socialism as the more humane of the alternatives. Furthermore, it assumes that environmental problems are structural and systemic, not isolated or unconnected. According to this view, a primary goal is the preservation of biotic systems, as left biocentrism recognizes that the destruction of biotic systems leads to uneven impacts on humans, with the less-privileged potentially bearing higher costs or impacts than the wealthy. Thus a sustainable society requires social and political structures that encourage good environmental practices and that demarcate environmental limits to growth. Again, what differentiates this group of environmental philosophers is their concern with articulating an entirely new ethical vision or framework for addressing environmental concerns, rather than patching up any traditional ethical theory.

The basic differences among environmental philosophers can also be seen by conceiving of their ethical views as lying along a spectrum running from anthropocentrism (or light green environmental ethics) to ecocentrism (or dark green environmental ethics) (Curry, 2006). Where any theory lies on this spectrum will depend on what the theory regards as having intrinsic value. Thus a theorist who argues that human well-being is the only thing of intrinsic importance and that environmental policies should be directed toward human fulfillment or well-being may be regarded as promoting a "light green" environmental ethics. This sort of theorist may defend any number of environmental policies (e.g., green spaces in cities, pollution restrictions, etc.) on the grounds that they are necessary to promote human well-being. However, as we move along the spectrum and get into darker green terrain, the area of moral concern expands, and a larger number of interests are regarded as having intrinsic value. Thus at the other extreme of the spectrum, ecocentric theorists would argue that entire ecosystems (and not merely just certain particular members of ecosystems) have intrinsic value and that the aim of environmental policy should be to maintain the integrity of ecosystems as a whole. Meanwhile, in the middle of the spectrum, would lie the views of those theorists who regard the area of moral concern to extend farther than just human beings, but not as far as to include entire ecosystems as such. The theories of those concerned with animal welfare, such as Singer's utilitarianism and Regan's animal rights theory would fall here and could thus be appropriately described as "mid-green" (or "biocentric") environmental ethics. Again, what determines where a given view would lie on this spectrum is the breadth of moral concern advocated by the theorist and the corresponding locus of intrinsic value.

## ENVIRONMENTAL ETHICS: THE VIEW FROM THE BUSINESS LITERATURE

The three general views of environmental ethics addressed in the philosophy literature (light green/anthropocentric, mid-green/biocentric, and dark green/ecocentric) are also evident to a considerable extent in the management and organizational literature dealing with environmental management. For example, Judith A. Clair, John Milliman, and Karen S. Whelan (1996) provide an important discussion of the different "ecophilosophies" used in business. As they define the term, ecophilosophies are collectively held values about the natural environment that are related to corporate environmental action. Basically, Clair et al. assert that ecophilosophies influence the environmental management approach taken by companies and this in turn influences organizational performance and effectiveness. Paralleling to a considerable degree the discussion in the philosophy literature, Clair et al. emphasize that an important feature of ecophilosophies is their theory of value of the nonhuman world, and they go on to discuss two different theories of value. The first is the instrumental theory of value reflected in anthropocentrism: the nonhuman world lacks value except where it fulfills instrumental purposes for humans. This view emphasizes wealth and growth as goals for business. The second perspective is the intrinsic theory of value of ecocentrism, which argues that there is inherent value in the natural world. It thus argues it is unethical to exploit, abuse, or degrade aspects of the natural environment that are morally considerable. This view also emphasizes spiritual and psychological growth among people as important objectives for businesses and organizations.

Based on these ideas, the authors develop a model to categorize ecophilosophies of business organizations. The first category is *unrestrained economic growth,* where organizations pursue wealth and growth with few restraints or environmental considerations. This is a strong form of anthropocentrism that assumes the use of natural resources or exploitation of natural resources could continue forever. In addition, this view assumes that technological and scientific advances can remedy any capacity for harm that emerges from organizational actions. Given the limited value assigned to the natural environment, companies that hold this ecophilosophy often deny environmental problems and focus on avoiding regulation. Clair et al. (1996) suggest organizations that reflect this ecophilosophy are likely to have considerable crisis potential and to be low environmental performers, in part because the assumptions of unlimited resources and of technological remedies to technological harms are incorrect. One can argue that unrestrained growth has been a common and traditional ecophilosophy for many businesses and governments. Indeed, this view of the world is still widespread and probably dominant in many business and government organizations.

A second view based in anthropocentrism is *social consciousness* (Clair et al., 1996) that emphasizes the sustainability of a valued environment during economic growth. Thus although the environment is to be used or exploited for human purposes, organizations that reflect this view also assume there are limits to natural resources and to humans' ability to remedy environmental harms. The perspective is socially conscious because the organization is concerned to protect stakeholders from environmentally-based health and safety threats, while the main focus is on sustainable growth. Organizations using this view gear their operations toward meeting or exceeding environmental regulations. However, the perspective is limited because the focus on human use-values is generally accompanied by a limited understanding of the natural environment and absence of comprehensive or coherent environmental visions for the organization. As a result, deeper-level environmental problems are often not addressed. Furthermore, given that the perspective emphasizes economic growth, organizations that hold this view often fail to alter broader social assumptions about growth that are relevant to making a profit. Organizations using a socially conscious perspective are often moderate environmental performers.

The third ecophilosophy is *environmental consciousness* (Clair et al., 1996) that focuses on the sustainability of an inherently valued environment. This view adopts some aspects of an ecocentric orientation by giving inherent value to the environment. Those who hold this view tend to critique traditional anthropocentric assumptions and business practices, regard them as bases for current environmental problems, and believe that destructive environmental practices must cease. Thus, sustainable development is a key focus in this view. There is a strong commitment to environmental programs and adherence to environmental regulations. Indeed, companies taking this view often spearhead stronger or improved regulations and practices. Environmental management is often a part of the core business operations of companies taking this view, which leads to a high level of environmental performance. There are, however, limits to this view. First, this view is not the norm in business; hence companies that take this view may experience limits on competitive advantage that are not experienced by less environmentally conscious firms. Second, environmental programs can be costly, so attention is needed to balance the costs and benefits of environmental programs. Third, it is not clear how an organization can become fully sustainable or minimize environmental problems. Finally, it is not fully clear what an ecocentric ecophilosophy would mean for business practices.

Although the unrestricted growth view has long dominated the business literature, the discussion above suggests that the issue of ecocentric versus anthropocentric business management has become central to the debate on environmental ethics in the organizational literature. Scholars in the field (e.g., Purser, 1994; Purser, Park, & Montuori, 1995; Shrivastava, 1995, 1996; Iyer, 1999; Hanna, 1995; Johnson, 1996; Balakrishnan, Duvall, & Primeaux, 2003) have attempted to distinguish features of ecocentric and anthropocentric management. An important question in the field is whether it is necessary to adopt a new ecocentric management paradigm to be environmentally responsible, and, if not, how traditional management theory could be made more environmentally responsible. This debate within the management literature then parallels to a significant extent the debate within the environmental philosophy literature between those advocating the amendment of traditional ethical theories and those advocating for entirely new ethical frameworks.

For example, Purser et al. (1995) distinguish between two broad management paradigms: the environmental management paradigm and the ecocentric responsibility paradigm. According to the ethical spectrum we have outlined above, the environmental management paradigm would be an example of a lighter green approach to business management (or, in Clair et al.'s [1996] terms, it would be similar to an ecophilosophy of social consciousness.) Thus, according to the advocates for this paradigm, there is nothing fundamentally objectionable about economic growth as such and companies would not necessarily encounter any fundamental obstacles to pursuing environmentally responsible policies within the existing basic framework of a business environment dedicated to the maximization of profit. "Win–win" situations may develop because it will often be the case that the profitable course of action for business will also turn out to be environmentally responsible. And in those cases of deeper conflicts of interest between business operations and the environment, environmental policy should be dedicated toward "sustainable" development, again with the implication that there is nothing objectionable as such to economic growth. According to this view, the environment is a resource that may be appropriately and unproblematically "managed" for the benefit of human well-being.

However, against this view, Purser et al. (1995) defend an alternative ecocentric responsibility paradigm that reflects the themes found in the deeper green ethical theories within the philosophy literature. They propose seven principles of ecocentric organization development: (1) to appreciate the natural environment; (2) to search for environmental health; (3) to encourage environmental self-development; (4) to take an anti-bureaucratic posture and encourage democratization of work; (5) to legitimate the role of citizens and the community as stakeholders in environmental issues; (6) to value diversity, stability, and cooperation; and (7) to use nature as a model for organizational design. They view ecosystem integrity as something intrinsically valuable and as a fundamental limit that business ought to respect. Again, these are themes echoed throughout the deep green philosophy literature.

Similar to Purser et al. (1995), Shrivastava (1995) developed a version of an ecocentric management paradigm that emphasizes the importance of harmony with nature and a move toward business organizations that are nonhierarchical in structure and that make use of participative modes of decision-making and decentralized authority. What these views have in common is the notion that traditional management theory is at bottom too anthropocentric to deal with current environmental problems and that a fundamental ecocentric paradigm shift is therefore required, a view similar to the view in philosophy that a fundamental shift is required away from traditional anthropocentric ethical theories toward theories that take an ecocentric approach. However, just as we can find lighter green environmental philosophers willing to defend traditional approaches to ethical theory, we can find management scholars willing to defend more traditional management paradigms.

For example, Hanna (1995) discusses Shrivastava (1995) and argues that "the traditional managerial paradigm is not so flawed as to need replacement by an ecocentric alternative" (p. 797). He goes on to suggest that, rather than being the core of a new management paradigm, ecocentrism is better regarded as a kind of New Age religion, something far removed from the everyday practical concerns of most people today. Somewhat less polemically, Hanna (1995) asks whether the abstract nature of the "paradigm debate" is really all that helpful for considering how to grapple with the concrete problems facing business managers as well as citizens of liberal democracies. As he asks rhetorically, "Who would define the value of avoiding the risk of a future environmental hazard when that implies altering a starvation risk, or a health risk for a large biological population?" (p. 797). In other words, Hanna raises the question of what we are to do when important values conflict in particular cases (e.g., maintaining environmental integrity versus keeping people from starving), and how we would know when one claim should trump another. As he writes, "what level of environmental disturbance would make it appropriate to close a plant or shut down a business (thereby significantly stressing and placing at risk a human community)?" (p. 797). Thus for Hanna, rather than developing a new ecocentric management paradigm, what is needed is the amendment of traditional paradigms to take into account the value of the environment, for example, through "establishing ownership rights for natural resources and . . . appropriate accounting for resource use" (p. 798).

In a similar vein, Johnson (1996) raises other objections to the operational practicality of ecocentric management paradigms. Endorsing Hanna (1995), Johnson argues that anthropocentrism "can be a strong foundation for the development of an environmental conscience" (p. 610) and that if "one elevates the well-being of the entire human species, now and in the future, to the center of moral consideration, it becomes impossible to escape the conclusion that the well-being of humans and the well-being of the ecosystems on which we depend are inextricably linked." Moreover, Johnson echoes the rhetorical questions raised by Hanna and suggests that "[s]pecific questions about the ethical principles and reasoning processes we use to mediate interspecies conflicts (particularly between 'vital interests' of humans and other species) are the tough ones" (p. 610). Business paradigms as such are insufficient for addressing such issues and "the hard work of operationalizing an ethic or a paradigm really begins" (p. 610) through engaging with the sort of hard, practical questions raised above.

## HABERMASIAN CRITICAL THEORY AND PUBLIC DECISION MAKING

Given that business managers and citizens of liberal democracies are often faced with the sort of hard ethical dilemmas (or trade-offs) noted above, trade-offs where gains along one dimension of value (e.g., maintaining the integrity of an ecosystem) come at the expense of another important dimension of value (e.g., preserving the economic well-being of a community), how are we to ensure that collective decisions are made fairly? Our brief survey of the debate about environmental ethics within the management literature has revealed that the debate actually turns on very difficult metaphysical questions, questions that reach to the core of what "nature" is, and the place human beings occupy within it. Thus the debate among management scholars over environmental ethics is in essence philosophical and covers a lot of the same territory as the debate occurring among academic philosophers. For example, in his response to the criticisms made by Hanna (1995), Shrivastava (1996) is eager to defend himself against the charge that an ecocentric management paradigm is tantamount to being a "religion." However, Shrivastava does observe that ecocentrism is "an ontology (assumptions about reality that underlie theories)" (1996: 10). Thus, regardless of whether or not it is fair to characterize ecocentric philosophers as promoting a "religion," they are involved in making strong claims about the nature of nature as well as strong ethical claims about how human beings are to live in the world.

However, it is precisely these kinds of arguments about "the nature of nature" that are so difficult to resolve to everyone's satisfaction. As we have been discussing above, anthropocentrists and ecocentrists disagree radically over such ontological matters, and this disagreement over fundamental premises carries over into disagreements on practical matters. Moreover, this disagreement seems very difficult to resolve theoretically: other trends from within philosophy, including pragmatism and postmodernism, not to mention earlier accounts of logical positivism, have deeply questioned the ability of philosophy as such to provide valid ethical or practical guidance. Yet given such disagreements on fundamentals, how can collective decisions be made on a fair basis?

In our view, the critical theory developed in the work of Jurgen Habermas provides a valuable approach for theorizing about how collective decisions can be made on a fair basis given the fact of radical disagreement on deeper-level ontological premises about nature and human nature. It is a theory of social development and change that seeks to further the Enlightenment goal of improving the condition of human beings by identifying unreasonable and illegitimate constraints on human practices and replacing them with consensual norms based on reason (Whitebook, 1979). Habermas's critical theory begins by accepting the fact of radical disagreement among citizens on ethical matters, but, unlike philosophic attempts to demonstrate the correctness of any given ethical theory by arguing to (or from) controversial ontological first principles, instead attempts to highlight certain general norms implicit in acts of communication among human beings, and to show how these norms could be viewed as establishing the basis of a noncoercive, democratic mode of politics. This project is discussed in Habermas's *Theory of Communicative Action* (1984, 1987), and below we very briefly outline this theory in order to demonstrate what it could mean for environmental ethics and business management.

Habermas's theory examines how communication lies at the heart of social order, and how in order for human beings to use language at all, they must rely upon a particular set of normative presuppositions. These normative presuppositions include: (1) that what each speaker says is intelligible or meaningful; (2) that what each speaker says is true in terms of the propositional content of the statements; (3) that each speaker communicates truthfully and sincerely; and (4) that what each speaker says is rationally justifiable (Eckersley, 1990). For Habermas, communication requires human beings to rely upon these presuppositions. Communication simply would not be possible without the assurance that people are being sincere when they communicate, with an eye to ensuring what they have to say is intelligible and rationally justifiable. And it is from these norms of speech that Habermas derives the notion of a hypothetical "ideal speech situation" that can provide an idealized model of what a noncoercive and democratic politics could look like.

In Habermas's ideal speech situation, human beings deliberate over a common course of practical action by rigidly adhering to the normative presuppositions that ultimately make communication possible. This is to say, within the ideal speech situation "it is assumed that the actors can express their goals truthfully and without reservation, that all pertinent evidence can be brought into play in the discussion, and that the agreement is based on reasoned evidence" (Brulle, 2002, p. 4). It is an attempt to envision a noncoercive situation in which people are free to air their opinions on a common course of action while respecting others' rights to do the same, and while maintaining fidelity to basic norms of nonduplicity and reasonableness. Thus, in doing so, "a mutually agreed upon definition of [a] situation is constructed which describes the relevant states in a situation, places the interaction within the ethical criteria of a specific historical and social context, and ties the individual's personal identity to the interaction" (Habermas, 1984, p. 136). In this way, a course of action can become normative provided that all participants can endorse it in the absence of any explicit or implicit coercion. This idea is at the core of what Habermas refers to as his Discourse Principle, which states: "The only regulations and ways of acting that can claim legitimacy are those to which all who are possibly affected could assent as participants in rational discourses" (Habermas, 1996, p. 458). In other words, Habermas argues that in order for norms to be legitimate, they need to be validated by human beings under noncoercive conditions approximating the ideal speech situation.

But what does this mean for environmental ethics? First, we would like to make the general point that given the quite radical disagreement among environmental philosophers on the level of ontology, we find Habermas's approach to be attractive as it may provide a way to advocate environmental concerns seemingly without relying upon controversial metaphysical principles and while maintaining fidelity to the pluralism that is at the core of life in liberal democracies. Again, Habermas's theory intends to provide a "post-metaphysical" way of thinking about normativity, given that the epistemological and ontological questions that arise from more ambitious "metaphysical" accounts of ethics are so difficult (and perhaps irresolvable) on the level of abstract theory. As we have alluded to above in our discussion of the management literature, it is one thing to say in the abstract that an ecosystem has inherent value; it is another thing entirely to demonstrate this sufficiently in a particular case, especially when the question becomes one of saving an ecosystem at the expense of a human community. These are the kind of dilemmas that present citizens with hard choices—choices involving good versus good, rather than good versus bad. Given the immense complexity of such matters, the value of Habermas's approach comes to light in that it attempts to lay the groundwork for these issues to be debated democratically, under fair conditions, and with adequate attention paid to the numerous particulars involved in the debate over any concrete policy. Again, Habermas's approach takes this pluralism seriously and recognizes the difficulty it poses when it comes to public deliberation on these matters.

We return to this point later in the chapter. However, before we elaborate any further on this issue, we also observe that just as environmental philosophers have criticized traditional ethical theory and management theory for their explicit or implicit anthropocentric biases, Habermas's critical theory has also been criticized by some environmental philosophers on the same grounds. Therefore, it is important to review this "green critique" of Habermas in order to determine whether his theory of communicative action could be truly compatible with ecocentric concerns.

## THE GREEN CRITIQUE
## OF HABERMASIAN CRITICAL THEORY

Habermas's critical theory has addressed the triumph of instrumental reason and the domination of nature within modern society, two important starting points for green or ecocentric theorists (Eckersley, 1990). Hence an important question is, why has critical theory had so little influence on environmental ethics, and on green theory and practice (Eckersley, 1990)? Essentially, Habermasian theory has been subject to an extensive critique by green theorists who argue that it is unnecessarily rigid and anthropocentric, and that Habermas's solution to the environmental crisis is overly instrumentalist (Eckersley, 1990).

This critique was initiated by Whitebook (1979). He argues that Habermas's 'transcendentalism' precludes any reconciliation with nature. According to Whitebook, Habermas has argued that the logic of instrumental reason should govern the relationship between human beings and the external environment, whereas the logic of communicative rationality should govern relationships among human beings. This, however, is an elevation of reason to an apparently transcendental phenomenon. This occurs because Habermas uncovers his categorical frameworks of instrumental and communicative reason by reflecting on the evolution of our species. Reason thus transcends the conditions of its genesis and achieves some autonomy. Furthermore, Habermas denies it is possible to conceptualize nature under categories of communicative rationality. As a result, nature is exclusively an object of domination and can only be known through instrumental reason as an object of technical control.

Whitebook (1979) also argues that the promise of critical theory is limited in terms of addressing environmental crises because Habermas's communicative ethics is thoroughly anthropocentric. Man is assumed to be the sole organism that has a broad communicative capacity and is the only value-bearing being. Therefore, all value in nature must be derived from what is valuable for our species, and nature cannot be treated as an end-in-itself. This raises the important question of whether we can deny all worth to nature and view it instrumentally without undermining the preconditions for the existence of people. As a result, he suggests philosophy in general, and Habermasian critical theory in particular, need to rethink the givens of philosophy so that nature is no longer treated as a "mere" object.

Eckersley (1990) continues the critique of Habermasian critical theory by providing a perspective based in the "radical, ecocentric wing" of the emergent Green political perspective. She observes that Habermas regards the Green movement as an indicator of motivational and legitimacy problems in society, rather than as the bearer of emancipatory ideas. Habermas views radical ecology as defensive and neoromantic, and argues that technical and economic solutions to the environmental crisis must be globally planned and implemented administratively. Furthermore, problems in advanced capitalism do not stem from technocratic rationality per se but from the fact that technocratic rationality is used without rationalized social norms in the sphere of communication.

Eckersley's (1990) ecocentric critique addresses two themes: the kinds of dealings humans can have with the nonhuman world, and the interhuman communication that is involved in Habermas's ideal speech situation. In terms of the first theme, she criticizes Habermas's rigid classification of cognitive interests and his claim that we can only know nature instrumentally. Eckersley notes that we cannot solve all problems with instrumental reason and environmental problems will remain intractable unless instrumental reason is limited by alternative sensibilities. Furthermore, the environmental crisis is seen as due in part to the overuse of instrumental reason. Indeed, instrumental reason may not be the best form of reasoning for human well-being and survival.

Second, Habermas's theory is problematic for Eckersley because he seemingly cannot adequately integrate concern for nonhuman nature since he only considers the development of norms between mutual participants in a discourse. This omits consideration of the fate of other species that are not capable of participating in such a dialogue. Thus Habermas's theory ultimately privileges human emancipation over the emancipation of nonhuman beings and cannot serve as a basis for informing a cultural practice that would fully protect biodiversity. In Eckersley's view, while Habermas's theory is based on respect for the relative autonomy of the human subject, nature should be accorded this respect regardless of its level of communicative competence. To realize this moral requirement, an addition to Habermas's Discourse Principle is required as follows: "A just common structure of political action must be common to all those affected, irrespective of whether they happen to be able to speak or gesture." The practical question regarding nature would then become: "If what is affected could talk and reason, would it agree to the proposed norm?"

Eckersley's critique of Habermas has opened up the question of how nature could be accounted for in a Habermasian framework where practical norms are supposed to be mutually agreed upon by participants in a discourse. Since other parts of nature do not have the same level of communicative competence or rationality as human beings, how could norms regarding the treatment of nature be fairly generated? If, according to Habermas, one must possess a roughly human level of communicative rationality in order to be counted as a moral subject, then it may seem that there is nothing to guarantee that human beings would not agree among themselves to generate the kind of anthropocentric norms that legitimate current levels of environmental exploitation. Given that Habermas's understanding of human liberation is defined by being able to take part in a free and rational discussion on practical action, how could this seemingly anthropocentric view help us think about what to do about environmental problems?

The issues raised in these criticisms are very complex, and we can do no more than sketch a response to them here. Briefly, there have been two general theoretical responses to these issues, both of which attempt to show that meaningful environmental norms can still be generated from within a Habermasian framework. One of these responses, found in the later work of Eckersley (1999) and further developed by Whitworth (2000, 2001), attempts to make the case for the notion of environmental advocacy. This is the notion that while non-human nature may not have a "voice" per se, or be able to articulate to us its own concerns, human beings can engage in imaginative representative thinking on behalf of the rest of nature in order to determine the answer to Eckersley's question: "If what is affected could talk or reason, would it agree to the proposed norm?" This is to say that human beings would be able to act as nature's advocate in any free discussion on practical norms, and through this kind of imaginative representative thinking can give voice to what was previously voiceless. Through this notion of environmental advocacy, then, Habermas's general framework could still be maintained and environmental concerns could be given standing.

However, this sort of response might seem to generate its own kind of problems. Just who, precisely, should then be regarded as nature's "true" advocate in any practical situation? Aren't there a multiplicity of groups each claiming to hear from nature quite different things? As Whitworth (2001) observes, in a debate between people opposed to the practice of fox hunting and those who argue that it is an important cultural tradition that helps keep the population of a bothersome predator at manageable levels, both sides can claim to be nature's advocates and yet end up by advocating different and opposed normative courses of action. Fox hunters can claim to be "true environmentalists" who, by keeping the fox population down, enable other species to thrive, while those opposed to the practice argue that the practice is so savage and barbaric that nothing could justify it. This is to say that while advocacy on behalf of nature might be a way of representing nature in Habermasian discussions of norms, the notion of advocacy itself provides no way of telling us who is entitled to speak on nature's behalf and what to do about conflicts that arise between different advocates.

Moreover, it could also be argued that such "representative" thinking on behalf of nature simply reads into nature our hopelessly anthropomorphic prejudices of what "nature" is. As Whitworth himself observes (2001, p. 34): "Environmental discourses are ... particularly open to bias, distortion, co-option and so on because the fundamental appeals are easier to 'translate' into the desired form, and harder to argue against, as any counter-stances are not wholly confirmable either." Given that we have no access to a "nature" apart from our own very partial representations of nature, what would this mean for the very notion of environmental advocacy? Wouldn't we merely be advocating for our own very partial interests and not those of "nature" as such?

The difficulties involved in the notion of "representing nature" have led to another kind of attempt to show that meaningful environmental norms can still be generated from within a Habermasian framework, even though the very notion of "nature" may be problematic. This perspective is outlined in Brulle (2002). In this paper, Brulle raises theoretical and practical concerns with Eckersley's ecocentric variety of critical theory. For Brulle, the most problematic aspect of Eckersley's ecocentric approach is that it relies upon an "autopoietic" intrinsic value theory where parts of nature (e.g., ecosystems) are theorized to be primarily and continuously concerned with the regeneration of their own organizational activity and structure, giving them a level of "self-directedness" similar to human beings. However, Brulle argues that this view of nature is not universally held; in particular, it is in tension with the view from evolutionary ecology that maintains that nature is best viewed as a chaotic system, in which chance and random events, as well as linear and nonlinear interactions, govern. The result of this thinking is that one cannot use environmental science to define what the "essence" of nature really is. In other words, Brulle argues that Eckersley conflates living processes into an "agency" of nature, which is a social construction that highlights the self-determining components of nature and downplays the more mechanistic and random aspects of nature. Furthermore, by claiming to see the "essence" of nature as an autopoietic or self-determining entity, and then inferring a moral necessity to treat nature as an "end-in-itself," Eckersley ends up by committing the naturalistic fallacy. These are theoretical weaknesses that, in Brulle's view, cripple Eckersley's efforts to unite environmental ethics with Habermasian critical theory. Moreover, from a practical point of view, Brulle argues that it would be unwise to ground environmental ethics on such a narrow basis as the autopoietic intrinsic value theory, since it could prevent a broader-based movement to protect the environment from emerging, and that it is in some tension with the idea that we live in a democratic and pluralistic society with multiple definitions of the good life. In other words, if we are required to endorse the autopoietic intrinsic value theory in order to articulate environmental concerns, it will be very difficult to achieve any broader environmental consensus with others who cannot accept the theory, or who have other reasons for wanting to protect the environment.

For Brulle, rather than trying to represent nature as a kind of potential moral subject that we could imaginatively engage with, we should accept that no one kind of ethics or argument for the protection of the environment will be applicable in all situations or will be acceptable to everyone regardless of cultural background. As Brulle writes (2002, p. 15): "Decisions regarding protection of the natural environment will always be partial, temporary, and contingent. So a universal morality guiding our treatment of nature is most probably an impossibility." It is largely unavoidable that the kinds of reasons we use to defend the value of nature will turn out to be instrumental (i.e., utilitarian or aesthetic), and so rather than trying to dodge this by thinking we can represent within our practical discourses the voice of a nature that ultimately cannot be represented anyway, we should try to ensure that our concerns about nature are given fair hearing along with other concerns at stake and "where the industrialist presuppositions of profitability would not be the deciding force" (Brulle, 2002, p. 16). This is to say that while Brulle finds the notion of representing nature as a potential moral subject problematic, the sorts of concerns we have about nature (e.g., depleting resources, pollution, climate change, loss of biodiversity, etc.) can still be articulated from within a Habermasian framework without any essential problem. There is no valid reason why such concerns should be set aside a priori in deliberative situations, given relatively unproblematic assumptions about what human beings require in order to lead minimally decent lives.

Without resolving the complex debate among Brulle, Eckersley, and Whitworth on the notion of representation, we note that what their perspectives do have in common is the Habermasian notion that structural change is ultimately necessary before environmental concerns can get a fair hearing. Despite their differences on the issue of environmental advocacy, both Brulle and Whitworth see the ultimate strength of Habermas's approach in its emphasis on the need for meaningful deliberation and the need for structural change toward this end. Meaningful deliberation (the kind of deliberative situation that approximates Habermas's ideal speech situation) is necessary precisely because the issues are so complex. Given human fallibility, the complexity of the subject matter, and the plurality of considerations that must be taken into account, important public decisions require public deliberation in order to hear all sides of an issue and to ensure that no considerations are being illegitimately excluded. Moreover, as Whitworth observes (2001, p. 34), "all real decisions involve some sort of trade-off, and it is whether such trade-offs have been discursively redeemed that makes the discourse more or less communicatively rational." This is to say that given the inevitability of hard choices in public decision making, these hard choices require "discursive redemption" whereby all sides of an issue first need to be given fair hearing in order for a public decision to have any sense of legitimacy. This is a notion of democracy that has much in common with themes from the deep green philosophy literature, which emphasize the need to move toward a society based on nondomination and broader-based decision-making practices.

## CONCLUSION

This chapter has shown that the debate concerning anthropocentric and ecocentric philosophies is important in the philosophical literature on environmental ethics. Anthropocentrism has been challenged by advocates of ecocentric ethics who seek to establish a new philosophy that does not privilege human interests over nonhumans. We have also outlined a range of positions related to this debate that are defined by the breadth of extension of moral concern. These include light green or anthropocentric views, middle green or biocentric mixed views that incorporate ecocentric concerns along with anthropocentric concerns, and deep green or fully ecocentric views. The views on environmental ethics in philosophy are paralleled in the management literature on environmental ethics where three basic views have been identified—unrestrained growth (anthropocentrism), social consciousness (a mixed view), and environmental consciousness (full ecocentrism).

The debate over anthropocentrism versus ecocentrism also emerges in the debate concerning the relevance of Habermasian critical theory to environmental ethics. Habermasian critical theory has been criticized for being overly anthropocentric, for addressing nature only instrumentally, and for its failure to address the nature of nature. These criticisms have been addressed by scholars who argue there is no human view or understanding of nature that is free of human influence; that ecology cannot inform us of the nature of nature; and that through Habermas's critical theory, one can deliberate environmental issues in normative and aesthetic terms as well as instrumentally. There is thus nothing inherent in Habermas's critical theory that prevents it from informing environmental ethics and politics. Indeed, Habermas's critical theory provides a valuable approach for theorizing how collective decisions can be made fairly, given the diversity of values and views about nature that exist in society. The central core of his critical theory is the theory of communicative rationality, which outlines the normative conditions for free and rational debate.

Theorists from both anthropocentric and ecocentric perspectives do, however, agree that there is need for structural change in society if it is to better address the natural environment. Interestingly, theorists from a wide variety of perspectives argue that we need to move from rigid, hierarchical organizations and institutions run in autocratic manner to flexible, participative organizations that operate democratically. Since Habermasian critical theory has been fundamentally concerned with developing organizational and institutional conditions that enable human emancipation, the concerns and perspective of this critical theory would seem to have much to contribute to the agendas and programs of many of these perspectives.

We argue that if one cannot discern the essence of nature through environmental knowledge as a basis for environmental ethics, then the nature or meaning of nature must be debated and negotiated, and a genuine consensus or agreement reached in key settings or situations of environmental concern. Since all the views we have reviewed endorse structural and institutional change in society as a necessary basis for better incorporation of nature into human action, this area of structural change may be one of the most important areas where Habermasian critical theory can contribute to environmental ethics. That is, before we can move toward a more ecocentric position, we need to solve key human problems and to reconstitute nondemocratic structures in democratic form (Brulle, 2002). Habermasian critical theory can help protect the natural world by changing the conditions under which decisions are made regarding the natural environment to ensure that environmental considerations are given fair hearing (Brulle, 2002).

At a general level, from a Habermasian perspective there is a need to create a strong public sphere including public forums for undistorted communication and debate where environmental issues can undergo public deliberation to reach shared agreement. Current forums and institutions need to be revitalized so that they allow and encourage open, fair, and rational debate. In such public deliberations, aesthetic and hermeneutic aspects of environmental issues need to be given consideration along with scientific and technical issues. Industrialist presuppositions of profitability would not be the driving force in such debate. While one should not expect ecology or science as such to tell us what to do (Szerszynski, 1996), the principles and values of deep ecology should be debated and discussed. Furthermore, Habermas's democratic and discourse principles need to be discussed and implemented as well in such deliberations.

Although the creation of a public space for debate on environmental ethics will not necessarily produce a situation where decisions always favor protection of nature, such public spaces are an essential step for humans to be able to actually consider and address environmental issues in a meaningful manner (Brulle, 2002). Brulle (2002) provides three examples of projects designed to improve environmental decision making in ways consistent with Habermasian critical theory. The first project involves changing decision making in government agencies that deal with environmental issues. An approach known as "analytic deliberation" involves use of "a democratic method for development of government policies" and provides techniques to "integrate practical, normative and aesthetic concerns" (p. 15) into democratic decision making. Second, there have been a number of planning practices developed to implement the democratic morality of critical theory. Third, there have been several society-level decision-making processes developed that seek to encourage and enable structural change in political and economic institutions in relation to how institutional structures enhance or hinder ethical consideration of nature.

To conclude, Habermasian critical theory contributes to environmental ethics by suggesting communicative practices and norms necessary for meaningful, fair, and valid practical debate that can produce normative decisions and actions. Although it does not itself prescribe any particular ethical content, it establishes norms for valid and fair democratic communication necessary to rationally debate environmental issues and to address and hopefully resolve fundamental environmental questions that emerge in a pluralist, liberal democracy.

## REFERENCES

Attfield, R. (2003). Environmental ethics: An overview for the twenty-first century. Cambridge, UK: Polity Press.

Balakrishnan, U., Duvall, T., & Primeaux, P. (2003). Rewriting the bases of capitalism: Reflexive modernity and environmental sustainability as the foundations of a new normative framework. *Journal of Business Ethics, 47*(4), 299–314.

Beck, U. (1992). *Risk society: Towards a new modernity.* London: Sage.

Benhabib, S., & Dallmayr, F. (Eds.). (1990). *The communicative ethics controversy.* Cambridge, MA: MIT Press.

Brulle, R. J. (2002). Habermas and green political thought: Two roads converging. *Environmental Politics, 11*(4), 1–20.

Clair, J. A., Milliman, J., & Whelan, K. S. (1996). Toward an environmentally sensitive ecophilosophy for business management. *Industrial and Environmental Crisis Quarterly, 9*(3), 289–326.

Curry, P. (2006). *Environmental ethics: An introduction.* Cambridge, UK: Polity Press.

Eckersley, R. (1990). Habermas and green political thought: Two roads diverging. *Theory and Society, 19*(6), 739–776.

Eckersley, R. (1999). The discourse ethic and the problem of representing nature. *Environmental Politics, 8*(2), 24–49.

Gephart, R. P. (1984). Making sense of organizationally based environmental disasters. *Journal of Management, 10*(2), 205–225.

Habermas, J. (1984). *The theory of communicative action: Vol. 1. Reason and the rationalisation of society.* London: Heinemann.

Habermas, J. (1987). *The theory of communicative action: Vol. 2. Lifeworld and system—a critique of functionalist reason.* Cambridge, UK: Polity Press.

Hanna, M. D. (1995). Environmentally responsible managerial behavior: Is ecocentrism a prerequisite? *Academy of Management Review, 20*(4), 796–799.

Hill, T. (1983). Ideals of human excellence and preserving natural environments. *Environmental Ethics, 5*(3), 211–224.

Iyer, G. R. (1999). Business, consumers and sustainable living in an interconnected world: A multilateral ecocentric approach. *Journal of Business Ethics, 20*(4), 273–288.

Johnson, P. C. (1996). Development of an environmental conscience: Is ecocentrism a prerequisite? *Academy of Management Review, 21*(3), 607–611.

Purser, R. E. (1994). "Shallow" versus "deep" organization development and environmental sustainability. *Journal of Organizational Change Management, 7*(4), 4–14.

Purser, R. E., Park, C., & Montuori, A. (1995). Limits to anthropocentrism: Toward an ecocentric organization paradigm? *Academy of Management Review, 20*(4), 1053–1089.

Regan, T. (2004). *The case for animal rights.* Berkeley: University of California Press.

Shrivastava, P. (1995). Ecocentric management for a risk society. *Academy of Management Review, 20*(1), 118–137.

Shrivastava, P. (1996). Ecocentric versus traditional management: Some hints to Hanna. *Academy of Management Review, 21*(1), 9–11.

Singer, P. (2002). *Animal liberation.* New York: Ecco Press.

Szerszynski, B. (1996). On knowing what to do: Environmentalism and the modern problematic. In S. Lash, B. Szerszynski, & B. Wynne (Eds.), *Risk, environment and modernity: Towards a new ecology* (pp. 104–137). London: Sage.

Whitebook, J. (1979). The problem of nature in Habermas. *Telos, 40,* 41–69.

Whitworth, A. (2000). Communication with the environment?: Non-human nature in the theories of Jurgen Habermas. *Politics, 20*(3), 145–151.

Whitworth, A. (2001). Ethics and reality in environmental discourses. *Environmental Politics, 10*(2), 22–42.

Printed in the United States
123461LV00002B/109-120/P

9 781593 117856